INTRODUCTION TO FAMILY PROCESSES

FIFTH EDITION

INTRODUCTION TO FAMILY PROCESSES

FIFTH EDITION

RANDAL D. DAY

BRIGHAM YOUNG UNIVERSITY

Routledge
Taylor & Francis Group
New York   London

Please visit: www.family-studies-arena.com

Routledge
Taylor & Francis Group
270 Madison Avenue
New York, NY 10016

Routledge
Taylor & Francis Group
27 Church Road
Hove, East Sussex BN3 2FA

© 2010 by Taylor and Francis Group, LLC
Routledge is an imprint of Taylor & Francis Group, an Informa business

Printed in the United States of America on acid-free paper
10 9 8 7 6 5 4 3

International Standard Book Number: 978-1-84169-761-1 (Hardback)

Library of Congress Cataloging-in-Publication Data

Day, Randal D., 1948-
    Introduction to family processes / Randal D. Day. -- 5th ed.
        p. cm.
    Includes bibliographical references and index.
    ISBN 978-1-84169-761-1 (hardcover : alk. paper)
    1. Family. 2. Family--Research. I. Title.

HQ519.D39 2010
306.85--dc22   2009026073

Visit the Taylor & Francis Web site at
http://www.taylorandfrancis.com

and the Psychology Press Web site at
http://www.psypress.com

This book is dedicated to my wife, Larri-Lea.
She has taught me much about the meaning of family, love, and companionship.

—RDD

CONTENTS

PREFACE

Families are complicated and this text attempts to explain the complex workings of inner family life. This is the fifth edition of this text. It began as a working project for introductory family classes being taught at Washington State University and Brigham Young University. Our original intent was to create a book that focused primarily on family processes and dynamics rather than sociological trends, political topics, or the individual psychology approach. It is written for undergraduate courses on family processes and family studies, the family, marriage and family interaction and relations, and family dynamics taught in family studies, human development, psychology, sociology, social work, education, consumer sciences, home economics, health, and nursing departments. This book also appeals to those who want to maximize the positive parts of family life.

This edition tries to stay true to that initial mission. To that end, in this edition there are several changes. First, there has been significant updating of chapters. Unfortunately, some of the topics of interest have not produced much new research, but, where possible, every attempt was made to make the topics current.

Second, there have been chapter additions and some chapter restructuring. This edition now contains a chapter on research methods. This is an introductory examination of how research is done in family sciences. Also new is Chapter 7, which introduces the discussion about how we choose relationships and how those choices live on in committed long-term relationships. In the previous edition, the chapter on change and life was combined with the theories chapter (Chapter 3). Some of the chapters appear in different locations in the text. Last, the activities for this text have been moved to a companion Web site at **www.psypress.com/family-processes**.

Third, I have inserted more research on families from diverse cultural and ethnic backgrounds and the impact of work and technology on the family (see Chapter 6), the changing nature of family structures including single parenting and gay unions (see Chapter 1), the role of gender and power and genetics and personality in relationships (see Chapter 5), and stresses in family life (see Chapter 13).

Last, the activities for this text have been moved to a companion Web site at **www.psypress.com/family-processes**. The book's Web site contains the Chapter Activity Questions that reinforce writing and critical thinking skills, Journal Activities to strengthen students' personal connection to the material, and Web Links to encourage further investigation into the material online.

Also available on the Web site is a section for instructors only. The instructor's portion features small group and in-class exercises, lecture outlines, topics for debate, suggested films, PowerPoint presentations, and multiple-choice, true–false, matching, and essay questions.

Each chapter in the book opens with a Preview and concludes with a Summary, Study Questions, Essay Questions, Key Terms, and Suggested Readings. Principle Boxes highlight key chapter concepts to serve as a study reference and a Glossary defines the key terms listed at the ends of the chapters.

As I have revised this text over the years, it has become clearer to me that studying and understanding family life is ever more important. It is clear that families and family life are ever changing and the study of family life is occasionally fraught with important but controversial issues. As in past editions, this text does not attempt to tackle all the social issues that attend the study of the family. Instead, I have made a conscious decision to speak mostly about how families (regardless of structure or ideological orientation) do the business of family life. This approach might not mesh well with those who want to focus their discussion about family on key cultural issues that typically attend the study of families in today's world. It is not my position that those issues are less important. It is my position, however, that a beginning-level text on family interaction cannot cover everything. I have chosen to devote my efforts to examining the *how* of family life instead of the *why*. In this text, we ask the question, "How do families interact within their private space?" Others, very legitimately, might want to ask questions about how family has changed over the last 100 years—or if one structural type is better or more effective than another. Although those are certainly interesting questions, I seek instead to gather what we know about how families interact with one another. There are times when structural issues come into play: For example, the interactional life of a step-family has some unique characteristics. Where possible, I have attempted to bring those issues to the fore within the discussion of different family process issues.

A strong and enduring theme of this book is that (to paraphrase a line made famous by Dickens in his epic novel *A Tale of Two Cities*) the family realm is the best of human life and it is the worst of human life. The best parts of family life are experienced as we find deep joy and the greatest pleasure from our interaction with those whom we love and love us the most. Family life is also a crucible that refines and tests and helps us grow and mature in ways that are noble, great, and wonderful. If we are wise in the way we manage this precious part of our lives, family life can provide satisfaction, fulfillment, love, security, a sense of belonging, and other beauties and riches that are difficult to attain outside the family realm.

The undesirable parts of the family realm reflect the worst side of human relationships. More murders are committed in families than anyplace else. Physical abuse is all too common. The privacy that allows intimacy and the deepest of love also allows sexual and emotional abuse. Family life is the source of some of the deepest frustrations, intense misery, immeasurable exploitation, and serious abuse that humans ever experience.

As I wrote this text, it was my hope that ideas assembled here would assist readers in finding ways to increase the positive aspects of family life, avoid the undesirable parts that can be avoided, and more effectively manage the challenges and obstacles that cannot be avoided.

Some of the positive things that can come from healthy family life are intimacy that is not stifling, bonds without bondage, meaning and purpose, growth and progress, maturation and beauty, and enough security and stability that we have a sense of being in a wholesome home. On the negative side, our goals are to avoid violence, exploitation, dominance, abuses, tyranny, negligence, and other forms of excess that bring pain, hurt, disappointment, and inhumanity.

The original goal for this book was to help families and those who help families better attain these positive parts of the family realm and avoid the undesirable parts. Thus, this book is written to and for those who live (or will live) in families and also for those who want to work professionally or as a volunteer to help families. Each of us can help in many ways. We can help our own families and our friends, and we can help in our professions and avocations.

Many contributions of our families, colleagues, students, and friends have played a key role in the intellectual journey that this book represents. There are several who have directly impacted this edition (and past editions) with ideas, support, encouragement, reactions, and suggestions. They include Wesley Burr, Kathleen Bahr, Denise Bodman, Tom Holman, and Alisa van Langeveldt.

I also want to thank those who reviewed this edition: Karen Schmid (Indiana State University), Denise Ann Bodman (Arizona State University), Julie James (Indiana University), Natasha Cabrera (University of Maryland), and Kathleen Ramos (California State University – Fresno).

—R. Day

CHAPTER 1

Adapting to Family Life in Our Times

☐ Chapter Preview

In this chapter, readers will learn:

- That the study of family life is about the everyday quotidian of common experience.
- Several reasons why studying family life is important.
- How the study of family is new but, at the same time, its emergence has a long history.
- That the study of family life is different than the study of families from a sociological, psychological, or historical point of view.
- How everyone who studies family life brings bias to that study.
- That our view of what constitutes family life and even how to define what is family is changing.
- How family processes are the strategies used by family members to maximize family goals.

☐ Introduction

> Cynthia and David were arguing about finances . . . (They seriously disagreed about how their saving should be spent—and they were fighting again). . . . Suddenly, Cynthia looked down . . . , "What happened to your socks?" Startled, David . . . commented, "I had to chase a raccoon out of the garden last night . . . ." They both laughed. (Driver & Gottman, 2004, p. 301)

This story was reported in a research project conducted by Dr. Janice Driver and Dr. John Gottman. It is one of dozens initiated by psychologist and family science researcher, Gottman at the University of Washington. Gottman and colleagues have been observing 130 couples once a year in a laboratory research experience since 1989. Each year these couples spend at least one weekend in the **Love-Lab**, as it is called. They cook dinner, have discussions, and continue with everyday life. Their movements, conversations, and activities are recorded on video and audio. Trained researchers carefully code each segment of their interactions later. In the study, researchers found that a husband's playfulness is directly related to his wife's playfulness. Another finding was that the husband's ability to be playful and his skill at making his wife laugh might be directly related to lower levels of conflict in marriage.

This study is a good example of the kind of research findings and ideas featured in this text. One unique aspect of this text is its focus on the inner workings of daily life. To explain this unique quality, let us introduce two words that capture the idea of examining ordinary daily life. Two key words for this chapter are *quotidian* and *prosaic.* Quotidian refers to the ordinary, usual, commonplace, and everyday events of daily life. In this text, the discussion centers on the commonplace, ordinary ways that families interact, solve problems, make decisions, communicate, and function, and it captures the everyday "sentences, paragraphs, and chapters" of daily living. Two important assumptions are underscored within the idea of the prosaic of everyday life. First, family scientists assume that learning about the daily routines, rituals, communication, and performance of life is important. For example, Gottman and his team of researchers frequently write about common topics like ordinary humor and its relationship to conflict. In contrast, many research studies have shown that conflict has strong and negative effects on the well-being of children (cf. Buehler et al., 1998).

Second, we assume that by knowing how some aspects of the daily prosaic of family life works, we can have some chance of altering how people request action from spouses and children, how they respond to demands, and how they structure important family rituals. By understanding these commonplace ideas about family life, it is thought that we have a better chance at changing those elements of daily life that could threaten the chances of our family staying together or developing strongly grounded relationships that help attain desired goals.

Studying family life is an exciting and interesting adventure. Many of us want to know how to make our own families stronger and how to assist other families as they struggle with life's difficulties. Often the lives of families are at the center of national news, political campaigns, movies, and heated congressional debates. We care about how families raise their children, spend money, decide where to live, and contribute to the economy. Much of the media and political discussions about family life focus on who people choose to marry, how many children they decide to have, and whether or not they divorce or stay married (or get remarried). In contrast, the primary purpose of this text is to examine the interior of family life. This text does not dwell on the larger political debates about families, public policy debates, and demographic issues about family life. Instead, the focus here is on the inner workings, dynamics, and patterns of family life regardless of who is present, how poor or rich they are, or where or if they work at certain jobs.

☐ Reasons for Studying Family Life

Family life has become a legitimate field of study. Many universities across the United States have degree programs dedicated to helping students better understand the complexities of family life. There are several reasons why it is important to study family life. First, information about family life can assist someone as she or he chooses to form and build her or his own **family of procreation**. A family of procreation is the family we create with a partner and refers to that partner agreeing to form a relationship (formal or informal) and include children (either by birth or adoption). Second, as we learn about family we can better understand someone's **family of orientation**. One's family of orientation focuses on the family in which he or she was raised. In both cases (i.e., reflecting on our families

FIGURE 1.1   Today's couples struggle with the daily task of trying to understand their changing world.

of procreation and families of orientation), when we understand family interaction (either from the perspective of procreation or orientation), we have the potential of increasing the quality of those relationships and increasing our chances of attaining the goals and desires that inevitably reside within families.

However, most of us who teach family science courses are not satisfied with the idea that this is only a self-help type of course. We assume that many (if not all) of you in introductory family science courses will at some point be working with people in your communities and effecting some type of intervention in the lives of those around you. This information, therefore, can serve as a foundation for understanding how to work with families who are not connected directly to you. Students who major in family science, social work, or sociology often find employment in community-based agencies that specialize in assisting families in difficulty. Examples of such agencies are community action centers, child protective services, adoption agencies, programs for the aged (e.g., Social Security), or adolescent group homes. Additionally, some students continue with their education and attend graduate school. Those who seek a master's or doctorate in family science usually find employment in therapy settings or choose a career teaching about family life in a university setting.

Others will find their life's work within settings that train others in how to aid families who need counseling assistance. Some will find a variety of opportunities to become advocates for family-related issues in their own communities. For example, most U.S. communities have a local branch of Habitat for Humanity (*http://www.habitat.org/*). This organization helps families build a suitable home. One of the important volunteer jobs within Habitat for Humanity is a committee that prepares families to do a better job of money and general family management. The information found in this text will help people be more effective in working for an organization like Habitat for Humanity by teaching about the interior of family life, how people use valuable resources, and how they make life-impacting decisions.

It is important to note that family science is relatively new compared to more established academic disciplines such as math or biology. Most university departments and programs that offer courses in family life have come into existence since the 1960s. Moreover, most family relations programs originated within "home economics" programs.

Prior to the 1970s, almost all land-grant universities ("state schools" such as Washington State University, Florida State University, Oregon State University, The Ohio State University, Kansas State University, etc.) were required to maintain an academic program (usually with women in mind) that focused on teaching the "art of homemaking." Some of the students in these programs eventually became home economics teachers in high school settings. However, the vast majority of home economics majors during this time were preparing to become wives and mothers, many in farm settings: Most of the nation's families used to live in rural agricultural settings. To help train and educate these agricultural-oriented wives and mothers during the 1890s, each state in the United States was given money to fund a land-grant school.

Typically, men sought degrees in agriculture and women were expected to learn the homemaking arts. Of course, there was a dramatic shift in our culture. Following World War II, many families moved away from farm life and into the suburbs. By the 1960s and 1970s, many of the nation's women began finding jobs and activities that took them away from home and from focusing only on the home arts. In addition, with the invention of the microwave oven, efficient washing machines, and preprocessed foods, the role of women in the home changed dramatically almost overnight.

During the same period, the federal government increased funding to develop social programs designed to alleviate family problems such as poverty, family violence, and unwed pregnancy. To meet the growing need for family community workers (e.g., social workers, day care providers, etc.), many universities created programs designed to train students in how to work with agencies and community action programs that served families. The overall result was that the interest in family studies and the role of family scholars also dramatically increased. Prior to the 1940s, scholarship about family life was geared toward assisting a mother (usually the woman was the target of this type of research) in making better use of her time, managing a farm household, learning to prepare meals, and preserving food through the winter. After the 1940s, the role of the family science researcher changed. During this era, family science teachers at the state schools began teaching students how to focus on intervention: Curriculum shifted to a focus on training students to work with families experiencing trauma. In the 1960s, the training took another turn as the U.S. government created a plethora of social programs designed to build a Great Society. Among those programs, the **Head Start** early childhood intervention preschool system was organized. Many of the state schools developed preschool centers to train students to work with young children, especially those from disadvantaged backgrounds.

Today, university-based family science courses have moved away from self-help programs to curricula that are designed to prepare students for work in the social and teaching agencies within communities. Generally, they are not designed primarily to help students have a better family experience. Of course, studying family life is always transferable to one's own situation and these courses often provide valuable insights about one's own life. However, most who teach family science seek to prepare students to reach a wider audience of families within their communities. Therefore, it is a key assumption of this text that those who study this topic will eventually have some type of role (either for pay or as a volunteer) in some kind of community or state-sponsored agency or community experience within which they will be asked to help decide efficient ways of helping families overcome difficulties. This text was developed with that audience in mind. Of course, working with one's own family is also an important and legitimate cause. The information found here is certainly helpful in that regard.

In sum, there are three ways that information from a course like this is used: First, it can be used to strengthen your own family. Second, you can use this information to strengthen or even, in a limited way, intervene in the lives other families. Finally, this material will help those who wish to go beyond the introductory level and become family science researchers, clinicians, and teachers. Also, keep in mind that it takes a great deal of training and experience to become a counselor or therapist. This book is a foundational platform from which the journey to becoming a therapist can begin. It is often said that a little information is a dangerous thing. So it is with studying the dynamics and processes of family life. Becoming a skilled family therapist takes hundreds of hours of supervised training. Reading this text and taking a family course for credit does not qualify one to counsel others in distress.

☐ There Are Other Legitimate Ways of Studying Family Life

It is important to understand that much of the study of families in society does not focus on daily family life or **family processes**. There are several academic disciplines that explore "different parts of the elephant" when studying families. Remember the poem about the blind men who encountered an elephant—some felt the tail, others the trunk, and still others the large midsection? Each of the wise men had a different story to tell. Metaphorically, the study of family life is different: It is about looking inside the elephant and watching how the internal organs interact, how blood flows, where food is processed, and what the elephant is thinking. Other family researchers in other disciplines focus on the outer view of family life. For example, anthropologists might focus on the differences in marriage patterns across several different cultural groups. Sociologists typically study marriage as one of many institutions in complex society. They might have great interest in how families have adapted to a changing society, how divorce rates change in times of national crises, and how family life is impacted by changes in employment availability. Historians, on the other hand, go to great lengths to discover the historical changes in marriage and how those changes can help explain better who we are. An example of the historical approach to studying the family could be a look at how people chose their mates in medieval Europe.

Psychologists are another group who study family life. For example, a psychologist might study family life by exploring how married relationships impact the psychological well-being of a particular family member. On the other hand, a research psychologist might want to know how family life pushes young women toward anorexia or other eating disorders.

Demographers, yet another group of scientists who study family life, are typically interested in descriptions of how families are changing demographically in our culture. They might, for example, want to know how many families have children, how many live below the poverty level or how many remarry. Demographers are also interested in the economics of family life, how much money families spend, and the intricacies associated with general resource allocation.

It is important to remember that the study of inner family life or family processes is much newer than these other disciplines. Although this metaphor sounds messy and distasteful, the study of inner family life is about climbing inside the live elephant and trying to find out what makes it work. Only recently have researchers begun to ask questions about the intricacies of inner private family life. One reason for the relative newness of studying family processes is that most families resist the type of scrutiny necessary to understand the events of daily life. Families are very cautious about allowing researchers to enter their homes and do research. Additionally, in-depth family research is expensive. These and many other limitations make it difficult to conduct research about family life.

Instead of spending our time on the demographics of family life or attempting to create an encyclopedia of family life research findings, we instead focus on a few compelling key family processes. That means most of the discussion in this text is about what families do, how they solve life's dilemmas, and how they use various strategies to achieve goals. We realize that most of the goals families have are not very explicit. We also acknowledge that most of the choices we make as family groups are made with a vague notion about why we are doing them. Moreover, in many cases, it might be that not all family members agree on the family's direction, goals, beliefs, or choice. This ambiguity about family life makes it both rich and exciting to study, but also makes it very difficult and challenging.

☐ Studying Family Life Is Not the Same as Living Family Life

Unlike other academic pursuits (e.g., chemistry, math, or music), nearly everyone experiences family life firsthand. Although more general life experience can be helpful in understanding larger principles of inner family life, our personal unique perspective can sometimes get in the way of objectivity. Think of how many times you have been in a bank. It might have been dozens or even hundreds of times. Just because you have been there and have borrowed money for a car, paid a loan, or deposited or cashed a check does not necessarily mean that you know how to run the bank. Biochemistry provides another example of this principle. Most of us know very little about the chemistry of life even though we use chemicals and our bodies certainly perform complicated chemical reactions every second of life. Some of us might have a superficial understanding of simple chemical interactions, but the point is that having food transformed into energy within your body is not the same as understanding how that happens. We live daily family life without really thinking about it, knowing how, or having to understand how it all works. In this regard, family scientists have something important to contribute.

Union gives strength. (Aesop)

PRINCIPLE 1.1   FAMILY EMPLOY PROCESSES AND EFFECT GOALS

Family processes are the strategies and daily sequences of behavior employed by family members to achieve goals: Those goals are often implicit and the goals might or might not be shared by every family member equally.

☐ Why We Care About Families

We care about family processes because:

1. Most people get married and stay married to someone (Simmons & O'Connell, 2003). Therefore, these processes are of great interest to a wide number of people for whom these close relationships are of high importance. The well-being of individuals is affected by what goes on in close family relationships.

2. About 80% of women who marry will bear a child (Downs, 2003). Because most people who get married have children, it is in the interest of all community members that we find ways of rearing and caring for children in ways that create the best outcomes for those children. In general, when children are emotionally, socially, spiritually, and economically stronger, the larger community does better.

3. When things go wrong in families, it is costly (Dalaker, 2001). Those costs are incurred not only by the individuals involved, but the community at large. For example, divorce incurs high costs (financial, emotional, social, etc.) for the individual, but it also costs employers, causes disruption in the lives of children, and often results in intervention from costly government programs (such as **Temporary Assistance to Needy Families** [TANF]). In an important government document, Dalaker (2001) showed that family type is a significant predictor of children living in poverty. About 33% of all children who live in a mother-only-headed home reside in economic conditions that are below the poverty level. Not all of those children are in single-parent families because of divorce, but the majority of them are in some type of transitory relationship—many of them because of divorce.

PRINCIPLE 1.2   FAMILIES ARE IMPORTANT

We care about families because of the value they have to individuals, society, and the economy.

☐ Families Struggle Throughout the World

To begin our voyage into inner family life, consider the following information to comment on how you feel about family life and its challenges. In your accompanying workbook, there is a place to record your thoughts for primary ideas within each chapter. The purpose of these Journal of Thoughts exercises (JOTS) is to encourage you to think past the clichés of our family existence and to begin thinking more analytically and specifically about what happens in families on a daily basis as they try to solve problems, make decisions, allocate resources, and make sense out of a very complicated world.

During the deadly Hurricane Katrina, there was terrible family devastation. The following story, posted on the Internet just after the storm hit New Orleans, reflects a special kind of family devastation:

September 3, 2005 | Franklinton, La., in Washington Parish is without any federal assistance, and there is only a small Red Cross office open. . . . We are panicking. . . . Not all food stores have power, and the ones that are open are only taking cash. (Crider, 2005)

In this woman's story, you can discern the panic and deep longing for that which has been lost. In times of loss and crisis, most people turn to family first, seek home as a refuge, and do what they can to save that most special part of their lives they call family.

Do you know how you would react to a local or national devastation? Are you prepared to have a loved one serve in the military and be in a dangerous place for months at a time? What resources do you have to call on? Among your resources might be your other family members, your religion, your inner strength, your decision-making process, and your skill

FIGURE 1.2   During Hurricane Katrina, citizens of New Orleans took refuge in local safe buildings, not knowing what had happened to their homes, relatives, or friends.

for solving difficult problems quickly. A primary theme of this text is that there is hope. Even if your family has experienced or will experience difficult times or even the usual stresses of daily living, you can make your family experience one that helps you cope and even survive.

In addition, some readers of this text will find themselves working with families who experience tough decisions and difficult life events. How will you react to their problems and how will you be able to assist them as they struggle for stability and try to meet the goals they have in mind? My hope is that these principles and ideas can be of assistance.

☐ Biases in the Study of Family Life

On a plane to Washington, DC, recently I could not help but overhear the conversation of a young married couple in the seats next to me. As they talked, it was clear that they were struggling with many relationship issues. After some time, the young man turned and asked me if I were married. I replied that I had been married for 38 years to the same person. He was incredulous and reacted as though he did not believe me. I showed him some pictures of my family and that seemed to convince him. His next question still haunts me: "In today's world," he puzzled, "everyone gets divorced, very few of my friends want to get married, and they are not too thrilled about the idea of having kids. How is it that you are still married? How did you do that?" I am sure my answer did not really help him much. I said something about commitment and working hard. I also said that my relationship with my wife has not always been smooth and that staying together takes great effort.

An important aspect of this story is that each of us who writes about family science issues brings to his or her writing a personal history. Therefore, the first type of bias that I bring to the writing of this text comes from the experiences I have had raising five children with my wife. These events have greatly influenced my ideas about marriage, relationships, and family life. In addition, where I grew up, the experiences in my **family of origin**, and even my personal religious beliefs influence how I approach the writing of this text; conversely, your experiences influence how you read, interpret, and use the information found here.

Second, each author (at least in the social sciences) brings to the creation of a text or research article an education-based bias; authors write from the biases of their training. Theories, research ideas, and the type of training they bring to the project influence them. Although each of us tries to be as objective as possible, often our experiences, beliefs, and training shine through.

You should know from the outset that I believe that family life is an essential, enduring, and critical aspect of the human experience. You could say that I am biased in that regard. In addition, I assume that you, the reader, approach the study of family processes with biases. We cannot avoid our personal views of life, but we can acknowledge how those views might influence how we think about family life.

It goes without saying that most people realize that family life is a double-edged sword; it can be a source of love, compassion, and fulfillment, but it can also be a harbor of destruction, oppression, and violence. Either condition is possible; however, I believe it is the responsibility of each family member to learn how to make family life better for all involved. Therefore, another goal of this text is to convince you that by understanding the processes that occur in daily family life, one can change the quality of family life. In other words, a primary assumption of this text is the idea that family members can make a difference in the quality of their family life.

In the next sections, several ideas are presented that should assist you as you begin the study of family lie. First is a discussion of how family life is changing. It is critical to realize that there are several basic changes occurring in family life that make us rethink what families are and what their function is. You will be asked to evaluate whether family life is disintegrating or merely changing with the times. Again, this is an area where one's strong beliefs shine through. Some family scholars view family life as the optimal forum for raising children and seeking personal happiness. Others view family life as mostly destructive and antiquated, and they loudly campaign for alternative lifestyles to emerge and replace family life.

Next, you are to consider what constitutes a family. This is a complicated discussion in which many family scholars reveal their personal biases about family life.

Finally, we explore family processes. Even though our idea of what constitutes a family might be changing, and even though family life might or might not be the same as it was in times past, a key idea of this book is that families must meet the challenges before them. They use strategies to solve problems, make decisions, and allocate resources. The study of family processes is the study of those strategies families use to maximize the goals they set out to achieve.

☐ Our View of Daily Family Life Is Changing

What families do (e.g., have and rear children, solve problems, take care of each other) has remained relatively unchanged for centuries. However, how those activities are performed and who is present (i.e., the composition of family life) is ever changing over time and varies from family to family and culture to culture. Later in this chapter, there is a more complete discussion of what is meant by the term *family*. It might not be apparent, but that topic alone could take the space of a book by itself. Clearly, however, how we define who family is and how families organize and carry out the prosaic daily life changes constantly.

A key to understanding our attitudes about family life is to realize that many Americans have uncertain, vague, and even ambiguous ideas about the value of family life. On the one hand, most of us would agree that family life could be essential, fulfilling, and even wonderful. At the same time there is so much violence and distress in today's families that some suggest we should rethink the value of family life. To illustrate this idea, the following is an example of how our thinking is changing rapidly about gay and lesbian relationships. Only a few years ago it was illegal in all the states of the United States to have a homosexual relationship. The following traces some key political, legal, and historical decisions that have changed our legal thinking about what can (or should) constitute a family.

> According to the U.S. Census Bureau, there were at least 600,000 gay and lesbian couples living in the U.S. in 2000, in virtually every county in the country. (Wolfson, 2004, p. 87)

Our story begins in Denmark. In 1989, Denmark was the first sovereign country to recognize same-sex partnerships. The Danish Registered Partnership Act stated that "two persons of the same sex may have their partnership registered . . . the registration of a partnership shall have the same legal effects as the contracting of marriage." It was not long before Norway, Sweden, Iceland, and France did the same over the following 2 years (Pinello, 2006). Within a few short years, The Netherlands, Belgium, Ontario, and British Columbia courts joined with that movement and declared gay marriages to be legal.

In the United States, much public press was given to the events of November 2003 regarding high court actions in Massachusetts and San Francisco. The Massachusetts Supreme Judiciary Court declared (*Goodridge v. Department of Public Health*) that it was, in essence, unconstitutional for Massachusetts to limit marriage to only heterosexual couples. They declared that a heterosexual-only marriage policy violated the Commonwealth's constitutional principles. Nine days later, the mayor of San Francisco instructed the county clerk to issue marriage licenses to same-sex couples who wanted them. These actions provoked a number of other communities to quickly move in that direction. From New Mexico to New York and Oregon to New Jersey, local mayors and state and county officials began allowing for **same-sex marriages**. By April 2004, more than 7,000 marriages of gay couples had been performed and by May 2004 more than 6,000 had been performed in San Francisco alone (Pinello, 2006).

In response to the actions of these state courts and local initiatives of mayors and county commissioners, more conservative elements of the U.S. government tried to intervene. Most conservative backers who were opposed to gay marriage referred to the language of those who had supported the **Defense of Marriage Act** (DOMA) that was passed by Congress and signed by President Clinton in 1996. It defined marriage by federal law as "only a legal union between one man and one woman as husband and wife." The bill was supported 342–76 in the House and 85–14 in the Senate. Although this act did not prohibit states from making gay marriage legal, it did provide that one state would not be required to recognize another state's same-sex marriage.

The Problem

The purpose of understanding this important social and political issue is that it makes an important point. Throughout history, at many times the very core structure of what many think of as a family has been challenged. If you are interested in this topic, you will find the book *The Way We Never Were* (Coontz, 1992) an interesting read. With regard to gay and lesbian marriage, there are several comments one could consider: First, one could say, "Who cares? If someone wants to be married to a same-sex person, why in the world should I care?" Another response might be, "I care about this because it is immoral and I want the rest of the country to recognize the moral position I have about this issue. We are losing our moral/Christian/ethical foundation in this country and that will hurt us." Yet another person might say, "I believe that when a gay couple marries—and there are children involved—it hurts those children and we just can't have that." Someone else might respond, "I am gay and I think I am being discriminated against. If I die, my life-long partner has no claim on my assets, and if I am in the hospital my partner cannot give any input into the medical choices should I not be able to respond. This is my life-long partner—why don't I have the same rights as others?" In your first Journal of Thoughts (1.1), you are asked to comment on each of these positions. What is your view and how did you arrive at the conclusions you have?

The point of these interesting public policy issues is that since the beginning of the United States' constitutional history there has been an ongoing debate about what power the federal (or state government) should have over individual, personal decisions, especially when those decisions have to do with personal property (as in the case of slaves), religious practice (as in the case of Mormon polygamists in the 19th century), or in the case of gay-rights activists, the right to marry whomever they want.

The gay and lesbian movement believes strongly that they have a right to love (and even marry) whomever they wish. Many who live in the larger community in which gays live have a moral difference with same-sex union, but many also have an aversion to a change in these laws. Pragmatically, many know that to allow gays to marry will cause large-scale policy shifts in many legal arenas, including changes in wills and contracts, inheritance designations, custody determinations, medical and insurance benefit offerings, and a host of other contractual issues. The reason we dwell on this issue here is that it raises key questions like these: What is family? What family forms should our legal and financial systems attend to? Who should have the ultimate say about individual matters? Who should have the ultimate say in matters that may influence children? And, does a government have the right (or responsibility) to dictate moral direction? If the government does have the right or responsibility to promote a particular ethical or moral view, which of the myriad of competing moral views should they adopt? These highly charged political issues find their way into elections, public debate, and even the Supreme Court. The usual way the average person expresses his or her views on these topics is through the voting process: The public votes for politicians who then make laws and statutes and appoint judges who declare opinions about such issues when necessary.

☐ A Statistical Overview of Families in the United States

For a moment, reflect on the image that comes to mind when one says "families in the United States." What kind of family came to mind? Probably one like yours. Now let us think about the kinds of changes that families might have gone through in the last 100 years. What would you list as key changes? In the United States today, about 50% of all households claim to have a married couple present where there is a child (U.S. Census Bureau 1998, Table 69; 2003, Table 66). That could mean that the child is biologically related to one or more of the parents. However, it is important to note that those children could alternatively be there as the result of one or more other life situations such as they are adopted, they are part of a stepfamily, or they are in foster care.

It is also important to note that about 32% of all households are comprised of relationships that are labeled by the U.S. Census Bureau as "non-family households." These households include cohabiting couples, same-sex unions, and others who are living together and might not be related but are not in a marital or sexual union.

The percentage of people marrying today is declining. Not only are fewer people getting married but they are also getting married later than they used to. Currently a little over 50% of all households contain a married couple with a child. In 1970, that number was about 71% (U.S. Census Bureau 1998, Table 69; 2003, Table 66).

In addition, cohabitation is on the rise. The U.S. Census Bureau has been carefully charting the emergence of couples who are living together in one household but are not married. It is estimated that in just one decade (1990–2000) there was a greater than 70% increase in cohabitation (Simmons & O'Connell 2003).

☐ What Is Family?

Defining family is not an easy task. In the late 1970s, then President Jimmy Carter organized what came to be known as the White House Conference on Families. Unfortunately, very little of the original agenda was discussed. Most of the conference energy was spent on the key question of what constitutes a family. The various participants had specific agenda items to bring to the discussion but directions and answers to other key questions almost always depended on how one defined family. An acrimonious battle ensued: The more conservative participants did not want the conference to use the language "families" but, instead, wanted the designation "family" to prevail. Of course, the agenda of the more conservative participants was that using the term *family* would help the conference focus on a more widely held view (by their estimation) that family issues were about men and women marrying and having children. They further suggested that the focus of family life for the conference be limited to situations in which the mother was living at home and taking care of the children.

Those promoting a more liberal agenda insisted that restricting the conference to a discussion about one type of family configuration (i.e., man–woman–child, with the mother staying at home with her children) would necessarily exclude a discussion of family life that should encompass many individuals who were involved in family life but did not fit that rather narrow definition (e.g., single parents, gay couples, etc.). Unfortunately, for the conference, the battle over this single issue ended the conference with virtually nothing else of any significance to family life being discussed.

Among the strongest public voices in the United States today are fundamentalist religious organizations that adopt the position that family life is sacred. One example is the Roman Catholic Church, in which marriage is seen as one of the essential sacraments of religious worship. Many conservative fundamentalist religions take a very "pro-family" stand on what marriage should be like and many discourage or even prohibit divorce. Certainly, most are overtly opposed to same-sex marriage.

One example of this type of conservative stance emerged in the late 1990s with the development of the "covenant marriage" concept. In an effort to discourage divorce, Louisiana enacted an optional "covenant marriage" license in June 1997. According to this law, those who wish to enter into a **covenant marriage** must agree to premarital counseling. Additionally, the petitioners must sign an agreement that if they wish to divorce in the future, it has to be proven on specific grounds. This last item is in response to the **no-fault divorce** laws passed by every state in the United States during the 1970s and 1980s. In a no-fault divorce situation, partners can divorce without having to prove that the other spouse was at fault (e.g., committed adultery, became a convicted felon, etc.).

Public policy scholar William Galston (1998) proposed that:

Evidence indicates that . . . (with regard to children) the intact two-parent family is generally preferable to the available alternatives. It follows that a prime purpose of sound family policy is to strengthen such families by promoting their formation. (p. 149)

He asserted that it would be absurd to suggest that all single-parent families are "dysfunctional" or that it is reasonable to hope that all families would have two parents. Instead, the suggestion is that two parents is the optimal family pattern.

The Separation of Marriage, Sex, Childbearing, and Child Rearing

In times past, many living in North American cultures (and many cultures around the world) believed that sex with a person of the opposite sex, marriage, **childbearing**, and **child rearing** were a package deal. That is, an ethical, moral, religious ideal prevalent in Western society for hundreds of years has been that one had sex only with one's married partner and that having and rearing children were an extension of a marriage relationship.

Over the last 50 years, there has been a cultural shift. In the early years of this century, U.S. culture was more family centered. Many today would describe U.S. culture as more individualistic or person centered. Prior to the 1900s, families were much more patriarchal and collective in nature. Because family members relied on each other for survival, there was a sense of collectivity that pushed people to remain associated with the land, farm, and other family members. That association also demanded obedience, followership, and autocratic control. It really was not practical or effective to have families operate by any kind of democratic ideal. Instead, the father (or father figure) was in charge and his will was to be obeyed.

By the 1940s things began to change dramatically. Before 1940, all but a small percentage of children were born into some form of family in which a marital union had occurred. During the last 50 years, our culture has taken on a radical experiment in which the focus is on the well-being of the individual instead of the family group. We are experimenting with the idea that we should empower and enhance the well-being of the individual directly rather than through the support of family-centered efforts. One result of this shift to radical individualism as a cultural mandate is that sex, close relationships, and child rearing are moving from a family-centered activity to an individually centered activity. It is proposed by proponents of this approach that sex not be tied to marriage or even to close relationships, that sex not be tied to childbearing (i.e., birth control), and that the birth of a child not necessarily be tied to a single monogamous relationship. More than one out of four children in the United States are born where a marriage union is not present. When considering children born to African-American mothers, the figure rises to more than 70% not born into a marital union (Waite, 1995).

Many factors contribute to this cultural change in our thinking about marriage, parenting, and family life. Among the most visible reasons are changes in national economics, shifts in religious orientation, and a reevaluation of how we perceive women's role in a changing society. Those ideas can be examined when we consider fundamental changes that have occurred in how families live in a variety of cultural and work-defined arrangements.

For example, in an agricultural society, women and children are much more of a resource to the family enterprise. The more children one has to share the workload, the more productive the overall operation of the farm, orchard, estate, or ranch. In times past, it was much more critical for individuals to bond and band together for protection, common task completion, and general self-preservation.

In sharp contrast, U.S. society since World War II has seen the rise of individual enterprise by men and women. There are few jobs left in any commercial sector that women cannot perform as well as men; physical strength is no longer a prerequisite of job performance in most cases. Additionally, there has been a significant change in attitudes about whether or not a woman *should* do the same types of jobs historically performed only by men. For example, it has become common practice for women to serve in the military, once a prime example of the male-dominated workplace.

Many believe that caretakers can rear children just as well as parents. It is hard to imagine a time in history when parents have been as willing to relinquish the rearing of children to nonfamily members. This change in child-rearing practice was made possible only as we moved away from rural agricultural living. Today, only about 2% of the U.S. population lives in a residential situation in which agricultural production is the primary source of income. This move away from agricultural-based income has had a significant impact on our attitude toward child rearing and fertility itself. In a fast-moving, individually based, entrepreneurial society, many consider children something of a liability. In many Western countries, governments have resorted to offering large cash and goods incentives to parents who birth children. In some countries and certain segments of U.S. culture, fertility rates have fallen "below replacement"; that is, there are not enough children being born to replace the parents when they die.

Therefore, studying daily family life has a greater purpose than teaching individuals how to enjoy each other's company and be more fulfilled in close personal relationships. A major assumption in this book is that understanding the daily life of families is a critically important issue that affects every sector of our society including the well-being of our communities in general.

How Family Life Is Defined in This Text

As previously discussed, there are many forms and styles that families can adopt. For example, when a remarriage is involved, we usually refer to this configuration as a stepfamily. There are also single-parent families and even polygamous family types. In fact, **polygyny** (one man marries two or more women) has been practiced by more human societies than any other form of marriage. Most simple, preindustrial societies and Muslim societies still allow for this type of family arrangement.

Society's definitions of family life have changed over time in response to many cultural, religious, and economic transformations. Within each general historical period, there have been a variety of idealized marital concepts. Because it would be impossible to capture all of those idealized notions about family in one definition, it seems reasonable to follow the lead of two prominent family scholars. In their book *Family Systems in America*, Reiss and Lee (1988) suggested that one should define family in terms of what family members do and not its structure. That is, instead of trying to capture all of the possibilities of who could be found in a family, it is a more useful approach to ask what family groups do with each other. They suggested four central functions of family life: providing sexual intimacy, reproduction, economic cooperation, and the socialization of children. According to most anthropologists, families found in most cultures and subcultures of the world perform these functions. Therefore, in this text, a family is a group of individuals in which there is a generational connection present (i.e., a parent–child relationship is found). Additionally, family members provide close intimate contact (usually characterized by deeply held commitment, trust, respect, and a sense of long-term obligation). It is assumed that sexual intimacy is an element of the relationship between the parents and that this family group seeks to achieve goals by acquiring, allocating, and distributing resources (i.e., time, money, space, and close personal contact).

It is also assumed that individuals choose to participate and contribute to the core sense of family life with varying degrees of enthusiasm. In some cases, the federation of individuals is loosely connected and the beliefs, ideologies, goals, and values of the individuals do not overlap as much. In other cases, there is a stronger sense of the family group in which the individuals with the family share, subscribe, endorse, and contribute to central family ideals, ideologies, beliefs, and goals.

☐ Why Is the Study of Family Life Important?

Many family scholars believe that the study of the family is important and useful in solving many of the problems facing our society for the following reasons.

- *Families are a fundamental unit of society.* This idea reflects a belief that people everywhere in virtually every society have selected family life as the preferred way of joining for survival and strength. Somewhere in our prehistorical past, individuals found that they could do better if they formed small, intimate family groups. Society seems to begin when individuals claim a family group. We have all seen pictures and movies of animals that begin their lives and must be quite independent from the beginning. You might have seen documentaries about animals such as baby wildebeest that can be up and running from a hunting lion within a few hours of birth. Contrast that image to the helplessness of a human infant. A newborn baby is very reliant on its mother for several months and is quite dependent on sustained family life for several years. Therefore, the family unit is fundamental to society because it helps the human race survive to the next generations.
- *The best way to rear children is in families.* Family researchers and family observers believe that the most effective forum for raising children is the family. A child's mother and father are more likely to take special and attentive interest in the well-being of their children. That is not to say that they always do a good job. Rather, overall, the job they do is usually better than that of a disinterested third party. Parents are more likely to make better decisions about their children than would someone else.
- *Better family life means stronger community well-being.* Etzioni (1993) has created an intellectual movement in which he suggests that strength in family life creates community strength. He suggests that when children perform better in school, are arrested less, are more responsible to civic law, and experience less violence in homes, each of us in a community of families benefits. That is, the social and economic standard for all increases and each individual is better able to reach his or her desired life goals.

☐ Family Processes

In our study of the family, it is critical to understand family processes, the strategies used by family members to maximize family goals (Day, Gavazzi, & Acock, 2001). For example, a family goal (derived from a core belief or **ideology**) might focus on education, with the goal that family members will have the greatest chance of doing better in life. Therefore, family processes are those strategies used to reach that goal, which could include tactics like saving money, insisting on certain family habits, and restricting time use. The communication we use, how we solve problems, and how we set and maintain boundaries are all examples of family processes.

It is a basic premise of this text that family goals are founded on core ideologies; that is, families are composed of individuals who have expectations, goals, ideals, and desires. The family represents the intersection where the expectations, goals, ideals, and desires of family members overlap. Therefore, sometimes families have some beliefs and ideas that are strongly held by the group. Of course, not everyone in a family unit totally subscribes to the beliefs and ideologies held by the other family members. However, the core ideas shared by family members become the core of family life. The study of family life is also about families in which there is a loose federation of individuals who share very little. In such cases, the expectations, desires, goals, and ideals of the individuals might have more power to direct how family resources are distributed and allocated. In some families, the connection among family members might be so tenuous that the only thing they share is a common place to sleep.

The preceding idea suggests that there are at least two distinct ways of examining family life. The first way is to examine the family as a definitional unit in which the actual structure of the membership is the focus. By that, I mean we would study family membership (who is there and who is not) and changes in membership (divorce, birth of a child, remarriage, etc.). On the other hand, another legitimate focus of study is the examination of the shared beliefs that family members hold, regardless of who they are, and the strategies families use to achieve goals.

This book is about trying to explore and discover what those beliefs and ideologies might be, how families organize around those ideologies, and how those ideologies are acted out in everyday life. Ultimately we want to know what strategies families use to reach the goals they have and if there are ways to assist them so that they can more successfully reach those goals.

It is also important to realize that the study of daily family life is relatively new. Only recently have scholars and teachers turned their attention to this field of study. Although students and sociological researchers have studied the family as an institution for many years, only a few scholars have turned their attention to inner family life. For more than 100 years, social scientists have been intrigued with the study of the mind of the individual; of course, we call that discipline psychology. This text focuses on the aspect of life that falls somewhere in between the study of the individual and the study of groups in society. Said differently, an important feature of this book is its focus on what happens behind closed doors. Moreover, again, it is assumed that by studying the intricacies of daily life, we can have some chance of assisting individuals as they try to make daily family life better for those involved.

Not only have most social scientists studied families from the larger, macro view and looked at the family as an institution, but also most family scholars investigate the extraordinary. That is, they are interested in family crises such as divorce, the death of a child or spouse, the effects of catastrophic poverty, or violence in families. The study of these problematic areas of family life is important and has alerted us to the many challenges facing today's children and parents, but there is another side of family life characterized by the ordinary, mundane, prosaic, everyday events of life. In this book, we spend most of our time talking about the ordinary choices and everyday decisions families make. There is a growing awareness that the ordinary acts of daily living have a special power. It is often the routine acts of daily life that shape who we are and how our lives "turn out." Occasionally, a dramatic event will severely alter a family forever. Nevertheless, for most people, lives are filled with the routine acts of daily living that combine together to form and shape who we really are.

☐ The Protean Family

In Greek mythology, Proteus was a lesser known but important god of the sea. His claim to fame was that he could change his shape into various forms at will. The derivative word **protean** describes someone or something that has this same ability. The family seems to fall into this category. Families themselves take on many forms; they are changeable, polymorphous, and versatile. Additionally, the definitions of family life are also protean. Those who think about family life and decide which type of small group is a family and which is not choose from among the many definitions available and select the one that best suits their purposes and ideological orientation.

For example, businesses or governmental agencies define the family in ways that serve a particular purpose and are usually very specific and precise. Billions of dollars are meted out each year in transfer payments to "family members." For example, insurance companies will only cover the medical expenses of family members that fall within their very restricted family member definition. Some authors (e.g., Cherlin, 1999) suggest that such definitions fall into our notion of a public family.

Those wishing to broaden the definition of the family seek to make private family life (as opposed to public family life) an individual choice in which a variety of styles, configurations, and combinations are acceptable. Those who approach the study of family life from more traditional business or governmental points of view might seek to limit and constrict the definition of the family for economic reasons. In addition, those who view the family as a sacred religious institution will suggest a particular configuration and even gender role assignment within the family based on doctrine and beliefs that support their point of view.

FIGURE 1.3   The family has to change overtime as different cultural and physical demands change.

PRINCIPLE 1.3 FAMILIES ARE PROTEAN

Families are very adaptable and change structure and even what they do within family life (function) to meet the demands of a changing and volatile world.

☐ Summary

It is not the purpose of this text to suggest to a wide and diverse audience which of the many definitions of family life one should adopt. Instead, it is a stated goal of this chapter that the reader should carefully consider this issue and be able to articulate a position about one's personal definition of what constitutes family life and be able to show how that definition flows from a central, ideological, or even practical notion.

In designing your definition of a family, you might wish to consider the beliefs of your parents, community members, friends, and other family members. From these you might be able to find and identify your personal private family definition. The last task in this set of thought exercises is to consider what would be the optimal family, in your opinion. Too often, we design our definitions and make moral decisions while attempting to be overly inclusive, and in our attempt to be fair, we try to consider every iteration of a complicated matrix of possibilities. Instead, this exercise asks you to define family from the perspective of ideas, ideals, beliefs, and ideologies that you hold. In other words, what does family life mean to you specifically and to those with whom you come in contact? What is your personal ideal about family life?

☐ Study Questions

1. What types of family difficulties might one study in the field of family science?
2. What does the term *protean family* refer to?
3. Is it possible to study the family without bringing a bias to that endeavor?
4. Explain what we mean by the idea that in U.S. culture there has been a move away from the idea that sex and child rearing are strongly linked to marriage? What evidence can you present to substantiate that claim?
5. What do we mean when we say that family life is unique?
6. Define what we mean by *family processes*. Give several examples of different family processes.
7. What is a family process? How is that term defined and used in this text?
8. What do we mean when we say that we are defining family in terms of function instead of structure?
9. Explain in your own words what Principle 1.1 means when it says that families employ processes that effect goals.
10. Why do we (the family science scholarly community) care about families?

☐ Key Terms

Love-Lab
Quotidian
Prosaic
Family of procreation
Family of orientation
Head Start
Family processes
Temporary Assistance to Needy Families
Family of origin
Same-sex marriages
Defense of Marriage Act
Covenant marriage
No-fault divorce
Child rearing
Childbearing
Polygyny
Ideology
Protean family

☐ Suggested Readings

Amato, P., Booth, A., Johnson, D., & Rogers, S. (2007). *Alone together.* Cambridge, MA: Harvard University Press.

Brodrick, C. (1993). *Understanding family process: Basics of family systems.* Newbury Park, CA: Sage.

Coltrane, S., & Adams, M. (2008). *Gender and families.* Lanham, MD: Rowman & Littlefield.

Coontz, S. (1992). *The way we never were: American families and the nostalgia trap.* New York: Basic Books.

Kowaleski-Jones, L., & Wolfinger, N. (2006). *Family families and the marriage agenda.* New York: Springer.

Roopnarine, J., & Gielen, U. (2005). *Families in global perspective.* Boston: Allyn & Bacon.

Thornton, A. (2001). *The well-being of children and families.* Ann Arbor: University of Michigan Press.

How We Study Families

☐ Chapter Preview

In this chapter, readers will learn:

- How personal inquiry is a key way in which we understand the world. However, it is one of the least reliable ways of substantiating a research hypothesis.
- That the research process can be broken down into three elements: goals, strategies, and tactics.
- How empirical or quantitative research attempts to systematically measure or assess the world of the family by interviewing or observing them directly.
- That field research seeks to understand the stories of family life by using the techniques of in-depth interviews and participant observation.
- That it is important to understand the difference between a construct and a variable and between correlation and causation.
- How validity and reliability are key notions in family research is validity and reliability. A valid measure assesses what we think it is supposed to measure and a reliable measure assesses the same idea time after time with the same precision.

☐ Introduction

Those who embark on the journey to study family behavior soon discover the intricacies of the science of family life. The family science community of scholars struggles with some of the core problems of human existence: Why do some families endure and others dissolve? Why do some excel at collecting and using resources wisely and others do poorly? Why are some families plagued with chronic and destructive violence as a feature of their daily life and others are relatively violence free? To that end, family scientists collect data of various kinds, analyze ideas, apply theoretical notions, and try to make sense out of the world of family life.

This chapter explores how family scientists research inner family life and how they think about core theoretical positions that describe interactions in families. In the first section, we explore the language and methods of social science and provide examples of how research about families is collected. In the second section, we explore some of the theoretical language used in family science. It is not the intent of this chapter to dig deeply into research methods, statistics, or theoretical ideas used in this discipline; however, the constructs presented here are important. They help us understand how to better evaluate the research we read and use as we attempt to intervene in the lives of families—be it our own family or other families we aim to help.

☐ Concepts in Family Science Research

Family scientists use a variety of research methods to discover new information about family, verify theoretically based hypothesis, or design some kind of intervention to make family life better. In addition, some family scientists design research to evaluate the effectiveness of family-based programs. It is important for students of family science to become familiar with the language and reasoning processes of science. As was mentioned in Chapter 1, the study of families is more than a self-help journey. You might find pieces of information in your study of family life that will, in fact, help you and your family personally. The study of family science, however, seeks to transcend the idea of self-help, goes further than even helping other families (i.e., this text is not really a book about how to intervene in the lives of families), and, instead, focuses on the collected body of knowledge that encompasses the discipline of the study of the family. With that in mind, the first way that people usually think about approaching their understanding of family life is what we call **personal inquiry**.

Personal Inquiry

As you sit in the doctor's office, you spy a recent edition of *Working Woman*. You notice a short two-page article on day care. The writer provides a short list of "dos and don'ts" for mothers with children in day care. For example, according to this article, one should check to see if the day care facility keeps a daily log of your child's activities, needs, and problems. It also suggests dropping in unannounced and checking out the situation during the day when you are normally not there. How would you rate this kind of research approach? Is this truly research? Now, suppose you turn to the man next to you with a crying 2-year-old and ask his opinion about day care. It turns out that the two of you have similar views. You conclude that day care is a good option, and in your opinion, it appears to the two of you that your children are doing just fine, thank you. On what have you based your view? Why did you come to that conclusion or a different one? How do your values and beliefs fit into your answer? What role did research play in your conclusion? Have you actually read studies about day care and its effects (or lack of effects) on children? Even if you did read a well-crafted research article about this topic—and it differed from your view—would you hold to what you believe or could your belief or ideal be shaken by research? All of these are important questions that we hope to explore within this chapter. We begin by reminding you that your personal opinion about any issue is very complex and its sources are varied and difficult to identify. You could have picked up your view from an older sister, a troubling scene in a movie, a sermon given by a minister, or it could just be built on a "gut feeling" you have. It is not our intent to discount those sources from which we all derive opinions. However, there are other ways of exploring and confronting the knowledge of life. It is important to remember that science, per se, is not about finding ultimate truth: We will leave that to others. Science is about working with truth like ideas—all of which, by definition—have to have the possibility of being proven false. We do the best we can at searching for ideas that are usable, make sense, and seem to stand the test of research practices. Ultimately, though, final truths fall into the realm of theology and belief.

Experiential Reality

It is important to understand that your **personal experiences** are valuable. They mean a great deal to you; they define who you are and how you experience and approach life, make decisions, and solve problems. However, your **personal experiential reality** (Babbie, 2006) has limitations. For one thing, it might color what you see and what you believe. Consider the preceding example. Were you raised in a family within which day care was used frequently? Did you go to day care as a child? Perhaps you left your children at day care or someone close to you has made that choice. In addition, you might have strong feelings about that choice. Perhaps in your family of origin there is a strong ideological orientation that calls for all family members to work outside the home if they can or want to. It could be that you were raised in a home with a stay-at-home mom, or you might have been home schooled. According to the National Center for Educational Statistics (2008), more than 1.5 million children in the United States were home schooled in 2007. That is nearly a 30% increase from the number being home schooled in 1999. If you are one of those who came from a home school environment and no day care, your personal views about day care and its effects on children could be much different than those of someone who grew up participating in day care.

The process of doing family science research is designed to go beyond personal experience and look at the world of family life in a scientific and more objective way. It is not designed to confirm the lifestyle of a single participant, nor is it designed to validate the religious, ideological, or political views of potential research sponsors. By the same token, the experience of a single person is (or can be) interesting and can even lead to future research, but students in class are asked to think more broadly than the isolated experience of one individual.

PRINCIPLE 2.1   FAMILY SCIENCE RESEARCH

Sound family science asks us to go beyond our personal experience.

Problems With Personal Inquiry

One of the first problems with using personal experience or personal inquiry as the basis for making general statements about family life is what we call **sample bias.** When we conduct social research, we are trying to discover or understand a problem within a **population.** A population is the group we are interested in making statements or generalizations about. Populations tend to be fairly large, so researchers will look at only a portion of the population, referred to as a **sample**. Researchers try very hard to make sure their sample is representative of the population they are studying; in this way, they are better able to generalize their findings from their sample to the target.

For example, some family scientists are interested in male prisoners in the United States. Within this population are various subpopulations, including men who have children and are going to be released back into family life within 3 months. You can imagine that men who have children might have different characteristics and beliefs from those who do not. A researcher might randomly choose 2,000 of the total population of fathers about to be released (i.e., a sample of the population) to study on a particular topic. The prisoners would be chosen randomly in an attempt to make sure they represent the entire group.

Compare that approach to asking a class member if he or she has a relative who has been to prison and asking her or him to share what she or he thinks about the fairness of the prison system. With a sample of one person, we very likely will get a **biased** view. Take a moment to look in the dictionary to see what biased means. You will find that your dictionary defines biased as a tendency or inclination that causes someone to be prejudiced. In statistics, we often say that bias means that there is **systematic** (as opposed to **random**) **distortion** of a statistical result. Therefore the one person who comments in class might not (usually does not) represent the condensed, distilled, well-rounded opinion that we might get if we interviewed 2,000 people.

Seeing What We Want to See

Another problem with the single observer and personal experience is that one tends to see what one wants to see. This is not a flaw, per se; instead, it is a human condition. When we are faced with making sense of our world, we often respond to what Babbie (2006) called **agreement reality**. That is, we are immersed with groups of people we love, we respect, and we want to love us. The stories and tales we hear about prison life, for example, come from one person's perspective and are usually told to a group. That group coalesces around an idea and then promotes that point of view. Sometimes, this agreement reality is not even discussed openly. For example, we "just know" that we are to agree with certain opinions or behave in certain ways in the group; we know that it is not our place to have a conversation about why we have these rules. Therefore, taking the opinion of one person and acting on it (in the case of research questions) is problematic. That person might not even be aware of the bias brought to the discussion.

Another reason we often seek opinions from multiple people rather than a single individual is that the individual's view of the world is frequently off center. That is, humans are notorious for **reporting inaccuracy**. This does not mean that all humans are liars. Instead, it simply means that we are not very good social observers, we have remarkably poor memories, and we filter what we see and hear through years of personal experience. Now, one could easily ask, "What, then, is the point of asking 2,000 people if all of them are poor reporters?" Good question. The answer is that most social scientists would rather stand on a research finding that was the predominant response of 2,000 relatively independent (i.e., they do not know each other or are not all alike in some obvious way) observers than to just ask one or two people. At least with 2,000 participants, one might have some notion about how the event or attitudes varied across those 2,000 people (taking into consideration that some may be rich, some poor, some African American, others European American). Statistically, we could compare their responses and find out if that event or their behavior was seen in a similar way by small groups within the sample of 2,000. For example, one might compare parenting ideas of prisoner fathers who grew up in poverty with the ideas of those prisoner fathers whose families were better off.

We could even examine those whose responses were so different or odd that we call them **outliers** (or unusual respondents). Scientists can learn much from those who respond in a significantly different way, but they must be careful not to inadvertently think that the outlier represents the majority of the population. This latter problem is referred to as **overgeneralizing**. To overgeneralize means to take the opinions of one person or a small, nonrepresentative group of people and assume that what those people think or how they behave is representative of a larger group.

In sum, practically everyone has vast experience in family life. It turns out, however, that your personal experience in that one family (or even two or three families) is very limited and is, by definition, biased. That is not a critique of you, personally, but it is a caution to those who would take their personal family experience, whatever it might be, and overgeneralize that idea to the vast population of families that are not their own.

☐ Research Goals, Strategies and Tactics

Social science research involves the use of goals, strategies, and tactics. **Research goals** refer to the overarching questions researchers are interested in asking. **Research strategies** are the overall plans and methods used to solve a specific research goal, and **tactics** are the procedures or modes of attacking a problem. The goals scientists have will influence which strategies and tactics they choose. Let's examine a real-life example.

Researchers have often wondered how family structure (e.g., whether a family has been divorced, has stayed intact, or is a stepfamily) and family processes combine to influence the healthy outcomes of children. In 1995, researchers at the University of North Carolina initiated a study of more than 20,000 families (see *http://www.cpc.unc.edu/projects/addhealth*for a complete description of this important study). This study, the National Longitudinal Study of Adolescent Health (or Add Health, for short), is the largest, most comprehensive survey of adolescents ever undertaken.

The general goal of the Add Health project is to examine how social contexts (families, friends, peers, schools, neighborhoods, and communities) influence adolescents' health and risk behaviors. The research strategy mostly involved conducting in-depth interviews with more than 20,000 families across the United States. To date, there have been three waves (or sets) of data collected (1995, 1996, and 2001). More than 1,000 research studies have been produced from the Add Health data set, and many of those research findings have altered how we view teens and their parents. The tactics used by these researchers included, first, an in-school interview with a nationally representative population of teens in Grades 7 through 12.

As discussed earlier, researchers want to avoid sampling bias. The Add Health study tried to address this issue by finding study volunteers in a variety of kinds of schools, locations, and socioeconomically mixed neighborhoods across the United States. Based on the quality of the data and the number of first-rate publications that have emerged from this spectacular effort, researchers are fairly certain that this sample, although not perfect, is reasonably representative of family life in the United States.

We frequently refer to this type of research effort as a **quantitative research strategy,** meaning that the responses of the individuals are reduced to a series of recorded quantifiable

FIGURE 2.1 The Add Health project has surveyed more than 20,000 families in their homes, asking a myriad of questions about their personal lives and about their family.

numbers. Using sophisticated statistical techniques, researchers can then analyze the data to answer a variety of questions about adolescent health, family life, and the transition into adulthood. Hundreds of graduate students from around the world have written their master's theses and doctoral dissertations using these data. Such data are relatively inexpensive to obtain and most of the information is available to the research community. Sharing of data and publishing findings are basic tenets of the scientific endeavor.

PRINCIPLE 2.2   FAMILY SCIENCE NOT ABOUT TRUTH, PER SE

Family science is uncovering our best guess about the ways things work in families. It is not about discovering absolute, immutable truths. Hence, every research project has limitations and biases.

As Principle 2.2 points out, every research project, however, has limitations. The Add Health data set is somewhat limited in its data about inner family life. For example, there are few questions asked of the family about family routines, family rituals, and other in-depth family processes. Still, there are enough different types of questions that were asked of each family and asked over three different time periods that researchers will be busy with these data for years.

☐ Causation and Correlation

Researchers (like everyone else) are interested in knowing what causes things to happen or what causes people to be the way they are. Unfortunately, simply collecting data does not always tell us the cause of things. Sometimes, it appears that we know the cause, but often, we are making a mistake by assuming **causation**. One of the biggest errors one can make is to assume causation based on correlational data. A **correlation** is simply collecting two sets of data and seeing if they relate ("co-relate"). Just because two things appear to happen together does not mean that one is causing the other to happen.

Let's examine a research finding from the Add Health research project. In one study (*http://www.youthdevelopment.org/articles/fp010001.htm*), researchers found that both family structure (i.e., the family is composed of the original biological parents, remarried parents, or single parent) and the number of times per week a family has meals together are related to the probability that a teenager in the family will have an early sexual experience. For example, if both parents were the biological parents and the family has more than five meals together weekly, the teen in the home was more than twice as likely to have not had an early sexual experience. Please be careful here: The topic is causation. Does this finding imply or demand that there is a causal sequence? Can one say, "Not eating meals together as a family causes teenagers to engage in early sexuality" or "Families that eat together won't have to worry about teen pregnancy"? An important element of research (in any discipline) is realizing what we can say from our research and when the research is being abused.

Spurious Relationships

In this case, we introduce the term **spurious relationship.** A spurious relationship is one in which two events are seemingly related, but on further examination, we find that both of them are, in fact, the result of some other third event. Here is an example: On the Oregon coast, as the number of hot dogs sold in local stores rises, there is a dramatic increase in the drowning deaths at the nearby beaches. So, therefore, one might conclude that the sale of hot dogs *causes* drowning in the ocean. Is this correct? Not really. A third event connects hot dog sales and drowning. What is it? You guessed it—both occur in the summer.

Using the notion of spurious relationship, then, what could be said about the dinner time and sexual activity table? Here is a quote from the Add Health lead researcher Kathleen Mullan Harris: "Obviously it is not the dinner meal that is reducing [sexual activity]. There is something about sharing this time on a regular basis that promotes healthy development. I think a multi-faceted process is going on" (*http://www.youthdevelopment.org/articles/fp010001.htm*).

In addition to just thinking about dinner time and what goes on there, perhaps another explanation for those fascinating findings is that some parents have a slightly different way of organizing their lives, and dinner just happens to be a part of the special relationship or organizational pattern found in certain types of families.

☐ Constructs and Variables

The preceding dinner time example illuminates another aspect of social science research: Researchers spend focused time identifying important constructs and variables within the research endeavor. In the research world, a **construct** is an idea or formulation we deem relevant to a particular theory or research question. A **variable** is an extension or way of assessing or measuring a construct. It is also obvious that a variable varies. That is, we usually think of a variable as having breadth, depth, length, or some other dimension. Returning to the dinner time example, the construct in this research formulation is (or could be) family time together. These researchers theorized that certain types of family experiences, such as time together, might be a signal or marker for some other more difficult-to-measure family process. In this case, that construct was measured using the variable of number of meals eaten together in a week. During the research project, family members were asked to report how many meals they ate together. In addition, the teenagers in the study (over time and retrospectively) were asked at what age they first had sexual intercourse. If you use your imagination for just a moment here, you can easily see how difficult a simple research problem can become. First, whose report of the number of meals are you going to use? Should you use an average of all respondents? In this case, they decided to use the mother's report—thinking that maybe her report was more accurate and reliable (see later discussion about reliability).

One could also ask if you believe that teenagers would really be honest about their sexual activity. What percentage of the 13,000 youth who were asked this question gave honest answers? When they were answering, for example, did they imagine that their parents might have access to the data? Did they also possibly imagine that it was shameful to have (or to not have) had a sexual experience at their age? In addition, what about the family structure variables used here? Nothing is said in this report about how many times the parents were married, divorced, and then remarried. They were simply listed as stepparents. We also are not given any information about the age of the parents. The parents' age, how many other children are in the family, and if the mother works outside the home could have significant effects on the dinner time experience. Finally, what about the income and ethnic differences that surely would make a huge difference here?

The point here is not to throw cold water on this interesting study; rather, it is to be careful when reading, citing, and using social science research. I have attempted to be careful in this text using the same admonition. Those of us who are social scientists love to dream up constructs (sometimes they turn out to be quite good—and other times quite silly). We love to find ways of measuring those ideas (but our methods are very primitive). We love to take our findings and try to help people (most of us in family science are do-gooders at heart). Your responsibility as a student, and eventually a community worker or family member, is to be careful with what you read. Try to dig deeper to make sure you have some idea that the information you are using is not bogus.

☐ Empirical Research

The process of doing family science research as already described is sometimes labeled **empiricism**. Empiricism is a philosophical tradition that tells us that to really know our world we have to rely on experience, but not just any old ordinary experience, experience that is as objective as possible. Did the ice melt or not? Is the earth kind of flat or perhaps spherical? Through a very elaborate series of experiments (relying on primary sensory experience), early scientists gathered "facts," examined the measurable variables, and proposed that, indeed, the world was not flat. That seems to have been well documented in recent years with pictures (another form of sensory evidence) from spacecraft. This approach insists that we do not accept (for the purposes of science) revelatory declarations, preferences of individuals, or proclamations by powerful public figures (remember the discussion earlier about truth). We have, within our Western cultural tradition, moved away from accepting the divine right of the king, pope, or other charismatic leaders to declare that some human condition is a given. For example, Hitler convinced an entire nation of people that Jews were "subhuman." All science aside and all empirical evidence to the contrary, he declared it and mandated that it must be so. The empirically based social scientist would counter such declarations and would say, "Show me the data!"; in other words, show me the evidence that Jews are subhuman. If you cannot do that, you cannot build your arguments (religious, political, or governmental) on that assertion.

PRINCIPLE 2.3   EMPIRICISM IN FAMILY SCIENCE

Empiricism is one way to tell the story of inner family life. It attempts to do so through numbers and statistics.

☐ Field Research

There is a type of research that does not focus so much on statistics, variables, and correlations. **Field research**, instead, focuses on the natural events, interviews, and case study analyses. There are at least three kinds of field research common in family science: **participant observation**, **in-depth interviews**, and **focus group** analysis. In this chapter, we focus on the two most widely used field research approaches: participant observation and in-depth interviews.

Participant Observation

In participant observation, the researchers immerse themselves in situations, family groups, tribes, or communities. There are several excellent examples of this kind of research. Dr. Barry Hewlett, for example, has spent the last 30 years regularly visiting the Aka people of Central Africa. Hewlett, Lamb, Shannon, Leyendecker, and Scholmerich (1998) explored how parents interact with infants in different cultures. The hypothesis was that European Americans focused their interactive attention with infants on verbal skills and interaction that occurs at a distance from the child. Imagine a mother or father leaning over the crib talking and cooing with the infant.

On the other hand, researchers have noticed that parents in traditional small societies spend much more time holding and carrying their infants. These findings have been collected mostly from researchers simply visiting a location and watching interactions for 1 to 2 hours. Hewlett and colleagues traveled to Central Africa. (Hewlett does this type of research on a regular basis, as was mentioned, so he has a 30-year working relationship with a number of villages.) How, exactly, did these researchers collect their data? In this study, the researchers lived in the villages of two small communities, known as the Aka and Ngandu. The Aka live in camps of 25 to 30 people, moving several times a year as they search for hunting locations. They live in small dome-shaped huts constructed by the women. These huts are large enough only for a very short bed (4 ft.) and a small fire. The Ngandu (the comparison group for this study) live alongside roads in rather established communities. They live in huts built by the men that are about 40 ft. by 20 ft. Most of the huts are constructed of thatch and mud. About 30% to 40% of the men have more than one wife (**polygyny**) and each wife has her own room or hut. The Aka are much less integrated into anything that represents a commerce-based society—they have no cash, nor do they buy or sell much of anything. They make their own clothes and kill or grow their own food. On the other hand, the Ngandu are more likely to have received some schooling and

FIGURE 2.2 Aka fathers hold their infants for safety.

might work at jobs for pay. In this study, the researchers wanted to know how the type of living style changed how parents interacted with their children. They hypothesized that as a group becomes more integrated into a commerce-based society, the more the parents would physically disengage from their infants. Think for a minute and speculate why that would be the case (see later for some suggestions).

In this type of field research, the researchers used a clipboard and coded score sheets. The codes for the behaviors they were interested in studying (infant interaction) were developed by other researchers over many years. These codes have high levels of validity and reliability. **Validity** means that the measures they used are, hopefully, measuring what the researchers think they are measuring. There are different types of validity that are not covered here (e.g., face, predictive, convergent); if you are interested in these you might want to find a research methods book or explore this term online. **Reliability** speaks to the idea that each time researchers use the measure they get similar results. Suppose you walk into a clock store, and there are hundreds of clocks on the walls. You notice that they are all set to the same time. If the time on all the clocks matches the satellite broadcast of the actual atomic clock used to measure time (*http://www.time.gov/*), you could say that the clocks in the store have a valid measure of the correct time. Reliability, on the other hand, speaks to the long-term accuracy of the clocks. So, a clock could be very reliable—it just keeps on ticking and its hours and minutes are right on the mark. However, if it is set 16 minutes too fast it is not really expressing a valid time—just a reliable time.

With that in mind, these researchers had to have a good working relationship with the people they were observing and had to be skilled at what to look for. They had to have excellent reliable and valid instruments (their code behavior on the clipboards) to be assessing clearly thought-out constructs tied to a theoretical idea. The research tactic used by Hewlett and colleagues was simply to sit in a corner of the hut or nearby and code the infant–parent interaction while the families went about their everyday lives for days at a time. They had to make sure their presence did not in some way alter the daily living routines of the villagers, and they had to try to administer their behavioral coding assessments in a reliable, consistent way.

What did they find? In fact, they discovered that Aka parents held their children much more than did the Ngandu. The Ngandu were more likely to talk and verbalize with their children. Why? These researchers suggested several reasons. One thought has been that in more primitive cultures, especially hunting-based societies, people must live in more remote and more dangerous settings. The parents might hold their children more to keep them from insects, snakes, and other "on-the-ground" hazards. Hewlett disagreed with this reason. In his observation, there were just as many snakes, insects, and hazards in the Aka settings as there were in the Ngandu villages.

Perhaps the difference in holding is related to nutrition. The Aka do not store food, per se, and the infants might need more contact through nourishing. That hypothesis did not prove to be the explanation either. What these researchers concluded was very interesting. The primary finding was they really did not know why the two groups were so different. They made a very important point relevant to our discussion about research. In essence, they say that they (the European American and European researchers) were bringing their own bias to this problem. That is, all of the potential reasons for differences that they generated were ideas that came from the minds of people who were raised in the suburbs of Western civilization and not on the jungle floor of Central Africa. They then ventured some other guesses about the number of yearly relocations each group experienced and also suggested that their worldviews about family life, egalitarian lifestyle, and the value of children might be at the heart of the difference. You are encouraged to read this interesting article and see if you have other ideas.

In sum, there are several key points that this article helps us with. First, we learn that participant observation field research is difficult and costly but provides wonderfully rich data. These kinds of data provide an illuminated image of how people conduct the prosaic of everyday life. Second, participant observation research does not rely on a random sample or population-based demographics, nor is it even necessary that the participants really know what the research is about. These participants were not literate and could not fill out a questionnaire, nor would they even know what to do with a semistructured interview. Third, most field research requires in-depth training and, in most cases, years of experience and preparation. Most graduate students and young social science professionals are unwilling to load their backpacks and head into the jungle of Central Africa to live with the Aka for 3 to 4 months at a time. The results can be wonderful, but often the costs are high.

In-Depth Interviews

A second type of field research is the in-depth interview. In this type of research, researchers locate and interview a group of individuals who share a common life experience. For example, one could interview women whose husbands are about to be released from prison, or researchers could interview couples who have had a child suffer a spinal-cord injury. Usually, these researchers do not attempt to sample the whole population of possible participants, but instead, they will interview a relatively small number of individuals who are willing to tell their story. As participants tell their story, the researcher takes careful notes, often recording the interviews for analysis at a later time. Once the interviews are completed, the researchers have a word-by-word transcript created of each interview. This can be a lengthy and expensive process. Interviews continue until the researcher reaches a **saturation** level; that is, new interviews do not seem to be yielding any new information.

Here is an example of the use of in-depth interviews. In 2004, an article was published in the *Journal of Marriage and Family* about parents in Bangladesh and their views on having girls instead of boys. The researchers, Ahmed and Bould (2004), interviewed 120 mothers who were employed at a garment factory in Dhaka. They began the article by noting that only 20 years ago, researchers were very pessimistic that women in Bangladesh would ever have an avenue to equal power in family relationships. These families are very poor and most of them are without land, and the husbands have either no job or one that pays a very low wage. Over the last 20 years, the women of the family have begun to find work in garment factories, and with those wages, they have begun to be able to make choices independent of the men's wishes for them. Most researchers, until recently, have written that families in Bangladesh are extremely patriarchal. That is, the husband's word is law, and women have traditionally had very little say in family and household matters. With this newfound independence, these women are creating a better life for themselves and their families, according to these authors.

In this type of research, there was no questionnaire, per se, filled out by the women. No attempt was made to generate an unbiased sample, nor was there any attempt to show how attitudes change over time, or vary by the number and gender of the children in the family. In this type of field research, the researcher must be careful to not infer spurious causal connections. Instead, the researcher tells the story, in this case, of a small number of women who are struggling with provisioning and surviving. The researchers looked for themes in the stories of these women. In addition, there was care taken in this type of research to note the cultural or community contexts that might be relevant. For example, these authors used several pages to describe how there is great pressure on these women to have sons because sons are the key to security in old age. The women in rural Bangladesh must (at least in the past) rely on their fathers to begin with, then on their husbands; and if the husband dies, the woman must look to her son for support. Women without men in their lives are extremely vulnerable. In this study, however, the women who worked in the factory seemed to have changed their attitudes, and less than 10% of them reported that the ideal family had sons in it. Instead, they seemed to be hoping for daughters who could work with them and help bring in income. These women's power also seemed to increase when they were able to direct some of their income to their kin and help support them.

In field research, the goal is not to present a statistical comparative picture of family life. Instead, the goal is to provide more rich description of how the family works through the eyes of those reporting the **lived experience.**

☐ Summary

Which of these approaches is best? The answer is all of them. They are all ways of telling the story of the human condition and both are very valuable. Often those who do the more quantitative or empirical work rely on the lived experience world of the field researcher. In a like manner, the field researcher pays close attention to the findings of larger empirical, longitudinal, statistical-based research findings. Those findings inform and enlighten his or her efforts.

In this chapter, you have read about how family science researchers go about the task of trying to discover how to better understand family life. There are many ways researchers collect information about families. Sometimes, we use large-scale data sets like those created by government (e.g., census data), sometimes researchers rely on historical accounts, others collect information from within clinical settings, others complete in-depth interviews with families, and still others ask family members about their beliefs and attitudes about their lived experiences. All of these methods are legitimate and useful when done carefully and with precision. All of them are attempts to tell the story of family life. It is not helpful to claim that one of them is better than another; instead, each contributes to the story of family life in a different way and each helps build a wonderfully rich mosaic—a mural of family life. When we step back and look at all the stories told by all the means possible, only then can we begin to the see the richness of the whole picture.

☐ Study Questions

1. Explain what is meant by experiential reality and why this idea is presented with the topic of personal inquiry.
2. What is sample bias and how is this issue addressed in family research? Give an example of sample bias and show how that bias could render research findings problematic.
3. What is the difference between a strategy and a tactic according to the text?
4. Define what is meant by quantitative research.
5. What is the difference between a construct and a variable? Explain each and provide a an example (not found in the text) of each.
6. Contrast the idea of empirical or quantitative research with that of qualitative field research.
7. What are the two primary types of field research explained in the text? Explain, define, and provide examples for each.
8. Why do we care about the idea of causation and correlation? In your answer, include (and define) the idea of spurious relationship.
9. Describe the study reported in the text about the Aka and Ngandu peoples. Why was this study used as an example? Why didn't the researchers use more qualitative methods in their research?

☐ Key Terms

Personal inquiry
Personal experiences
Personal experiential reality
Sample bias
Sample
Population
Biased
Systematic and random distortion
Agreement reality
Reporting inaccuracy
Outliers
Overgeneralizing
Research goals
Research strategies
Tactics
Health
Quantitative research strategy
Causation
Correlation

Spurious relationship
Constructs
Variables
Empiricism
Field research
Participant observation
In-depth interviews
Focus group
Polygyny
Reliability
Validity
Saturation
Lived experience

☐ Suggested Readings

Babbie, E. (2006). *The practice of social research*. New York: Wadsworth.
Glenberg, A. M., & Andrezejewski, M. E. (2008). *Learning from data: An introduction to statistical reasoning* (3rd ed.). New York: Lawrence Erlbaum Associates.
Seccomb, K. (2008). *Families and their social worlds*. Boston: Allyn & Bacon.

CHAPTER

Theories About Family Life

☐ Chapter Preview

In this chapter, readers will learn:

- That theoretical orientations flow from deeper philosophical traditions. Among those are the traditions of rationalism, empiricism, and existentialism.
- How theoretical approaches assist us in our study of family life. Among them are rational/exchange, developmental/family life cycle, symbolic interaction, conflict, and systems theory.
- That individuals join together to form a family and a family is an entity.
- How an entity or group of individuals can be tied together by a common set of goals and beliefs, and how families have systemic properties. This is sometimes called "wholeness" and refers to the idea that a system is a complexity of elements standing in interaction as an underlying pattern or structure.
- That family groups or systems attempt to maintain stability over time. This is called homeostasis. Family systems also must adapt and change over time and this is called morphogenesis.
- That it is difficult to speak of causality when referring to system processes. Instead, one tries to identify patterns of interaction.

☐ Introduction

The theories we use in social science are representations or models for something tangible and real. Remember the discussion in Chapter 2 within which I proposed that empirical and theoretical ideas change and develop over time and are never meant to represent a position of truth, per se. Instead, theories are perspectives that help us understand reality and are merely constructs that we use as tools to approximate our understanding of the "real" world. An important question to ask in response to that last statement could be "Is there a real world?"

It is also important to realize that most of the methodological and theoretical ideas and terms presented here did not originate in the young discipline of family science. Instead, these ideas have, for the most part, a long and rich history in other disciplines such as sociology, economics, and psychology.

Within the pages of this chapter, several theories used in family sciences are presented. There are two important limitations you should know about the following synopsis of these theoretical ideas. First, each of the theories mentioned has a prominent history in the social sciences. Our glimpse of these complicated ideas only captures a small portion of the volumes written about each.

Second, these are not the only theories used by family scholars. The following overview represents a quick look at the theories most frequently used. If you continue studying family science, you might wish to take a course that examines these and other theoretical ideas in depth. Additionally, the suggested readings at the end of this chapter provide a starting place for extended study about theoretical orientations in the discipline of family science.

☐ What Is Theory?

The word *theory* can sometimes produce a chill in everyday conversation, but an understanding of theoretical ideas is essential when embarking on voyages of scientific discovery. Theoretical ideas have inspired discoveries in astronomy, biology, economics, and medicine. Whether one wants to discover new knowledge or to apply ideas already known, efforts are much more effective if they are done within the context of established theories.

When scholars or application specialists try to answer the question "What is going on here?" they are always building on the accumulated findings of others. In everyday life, people refer to this phenomenon when they say there is "no need to reinvent the wheel." One of the most important tasks of scholars and thinkers in family science is the work of collecting and organizing ideas into theories. From these core, fundamental ideas and principles of family life, come a wealth of notions that can assist us in explaining why people do what they do. These constructs also can assist when we decide to change behaviors in our life that do not help meet the goals we have in mind.

In sum, theories are combinations of hunches, collected facts (or ideas we think are facts), and the accepted wisdom about aspects of a situation. They provide a common language for discussion about a topic and provide suggestions for research and application directions. Most of the theoretical ideas presented here will sound familiar and you might discover that many of them are rather commonsense notions. However, these collected ideas represent a "language"; in other words, terms and constructs summarize our best thinking about the ways families and individuals in families set out to solve life's problems, build stronger relationships, and make daily decisions. The following are several key terms, constructs, and ideas that constitute many of the theoretical viewpoints discussed later.

Reductionism

One of the more important questions in studying families (or any other social process) is how we approach the complexity of social life. An ongoing debate in social science centers on the topic of **reductionism**. On the one hand, some believe that it is inappropriate and ineffective to "reduce" life to small fragments or parts of behavior. For example, a reductionist-oriented researcher would try to identify the tiny pieces of daily behavior that make up life. He or she would attempt to show that the parts matter and are connected.

FIGURE 3.1   This family is being reduced to small fragments—we call that a kind of research reductionism.

Additionally, a reductionist would suggest ways of intervening in a problem by targeting one or more of the parts for change.

A reductionistic perspective takes the view that one can successfully focus on the small parts of a family and figure out what that family will do in a variety of situations (Sprey, 2000). The small parts are usually the people within the family. The approach for many years in family studies, therefore, has been to focus on each person in the family and note what **roles** each one plays (i.e., father, provider, caretaker, defender, etc). For example, to measure marital satisfaction, each partner was asked a few questions about how he or she thought the marriage was going. Sometimes the responses from both partners were statistically merged and guesses were made about how "happy" the marriage was. This created some problems for theorists and researchers. Many began to realize that marriages and families were more dynamic than merely the sum of the two scores.

PRINCIPLE 3.1   REDUCTIONISM

Reductionism focuses on the small atomic parts of a system. Many scientists, especially those who study physics, math, and chemistry, for example, believe that understanding comes from studying the smallest atomic fragments of a system as a strategy to understanding how the system works. This philosophical orientation was made popular by such scientists as Galileo and Newton. Applying reductionism to social science is a pragmatic approach but has serious limitations.

In other words, one point of view is that it might be very difficult if not impossible to measure the wholeness of a family by gathering information about each of its members and then somehow combining their answers to get an overall picture of the family. As a result, it seems there are only a few theoretical choices with regard to the study of the family.

First, we could continue with the typical questionnaire-based approach in which a researcher asks a family member (and usually it is only one member) some questions about his or her experience in that family. Using this method, we would have to assume that one person's view of the larger activities and beliefs of a group of people is sufficient. We would assume that this person's analysis of family life (and often it is the mother's view) is accurate enough, so we use that view as a summary for what the entire family believes, thinks, and does behaviorally—and we treat that one view as reality.

For example, suppose we are measuring something like father involvement (Marsiglio, Amato, Day, & Lamb, 2000). Many researchers want to know if father involvement really matters in the lives of children. Although the research in this area of study is relatively new, the findings have a wide variety of implications for public policy, custody issues, and what we think about children's well-being.

Most of the research about father involvement, however, has been done by asking mothers what fathers do in families. Does that seem odd to you? Many researchers think that approach is odd and have begun trying to get information from fathers. However, fathers are more difficult to find and they typically do not like to answer surveys, so in general, they are a more difficult group (than mothers) with whom to do research. A reductionistic approach has been to gather a few pieces of data from mothers about fathers with regard to a few activities he might do in family life. Then researchers would make some guesses about what that means for family life. To many researchers, that approach has seemed less than adequate.

Another approach that is gaining popularity is to move away from a purely reductionistic view, gather information from several people in the family, and then, using sophisticated statistics, researchers could find shared beliefs about what has happened in a particular family. For example, if we wanted to know more about father involvement we would ask mothers, fathers, and even children for their perceptions about what the father does and what it means to them. The idea is that by combining the views of several people we might get closer to understanding the processes that occur in family life. This type of research is costly and still only provides an approximation about inner family life.

Still another approach rejects the idea that we can research inner family life by asking simple questions like "How many times did you spank your child last week?" Instead, qualitative researchers approach the study of family life by gathering narrative stories, observing the families in their homes, and then extracting from what they see and hear any patterns or themes that reemerge.

The Approach in This Text

The information used within this text is taken from many different kinds of research studies, some of which are extremely reductionistic in nature and others that are excellent examples of narrative-qualitative studies. My belief is that each of the approaches we use has strengths, limitations, successes, and problems. Each is another way to tell the story about family life behind closed doors. However, a clear bias found in this text is that I believe that it is important to at least attempt to study families rather than only focus on the individuals within families.

☐ Family Systems Theory

One metaphor that is often used to understand family life is to think of families as an interactive system. Systems are often defined as a group of interacting parts (Broderick, 1993; Klein & White, 1996). This idea simply means that when describing any **entity** (a football team, a habitat in the forest, or a complex factory), it is assumed that all of the parts are somehow connected and interrelated. In the case of family science, families are not a closed system like an airplane. A modern jet passenger plane is a self-contained closed system.

FIGURE 3.2   Sometimes people use the metaphor of a factory to try and explain family systems theory. This approach does not capture what systems theorists had in mind. A family system is more organic than mechanistic; that is, it is like a small ecosystem.

All of the parts (e.g., the compass, engines, and rudders) are parts of a complex group of parts collected together in one place and labeled an airplane. The airplane does receive fuel and supplies from outside sources and from time to time the pilot gets messages from other systems outside plane (e.g., other airplanes and the control tower). The pilot, one could argue, is not really a part of the plane system, but he or she uses that systemic object to get from point A to point B. For the most part, the airplane, itself, is a closed system of parts and it has a rather singular mission.

Families, on the other hand, are a relatively open system (Broderick, 1993). The **boundaries** of a family are rather permeable. Boundaries, by definition, are "invisible lines drawn within and among family members that form subsystems—for example, the lines within the individual self, the marital coalition, and the children" (Sauber, L'Abate, Weeks, & Buchanan, 1993, p. 38). Boundaries are discussed in more depth later in this chapter.

The Family as a Whole

A basic notion proposed by systems researchers and family intervention workers is that it is impossible to understand family life without viewing the family as a whole (Broderick, 1993; Hall & Fagen, 1956; Klein & White, 1996). In Freudian psychology and other general social science approaches, the unit of analysis is almost always an individual, with other family members playing a supporting role in the story. In a systemic view of family life, the primary story centers on what the whole family is doing and the focus on a particular individual (even if she or he is the person with the most obvious "problem") is secondary to understanding how family life works. Indeed, solving an individual's "problem" often involves changing patterns that involve other family members.

Often when researchers examine family life, the interaction in families is viewed as larger than any one person or even any one rule or pattern. Okun and Rapport (1980) summarized this idea as follows:

> The system in an integrated coherent entity is more than the mere composite of independent elements. This wholeness transcends the sum of the system's component elements . . . a change in one part of the system may cause a change in many parts (subsystems) of the larger system and in the larger system itself. (pp. 8–9)

We cannot understand the Browns simply by understanding each individual member of the family. We must also understand (i.e., we have to observe, take note of, and record) the relationships and interactions that occur with this family entity (or systemic unit). Another way to say this is that each role found within the family is dependent on the others. For example, one cannot be a mother unless there are people to "mother."

PRINCIPLE 3.2   THE FAMILY UNIT AS A WHOLE

When using a systems approach to understanding family life, one has to view the family unit as a whole and, therefore, not use the individual as the primary focus of interest.

Families are thus not a closed a system like an airplane but, in many ways, are more complicated. Some family systems scholars consider the people in the family to be the "parts," but others write about the family system as being even more complicated than simply a collection of people. For these family scientists, the unit of analysis is the interaction found within the inner life of the family. That is, many family science researchers examine how patterns of interaction are formed, what effect those exchanges of feeling and information hold, and how family interaction can be changed.

One way to think of family interaction and the difficulty of studying it is to imagine you are doing research about families. If you were approaching family life from a mostly reductionistic point of view, you would seek information about the family from one or more of the family members. Possibly, you would ask each one what he or she thinks about the quality of the relationships within the family. However, if you were trying to assess a family-level measure, you would have to find a way to measure some attribute or aspect of family life that exists or inheres within the group. For example, we could give them a difficult interpersonal task to solve and with the video camera running (and the interviewer out of the room) we could capture how they solve this problem. Trained coders could then evaluate the recorded interaction and try to assess some family-level characteristic that transcends any one person.

We could, for example, code their interaction with regard to playfulness, contention, cooperation, or intrusive control. We would not get those family-level measures just by asking one person her opinion of how she feels about cooperating in these kinds of situations. Instead, a disinterested third party (like the judge in a courtroom) codes and rates the collective notion of cooperation as viewed in real time. We would, of course, have to make sure that the coder was well trained to recognize the elements of playfulness, cooperation, and so on. In addition (remember Chapter 2), we would want the coder's scores to be valid and reliable.

Systems theory posits that when theorists invented system theory, they were, for the most part, interested in closed systems consisting of machine parts (e.g., radar, rocket ships, and robots). Although families, family members, and the interactions found within a family system are not nearly as predictable as pieces of metal and wire, there are some attributes of family life that are system-like. For example, the first idea we explore here is the notion that systems theory assumes that every system has an underlying "structure."

Underlying Structures

A primary theme of family science research from a systems point of view is the idea that the role of the therapist or researcher is to discover underlying, hidden "structures." There are many social science researchers who have adopted this theme over the years. For example, this idea is at the heart of the writings of Sigmund Freud. In the Freudian approach to understanding the human psyche, the notion is that the skilled observer can detect hidden patterns or undiscovered, unresolved conflicts deep within the subconscious of the individual. By finding, identifying, and revealing those hidden conflicts, one can attain a higher level of mental health.

This type of idea also extends to theories that describe the cognitive abilities of children and adults. Piaget, for example, suggested that there were hidden, internal schemata or mental structures that direct our ability to solve problems and make sense out of life's puzzles. Likewise, several writers of family theory have suggested that within family life there are underlying structures or patterns of interactions that direct what occurs in family life. As mentioned earlier, though, families are not mechanical entities. The metaphor of a system is easier to understand if one thinks of a mechanical device or group of devices welded together and designed to solve some problem in a factory. Think of a complex factory, for example, in which there are hundreds of steps performed by hundreds of machines to produce an item, like an automobile, for example. Most systems like the automobile factory receive inputs (e.g., metal, plastic, paint, and glass) and the parts of the system (e.g., the metal press, the paint robots, and the glass-installing arms) work together to solve a central problem (i.e., to have an automobile exit the output door, completed and working and looking like it is supposed to). The workers in the factory are really extensions of the robotic arms and levers, moving in unison (if all goes well) to produce a specific goal. The patterns of interaction (e.g., the metal is pressed and cut before it is painted) are all thoughtfully mapped out, timed, and executed according to a massive collaborative effort by all involved.

In the world of human and family systemic thinking, the idea is that you can observe the movement of the actors, how they communicate, what comes into the system, and what happens to the system (whether it be factory workers or family members). Based on those observations, one could deduce what the goals of the system are and how effective that particular system is at achieving its apparent goals.

Like Freud trying to discover the underlying patterns of the mind, the researcher or therapist who works with family systems theory tries to understand the underlying patterns of family life by watching how families solve problems, how family members communicate with one another, and how they allocate **resources**. So, family systems theorists are fond of saying, "a system is a group of interacting parts that comprise a whole."

Families Have Goals

This view of the world reflects not only the system perspective, but also the social-exchange and conflict theory ideas. All of these approaches assume that the system is goal seeking: Families have goals they are trying to achieve. For the most part, this process is not really apparent to a typical family. They rarely sit down and discuss the overall meaning or goal of their family. In fact, it probably takes a skilled observer from the outside to watch the repeating patterns of a family before some of the underlying themes or goals surface.

> ### PRINCIPLE 3.3   FAMILIES ARE GOAL DIRECTED
>
> Families are a collective and usually form an entity. Such entities are thought to be goal directed. That is, whether the actors know it or not, groups have a tendency to try and achieve stated or implicit goals. Understanding family life is about understanding how efficient a particular family group is at achieving appropriate goals and aims.

Subscription and Efficiency

These goals vary widely from family to family (see Chapter 8 for more on this topic). In addition, there is always a good chance that one or more of the family members will not subscribe to the overall family direction, goal, aim, purpose, ambition, or aspiration. We do not know very much about this idea, as few family researchers have attempted to assess it. However, one can imagine that if the subscription rate were low in a family—that is, there was low consensus about what that family's mission, aim, goal, or purpose was—we would speculate that the family would be less efficient in solving problems, making decisions, and getting the daily business of family completed (Day et al., 2001). Why? Efficiencies of goal achievement (getting children educated, saving money, becoming healthy, etc.) are more likely to be achieved when all involved agree on the desired outcome. If some family member only half-heartedly subscribes to the idea of education for all then it will take much more effort on the part of those who do value that goal to make it happen.

Therefore, there are three take-home ideas from this discussion. The first is that a system (including a family system) is a group of interacting parts (family members and the patterns of interaction that occur). Second, families have aims, goals, themes, and missions they are trying to attain. Further, families use strategies that are pattern-like to make those goals happen. That is, they are more likely to do the same routines over and over than they are to try some new approach to achieve goals and deal with problems that might affect goal achievement. Third, there is a subscription rate involved in the family goal attainment process. Consequently when family members are fully subscribed and focus their energy and resources on a given theme, aim, or goal, the goal will be easier and faster to obtain.

Equilibrium

Another useful term that comes from the systems perspective is equilibration or **equilibrium.** Of course, this idea refers to the balancing act that families must perform. As family entities attempt to reach goals, they have to respond constantly to the changes that happen in their world—money comes in, children get sick, the local factory announces layoffs, the mother is depressed, and so on. Family units are not static systems. A closed system, like a watch, can be wound and then you do not have to bother with it until it needs winding or a battery. On the other hand, families are interactive systems that require constant adaptation, change, and response. One cannot get a family organized, arranged, thought out, and defined and then walk away as you would with the clock. Instead, on a daily or

FIGURE 3.3   Families try to maintain balance and return to that balance even though events and stresses disrupt that stability.

even hourly basis family members are changing and influencing the other family members. Therefore, family units try to reach goals by keeping life's events in balance. We have to change the rules, adapt our traditions, and alter how we get daily chores done.

Morphostasis and Morphogenesis

Morphostasis and **morphogenesis** are two forces that occur each day in family life. According to the family systems way of thinking, as various events occur (e.g., a child is injured on the playground), family entities try to keep the rules of everyday living intact and keep life moving along. Morphostasis means that we want there to be continuity and sameness. The other pull is that families realize that there is constant genesis or creation and change. So, when the child is injured on the playground, we collectively ask if the old way of doing things will work today. Does someone else need to make the dinner? Who can help with homework tonight while someone takes her to the doctor? Who will call her friend and tell her she is not going to be able to play? Later in this book, we talk much more about family crises and how families adapt to events that change the nature of family interaction as the Browns try to keep the daily events of life running smoothly and at the same time re-create how they meet the changes that occur as people get older and the family is altered. (See Chapter 8 for a more detailed explanation of these ideas.)

Boundaries

As mentioned earlier, families are rather open systems that have permeable boundaries. The idea of a boundary is a key to understanding systems thinking. System boundaries occur where two or more systems or subsystems interface, interact, or come together. They are borders of a system. Sometimes these boundaries can be very solid and rigid and other times they are very permeable. Boundaries occur at every level in the system and between systems. Often, we understand where a boundary is by listening to the rules families construct about where people can and cannot go, what they can and cannot do, and who is allowed in the family and who is not allowed to leave. For example, some families might have a very open system and family members are allowed to come and go without much restriction.

> ### PRINCIPLE 3.4   FAMILIES ARE SYSTEMS WITH BOUNDARIES
>
> Like all systems, families develop, maintain, and use boundaries. These boundaries define membership and information flow. They also help specify membership expectations.

When we say that system boundaries are permeable, we mean that the system is not tightly closed. In fact, in some families they are so permeable they are like a sieve. Other families are more protective and they construct boundaries that resemble castle walls. The "drawbridge" is only lowered for certain events and a castle-family member has to return on time or trouble will ensue. Likewise, there might be strict rules about who can enter other family members' rooms or study areas. We speak more of this issue in Chapter 9 on rules and patterns of interaction.

Boss (1998) illuminated another type of boundary issue. As a family scientist, she has researched the idea of boundaries in many settings and recently applied her work to the problem of families who have a member with Alzheimer's disease. In her book, she shows how the physical and mental awareness of family members can greatly influence our ideas about family membership and responsibility.

Subsystems

Within the family system there might be smaller units of analysis. Another element that researchers speak of is the idea of **subsystems** within the family realm. There are several possible subsystems, which include the spousal or executive subsystem, the parent–child subsystem, and the parental subsystem (in which the husband and wife relate to each other with regard to a parenting role). One of the key tasks of subsystems is boundary maintenance.

Family therapists have long known that a sure sign of a family in difficulty is when their subsystems are not kept separate and distinct (Minuchin, 1981, 1996). For example, when family members build coalitions across subsystems, the family's ability to achieve goals is weakened. If a mother builds a stronger relationship with a child than she does with her spouse, then the family system is weakened. If a parent (in this case often the father) blurs the boundaries between himself and a child emotionally and sexually the entire family system is weakened and can even be destroyed, as is often the case when incest occurs.

The concept of the subsystem helps us understand that the primary "parts" of the system are not the individuals but instead are the interactions between and among the various subsystems within a family group. The father influences his partner, and in turn, the response of those two people influences how they allocate resources, make decisions, and monitor their children. The great American playwright Arthur Miller once said "all human interaction is 98% historical," referring to the simple idea that the patterns of previous interactions and decisions live on and direct the next thing we say to a family member in the next situation. The study of those patterns of interaction is a characteristic of the study of the family using a systems approach.

Equifinality

One of the more unique concepts used in family system thinking is the idea of **equifinality**. Simply put, equifinality captures the idea that "many beginnings can lead to the same outcome, and the same beginning can lead to quite different outcomes" (Bavelas & Segal, 1982, p. 103). In other words, any outcome you can imagine can be brought about by multiple causes. Further, because there are so many events that can cause a given outcome, paying attention to this idea turns our attention away from worrying about those causes as much as some other theoretical orientations do.

For example, we know from various studies on parent–child interaction that parental overinvolvement can lead to two very different outcomes in children. Being an overresponsive parent can push children to overachieve and it could push some children to underachieve. Friedman (1985) listed several research ideas that seem to lead us to the conclusion that one beginning can have many different outcomes. Having an alcoholic parent could produce children who are diametrically opposed to drinking or children who abuse alcohol themselves; if a parent takes a stand on some ideological issue (e.g., a strong religious conviction) children might see the parent as a hero or a controlling, demanding dictator.

Likewise, the same effect could have come from very opposite causes. For example, the death of a child could bring a family close together and their level of functioning could dramatically increase, or it could devastate them and great distance and unresolved negative feelings could result.

Equipotentiality

In like manner, there are several factors that can lead to early sexuality, including early menstruation, contact with other youth who are sexually active, influence from a sibling who is sexually active, low sense of self-worth, and so on. There are thus many causes that can lead to one single outcome.

Thinking more systemically, the search for single causes and single outcomes takes a back seat. Instead, at center stage are the search for outcomes and their related processes. In the example of the death of a child, a family systems researcher focuses not on the events of the child's death but rather on how the family entity responds and tries to adapt. The focus would be on the strategies they use to resolve the loss.

When using a family systemic way of thinking, one asks "what" questions rather than "why" questions. The systemic way of viewing family life is to focus more on what can be done once some event happens, rather than a postmortem approach to find out why something happened. By examining how families and family members respond to daily life, we can make guesses about what they value, how they solve problems, and how they think about the world. Armed with those insights, family systems researchers believe they have a better chance of helping families cope with life's difficult events than if they focus only on why the child died, why the farm lost money, why the unmarried teen got pregnant, and so on.

PRINCIPLE 3.5   FAMILIES REACHING GOALS

Family members are more effective in reaching goals when they focus more on the "how and what" part of life than spending their energy on the "why" and causal aspects of daily life.

Imagine a family floating down a river in a raft. The river is in a scenic wilderness. The surroundings all contribute to the experience of the family. Specifically, the slope of the river as it cuts through a canyon will determine how fast the water is flowing. Although

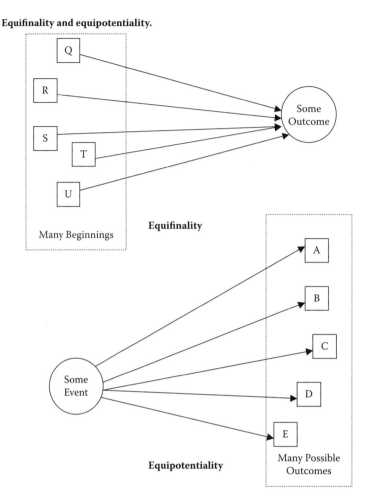

FIGURE 3.4 This diagram illuminates the two terms equifinality and equipotentiality. Equifinality describes the idea that many beginnings can lead to the same outcome. Equipotentiality refers to the notion that one beginning can have a variety of outcomes.

the family members might note these determining factors, such as the speed of the water, the number of rocks, and the position of the raft in the river, it is the rowing that is the focus of their attention. No one pays too much attention to why a rock is there; it is simply there and must be avoided. In only a few instances (like if my mother were there) would a family member be rehearsing why he or she came here in the first place. Certainly no one would be thinking much about how the family formed and why they were born with children who could not row better (although it might cross someone's mind). Instead of focusing on causes, the most effective families learn to focus on the problem at hand.

As you can see from this example, our focus has shifted from thinking about the researcher to the family itself. Both family researchers or therapists and family members themselves can benefit from the principle of equifinality. Certainly, there is a never-ending list of causes that one could examine in the river example. However, strong families and researchers who use this perspective spend most of their energy focusing on rowing better, spotting rocks earlier, and having some fun while the event is in progress. According to this perspective, researchers have less impact when they focus on the reasons why the family is rafting in the first place. Families are less effective when family members evaluate, rehash, rehearse, and criticize family activity instead of learning how to row better, so to speak.

☐ Theories of Change and Family Development

One of the giants and founders of family science research was Rubin Hill. As early as 1949, Hill developed the idea that a family was composed of social roles and that the nature and assignment of these roles changed over time (Hill & Hansen, 1960). Theorists who use this perspective make several key assumptions, as described next.

The first assumption found in this approach can be labeled the change assumption. The change assumption states that any living system (be it the individual or a complicated family group) has a path it follows and that all living entities change over time. The job of the researcher is to note those changes and find out how they influence individual or family decisions.

PRINCIPLE 3.6   CHANGE HAPPENS

Individuals, family structure, and interactions among family members change over time.

The second assumption we learn from family life course theory is that changes over time in family life have to be examined from a number of different levels. This idea surfaces in many theories about the family and has several different labels. Basically, the idea is that individuals live in some type of family group. Obviously, there are exceptional cases in which some children do not grow up in some type of family group, but that is clearly atypical. Family groups (whatever the makeup) are social by nature. By that we mean that a primary purpose of families is to care for, nurture, and facilitate an optimal outcome for each member. Again, a basic notion of this theory is that family groups organize around the idea of well-being. In every culture and in every historical time period, there are no examples of cultures that we know about in which the individuals have not banded together in these intimate family groups with the overall goal of helping each other "do better." Said differently, in every culture we know about, families exist in some form and are not established with the intent of destroying each other.

At the next level of complexity is the community. Each community in the world is composed of clusters or groups of families that are more alike or homogenous than they are different. A small community of families living in northern England is probably more alike than different and the same would be true of a community of families living in Egypt, Bolivia, or Japan. Although the similarity begins to fade the wider we cast our community net, it also true that families living in the United States, generally, are more similar in ideology, beliefs, and organization than they are dissimilar. Additionally, it is important to understand that individuals are connected to families, families are connected to communities, and larger communities are formed from collections of smaller local or proximate communities. Each level influences the other levels: To more fully understand the complexity of family life one must take into consideration how the larger and more distal community influences family life and how local family life influences the larger community. Chapter 4 explores this idea in depth but the principle of community life captures the core idea.

PRINCIPLE 3.7   FAMILIES ARE CONNECTED

Family development is influenced by the connections families have to their proximate and distal communities. Likewise, larger community life is influenced by smaller collections of families (i.e., one's proximate community) and by individual families themselves.

Another key assumption that is a feature of the family life course perspective is the notion of transitions. Transitions occur in families as they change and try to adapt to the events that happen over time (Klein & White, 1996, p. 128). This concept will be explored in depth in Chapter 8, but the central idea is simply that the transitions we make in family life, such as getting married, having and raising children, and divorcing and remarrying, create a path of possible events. Depending on the paths one chooses, other events are more or less likely to result. For example, once a child is born into a family, family members find a new set of paths that were of little concern before the child was born. In a few short years, the child might be attending preschool, and parents might begin thinking ahead about other school plans, the child's future, and how their family will be a part of the child's future.

PRINCIPLE 3.8   ANTICIPATING TRANSITIONS IN FAMILY LIFE

When a transition occurs in family life that is unanticipated or does not occur when it was generally expected to occur, that transition is more likely to have a negative influence as that family attempts to achieve its goals.

There are two very important principles that emerge from this simple idea. First, is the idea of off-time transitions. Younger unmarried women who conceive and bear a child are less likely to contribute to their personal and family goals than are those young women who have children within a range of years that is more "on time."

Epigenesis

A second important idea is the notion of epigenesis. Again, this is a simple idea that is useful and powerful in understanding everyday family life. What we do in life early on has a significant impact in our lives later. The choices we make early in our lives affect who we are, the type of family we raise, and the life we will lead later. This does not mean we cannot overcome the choices we make in times of family transitions, but those choices have the power to strongly influence our futures. For example, if a young couple decides to have several children early in their marriage, for better or worse, it will not only have an economic effect on future choices available to them, but can influence the resources available to their children, choice of family activities, where they can and cannot live, and even the educational pursuits of the parents.

> ### PRINCIPLE 3.9   EPIGENESIS OCCURS IN FAMILY LIFE
> What we do in life early on has a significant impact in our lives later.

In sum, family developmental theory is a useful perspective and some of its ideas help us understand important family processes. Throughout this text, two of its most powerful ideas are referred to frequently: First, family life has a course and that course can have many paths. Second, as family members make transitions, the choices they make within those transitional times can (and usually do) influence future opportunities and choices available to each family member.

☐ Rational Choice/Social Exchange Theory

One of the more frequently used theoretical ideas in family science is called rational choice or social exchange theory. At the heart of this perspective is the idea that each individual seeks to maximize individual self-interest. That is not to say that all people are necessarily "selfish" per se, but it does assume that each person acts with his or her personal welfare in mind as a primary motivating force (Klein & White, 1996).

The rational person goes about the task of maximizing. That is, he or she maximizes his or her position in life by avoiding situations in which the rewards are less than the costs. By definition, a reward is anything that is "perceived as beneficial to an actor's interests" (Klein & White, 1996, p. 65).

> ### PRINCIPLE 3.10   FAMILIES CAN MAXIMIZE RESOURCES
> Individuals maximize self-interest by rationally making choices that result in the most personal reward, and individuals avoid choices that are not rewarding or are otherwise costly.

Likewise, costs are defined as outcomes that are not beneficial to one's interests. For example, when we make a decision to buy a car, choose a spouse, name a child, or select an occupation, those who subscribe to this point of view suggest that we weigh the costs and rewards and choose what we believe to be in our best interest at the time of the choice. This is called a rational theory because it assumes that each of us has the power to use our intellect in the selection process. It also assumes that (unless someone has a serious emotional problem or is under extreme distress) we do not make choices that are deliberately bad for us.

Another way to say this is that we make choices that seem to assist us in reaching goals we have selected as important. The concept of rationality does not suppose that people make good choices all of the time (or even most of the time). Nor does this approach assume that goals that have been consciously or implicitly selected are appropriate or worthy. Instead, it assumes that people weigh their choices, balance the costs and rewards, and try to do the best they can at the time.

Social exchange theory also helps us understand the nature of relationships. As explained in Chapter 6, when relationships are based on a principle of equity they will thrive and be more likely to achieve the desired goals. Equity means that partners in a relationship work toward a balance of resources that each brings to the relationship and a climate of fairness pervades their relationship. When the balance is absent and one person has more resources (e.g., money, talents, or physical goods) it is assumed that the relationship will not be as effective in reaching the goals they set.

PRINCIPLE 3.11   EQUALITY IN RESOURCES

When partners in a relationship are more equal with regard to the resources they bring to the relationship, it is more likely the relationship will be stronger and is more likely that systemic goals will be achieved.

For example, we know that people who are of the same social or economic status tend to choose each other for marriage, and how decisions are made, resources are allocated, and time is used is reflected in the resources each person brings to the relationship.

There are two important criticisms of this approach that need to be mentioned. First, this perspective has a difficult time with the concept of altruism. Altruism reflects the idea that sometimes people seem to act without calculating the cost–reward ratio (e.g., when protecting a child). A perpetual discussion by those who write about social exchange ideas is the struggle to explain behavior that seems to not be "rational," or in other words behavior that seemingly does not result from a cost–reward calculation.

Feminist writers have focused on this notion to show that this approach undervalues the contribution women make in relationships. For example, Sabatelli and Shehan (1993, p. 396) suggested that social exchange theory does not do a good job of considering the part played by family members whose mission in the family might be to create solidarity at the expense of individual gain. This is really an extension of the problem that social exchange theory has explaining seemingly selfless acts of contribution. That leads us to a brief discussion of the notion of tautology.

The concept of tautology is the label given to reasoning that is circular and there is no way of proving your assertion (Klein & White, 1996). In the case of social exchange theory, every aspect of the theory assumes that people act only when a reward is forthcoming (or to avoid cost). Therefore, it is impossible to find examples of someone doing something that is not rewarding (according to this theory). Scholars frequently bemoan this type of tautological thinking because it does not seem to be very helpful in understanding more complicated human interaction. In other words, it does help us to simply know that a "reward is something that is rewarding."

Family as an Entity

Another difficulty with this approach is the idea that many family scientists are becoming more interested in studying the family as an entity. That means we want to see the family as a whole unit rather than trying to imagine all of the calculations that apparently occur in each family member's mind. Social exchange theorists have only recently begun to talk about how this theory can move from describing only the behavior of individuals to describing the complex behavior of several people in a close-knit group like a family.

Like all theories, this one falls short of explaining everything we wish it would in family life. However, there are some aspects of family life that are easily explained and understood using the language of social exchanges. For example, I suggest later in this chapter that families, like individuals, have goals and do maximize resources to attain those goals. The language for that construct comes from social exchange theory and it suggests that a unit, like a family, moves forward with a belief about what they would like to accomplish and, for the most part, they do not deliberately set out to fail.

☐ Conflict Theory and Family Science

The essence of this theoretical approach is to answer one central question: As family members come and go, age, and change, how is order achieved in such seemingly complicated and chaotic situations? The question of obtaining order out of chaos is one that has been asked for several hundred years (cf. Hobbes, 1651/1947).

At first glance, one might think that **conflict theory** is simply about why people argue and fight. That is too simple and does not capture the intent of this theoretical perspective. Instead, conflict theory is the struggle that we all have (in and out of family groups) to survive. This theory suggests that there is a natural state that humans live in that is rather unruly, nasty, and carnal. All men and women are in competition with each other because, in life, resources (e.g., money, time, space, etc.) are scarce and each person wants to not only survive, but also to compete for those resources and have the freedom to choose a personal direction. One person might want to buy a new car, whereas someone else wants to keep the old car and use the extra money to pay off debts.

A key idea in understanding conflict theory comes to us from German philosophers such as Hegel, who viewed the human condition as one of struggle. He suggested that although each of us is primarily self-interested (as in the exchange perspective from earlier), the process of struggling is a good thing. He did not say that fighting or having wars is an effective strategy. However, when we try to solve life's difficult problems (like how to spend family income, who should sleep in what room, or who should do the dishes) and a family member suggests who should do the dishes, the resulting exchange can either build strength in the family system or it can tear it down. If prolonged conflict ensues and the balance of power is uneven, then families will be less likely to meet their goals. When families struggle together and are successful at reaching a consensus then they become stronger.

This process idea has the following elements. First is the original idea and we call this the **thesis** ("Sandra, I would like you to do the dishes tonight"). The thesis or original idea always comes attached to the other side of the coin, the **antithesis**. The antithesis is the opposite point of view in which someone says, "No, I don't think so, it is your turn to do the dishes," or "I think it would be better if we spent the tax refund on tires for the car," or "Our apartment is not a big as you would like. You will have to share your room with your younger brother." In this way a dialogue or dialectic emerges, or in other words, a struggle arises. When members of a family group struggle together and make decisions that consider both the thesis and antithesis, the hope is that a **synthesis** will emerge. When a synthesis occurs, it is assumed that this creates strength and the family is more effective. When there is no synthesis or consensus and agreement, the family is weakened and is less likely to meet its goals.

Scarce Resources

At the core of this theoretical idea is the notion of scarce resources (Klein & White, 1996; Sprey, 1979). Resources are more than just money, however (Klein & White, 1996). Resources can be problem-solving skills, talents, abilities, or even the ability to control or exercise authority in a family. This theory also indicates that in most cases conflict is inevitable. That is, there is almost always an imbalance of resources or power in family relationships, and therefore conflict emerges.

The first principle of conflict theory is therefore the inequity principle.

PRINCIPLE 3.12   INEQUITY CREATES CONFLICT

Conflict arises in families when resources are not evenly distributed, and they are almost never equitably distributed.

There are many aspects to this perspective that I am not mentioning here. Many of the constructs and ideas that emerge from this perspective are used to describe how larger groups of people (e.g., a labor union and factory) struggle together to resolve their conflicts. However, in terms of the family, there is one more idea from this perspective that needs to be restated from earlier. This is the idea of struggle and synthesis. It is assumed that all families struggle as they allocate resources. Those families who are better able to meet their goals are the ones who share resources more equitably and are better able to experience true consensus and synthesis rather than prolonged conflict when allocating family resources.

PRINCIPLE 3.13   FAMILIES STRUGGLE WITH RESOURCE ALLOCATION

It is assumed that all families struggle as they allocate resources. Those families who are better able to meet their goals are the ones who share resources more equitably and are better able to experience true consensus and synthesis rather than prolonged conflict when allocating family resources.

The ideas from conflict theory are used in later chapters. In particular, we refer to these ideas in Chapter 10, Communicating in Families.

It is also important to note that from this intellectual tradition a strong, gender-oriented feminist critique of family life has emerged. In this view, social historians, family scientists, and feminist writers illuminate the idea that men have traditionally controlled most of the tangible resources and have typically had more power in family life. Therefore, when the power is unbalanced and the resources are not distributed equally, families are not as effective. This imbalance ensures the privilege of some (usually the males) in the family at the expense of others. This issue is more fully addressed in Chapter 5 on gender in family life.

☐ Symbolic Interaction Theory

Symbolic interaction theory is also a widely used perspective in family science. Originally, those writing from this perspective were describing individual psychological processes about how individuals place meaning on the events that happen to them. For example, when a researcher uses this perspective he or she might ask someone why they got a divorce or inquire about who is responsible for the financial decisions in a family. Researchers who begin with these types of questions want to know what the family member thinks about the specific event being asked. In other words, what does it mean or symbolize, and how does the meaning or interpretation of their view of what happened affect how they reacted. The assumption is made that the meaning we bring to the situation has a significant impact on the decisions we make and the ways we interact with other people

Symbols

For example, when we ask an Irishman what the word *da* (the common Irish word for father) means to him, he might have a complicated and involved response that includes elements of his biological father, someone who was supportive and involved, or a strict authority figure. The symbol *da* represents a very complicated collection of feelings, thoughts, and ideas. These ideas might be tied to his own experience with his own da; images he has collected from movies, books, and television; and even impressions from watching other fathers interact with children. In terms of a family science application, scholars have for many years been asking family members what certain aspects of family life mean to them. A basic principle that we use when we search for the meanings family members place on the events, outcomes, and activities they experience is the idea of perception as reality. Family members define the activities, behaviors, and outcomes of family interactions, and the way they define those activities, behaviors, and outcomes is real for them. In other words, one's perception of an event is that person's reality and the perception has the power to contribute to consequences and outcomes.

In several places throughout this text, we explore this idea and show how our perceptions and definitions of events and activities in family life become expectations and goals that direct what we do and how we evaluate family life. For example, it has often been noted that if our performances within our families do not match our expectations or the expectations of others, we feel less satisfied with how we are doing with that particular family role.

Roles

An important concept in symbolic interaction theory has been the **development** of the idea that each family member adopts and "plays" certain roles within the family. For example, a very important topic in the study of family life focuses on father involvement. Some family scientists approach this topic by asking first what roles fathers are expected to perform in families in the United States. Some have suggested that the most common response to this question is that fathers are providers, protectors, and nurturers, and that these larger ideas construct a father's identity as he evaluates his performance within that particular role (Marsiglio et al., 2000).

Another example of how this theory can be used is found in Chapter 13. When we study families experiencing crises, we often want to know how they define the event. Even the death of a family member could have several different meanings to different family members. It becomes critical in studying family life to know how each person is affected by life's events, how events are defined generally by the family (as an entity), and how a family is generally affected by the struggles and challenges of life.

Our perception about our role performance in family life influences not only how we feel about our family experience, but it is important to note how much consensus there is among family members about the collected idea about how a role is performed (Burr, Leigh, Day, & Constantine, 1979). This is a good example of a family-level idea that is used in the symbolic interaction tradition. Let's return to our father involvement research.

One example of a research study that could be done would be to find out how all family members (a multiperspective research approach) felt about what was expected of the father in a family. The following principle would suggest that when family members have more agreement about what a father should do in his father role, there would be less strain on all family members as he performs that role. One of the problems with the changing nature of family life is that many of the roles we have assigned to us (or we choose voluntarily) are changing rapidly.

PRINCIPLE 3.14   CONSENSUS DECREASES STRAIN

The more consensus family and community members have about what should occur in a family role, the less strain a family member will have as he or she enters and performs that role.

A young father might not have a clear idea of what he should be doing as a father because the people around him (i.e., family and community members) do not have much consensus about what it is he should do in that part of his life. Therefore, this theory would suggest that as a young father enters the fathering role (e.g., at the birth of a child) he might feel anxiety and strain as he considers what he should do.

In roles where there is high consensus about what a person should do in the role, we would expect that the person would have much less anxiety as he or she takes on that new role.

In summary, symbolic interaction theory helps us understand that humans are thinking, choosing, and deliberate creatures. We humans place meaning on what we see and the events that impact us. Those who study families using this perspective pay attention to those meanings that family members hold. Additionally, family scientists attend to the roles performed in family life and the ease of adopting or exiting roles (e.g., becoming a parent, losing one's parent, changing partners, gaining a partner).

☐ Summary

All of the theories examined in this chapter can be used to describe and understand family life. From rational exchange theories we learn that individuals and groups of people (e.g., families) have a goal of maximizing self-interest. Within that idea, we expect families and family members to rise above individual interest and contribute to the well-being of the group. This is difficult for many and is a constant struggle for some.

We also note that family members and families change over time. This added complexity adds rich variety to family life as children get older and eventually leave the nest. Relationships change and effective families figure out how to adapt to a changing and chaotic world. Regardless of the changes, families (as entities) try to do the best they can (for the most part) and they make the best decisions they collectively can. It is my position that most families try to succeed and very few (only in excessively troubling situations) set out to fail. Families work each day at trying to find the best way to allocate the scarce resources they have in ways that meet the deeply held goals and ideologies to which they subscribe.

We also note that the family can be thought of in terms of a system. The interactions that occur within that system are pattern-like and can be studied. The individuals within the family system are symbol-making, thinking individuals who bring personal meaning and definition to the world in which they live. It is critical to consider the ways in which family members view the family experience they create. As these individuals inevitably struggle together and make daily decisions about how to solve life's daily problems, they either learn how to reach consensus and equity or they are unskilled in this attempt and long-term conflict erodes their ability to make decisions effectively. The task for each day is to find ways of rising above selfishness and conflict to create effective family units that turn chaos into productivity and success.

It is quite clear that some families seemed to be very skilled at accomplishing this feat, whereas others struggle and even fail at this daunting task. As you read the following chapters about family processes and daily life, you will begin to form a position statement about family life. It is your task at the conclusion of this chapter to begin writing some of your ideas down about how families can better succeed at the difficult task of family life. Activity 3.1 is designed to assist you in thinking about your view of family life and how that view was formed.

☐ Study Questions

1. What do we mean by the idea of reductionism?
2. What is a theory and why do we care about them in family science?
3. Explain what is meant by equilibrium in a family system.
4. What is a family system?
5. Give an example of equifinality and explain how this idea can work in family life.
6. Look up the word *entity* and see how this term can be applied to a family.
7. What is the difference between a thesis and an antithesis?
8. Why is the idea of roles so important in the study of the family?
9. Pick your favorite theoretical orientation explained in this chapter and defend why it appeals to you.

☐ Key Terms

Reductionism
Roles
Entity
Boundaries
Resources
Equilibrium
Morphostasis
Morphogenesis
Subsystems
Equifinality
Thesis

Antithesis
Synthesis
Symbolic interaction
Conflict theory
Development

☐ Suggested Readings

Becker, G. (1991). *A treatise on the family.* Cambridge, MA: Harvard University Press.

Bronfenbrenner, U. (1979). *The ecology of human development.* Cambridge, MA: Harvard University Press.

Coleman, J. S. (1990). *Foundations of social theory.* Cambridge, MA: Belknap Press of Harvard University Press.

Klein, D. M., & White, J. M. (1996). *Family theories: An introduction.* Thousand Oaks, CA: Sage.

Walsh, F. (2002). (Ed.). *Normal family processes.* New York: Guilford.

White, J. (2005). *Advancing family theories.* Thousand Oaks, CA: Sage.

Families as Units of Change and Transition

☐ Chapter Preview

In this chapter, readers will learn:

- That family change is a fundamental family process.
- How life course theory is one way to describe the trajectories and changes that occur in families.
- About how some events (like births and weddings) trigger long-term and complex changes. Other events (like illnesses and relatives moving in) create short-term and simple change processes.
- That some changes in family life are not predictable changes. For example, divorce, remarriage, and a family member becoming handicapped are not routine changes.
- That there is some predictability in family life, and there is also great variability.
- That morphogenesis is change in the form, structure, or ways families do the business of family life.
- About how morphostasis (sometimes called homeostasis) is the tendency of families to resist morphogenesis (change).
- How ambivalence and ambiguity are universal and inevitable in families.
- About the epigenesis principle and how it helps us understand family changes.

☐ Introduction

In this chapter, we examine two important aspects of family life: life events that occur during the normal or usual course of family life and events that are less expected and are more severe or traumatic. In this chapter, we also discuss general changes in family life. It is important to note that this chapter is a continuation of Chapter 3: This chapter expands on the idea of a life course approach or theory of family life. Within that perspective, a key element of family life is presented, the element of change. There are two key aspects of family life that are captured in the writings of those who embrace a life course perspective. The first key idea of life course theory is the notion of trajectories.

A **trajectory** is a path or course that one follows over time. Of course, we do not all follow the same life course, as there are many different paths available. However, it is a hard fact that time marches on, people get older, couples form relationships, many of them have children, some couples stay together, and other couples do not. Some families are strong willed and resilient and others are weaker and vulnerable, but all change over time and find themselves on some kind of trajectory. Within the trajectories of life we find transitions that are embedded within (Elder, 1985). For more than 30 years, social scientists have studied work trajectories and the attendant transitions out of and into jobs; the trajectories of marriage and other close relationships and the transitions in and out of those relationships; and the course of childbearing, parenting, and the transitions that attend to having children in families.

Researchers commonly indicate that some of the changes that occur are expected, but sometimes they are a surprise. Sometimes the changes take family members away from us, and sometimes we gain new members. A key element of trajectories and transitions in families is that much of the change seems to be routine or patterned. Although the sequence is not always predictable, much of the time it is. Moreover, these changes occur both to the individuals in families and to the family itself.

☐ What Is Family Change?

The concept of family change is an important part of family science. The process of family change results from (a) events that help unfold the fairly predictable and typical processes that make up the family life cycle, or (b) other events that trigger unpredictable events that can result in turbulence and even crisis. These events center on the idea that change and transition are inevitable and inescapable. When we speak of family change and crisis we refer to processes that alter, convert, or modify what is happening in families. Much of family life involves change, transformations, evolution, instability, or an unfolding of potentials. It is also important to remember that change in families is more of a process than a single event. For example, if you ask someone when he or she divorced, that person might tell you the day the judge decreed the divorce, the time period when the relationship began to fall apart, or the day he or she moved out of the house. Divorce, like many of the changes we explore in this chapter, is filled with so many segments, pieces, and processes that it is difficult to tag one specific day or one particular time at which "the divorce occurred."

Although some events trigger change, change in families is usually a longer process that occurs gradually over a period of time. Thus the routine part of family life takes into account time, and it involves a series of sequences of what is happening. Changes in families include both dramatic changes in families and also some small or minor changes. Some of the more dramatic changes we experience are births, marriages, and deaths. These types of changes usually have complicated, long-term implications.

There are also many aspects of family life in which there are minor changes in form or structure. For example, when children start going to school, this usually creates adjustments that are easy to handle. When a new sibling is born into a family, it is difficult but often manageable. Birth creates a series of changes as the various family members adjust and accommodate to the new member. Another example of change that could be either dramatic or simpler is when a relative or friend comes to live with a family; it creates a different set of short-term change processes as the new member is assimilated into the family. When a family member starts to become very old and unable to help himself or herself, when someone suffers a serious injury, or when someone in the family develops a serious illness, these events create their own unique series of outcomes.

Another idea within the framework of life course theory is the idea of interlocking trajectories (Elder, 1985). If we move beyond an individual perspective as was discussed in Chapter 1, it is clear that a much better picture of family can be found by examining the overlapping and interlocking trajectories of several family members simultaneously.

PRINCIPLE 4.1   INTERLOCKING TRAJECTORIES

Each family member has a life trajectory. The individual's trajectory is probably different (even slightly) than others in a family, but because they are bound together in a family system, the individual trajectories interlock and each one is influenced by the other's.

The child has a life course, as does the mother and even the grandmother. Consider the following story that illustrates this point.

A couple in their mid-30s experienced the long-awaited birth of their child. Shortly after the baby was born, the husband was looking through the window of the nursery, waiting for the infant to arrive, and the doctor asked if he could talk with him. They had the following dialogue:

Bob: Is it really that bad? (long pause) Well, how can you tell? I mean . . . (fear and panic show on his face and in the way he talks) he's just hours old. How can you tell?

Doctor: It is the classical characteristics. He has the slanted eyes, the Simeon crease in the palm, the floppy muscle tone . . . and there's more. But it all adds up, and the hard fact is, Bob, your son has Down syndrome.

Bob: Well, . . . uh, there's got to be some mistake. . . . Joanna and I . . . we're good people. We're healthy people. And we don't fool around. We don't do drugs. We don't drink! I can't believe this. (Bob looks out the window as his eyes well with tears.)

Doctor: There are many different options you could consider. Sometimes, parents decide to institutionalize children who have this problem. Others find great strength in raising a special needs child. You should know, however, that raising a Down syndrome child is a difficult task and takes lots of family resources—money, time, patience, and you have to know that he will probably die at an early age. If you do decide to institutionalize him, you should do that right away, before Joanna and you are bonded with it.

Bob: (Outraged) A bond. The bond doesn't start today! That bond started the minute that baby was conceived! . . . Even before . . . . He's been in our dreams, our hopes for years.

Doctor: This is your decision to make with your wife.

Bob: This is going to break Joanna's heart. It just can't happen. It just can't.

In your workbook you will find a worksheet to fill out about this incident. It asks you to consider what you would do in this situation. It also asks you to comment on how others have handled this type of life change. The point of this story is to illustrate that many of the changes we face in life are difficult. It also illustrates the nature of overlapping and interlocking trajectories. The child has a trajectory, the mother who is a paid teacher has one, as does the father. Also, the grandparents were not present in this story, nor were the wife's sisters and their children. In many ways, the study of what happens in family life is the study of transitions within trajectories and the trajectories of many people as they overlap, interlock, and deeply influence one another. Truly, no person is an island, especially when his or her life is embedded within the lives of others.

☐ Family Change Versus Individual Change

> The individual life course takes place within the family life course, which is the primary context of human development. We think this perspective is crucial to understanding the emotional problems that people develop as they move together through life. (Carter & McGoldrick, 1989, p. 4)

The study of changes in families is different from human development. Human development refers to the systematic changes in individuals that occur between their conception and death (Shaffer, 1989, p. 6). The study of human development focuses on patterned changes that occur because of maturation and learning and it focuses on the cognitive, social, physical, and emotional development of individuals. It helps us understand that children and adults go through stages in their development. For example, most children go through a stage of negativism when they are about 2 years old. They say "no" frequently when they are asked to do something, and they are so negative that many parents in this stage of development think their child will never learn the word "yes." No does not mean the same thing to them that it means to an adult because they say it about things they like to do, and often they say "no" to something and are still willing to do it. The negativism is a stage that is part of their cognitive and social development.

Later, when children are about 8 years old, they go through a moralistic stage in which they are concerned with things being done according to the rules. If their parent is driving 3 miles per hour over the speed limit, they are likely to point it out. During this stage, children pay a lot of attention to following the "right" rules of games and activities.

Family change is different in that it refers to the patterned changes that occur in families rather than changes in individuals. For example, newly formed families begin with a formative period. In some cultures this first stage begins with courtship. In other cultures it begins when the parents negotiate a marriage, and in other cultures it starts when couples begin to live together. During the formative stage a family becomes more complex, more differentiated or separated from other family members, and, the goal is for family members to become increasingly more competent. This initial stage is a creative period because many new family rules or "understandings" are constructed.

PRINCIPLE 4.2   FAMILY CHANGE

Family change is different than individual change. Family change is about the change that happens to the system overall instead of a change in one's own life trajectory.

White (2005) suggested that the merging of family life course theory with family and human development theory be called transition theory. This is an attractive idea that informs much of this chapter. As White aptly pointed out, the Roman philosopher Heraclitus (536–470 B.C.) argued that only change and transitions were real, per se, and that stability is only an illusion. That is a tempting idea: Is there anything that is not in flux? Let's have no sniveling as you consider this important question. The ball is in your court, so to speak. Can you think of anything that is actually unchanging? Aside from esoteric theological discussions that transcend this chapter, I am guessing you are having a difficult time thinking of something that is not changing or at least changeable. Scientists would probably argue that every particle of the universe is decaying or transforming in some way. Before we get too abstract, let's back off from that extreme position for a minute and simply indicate that we use the concept of stability to denote rather ordinary observations of entities over time.

For example, when we do research about marriage we say a marriage is stable if there was no divorce reported from Time 1 to Time 2. But, as you can clearly imagine, the strength and veracity of a marriage could (and usually does) vary greatly from day to day. For the sake of reductionism and our attempts to take snapshots of entities like the family, however, we just say, "The marriage was stable for 20 years." It is much easier to consider stability if one simply looks at structure, such as divorce versus nondivorce or children versus no children. However, when we start to look at dynamic systems that are in flux and change, complete with life course issues of individuals with overlapping and interlocking trajectories, it becomes very dicey to glibly indicate that one system is stable and another is not.

Individuals occupy roles within the family entity. As those roles overlap and interlock, we begin to focus on the transitional nature of the individual and also on the collective group. Simply said, we want to know how effectively an individual or a group of individuals (a family in this case) makes the transition from one state to another, for example, from being married to being divorced, or from having no children to having several.

An important idea is that transitions are not simple. We do not just simply go from unmarried to married without a great deal of disruption. Not all disruption is bad, however, disruption and movement through time are inevitable. Elder (1985) commented on this notion and suggested that transitions are more like oscillations. That is, our well-being, functioning, ability to cope, and effectiveness during change oscillates. It is something of a rollercoaster. We revisit the idea of the oscillating rollercoaster in Chapter 12. For now, suffice it to say that change is inevitable, stability is probably a soothing illusion, and the job of life is to learn how to stay on the rollercoaster without getting too sick.

☐ Different Kinds of Change

Some changes in family life mean that people and families become more complex, more differentiated, and more able to cope with their life situation. This is especially the case when families are in the formative stage of the family life cycle. For example, when children start to arrive, families usually become much more complex and differentiated and a number of other predictable changes occur.

All changes, however, do not lead to greater ability and complexity, and they are not all desirable. Although we like to not think about it, life is a life-and-death cycle—again where nothing is static or stable. There are natural cycles for everything that is living, and these life courses all have ends as well as beginnings. When an older person's body starts wearing out, this, too, is a part of the course of life. For example, most athletic skills peak when athletes are in their late 20s, or, for the more durable ones, in their early 30s. After that the skills, coordination, and endurance are just not the same. Athletes are not very thrilled about being "over the hill" when they are 29, but it is a part of the natural progression of the human body.

The outcomes of some changes are positive and some are negative. For example, every family loses members to death. When death occurs, it leads to painful changes in bonds, feelings of love, and closeness. Also, it is a difficult time for most families when the needs of teenagers conflict with the needs of their middle-aged parents.

Many of the change processes and transitions in family life have a bittersweet quality to them. Weddings, for example, are often a time of joy, but also a time of tears. The launching of children is a time of excitement and also loss. The coming of children is rewarding but also limiting and constraining. The natural movement from the excitement and euphoria of new love during engagement and the early months of marriage is both a loss and a relief to most couples. The couple feels the euphoria, but the bride's mother might feel great joy and deep sadness at the same time.

There are many different types of changes that occur over the course of life, such as mental, physical, and emotional changes. People increase in their mental ability as they move from infancy to adulthood. Later, as they approach old age, their memory and other mental processes start to slip. Newborn infants do not see well, but their eyesight improves rapidly during the first month of life. Later, in their mid-40s, people need bifocals. Trifocals often come in the 50s, and for some a magnifying glass a little later. Young people are fairly adaptable, but older people usually do not have the same level of adaptability, and all these changes are parts of normal family life.

Families change in size, sex composition, complexity of interrelationships, expectations, help patterns, and patterns of emotional distance and closeness. The generational alignments evolve in several predictable ways, and the ways the family system copes with the environment changes.

In sum, transition theory is about the inevitability of change. One of the key jobs of all humans is to learn how to cope with change, learn from the past, and move into the next phase gracefully.

☐ Predictability and Variability in Family Life

When family scientists began to study family life in the 1950s (Duvall, 1955), they assumed most families moved through a very predictable series of stages. They developed the term *family life cycle* to describe this **predictable pattern**. One version of this cycle that has been widely used in recent years is the one suggested by Carter and McGoldrick (1989, p. 15), which includes the following stages:

Stage 1—Leaving home: Single young adults.
Stage 2—The joining of families through marriage: The new couple.
Stage 3—Families with young children.
Stage 4—Families with adolescents.
Stage 5—Launching children and moving on.
Stage 6—Families in later life.

Family scientists discovered, however, that very few families proceed in an orderly way through this series of stages. In fact, notice that this orientation focuses primarily on children and does not reflect the change sequence that many people actually go through.

FIGURE 4.1   Some people stay single and do not find a long-term partner.

It is only a small minority of families who experience this cycle without any interruptions or without an unusual arrangement of the stages.

In contrast, most families encounter several unexpected events that influence their life cycle. Notice, for example, how common the following events are that can influence the sequence of events in family life cycles:

- Many marriages end in divorce. Many remarriages end in divorce.
- About 12% of women who are of childbearing age have received infertility services during the last year (Stephen & Chandra, 2006).
- In many families one spouse dies before the couple reaches retirement age.
- Children can die before they reach the launching stage.
- Children sometimes leave home or need alternative living arrangements before the usual "launching" age.
- Sometimes a person will remain single following a spouse's death or a divorce and other times that person will remarry.
- Having a "blended" family usually changes the family life course.
- Adult children sometimes return to live with their parents after they experience a divorce or their spouse dies.
- Some children remain single but do not leave home until they reach a much older age than one would expect.
- There is a growing single population that never marries.
- There are an unprecedented number of young adults choosing to cohabit before marriage.
- About 70% of all children born to African American women this year will be born into a home in which there is no formal marriage partner.
- Overall, one in three babies born in the United States today has unmarried parents (Carlson, McLanahan, & England, 2006). In 1960, the rate was about 5%.

These different situations lead to several important insights about family life. First, they demonstrate there is great variability in the life course of families and individuals. Just as there are so many different types of families that we cannot talk about "the" American family or "the" English family or "the" Russian family, there are so many variations in family life that we cannot talk about "the" life cycle of individuals or families.

A second idea is that even though there are great variations in the cycles of family life, there are also some aspects of these cycles that are fairly predictable. Courtship, living together, or both precede weddings, and births (or adoptions) usually precede child rearing. One's own aging tends to come late in the cycle of family life, but coping with the aging of parents and grandparents comes earlier. Midlife crises do not usually happen to people in their 20s or their 80s. They tend to come when people are between 40 and 50.

There are, therefore, a number of rhythms and patterns in the ebb and flow of family life, and some of them are fairly predictable. The more we are aware of these patterns, the more we can help families prepare and cope with daily family life.

Patterns That Are Predictable

Research has discovered a number of processes that are more predictable. The following seven examples illustrate the kinds of family patterns that are fairly predictable in modern Western family life. These patterns seem to be ubiquitous.

**PRINCIPLE 4.3   SOME CHANGES ARE
PREDICTABLE AND OTHERS ARE NOT**

It is important to know that some changes in families are predictable and expected, whereas other changes are much less predictable and are usually unexpected.

Coping With Aging and Death

One of the most predictable events in family life is that members of the family die. Families eventually find themselves coping with the process of preparing for death and trying to find ways to adjust to the feelings and changes that are created by death. In our contemporary society, most people do not die until they are over 70, so death usually is preceded by a period of aging. This period usually involves illnesses, caregiving, decreased mental and physical abilities, and in some cases long periods of senility.

For most people, their first encounter with death is when their grandparents die. This is usually an important family process because parents find themselves helping their children learn how to cope with the kind of loss and change that occurs with the death of loved ones. At the same time that the parents are helping their children cope with the death of their grandparents, they are coping with the aging and death of their parents. These changes inevitably alter care patterns, visiting patterns, and patterns in the feelings of love and closeness.

Formation Followed by Maintenance

The formation period for a family begins when a couple starts to develop a serious relationship, gets engaged, or starts living together, and it usually continues for a period of time after most weddings. During this stage of the family life cycle the couple is creating their rules of transformation and daily, monthly, and yearly routines and cycles. It is also when they are constructing unique patterns of problem solving and decision making, and ways of relating to friends and relatives. They also begin establishing their family themes, traditions, and rituals. It is a period when most couples spend a great deal of time getting to know each other and deciding how their family will be alike and different from the families in which they grew up. It is a creative period because the new family is literally constructing the system it will have, its view of the world, and its way of relating to its environment.

The Maintenance Stage

Most families gradually move into a second stage that can be called the maintenance or management stage. The dynamics and processes of this next stage are different because the family system becomes relatively established and stable. The attention of the family shifts to different concerns, such as child rearing, economic survival, ways of relating to changes in the environment, and ways of finding fulfillment. The difference between the formative stage and the maintenance stage is similar to the difference between building a ship and then sailing in the ship or building a building and then using the building. The formative stage gets the ship constructed enough that it will float and can operate. The main attention then changes to use rather than construction. Some changes in the ship will be made while it is being used, but many concerns that were important when the ship was being constructed can be forgotten, and many things about the nature of the ship can be assumed.

Birth

The birth of an infant creates a complex set of predictable family events. It leads to some immediate changes in such things as routines, allocation of resources, the way time and energy are spent, and relationships among the members of the family. It also means that a different person is the youngest member of the family, and this changes relationships, privileges, and caregiving.

It also creates a predictable series of long-term and gradual family changes that will occur as the infant matures. When the child gets old enough to go to school, the family will need to relate to school systems, friendship systems, and recreational systems differently. Later, when the child moves into adolescence, he or she will introduce many new inputs into the family system such as new forms of music, recreation, ideas, anxieties, and aspirations. When children approach adulthood they tend to individuate and differentiate from the parental family, and eventually most children are launched from the family into families of their own.

As children become adults, the relationship between them and their parents changes to one of concerned fellow adults. Later, when the children become middle-aged and the parents become aged, the patterns of giving and receiving tend to reverse. The parent generation tends to be the receivers of attention, concern, and care, and the younger middle-aged generation tends to become the givers.

Parting Is Inevitable

Another predictable pattern is that weddings are followed by some type of marital separation. The traditional ideal is for marriage to last "'til death do we part," but some type of parting is a predictable family process. In earlier historical periods the vast majority of marriages ended with the death of one of the spouses. During the last century, however, an

FIGURE 4.2 The term empty nest refers to the time after the youngest child leaves home.

increasing number of marriages have ended with divorce. The divorce rate, however, has leveled off since 1979, and the present pattern is that about 50% of "first" marriages that occur in our society end with a divorce and about 60% of marriages end with the death of one of the spouses.

Idealism to Realism

Another predictable pattern in family life is that families tend to start out with considerable idealism, and this is gradually replaced with realism (Blood & Wolfe, 1960; Carter & McGoldrick, 1989). In many situations, the idealism is not replaced with realism, but with disenchantment, disillusionment, and despair. Most young couples have an idealistic view of the future of the family they are creating. They believe their love is unusually strong and deep, and they can communicate, relate, and share in unusually effective ways. As the years pass, the realities of a world that is, at best, complicated and unpredictable and often cruel and unjust gradually weaken the idealism.

The Empty Nest Stage Is Getting Longer

Several factors contribute to the empty nest stage of family life becoming longer. Life expectancy has increased dramatically in the last century. Most people now live beyond the age of 75, and at the same time the number of children in each family has decreased. Because most people have their last child before their mid-30s, parents usually are about 50 when they launch their last child. The result is that most people live more than 25 years after their children are launched.

Spending Years Single Is Typical

A final predictable pattern for American families is that most people are single for many years of their adult life. Many factors contribute to this pattern. One spouse usually dies before the other. Also, people tend to marry at later ages than in earlier times, and the higher divorce rate has increased the number of years people are single. This is especially the case for women because they do not remarry as frequently as divorced men. When an individualistic perspective is used, it is common to assume that single adults are not in a "family." However, from a family science perspective, being a single adult is a developmental stage most people experience in their family life cycle. Singles have parents, siblings, and grandparents, and many of them have children and grandchildren. Therefore, they are part of family life, and the family realm can be as important to them as it is to people who happen to be married.

Living Together Before Marriage Has Become Typical

During the 1950s and 1960s cohabitation was rare and pejoratively referred to as "shacking up." Today we live in a different world. Researchers estimate that there are about 5 million households in the United States maintained by heterosexual cohabiting partners (The National Marriage Project, 2006). It would be a rare thing if you did not know someone who has lived with a boyfriend or girlfriend. The phenomenon is so new that our language has not caught up with the trend. For example, how does someone introduce a partner with whom he has been living for 6 years, but to whom he is not married? He probably just says, "Hi, my name is Bert and this is Bernie." More to the point, family researchers can no longer build neat and tidy tables about marital and partnership transitions that fit most of the population. There are so many different patterns and possibilities that talking about one type of structural possibility is not very helpful.

Variability in Patterns of Change

Many factors create variability in family change. For example, some children leave home in their midteens. This pushes their families into the launching process earlier than most families. Other children never leave home, and this creates a different combination of change and stability. Death is inevitable, but it is unpredictable. Families never know when they will need to cope with the processes of dying, bereaving, and finding ways to go on without loved ones. This adds unpredictability and variability to every family's life.

People also respond to the processes of aging differently, and this influences patterns of daily family life. For example, some people experience midlife crises that dramatically change their lives, and this can influence the changes others might want to make or not make in their family.

The process of launching children changes the obligations and responsibilities of parents. There are many ways families can respond to these changes. Some families invest more or less energy in their careers, and others try new careers, move to new locations, or take up new educational or recreational pursuits.

The aging of parents and grandparents introduces variability and unpredictability in a family's daily life. When an aged parent needs emotional, financial, and physical assistance, it can influence career options, the way a family's financial resources are used, the way the rooms of the house are used, and how people relate to each other.

☐ Transitions

The concept of **transitions** was created when scholars realized that living systems usually do not have a constant rate of change. They tend to have periods of rapid change followed by periods of relative stability. The periods of rapid or dramatic change are called transitions and the periods of stability are called stages. Most of the major transitions in families occur when there are changes in the membership of the family or in the way the family interacts with its environment. Many of these transitions are fairly predictable and normal, and they can be anticipated. Some of them, however, are part of the unpredictable and variable parts of family life. Some examples of transitions that influence family life are engagements, starting to live together, weddings, birth of a first child, children starting school, children moving into adolescence, children leaving home, the death of a parent, retirement, the death of a spouse, and one's own death. Not all transitions in family life are routine.

In Chapter 13, we discuss events that are very unexpected and have a different texture to them in family life. For example, becoming unemployed or employed, onset of a serious and chronic disease such as cancer or a heart ailment, recovery from a serious illness, sudden fame or fortune, and sudden defamation or misfortune can create important transitions in family life, but they should not be thought of as routine changes. Some changes are created by biological factors such as puberty, menopause, and senility, and some are created by experiences.

For example, the process of experiencing pregnancy and birth creates many changes in the perspectives, insights, sensitivities, and concerns of the parents, and these experiential factors create part of the changes that occur in family transitions. The family emotional system changes over time, and changes often occur in the environment that also influence family transitions.

Some changes are created by a combination of factors. For example, the changes created by adolescence and midlife crisis are not caused by one event or process. They are instead created by the complex interaction of physiological, social, mental, economic, spatial, and emotional changes, and they create sizable transitions in the individuals and in the family.

Some transitions tend to be relatively easy and problem-free, yet others tend to be difficult. Also, some of them are easy for one family but difficult for another. For example, some families have a difficult time coping with children leaving home, but others find it an easy transition (Haley, 1987). Some families have a difficult time coping with retirement, but others find it easy. Some find the transition into parenthood easy, and others find it challenging. One important challenge for family scientists is to find ways to help families cope with transitions so that there are healthy periods of growth rather than excessive difficulty.

Fortunately, in the late 1930s sociologists such as Cottrell (1942) began trying to identify the principles that are involved in making transitions easy and difficult, and scholars have tried to use these principles to identify strategies that families, therapists, and educators can use to promote family health. The principles Cottrell identified are fairly specific (not general), and they have since been revised and updated in light of subsequent research (Burr, Leigh, et al., 1979). Three of these principles are now so widely understood and useful that they are included in this chapter.

☐ Anticipatory Socialization

These ideas refer to the process of helping people learn what will be expected of them in new roles and situations. The term *socialization* refers to the process of gradually learning the norms, scripts, attitudes, values, and subtle rules a person needs to know to be able to function effectively in society. Infants are in an unsocialized condition, but gradually they go through the process of being socialized by parents, teachers, siblings, and others who teach them how to act and feel.

Anticipatory socialization refers to learning that is done before people are in a role where they actually use what they have learned (Merton, 1968). In particular, Merton indicated that anticipatory socialization involved acquiring new abilities, skills, and, in some cases, changing one's reference or social group.

PRINCIPLE 4.4   ANTICIPATORY SOCIALIZATION

When one can anticipate a situation and learn from a previous experience (or an experience of someone else) then the next transition into a situation similar to the previous target experience will enhance the chances that the new transition will be smoother and more efficient.

Cottrell (1942) was the first scholar to develop the principle that anticipatory socialization helps people make transitions. Since then, other scholars such as Merton (1968), Burr (1973), and Bronfenbrenner (1979) have refined it. A study conducted in Norway illuminates this process. Waerdahl (2005) found that children making the transition from primary school into middle school at age 12 used symbolic objects and clothing that helped them practice and identify who they would become as they made this key transition. In Merton's study of soldiers making the transition back into civilian life, he noticed that they practiced being civilians by dressing in certain ways and using home-based language that replaced army clothes, hierarchies, and speech. In like manner, Norwegian children were more successful in transitioning into an advanced school when they were able to practice "being older" by dressing older and adopting the language and symbolic items of the older children. In Waerdahl's study, the key to success for these children was the ability to obtain the highly prized Levis jeans that signaled to others that they understood what was required to be a part of the older group.

In another study by Coleman and Hoffer (1987), it was found that students' successful transition into the workplace was guided by learning accurate information about working and work expectations. Parents were key facilitators of this pretraining, followed by friends and other family members. In both of these cases, the power of this principle is clear: Learning and practicing about a future role assists one in making the transition into that role. Although we know very little about how this process works for groups (as opposed to individuals) we could also speculate that when families practice transitions before they occur (e.g., moving to a new school, getting divorced, having a new baby, etc.), the group will have an easier time making those transitions.

This principle helps us realize that timing is important in trying to help people learn what they need to do. There are moments of readiness or teachable moments when people are eager and motivated and other times when they are less interested in learning (Guerney & Guerney, 1981). As we begin to make transitions into difficult or even pleasant situations, it is critical to prearm family members about the nature of the transition. This strategy decreases role strain.

☐ Role Strain

A second principle that helps people cope with transitions deals with role strain. **Role strain** refers to the felt difficulty people experience when they try to conform to the demands of a role. Some roles, such as caring for infants, are so demanding that there can be abundant role strain. When the parents both try to work full time and they try to keep up all of the other activities they were used to before the pregnancy, it can create one type of strain, an overload problem. To avoid this, couples need to learn that when they are expecting their first child, it usually helps to adjust and eliminate some of the competing roles they occupy. Frequently at least one parent and sometimes both parents need to adjust the amount of time they spend on their careers, leisure activities, educational pursuits, and other activities.

Sometimes, anticipating does not help much. There might be other cultural factors that trump one's prelearning. For example a study by Baxter, Hewitt, and Haynes (2008) found that information about the transition from cohabitation to marriage yielded interesting results. These researchers used data from the Australian panel survey called Negotiating the Life Course. They found that men were fairly constant in sharing household duties until the couple made the transition into parenthood. In Australia, about 75% of the couples cohabit before marriage. The question is this: Does this pretraining experience make a difference in who does which jobs in the household following marriage (when it occurs)? It turned out, in this case, that living together did not predict equality in marriage. Like many other studies, these researchers found that, over time, women were likely to do significantly more housework than were men. Further, over time, the amount of housework reported by husbands significantly decreased. This was magnified when a child was born. Even though there had been plenty of pretraining, the men in this study moved further away from household performance that resulted in increased role strain and tension.

PRINCIPLE 4.5   ROLE STRAIN

When role strain is high in a system or relationship, any transition into a new role or life course stage will be less efficient and more stressful.

Many things can create role strain. For example, it can be introduced by ambiguity about what a person is supposed to do in a new situation, and by conflicting expectations about what should be done. It can also be caused by having too many roles that one is trying to perform simultaneously.

Part of the role strain principle tells us that strain helps the transitions out of roles. For example, adolescence is usually a period of considerable role strain. The expectations for adolescence are ambiguous, and the important people in an adolescent's life do not agree on many of the expectations. Parents, teens, friends, and educators, for example, usually have different opinions. This makes the transition into adolescence difficult, but it usually makes the transition out of it much easier.

In fact most people are glad to have the teenage years behind them, and they are thrilled when they and others finally view them as adults, a stage of life where the expectations are clearer and there is less strain. Because the adolescent stage of the family life cycle also tends to be difficult for parents and siblings, they too, usually, find the transition out of the teen years a welcome breath of fresh air.

The main issues in applying this principle are knowing what role strain is, knowing the kinds of things that cause it, and finding ways to minimize or prevent it. Good anticipatory socialization can help because it gives people clues about which roles are more and less demanding. It also frequently helps people learn that some roles are fairly incompatible

FIGURE 4.3   Sometimes life comes at you hard. Role strain occurs when parents have multiple tasks to complete and a new role demand occurs on the top of a previous one before the new one can be resolved.

with others. For example, it is helpful to know that roles such as dating, being engaged, and being married are fairly incompatible, and trying to do more than one of these at the same time can create more than a little strain.

Goode (1960) identified a number of other strategies that can help minimize strain. One of them is to talk extensively with others to try to clarify the expectations and get a clear understanding of what is expected. This also helps create agreement with others about these expectations. Role theorists have a term for each of these two processes: getting *role clarity* and *role consensus*. Trying to get clarity and consensus is a natural process in many situations. For example, most engaged couples find it natural to talk for hours and hours, almost endlessly, about what they want and do not want when they are married and how they want to act and not act.

Another of Goode's strategies for coping with role strain is to compartmentalize certain roles. When two roles, such as being an employee and lover, demand very different ways of acting, it is helpful to separate the situations and places where people are in these roles. Being an employee during working hours and a lover at other times helps the employee, employer, and lovers all minimize their strain. A different example is that the roles of caring for infants and having a career are fairly incompatible, so people usually separate them.

A third strategy is to periodically examine the role demands we have in our lives to determine if we are overcommitted. Most of us go through short periods of time, such as during final examinations, when we have an overload, but it is an acceptable part of the ebb and flow of demands. However, sometimes we gradually take on one more obligation, and then another, and then another until we have inadvertently overcommitted ourselves. In these situations, it is an effective strategy to reduce our obligations by eliminating some roles. If we do not want to eliminate any of our roles, we can lower our "standards" in some roles.

☐ Transition Procedures

Another principle about transitions deals with the procedures that are used in making a transition. The principle is called the role transitions principle.

> **PRINCIPLE 4.6   ROLE TRANSITION PRINCIPLE**
>
> The clarity of the transition procedures helps the transition to be more efficient, smoother, and less stressful.

Imagine, for example, how difficult it would be if someone's wedding were spread out over several months. They would not know for sure when they were finally married. At what point would they have made the important commitments to each other, and when should their friends start thinking of them as a married couple? This type of ambiguity in the transition procedures would make the transition into marriage much more difficult than it usually is.

☐ Morphostasis and Morphogenesis

Morphogenesis

Morphogenesis and morphostasis can be understood easily if they are divided into their two root words. First, let's examine **morphogenesis**: The *morpho* part of this word comes from the Greek term *morpho,* which refers to the form or shape of something. The *genesis* part comes from the Greek word *genesis,* which means beginning or creating, and in this word it also refers to changing or altering. Thus family morphogenesis refers to changing or altering the shape or form of a family life. It means more than just changing the number or the ages of the people in the family, as it includes other things like changes in family dynamics, traditions, routines, emotional responses, rules, rituals, and other processes.

The main idea that family researchers have developed about morphogenesis can be called the morphogenesis principle: Some of the morphogenesis in families is routine and expected change and some of it is not. The difference is that routine changes are part of the typical life span or life cycle of individuals or families. For example, a member of a family might be paralyzed by an automobile accident, a family might win a large lottery prize, or someone in a family might go through a religious conversion. These and many other random and unforeseen events can create changes in the "form" of the families involved, but family scientists do not think of them as routine changes.

Morphostasis

The concept of **morphostasis** is the opposite of morphogenesis, and it is also easily understood when we break it into its two parts. *Morpho* refers to form, and *stasis* refers to static or stable. Thus, family morphostasis is the process of maintaining the status quo or avoiding change in a family life. Family scientists also sometimes use the term homeostasis rather than morphostasis. These two words are synonymous and interchangeable. For ease, the word morphostasis is used in this book rather than homeostasis. The morphostasis principle was one of the first principles to be identified after scholars began thinking with a family process point of view (Jackson, 1957).

PRINCIPLE 4.7   MORPHOSTASIS PRINCIPLE

Organized systems tend to resist change. A system will usually go to great lengths to keep the system working like it has done in the past.

When these ideas were being developed, the scholars who were creating them paid most of their attention to morphostasis, and they ignored morphogenesis (Jackson, 1963). This meant that during the 1950s and 1960s, family scholars who were developing these ideas assumed that family life was fairly stable and unchanging, and the primary tendency in family systems is to resist innovation and development. The current view in the field is that, on the one hand, there are always pressures, events, and processes that tend to create change in family life. At the same time, there are always pressures, events, and processes that tend to create stability and resist change. The two processes oppose each other and are incompatible, but both are inherent and unavoidable, and apparently they are natural and inevitable parts of family life. Unfortunately, there is virtually no research that would tell us if families (or systems in general) resist change. This is a powerful theoretical idea that needs to be researched more.

☐ Why Does Morphostasis Occur?

There are many reasons morphostasis is an inevitable and fundamental part of family systems. Three of these reasons are as follows:

1. Rules that are created in the early stages of a relationship become the first part of a complicated web or set of rules. Later on, if there are attempts to change the first rules it has implications for many parts of the web. One result of this pattern is that it creates some tendency to resist change.
2. A great deal of what happens in families is unconscious, or, using the iceberg analogy, it is beneath the surface and fairly invisible. Also, people have enough of a desire to control their lives that they like some degree of stability, security, and predictability. These tendencies lead to some resistance to change.
3. Family processes deal with many of the most fundamental and deeply experienced emotional processes that humans experience. For example, they deal with mating, reproduction, personal territory, intimacy, and belonging. People are highly motivated to arrange their life so these deeply felt affective experiences are comfortable. One example of this is the unbelievable trials humans sometimes go through to find a mate. When people get these parts of their lives organized so the inner and core affective conditions are comfortable, they have very strong, affectively motivated reasons to resist attempts to change things. This is one reason divorce and death are resisted so much, and why they are such tremendously disruptive experiences when

they cannot be avoided. They force us to reorganize some of the most fundamental parts of our lives.

☐ Practical Implications

Ambivalence

When we understand the twin processes of morphogenesis and morphostasis in family life, it gives us ideas that have several implications. One implication is that it helps us be aware that families always experience **ambivalence** when they encounter significant change. Ambivalence is feeling two opposite affective states or desires at the same time. Even when families encounter desirable changes like weddings, births, graduations, children going out on their own, career opportunities, and other new challenges and opportunities, there is always ambivalence in the family about them. The ambivalence is frequently uneven. This means that sometimes one side of the feelings for or against something are stronger than the opposing feelings. Usually, when a change helps people attain important goals, the dominant feelings are in favor of the change. When a change interferes with important goals or is threatening in other ways, the dominant feelings are against the change.

Sometimes perceptions determine the nature of the feelings, but perceptions are sometimes deceptive. Remembering the iceberg analogy, when a change has implications for the hidden parts of family life, people might not be aware of all of the pressures and processes. For example, a younger sibling might be relieved when an older sibling leaves home. They get a new bedroom. There is less hassle about the bathroom, no more getting picked on, and so on. The feelings of loss and emptiness can be very real and can have an effect on the child, but the child might not be aware of what is happening.

Early Intervention

Another implication of these two ideas is that, because systems tend to become increasingly rigid as time passes, generally speaking, the earlier in the life of an individual or family system we try to influence the system, the greater the impact we will usually have. In family science, there are many ways this can be applied. For example, we can make more difference in the way a couple relates by helping them early in their marriage rather than later. We can have more impact on people's lives if we influence them early in life than if we influence them later (Bronfenbrenner, 1979).

When we try to apply these insights, we also need to be aware of the readiness of individuals and families for change. People are ready at certain times and not ready at others. For example, we would probably have little impact on a person's life by trying to teach him or her something about careers when he or she is 3 years old. They need to be more ready than most 3-year-olds usually are.

It has become widely believed in our society that the first years of a child's life are the most important, and the principle of morphostasis is consistent with this idea. Family scientists, therefore, should do what they can to help parents find the resources they need to be able to exert the influence and care during this period that most parents want to have and children need.

Time Interventions Close to Transitions

Family scientists have discovered that periods of transition are a good time to try to influence family life (Klonsky & Bengston, 1996). Often it is most effective to try to create a change just before a transition or just after it. Some of the reasons transitions are a good time to try to make changes are because the morphogenetic processes are more powerful at transition points and systems are in a period of flux. After the transition, the family system tends to move into a new stage, the morphostatic processes take over and systems tend to resist change and promote stability.

An example of this idea is that just prior to the birth of the first child in a family is a good time for family scientists to help couples prepare to care for infants. The parents are thinking about the birth, anticipating it, and they are highly motivated by the emotions that surround birth and procreation. This is, therefore, a teachable moment or time of readiness for new ideas, skills, and ways of doing things. Attempts to help people learn how to cope with infants are not as effective before a couple is pregnant.

Another example is that it is not very effective to try to teach parents of infants how to deal with the transition into the teenage years. However, when the oldest child in a family is about 12, the parents are much more receptive to ideas about how to cope with teenagers.

However, this idea does not always work. Many other processes are always at work simultaneously in family systems, and we need to consider as much of the total system as possible. This is sometimes called having a holistic attitude or orientation. For example, if we just paid attention to the morphostasis and morphogenesis principles, we would conclude that the best time to help young couples prepare for marriage is just before the marriage. Experience in trying to help engaged couples, however, has revealed that the period just prior to a wedding is not a very good time to try to influence couples. Research about the effects of educational and counseling programs has revealed that they have very little impact when couples are in that transition (Druckman, 1979). Apparently what is happening is that the period just prior to weddings is such an intensely emotional time that couples are not receptive to new ideas. They are so concerned about the relationship and the preparation for the wedding that intervention programs have little impact.

Studies have found that premarital programs that have a follow-up phase about 6 months after the wedding are much more helpful than programs that just work with couples before marriage (Bader, Microys, Sinclair, Willet, & Conway, 1980; Druckman, 1979). What is apparently happening is that after couples have had time to settle into their marital relationship, they move into a period when they are more ready to learn than they were just prior to the wedding.

Epigenesis

Remember the epigenesis principle from Chapter 3 that includes three main ideas. One idea is that what is done during earlier stages of a life cycle sometimes limits future opportunities, and it can make later challenges more difficult. A second idea is that what is done during earlier stages of a life cycle also can expand future opportunities, and this can make later challenges easier to cope with. The third idea is that what is done during earlier stages of a life cycle tends to create habits or tendencies in family systems and in individuals' behaviors, and these tendencies are continued later even though the families or individuals have the capacity to do things differently. What this means is that such things as rituals, patterns, traditions, routines, themes, and mannerisms tend to be continued once they are established. Patterns, rules, and rituals are discussed further in later chapters. Each of these elements of family processes is a vital aspect of family life.

There are also many situations that illustrate this principle. One is that what couples do in the formative stages of their family life cycle can influence their options later. For example, assume a couple is beginning to get serious and they develop a pattern of talking openly and honestly about their feelings. In the process of developing this pattern, they create a complex set of rules about how they are going to interact in their relationship in their system. The rules are "understandings" about how they are going to act in relation to each other. Many of these rules are established without ever talking about them. They might develop rules such as agreeing they will try to be willing to take the time to listen to the other one when there is an indication they have a strong emotion. They will try to understand and they will try to avoid being demeaning or critical. They also will probably come to an "understanding" about such things as how hard they should try and what kinds of things, such as being "really tired," can interfere without it being a problem. In this example, we have only identified a few key "understandings" a couple could develop in this area, but if space were to allow, it would be possible to identify hundreds of these subtle rules about how a couple communicates about feelings.

The rules that are developed in the early stages of a relationship become the framework that is used to develop more elaborate and complicated rules and understandings. They also influence what can be done in the future. If a couple creates a pattern of being open and candid with their feelings, their system will then demand of them certain behaviors, and they will get certain things out of their system. The rules of openness demand that they take the time to listen to each other carefully and that they are patient and understanding whenever the other one wants to talk about feelings. They will get out of their system a certain degree of understanding, sense of belonging, closeness, and bondedness.

Some of these basic affective states are desires for territory, belonging, leaders and followers, a sense of meaning and purpose, maintaining the species by reproducing, sexual arousal, and being connected to each other in ways that are at least minimally secure.

Most of these emotional processes are so deeply experienced that we are not very aware of them. We do not have vocabularies to describe them well, and by and large they are imperceptible. The result is that they cause vague emotional feelings like anger, attraction, love, and desire. This means that we do not have very good access to these affective experiences to know how to deal with them consciously or deliberately, yet they are so powerful that they exert tremendous effect on our lives.

In sum, when people establish the "rules" they are going to have in their family they are dealing with many of the most fundamental emotional aspects that we humans experience, and when we get our "system" established, we find it a deeply disruptive emotional experience if we have to go back and renegotiate or change fundamental parts of it. The intensity of the affective aspects of these processes can be somewhat appreciated if we think about all of the elaborate human rituals, songs, dances, tokens, celebrations, covenants, and legal apparatus that are connected to the resolution of these processes.

Most of the discussion of this principle has focused on how it applies to family life, but it also applies to developmental processes in individuals. This means that what a person does in response to developmental changes and processes has important implications for what that person can and will tend to do later in his or her life. There are many examples of this process in individuals. If students do not apply themselves academically, they gradually eliminate future opportunities that demand educational excellence. If a person becomes proficient with a musical instrument, that person has choices that a person without that proficiency does not have.

When people learn early in life how to express themselves orally and in writing, these skills open up many avenues that would otherwise be closed to them. When people learn social skills, or when they do not develop social skills, these characteristics influence what they can and cannot do the rest of their lives. This principle is a useful idea, but there are many aspects of it that we do not yet understand, and more research needs to be done on the subject. For example, some of the "rules" that are created early in relationships seem to change easily at later times, but some are very resistant to change. We do not yet know very much about which "rules" operate which way and why. These are some of the unknowns that future analysis, theorizing, and research can help address.

☐ Summary

This chapter discussed ways human development and routine family processes influence what happens in families. Some are predictable. Families can anticipate them and prepare for them. Most families tend to be similar in these predictable processes. There are also many family processes that are not predictable. These unpredictable processes create great variability in family and individual development.

The chapter also discussed ways families can manage transitions so they are as manageable and growth-producing as possible. The processes of morphogenesis, morphostasis, and epigenesis were also discussed and illustrated, and several strategies for using these concepts were given. One of the main ideas in the chapter is that those of us who want to understand families should always be sensitive to processes of change. We should never ignore them, even when we are concentrating on other parts of family processes or other things that are known in the field.

Another implication of this is that the developmental ideas should be integrated with the ideas about the family realm, generational dimensions, and affect to form an increasingly comprehensive and helpful set of ideas.

☐ Study Questions

1. Name several "predictable" patterns of family life. Why do we pay attention to these?
2. Explain the idea that we move from idealism to realism as we get older. Think of a good example of this in your life.
3. Explain the concept of "anticipatory socialization."
4. What is the difference between morphostasis and morphogenesis?
5. How can the epigenesis principle be applied using the information from this chapter?
6. What is role strain?
7. How can you tell if a role you are in is stressful?

☐ Key Terms

Trajectory
Predictable patterns
Transitions

Anticipatory socialization
Role strain
Morphogenesis
Morphostasis
Ambivalence

☐ Suggested Readings

Bianchi, S., Robinson, J., & Milkie, M. (2006). *Changing rhythms of American life.* New York: Russell Sage Foundation.

Conger, R., Lorenz, F., & Wickrama, K. A. S. (2004). *Continuity and change in family relations.* Mahwah, NJ: Lawrence Erlbaum Associates.

Cowan, P., & Hetherington, M. (1991). *Family transitions.* Hillsdale, NJ: Lawrence Erlbaum Associates.

Noller, P., & Feeney, J. (2001). *Personal relationships across the lifespan.* London: Psychology Press.

CHAPTER 5

Genetics, Personality, Gender, and Power

☐ Chapter Preview

In this chapter, readers will learn:

- How genetics plays a key role in contributing to our self-definition and how we respond to the world around us.
- That gender role stereotypes inform family life and how men and women act toward one another.
- That the concepts of masculinity and femininity help us understand how home jobs, jobs outside the home, child care, and decision making get done in family life.
- How genetics is an important tool in understanding the differences between how men and women approach life.
- About the term androgyny and its reference to the blending of male and female roles within home life.
- That equalitarian role division describes the cultural movement toward men and women sharing the duties of home life in equitable ways. Equitable means fair, not necessarily equal.
- That the feminist framework since the 1970s has attempted to highlight cultural instances within which women's important contributions to culture and society have been underrecognized.

☐ Introduction

This chapter has four interconnected segments. The first segment introduces the idea that families are made up of individuals and individuals have unique biogenetic compositions. The biogenetic profile of each person contributes to his or her unique attributes. The second section addresses one collection of those attributes that is grouped together and labeled **personality** or temperament. Some of our personality is thought to be genetic and other elements of it are probably learned. In addition to those key elements, another essential aspect of the individual is **gender**. Gender begins in genetics but also includes a social construction to this important feature of daily living. Understanding the texture that gender brings to relationships is central to understanding other family processes found in subsequent chapters. The discussion of gender, in turn, leads to the core message of this chapter: Genetic, gender and personality differences often lead to power imbalances in relationships. Power imbalance is usually a destructive force within family dynamics. Within our discussion of power imbalance, we also discuss how destructive patriarchal control can be in relationships.

☐ Genetic Inheritance

Human Genome Project

Biology was routinely ignored as a feature of family studies until the 1980s. It was during this time that bioscientists begun unraveling the secrets of **genes** in the **Human Genome Project** (*http://www.ornl.gov/sci/techresources/Human_Genome/home.shtml*). Until recently, most family scientists operated on the assumption that the patterns of interaction in families (and even by individuals alone) were primarily the result of training or socialization. More recently, sociobiologists have discovered links between the genetic composition of the individual and certain family behaviors (e.g., choice of mate, parenting styles, sexual activity, etc.). In this chapter, we explore some basic ideas about the biology–familial connection. This topic is expansive and, therefore, what is presented here is a sample of the research and thinking that will be sure to come in the next few years as the genome project continues to uncover the mysteries of human life.

The U.S. Human Genome Project was begun in 1990. The development of this project was a coordinated effort between the U.S. Department of Energy and The National Institutes of Health. Billions of dollars have been spent in an attempt to identify all of the approximately 20,000–25,000 genes in human **DNA**.[1] Scientists from many countries are working feverishly to map the entire genetic code of the human. As they uncover the genetic code for each gene and for each gene combination, they are discovering how genes contribute to diseases and other serious problems and conditions, including how men participate in competitive activities, which seem to be linked to gaining, maintaining, or losing social status (Booth, Carver, & Granger, 2000; Mazur & Michalek, 1998).

The process of discovery involves mapping gene sequences. As of the writing of this edition of the text, approximately 92% of the mapping process has been completed. However, there are years of future research to be completed. Our brief emphasis here aims at mentioning a few examples of how genetic-based research can inform family processes. To that end, we present several examples under the rubric of **behavioral genetics**.

It is important to note that our **genetic heritage** rarely determines what we will become. Instead, our genes push or influence us in certain directions. Likewise, the environments in which we are raised (e.g., single-parent home, rural farming community, or inner city) do not "determine" who we are in and of themselves. Instead, who we are—or who we can or will become—results from our genetic heritage, the environment within which we grew up, and the individual choices each of us makes.

Our genetic heritage and our environments—including our parents and where we grew up—and other situations contribute to who we are. Additionally, we make choices that might be quite independent of (albeit greatly influenced by) our genetic, familial, and community profiles. Social scientists have struggled for decades with the important philosophical question that asks how much each of these influences matter.

In the mid-twentieth century, many psychologists decided that the genetic world was of little importance, and that the individual was shaped and fashioned by his or her surroundings and the people with whom he or she came in contact. Today, researchers and educators pay more attention to the genetic messages in each individual, the hormonal responses that are, in part, triggered by one's genetic profile. Of course we also believe that one's environment is a crucial aspect of the puzzle. However, social scientists are paying more attention to the inner biological person than ever before.

The study of behavioral genetics (Booth et al., 2000) examines the genetic influence on individual behavior vis-à-vis environmental influence. In a classic example of this type of research, a well-known family scientist examined antisocial behavior in twins (Reiss, 1995a, 1995b) and discovered that identical twins (who share 100% of their DNA code) were similar in their antisocial scores (.81 correlation) and fraternal twins (who only share 50% of their DNA code) were not quite as similar (.61 correlation). Using this relatively simple kind of research we can take a closer look at the influence of genetics and how it relates to environmental influence. Using a simple statistical procedure in this study, Reiss reasoned that about 60% of the influence to be antisocial (for the twins in this study) came from their genes, and only 40% came from these children's close environments.

Other studies using similar approaches have examined such things as intelligence, memory ability, impulse control, and risk-taking behavior (for further reading in this area see Booth et al., 2000; Plomin, 1994; Reiss, 1995a, 1995b; Rowe, 1994). This line of research has long suggested that physiological processes are elemental, critical, and essential components of human interaction (Booth, Johnson, & Granger, 2005). One of the key problems of this research in the past has been that the physiological researchers only considered the impact of social influence as background noise and not really part of the total causal picture. However some researchers (Booth et al., 2000; Booth et al., 2005; D'Onofrio, et al., 2007) have led the way in the shifting worldview of the nature versus nurture controversy. A central idea of this shift is that biobehavioral relationship interactions can be greatly changed by our social environment.

A study by Booth et al. (2005) delivers this point. These researchers collected information (both biological and social) from about 600 men and women (married to each other). They found an interesting pathway of linkages. They originally thought there would be a direct connection between high testosterone levels in men and relationship satisfaction. That is, other researchers have suggested that when testosterone was high, men were more likely to exhibit more aggression, domination, and risk-taking behaviors in relationships (Mazur & Michalek, 1998). Therefore, they supposed that when men had higher levels of testosterone they would be more aggressive in marital relationships. They discovered, however, that there was not a direct pathway between testosterone levels and marital quality. However, there was a clear link between the husband's perception of his role overload ("Is there too much to do?"; "I have things to do that I really don't want to do"; and "I can't get caught up") and marital quality. The connection between testosterone and marital quality was controlled by how he perceived his own stress overload. When he perceived his life as out of control or highly stressed, higher levels of testosterone did lead to lower marital quality. However, men who reported lower levels of role overload and higher levels of testosterone also reported lower marital quality.

The interesting aspect of this study is that one's genetic makeup, in this case his level of testosterone (usually fairly constant and a function of one's genetic profile) interacts with environment or, at least, our appraisal of our environment. In another study, this type of environment–genetics interaction was also found. D'Onofrio et al. (2007) conducted a landmark study in Australia with the offspring of twins. This three-generational study of family life is one of the few that have followed twins from an early age into the

FIGURE 5.1 Twins separated at birth, with parents who are very different from another, grow up to be remarkably similar even though they have never met.

childbearing years. This study began in 1980 when more than 8,000 twins were selected from the Australian National Twin Register. These twins were, at that time, entering young adulthood and responded to a self-report survey. The same twins were then contacted again in 1988 (with their spouses where possible) and they were again interviewed in 1992. By using twins (two people with the same genetic code, in this case) and by obtaining data about the twins' parents' marriages, these researchers could estimate the effects of social environment vis-à-vis genetic contribution to future divorce choices by this sample.

They found that these twin children who were raised with divorced parents were much more likely to divorce themselves when they got older and married. These researchers claimed that although environment and personal choice were all important contributors, something was passed along to the next generation that created potential problems with relationships. This type of research is not refined enough, as yet, to inform us about the mysterious

FIGURE 5.2 One strong trait programmed into humans is the fight–flight pattern. When there is high threat, humans are programmed to fight back or to flee.

"something" that gets passed on. Of course, it is not just one personality trait or one personal attribute that "makes" someone divorce. However, there is growing evidence that who we are and how we perform in relationships has a genetic component attached to it.

What should be the take-home message of this section? One could read this section and develop an attitude of despair: Who I am is immutable and unchangeable, therefore why try? Another approach is one of realization. When we find an area in our personality, temperament, or makeup that is destructive to relationships, we can target that problem and work harder to strengthen that area. You certainly should not come away from this chapter thinking that if you or your spouse (or spouse to be) came from a divorced family that there is no hope for you. Instead, if you have relatives who struggle with relationship problems, it means you will have to be on a higher alert status. You will probably have to work harder to stay out of relationship distress. Principle 5.1 captures this idea and states that once we realize that much of who we are physically, emotionally, and mentally is tied to genetic predispositions, we can respond accordingly.

PRINCIPLE 5.1   GENETICS AND FAMILIES

Families are more effective and efficient when family members realize that individual family members have different talents, respond to stress differently, and have different abilities and skills that might be rooted in genetics. Individuals should pay close attention to traits and weaknesses they have inherited. By attending to those challenges, we can increase our chances of doing well in relationships.

Sports metaphors are always dangerous, but I think the following one is on point for this topic. Michael Jordan was one of the greatest basketball players ever. Some have claimed he was the greatest ever for the position he played. Once during his illustrious career, he decided to take a break from basketball and try baseball. One of the most daunting athletic feats in all of sports is the ability to hit a speeding 95-mile-per-hour baseball with a rounded wooden bat. That is particularly true if the ball is spinning and curving.

Michael Jordan did not do very well at baseball, even though he was one of the greatest athletes to ever play basketball. The ability to hit a baseball includes several genetic components, including quickness, eye–hand coordination of a very special kind, the ability to see the spin on the ball, and muscular strength to swing a heavy bat at very high speeds. In addition to those skills, many of which are genetically based, one must also be mentally motivated to spend thousands of hours practicing and devote one's total energy, financial resources, and time to hitting a baseball. Of the millions of Little League baseball players in the United States only a few hundred thousand ever get to play in high school athletics. Of those, a very small number ever play for a college team. The highest level of professional baseball includes only about 700 players—from the millions who dream of it when they are 11 and 12 years old. Not everyone—not even Michael Jordan—could hit a baseball well enough to play professionally.

☐ Personality

The second theme of this chapter is that personality is a key element in understanding how people select mates, how well the relationship thrives, and whether or not it will survive. Before you continue, turn to Activity 5.1 in your workbook and fill out the questionnaire about your personality.

Defining Personality

What is your personality like? What do you think of when you say that "she has a certain personality" or personality trait? Another way to approach this topic is to answer a series of questions. The first one is this: How do you get energy? Do you acquire psychological energy by meeting new people, going to gatherings where there are lots of people present, or meeting a group friends for lunch? There might be some who get their inner strength from being alone, spending time reflecting, and taking a long walk.

Another way to think about personality or temperament is to think about what types of people you are attracted to. In one study of personality and gender, Pines (1998) found that men described themselves as more likely to be attracted to a woman's physical appearance, whereas women seem to focus more on such things as intimacy, commitment, and security. Thinking back to our earlier discussion about genetics, would you say that these findings are about gender differences (something that is learned from society) or about personality differences (something much deeper that comes from the core person you are)?

When we talk about personality we are speaking of the attributes or distinctive characteristics of a person. Your pet snake or even your car, for example, has attributes or characteristics that make it different from other pets or cars. I have a special guitar that is my longtime friend. I bought it when I was a teenager. It has special dents and scratches that make it different from other guitars and it sounds different than any other guitars I have played. It has a chunky, raw, homey sound that generates a certain mood when I play it. We sometimes hear people say that inanimate objects have a personality. My guitar "Rosy," however, is not really a person or even alive: Should we allow such inanimate objects to have personality? The guitar has attributes, but not thoughts and feelings.

Some have suggested that personality is just another term for person. They might claim that personality is just a collection of attributes of that person. To be more specific, Brody and Ehrlichman (1998) defined personality as "those thoughts, feelings, desires, intentions, and actions that contribute to the important aspects of individuality" (p. 3). Those collections of thoughts, feelings, desires, and actions make up who we are and form a kind of profile. Think of a dozen or more attributes on which a person could score high or low. Imagine a graph with the attributes listed along the bottom and the scores charted above. Some of the attributes might be introversion, attention to detail, cheerfulness, musical ability, and physical dexterity. Each of us has a different profile with different scores on hundreds of characteristics that make up who we are.

The purpose of this part of the chapter is to explore just a few of those attributes that make up our personality. The reason we are exploring this aspect of individual psychology is that many people have wondered if the type of personality they have has anything to do with how well they get along with one another in close relationships, specifically with other family members. For example, if someone is introverted and shy, is it better for him or her to seek out a partner who is engaging, extroverted, and reaches out to others? Or, should we encourage people to seek out partners who are more like they are? Of course, two of the primary goals in family science are to try and help people make better relationship choices and, once in a relationship, to find ways of making those relationships stronger. By understanding the qualities, differences, and special nature of each person, we believe one can build a stronger relationship with his or her partner.

Additionally, many researchers continue to pursue the idea that who we are (i.e., our personalities) can be tied to genetic foundations. Our personalities might also be tied closely to how we are treated with regard to gender as we grow into adulthood. Families are composed of individuals and the unique profile of each individual within a family contributes to how that family solves problems, makes decisions, and organizes life. We are not interested (at least in this chapter) in all of the attributes one brings to one's life. However, there are a few characteristics that seem to matter more than others.

Additionally, we focus here on the person instead of the single attribute. Early in the study of personality (cf. Allport, 1937) researchers suggested that it was much more effective to examine the "the unique individual (as) the point of intersection of a number of quantitative variables" (Eysenck, 1952, p. 2). So, rather than study whether being shy (a quantitative single variable) influences work performance, for example, the study of personality is about how one's profile of characteristics (the collection of many attributes) collect together within each individual.

Additionally, family scientists are just beginning to ask questions about what happens when there are different types of people with different personality profiles coming together in the context of family life. We suggest the obvious: Families are composed of individuals who are interesting, unique, and wonderful in their own right.

The study of family life examines what happens when an individual joins with another individual to form a (relatively) permanent relationship. The relationship is usually built on commitment and long-term goals, but the ability of the relationship to survive over time lies in the individual and his or her desires, sense of obligation, and investment in that relationship. Certainly, personalities, genetic makeup, and how we respond to issues of gender influence our commitment decision.

This part of the chapter is divided into two sections. The first is an explanation of several personality traits that have a long research tradition in the field of psychology. We explore five personality traits that seem to reappear in many different forms, but that nearly everyone agrees are essential and fundamental attributes of one's personality. Second, we make some suggestions about how to use this information in the context of family life.

The Big Five: OCEAN

Several researchers and writers (cf. Brody & Ehrlichman, 1998; Goldberg, 1990; McCrae & Costa, 1991) have identified a way to access five primary attributes of human personality. These attributes have a fairly long research history and many social psychologists agree that there is good reason to pay attention to these items. Goldberg (1990) surveyed a large number of people and administered 1,400 items. His work was based on other research (Norman, 1963), which began to collect any kind of word people use to describe the personality of another. Norman looked for words like anxious, quiet, shy, and creative. Goldberg then used a statistical procedure called factor analysis to numerically determine how people rated themselves when they saw these words. He found that there were common threads in the ways people linked certain words together into clusters as they described themselves.

As he read through the clusters of items, he labeled the themes in those groups of descriptors. Researchers who follow the work of Goldberg and others believe that the essential aspects of personality can be captured by five global terms they call markers.

Openness

Openness is the first factor. This refers to how open you are to experience. People who score higher on this part of the test are thought to be more creative and imaginative; they seek variety, and are more likely to focus on intellectual and artistic pursuits. The openness described here is about openness to life's adventures. Obviously, if one is more closed to experience, one would rate one's personality as less creative and less interested in seeking the new and different aspects of one's surroundings.

Conscientiousness

Conscientiousness is the second factor. This aspect of personality describes how organized we are. Think for a moment about how much you plan daily. Do you carry a day planner? Do you have a small electronic computing device that beeps every few minutes telling you where you should be? How thorough are you? How much do you fret over assignments and tasks that must be done? Conscientious people are organized and pre-plan most aspects of daily living. They usually love yellow sticky notes and make lists to remind them where their lists are.

Extroversion

How outgoing are you? Earlier I asked how you got your energy in life. When you go to a party, do you "work the crowd"? **Extroverts** need to shake everyone's hand, say a few words to every guest, and connect with larger numbers of people in every setting. At a party, they are likely to be more energized at the end of the party than at the beginning. Gatherings provide extroverts with vigor. At the end of a good party, an extrovert might take several hours to "come down" from the energy created by the experience. On the other hand, **introverts** are quieter, solemn, and restrained. If they do go to the party (and they might do anything to get out of going), they might find a corner to sit and talk with one person, or two at most. Instead of speaking with people superficially about a number of things, they usually find one person to explore a topic in depth.

Agreeableness

If you score high on this **agreeableness**, it means that you are warmhearted, trusting, and kind. It also means that others would probably rate you as compassionate. That means that you would understand the feelings of others and be empathetic. If you are lower on this

FIGURE 5.3 Some people are not comfortable interacting with others. Introverts might feel much more comfortable in life not connecting to others as much as extroverts do.

scale, it could mean you are more suspicious, less trusting, and perhaps more unsympathetic to the plight of those around you. Empathetic role taking is an important idea here. People who score higher on this measure are more likely to feel what others feel. People with lower scores are usually focused on how they feel and not what is happening to those around them.

Neuroticism

The final trait, **neuroticism**, describes how much a person sees herself or himself as emotional, anxious, and high-strung. A person who is less neurotic is less emotional, more even-tempered, and more self-assured.

Application: Please Understand Me

Keirsey (1998) explained that one of the most important messages in the study of personality is that it provides an important mechanism by which we can become more accepting and approach relationships with greater generosity. He suggested that each of us can learn that personality traits are neither good nor bad; they are just a part of our makeup. Of course, some change is possible, and some changes and refinements of habits and patterns of life are not only possible but highly desirable. At the core level of existence, though, it seems that most people change little during their lives. That is, their core personality and sense of who they are changes only slightly in most cases. Although we might change what we believe in, what philosophies of life we subscribe to, and even significant patterns of daily living (e.g., eating and drinking patterns), the core person that we are changes very little.

Therefore, our goal in relationships is not to change our partners, but instead to understand them. Keirsey (1998) has several axioms of relationship power that flow from our personality study. First, we should not assume that our goal in a relationship is to change the other person into a clone of who we are. Sometimes this requires courage and patience. Many of us become impatient with our spouses' and partners' nonconformity to how we see the world. Some people believe it is their duty, for example, to change their partner into an extrovert (because they are). They believe that the other person is defective if they do not live life in the same way they do. Relationships are strengthened when we learn to accept the nature of others. That does not mean that we have to accept abusive behavior, irresponsibility, or violation of deeply held values, but it does mean that each of us is a unique person whose way of approaching the world is valid and important.

Second, when we begin to think in terms of acceptance rather than change, only then can we really deeply bond and develop stronger loving relationships with others. On the other hand, if our primary goal in relationships is to try and change others into copies of us, it pushes people away and alienates them. According to Keirsey (1998), one of the more destructive relationship problems occurs when a person in a newly forming relationship takes the new partner into his or her life with the idea that the new partner could be a fine match with the change of a few traits. The person believes it is his or her job, duty, or even right to set about changing that other person. Instead, our primary job in relationships is to understand one another and discover the different ways that the other person sees the world and solves the problems of life.

These ideas seem to be borne out in a research study done about our selection of marriage partners. Perhaps one of the more well-documented theories of mate selection is the information that has been collected about assortative mating. Assortative mating is a theory that suggests that "birds of a feather flock together." In other words, when we are dating and looking for a partner, we choose someone who is like we are. That is probably true when it comes to personality characteristics (Botwin, Buss, & Shackelford, 1997; Bouchard, Lussier, & Sabourin, 1999). However, it seems that women are more attuned to that idea than are men (Botwin et al., 1997). Additionally, according to findings in that study, women expressed a definite preference for men who displayed a wide variety of socially acceptable personality characteristics (e.g., agreeableness and emotional stability). Men, on the other hand, were satisfied with fewer of these socially desirable traits and were probably focusing more on physical attributes. In addition, two other findings were reported. First, it turned out that finding one's ideal partner (with regard to personality traits) was probably more important than finding someone with identical personality traits. That is a finding that is worth reading again.

How we get along with a close companion in marriage might be directly related to whether that person matches our ideals. Interestingly, however, having a mate that does not meet your ideals later on does not dampen one's marital or sexual satisfaction. In other words, having a mate that meets or exceeds one's ideals can help but does not significantly detract. However, it did detract from marital satisfaction if one's partner was not similar to the personality of the other mate.

Researchers have speculated that certain personality traits were not so easy to overlook and embrace. For example, Hellmuth and McNulty (2008) completed in-depth interviews with 169 couples and found that higher levels of neuroticism were very predictive of interpersonal violent behavior toward one's spouse. In this longitudinal survey of couples living in a typical U.S. community, these researchers also found that there were several important moderators to this effect. A moderator is a factor (or factors) that can attenuate (or accelerate) a connection between two variables. In this case, it was true that husbands and wives who were scored higher on neuroticism were more likely to be violent and to be acted on in violent ways. However, over time, they found that couples who were good at problem solving or could find ways to lower their stress levels were not nearly as likely to be violent. This study brings up an important point about Principles 5.2 and 5.3. Both of these principles suggest that we should find ways of working around personality differences of other family members and even, if possible, find ways to embrace others for who they are. However, in situations where there is harm, violence, danger, and domination, one needs to be careful about condoning, sponsoring, or embracing behaviors that promote that dark side of relationships. Even if a person is neurotic (defined as a trait like propensity toward negative emotionality; McCrae & Costa, 1991), that does not give him or her license to hit, demean, or propagate interpersonal violence. The down side of embracing a person's profile of traits is that we might allow the unacceptable in the name of building a relationship.

PRINCIPLE 5.2   PLEASE UNDERSTAND ME

Learning about another's personality or temperament is best done in the spirit of understanding. When we merely "tolerate" others, we lose the best part of relationship strength.

PRINCIPLE 5.3   EMBRACING THE DIFFERENCES

When family members learn to embrace the rich diversity of human personality, there is less contention, better problem solving, and more efficiency in meeting desirable goals. Families struggle when members are told that who they are is defective.

Neuroticism is one personality trait that is difficult to embrace in general. Most of us want and dream of being happily married to a loving and caring spouse. Some find out within the first years of marriage that the person they married is different than they thought. Fisher and McNulty (2008) interviewed 72 couples immediately after their weddings. They assessed their sexual satisfaction, marital satisfaction, and the levels of latent neuroticism found in each partner. A year later, they revisited these couples. They found that higher levels of one's own neuroticism directly predicted decreases in marital satisfaction and decreases in sexual activity and satisfaction. These findings were true for both husbands and wives. Wives reported significantly higher neuroticism scores than did husbands and, interestingly, their scores were not correlated. That means that it was rare for a highly neurotic person to marry another highly neurotic person (or for a person scoring low on neuroticism to marry another low scorer). In addition, they found that if the couple reported frequent and satisfying sexual activity, the high neuroticism score did not matter nearly as much. These authors speculated that frequently being in a "bad mood" probably inhibited sexual activity. They also suggested that neuroticism probably contributes to one having more negative expectations about marriage and relationships in general.

Other elements of the Big Five Personality Inventory have been found to connect with other marital issues. For example, Botwin et al. (1997) found that three specific personality characteristics were key elements in predicting future marital and sexual dissatisfaction. These were identified by a lack of agreeableness, emotional stability, and intellectual openness. This is an exciting area of research that will continue to grow in the future. Our last example of research about personality and family life comes from the communications literature.

A study by Geist and Gilbert (1996) illuminates how communication and personality issues can be linked. In this study, couples were asked to fill out a number of questionnaires about their personality characteristics and how much relationship hostility there was, and to comment on the type of problems they argued about. The results of this study were that personality matters a great deal in how we argue with one another and how those arguments are resolved. Husbands who were more extroverted were more likely to express anger and contempt during times of relationship difficulty. The same was true for wives. Women who reported higher scores on the neurotic aspect of the personality scale were also more likely to berate themselves and consequently their husbands.

Their own feelings of inadequacy probably spill over in how they judge and criticize those close to them. These researchers also suggested that introverted wives might have difficulty interpreting and therefore understanding the needs of their husbands. Again, this example shows that our understanding of personality and gender can assist us in knowing why people do what they do in relationships. An often-used catch phrase is "first seek to understand." Relationships can be enhanced when we take that idea to heart, even though it is particularly hard for those who have personality traits that make that task difficult.

☐ Gender

The study of gender is an important key aspect of understanding family life. In this section, this topic is introduced and several terms are reviewed.

Elements of Gender

To understand how our gender is formed and shaped, let's examine a few studies that illustrate the process. Of course, **gender** is, first of all, a genetic trait based on **sex**: Biologically speaking, our sex is determined during the pregnancy process. Sex refers to the biological, chromosomal configuration resulting in physically observable sex characteristics. Second, it is beyond the scope of this chapter to review the key literature on gender. The discussion here is limited and focuses on a few key points that can help direct our attention to this important element of family life.

Gender Is More Than Sex

We are given our sex: For the most part, we learn our gender. Through gender socialization, boys and girls learn how to act within whatever immediate culture they are raised. Gender socialization occurs at the explicit and implicit levels of teaching. A mother might overtly teach her children to act in gendered ways (e.g., boys don't cry), but through family life and contact with culture, children also learn by watching and by other means of implicit or indirect teaching. Our teaching involves the selection of colors of clothing, styles and types of toys purchased, and even physical activities at an early age that are gendered.

For example, in Western society, female babies are usually treated more gently than are boys (Fagot & Leinbach, 1987). Children are socialized to perform in gender-appropriate ways. By appropriate, we mean whatever the parents think is appropriate. Parents usually teach their children about cultural norms and behavior similar to behavior they were taught as children, or in ways that represent certain ideologies or beliefs about the "right" way a child "should behave." For example, boys are usually more likely to be involved in active play with their parents, especially their fathers (Fagot & Leinbach, 1987; Parke et al., 2001).

In a fairly well-known study, researchers brought a baby into a small group of adults (both men and women). One group was told the baby was a boy, another group was told it was girl, and the third group was not told the sex of the child. The experiment was to see if the different groups would treat the baby differently just because of its sex. The group that did not know the sex of the child reported higher levels of uncertainty and frustration. They searched for clues about whether the baby was "strong" or "soft" as a way to tell its sex. Additionally, when the baby became fussy, the group who were told the child was a boy labeled the baby as "angry," whereas the group who thought the baby was a girl thought its fussiness was "frustration" (Condry & Condry, 1976). In these simple and unnoticed ways, parents tell us when we are young what our crying means, how active we should be when we play, and how aggressively we should respond to stimulation. They tell us different things depending on whether we are male or female.

For the most part, parents are unaware they are treating their children in gendered ways. Additionally, recent research suggests that babies' biological-hormonal states resulting from sex characteristics might push boys and girls to act differently when stimulated. This prompts the parents to then treat the baby more like a boy (or girl) and the cycle of socialization continues. (For a review of the emerging literature on biosocial influences in family life see Booth et al., 2000.) The result of how our parents socialize us, how we respond, and how they respond again is that men and women often develop characteristics that are gender specific.

Oakley (1985) identified several of these results. First, she suggested that children differ in what they are exposed to. Girls are far more likely to be exposed to "mothering" activities and are encouraged to become "mother's helpers." Boys, on the other hand are discouraged from such feminine pursuits. Second, Oakley found that children are channeled to gendered play activities and toys. For example, girls are given dolls and boys are given trucks. Third, we label children's activities with gendered tags. If a girl wants to play rough-and-tumble games she is labeled as aggressive, whereas a boy doing the same

FIGURE 5.4   Researchers have often wondered if the environment (e.g., the kinds of toys children play with) have an influence on the development of gender.

thing will be characterized as active. Fourth, parents often treat children in different ways from birth onward; they speak more softly to girls, tell them they are beautiful, and sooth them. Boys, on the other hand, are tossed and tickled and told to be big boys.

I observed a father at a social event take the small fist of his young infant, make it into a ball, and help the baby pretend to punch him in the face. The child seemed delighted. I wondered how delighted the father would be in a few years when the child did that on his own.

Research on fathers has shown that men are major players in socializing children to become gendered. In one study, Fagot and Leinbach (1987) demonstrated that men in families push boys more than girls to set high standards for achievement. Also, men seem to focus on developing emotional stability in girls, whereas they center on developing task completion and toughness in boys. From these beginnings, we cooperate in the formation of who we are. Who we are is partly genetic, linked to sex characteristics, and partly taught by our families. How we respond to our gender might also be due to deeply held characteristics of our personalities.

☐ Gender and Power in Family Life

In the 1960s, two prominent family scientists (Blood & Wolfe, 1960) suggested that historically men in the United States were in control of families because of a long history of patriarchal control. These researchers interviewed several hundred wives and claimed to have discovered that an egalitarian style of marriage was the marriage type emerging in the United States. However, several other researchers pounced on Blood and Wolfe's findings and suggested that there was still a great deal of inequality in relationships (see Monroe, Bokemeier, Kotchen, & Mckean, 1985, for a review). Most family scientists assume that historically men had the final say in marriage and were controlling and dominating.

Although we are probably not as egalitarian as Blood and Wolfe thought we were, we do seem to be moving significantly toward increased power for women in relationships. Scanzoni (1988) commented on this equality difference by claiming that, in U.S. society today, men are the "senior partner" in most marriages. As mentioned earlier, men and women are socialized and treated differently from birth. This differential treatment has the possibility of defining roles in marriage. It was originally hypothesized that women who work earn less than men, so men are more likely to control more of the family finances (Gupta, 2007).

Power and Economics

About 20 years ago, a world-famous economist (Becker, 1991) suggested that men and women are collaborators as they try to maximize the efficiency of a family unit. If you have ever taken an economics class, you, no doubt, have heard the term *utility*. Becker thought that men and women join together to share the duties of life in a combined effort to increase common goods and maximize utility. Men were "better" at earning more money and, therefore, spent more time doing so. Women were "better" at the homemaking arts and so spent more hours involved in those actions. A chorus of feminist critiques arose to challenge that idea (e.g., Blumberg & Coleman, 1989). Most of these researchers argued that men and women compete for the same resources (e.g., time, money, power to make decisions, etc.) and wives usually lose out and, therefore, end up with most of the "water jobs" (cleaning, laundry, doing dishes, etc.). It was argued that because women made less in the labor market (usually characterized by statements of gender discrimination), they were the holders of the short straw. Of course, this argument assumes that women's wishes and sources of identity are not tied to a certain or specific gendered role (i.e., mothering or homemaker). This theory is often referred to as the **economic dependence theory**: Women are economically dependent, not out of choice, but as a result of cultural discrimination. This power imbalance was characterized as resulting in a **reciprocal obligation**, which implies that the person with the most **power** (gained through earning potential and therefore decision-making reality) would ask the partner in the position of greatest interest to compensate him by providing a home and hearth.

By contrast, there are those who suggest that there is something more going on when a women (in this case) chooses to "perform gender" by keeping house, preparing meals, bearing children, and parenting (Burke, 2006; Gupta, 2007). In other words, women use household labor to make claim on their gender and proclaim their femininity. There are few conclusive studies that help us understand how these inner family bargains are struck and maintained. We also know very little about the ideological reasoning used by couples as they decide who does what and why. The work of Gupta (2007) comes the closest to helping understand these complicated negotiations. He suggested that neither of these approaches really captures the nuance of role division, power, and finances. He convincingly demonstrated that neither the husband nor the wife's earnings says much at all about time spent doing housework by women. Further, he suggested that most women (at least the ones in his study) act as independent economic agents as much as their earnings would allow. It suggests that we might be entering a new era in marriage.

PRINCIPLE 5.4   MARRIAGE PARTNERS IN OUR TIME MAY BE MORE ECONOMICALLY INDEPENDENT THAN EVER BEFORE

This independence has interesting implications for long-term commitment.

Typically, marriage, in the past, has been seen as a reciprocal partnership in which roles are shared to the advantage of both. It could be that men and women are choosing marriage and marriage-like relationships that are actually quite independent with regard to core activities and functions. Instead of power-dependent relationships, some suggest we are moving to a familial era of shared lives that have clear elements of independence.

☐ Your Marriage or Partnership

As you read the preceding information, keep in mind that it is presented in this chapter because the choices one makes about marriage, employment, and child rearing should play a significant role in selecting a partner. The way you view gender and power in relationships will guide how you decide to organize your family, divide household tasks, and direct what happens during daily family life. Take a few minutes now and fill out the Activity 5.1 worksheet in your study guide. This asks you the following: How equal should a marriage be (specifically yours)? Who should do the various tasks? What should happen if the role divisions are not what you think they should be? How should the roles and responsibilities in a marriage be divided? If you are a woman, do you expect to be a "junior" partner in the relationship? If you are the man, do you see your role only as provider, defender, and protector? Are you interested in a relationship based on equal division of providing, child care, household tasks, and financial decision making? These might be some of the more important questions one asks as relationships begin.

Power Dependency

One way to examine the role of power in relationships is through the eyes of social psychologists and economists. Recall from Chapter 3 the discussion of rational choice and social exchange. Principle 3.7 indicated that individuals in systems (like in family life) have a strong tendency to maximize gain to their own advantage. Theorists who subscribe to this idea believe that altruism does exist but is misunderstood. Altruism is often thought of as an act during which one's own welfare is not considered. In fact, altruism is, by definition, when we act and consider the well-being of another just ahead of our own. Our own needs do not leave the stage, but instead we consider the needs of another before we act on our own.

Within the themes of exchange and reward, the idea of **power dependency theory** has been used in social science for more than 30 years (Cook, Coye, & Gerbasi, 2006; Cook & Emerson, 1978; Cook, Emerson, Gillmore, & Yamagishi, 1983). In simple terms, power dependency theory helps us understand the social ties to others and how those result in mutual dependence. Within the framework of mutual dependence emerges the idea that individuals (within groups like families) have control over one another. Power and control go hand-in-hand. Power is the ability to make other people do something you want them to do but they do not necessarily want to do of their own volition. Control goes past the ability part of the equation and into changing another's behavior.

We have power over another when the other person needs some resource we have, and we not only have some of that resource but we have a way to transfer the resource to the other person. For example, Rob and Cindy are dating and thinking about getting married. He comes from a wealthy family who has given him large amounts of money to use in his personal account. Cindy comes from a poor family and has no money to add to the pot. We first have to ascertain if Cindy needs the resource(s) Rob has or if she values the resources he has. In addition, we need to know if Cindy has any type of valuable resource to add to the exchange. According to Cook and Emerson (1978) and Molm (2003) the power in a relationship is unbalanced when the dependencies are unequal. The result is that the relationship will be imbalanced and will struggle. This idea is captured in Principle 5.5.

> **PRINCIPLE 5.5   WE HAVE POWER IN RELATIONSHIPS (AND THEREFORE ABILITY TO CONTROL ANOTHER'S BEHAVIOR) WHEN THE OTHER NEEDS SOMETHING WE HAVE AND WHEN WE NEED SOME RESOURCE THE OTHER PERSON HAS**
>
> Relationships suffer when there is a power imbalance that results from one person having fewer valued resources than the other. Imbalanced relationships are less effective in attaining desired goals.

Let's imagine the types of resources that could be found in relationships. Of course, an obvious resource is money or the ability to acquire financial means. However, that might be one of the least important resources in marriage (and close) relationships. One could have the ability to acquire **social capital**. Social capital is probably more powerful in relationships than financial capital. Social capital is the quality relationship connection that inheres within close relationships. It is easy to imagine the social network of trusted friends that a person has cultivated. Those trusted friends, and the social capital that resides within those friendships, conjure enormous power—the power to make things happen in life. With social power, we can have an edge and prepublic knowledge about job openings, clever ways to solve difficult problems so we do not have to reinvent wheels, and access to hard-to-get knowledge, ideas, and solutions that give us an advantage. One of the goals of excellent, productive, strong, and effective relationships is assuring that each member of a couple has power within the exchange. If a person has no power, the strength of the relationship becomes one-sided, partners become bored and restless, and a spirit of contention and contempt is much more likely to arise.

The following are several ideas that come from thinking about power dependency theory. Many of these are, as of yet, untested in the family science literature but follow from the theoretical suggestions of those who apply this theory to economic game theory and the social psychology of business management. Each of the following ideas comes from the work of Cook and her colleagues (e.g., Cook & Emerson, 1978; Cook & Rice, 2001).

The first idea is that gendered relationships tend to be power imbalanced because men in Western cultures are physically stronger, have typically and historically controlled resources, and, in some cases, have relied on religious dogma to infer imbalanced relationship power.

When men take it on themselves to rule households through the process of domination, power imbalance, and control, they will actually have less ability to achieve the mutual well-being of all members of their families. And, because men are stronger, have typically controlled the wealth of family life, and have traditionally had exclusive access to education and the means to acquire social capital, there have been serious issues of power imbalance in family relationships for generations. It is only in recent years that women have been recognized as having a role of co-partnership with men in marriage.

Further, families are more effective and efficient when family members understand that the family environment is only one aspect of the decision-making process that influences the individual. In particular, as children get older, they make decisions that might be independent of ideology, training, and wishes of parents. When parents understand this principle, they will be more effective in providing support to children and other family members. Additionally, when family members realize that genetic predispositions and free will are in operation, even in younger children, parents are more likely to respond to family problems in effective ways.

When power imbalance is high, families are much less likely to be efficient in attaining desired goals. This type of efficiency is probably the result of many factors. One of them has to do with contention. When power imbalance is high, families are more likely to experience contention, unresolved conflict, and power-ridden competitive communication. When it is in a person's best interest (i.e., he or she stands to lose something valuable by being nasty) to be kind, generous, and helpful, he or she is more likely to be less contentious. In other words, if there is a power imbalance (meaning one person has fewer valuable resources to bring to the relationship) there are fewer barriers to prevent destructive power use.

When power imbalance is high, the satisfaction and well-being of close family relationships diminishes. As stated earlier, as power imbalance rises, contention, distancing, and disregard are also likely to rise. These conditions detract from the ability of a family to administer the nurturance and love needed. Additionally, when power imbalance is high, it is more likely that decisions will be made that favor the person with the most power. Obviously, when only one member of a group makes decisions for the rest, trouble is likely to follow. It should be obvious that input from all members of a group is likely to result in better decision making. In addition, when group members feel like their input is of no value, they will be less likely to endorse the decision.

These researchers have also noted that when power imbalance is high, it is more likely that divisions of labor, household routines, and the daily patterns of life will favor the person(s) with the most power. When people (male or female) have more power (and thus more control) they will (over time) most likely advantage themselves. That is, they will pick chores, jobs, and assignments that they like to do, leaving the worse jobs for those with less power.

It is also reasonable, therefore, that when power imbalance is high, families will be less likely to do well at resolving crises. Families within which one member has more power than another will be less likely to generate creative solutions and new resources in times of trouble. Having balanced power in relationships means that all members have a more vested interest in outcomes.

☐ Summary

In sum, this chapter has suggested that family members come to families with certain unchangeable traits that can and do influence what happens in families. We all come with a personality profile of some sort and we come with a sexual orientation that is magnified and enriched within culture becoming the elements of gender. From gender differences come (almost always) power differences that form a foundational building block of family life. Some families learn early on to dampen the effects of naturally occurring power imbalance. For most of us, it takes significant effort to generate power equity—but with that equity comes relationship strength.

It seems clear that gender or sex inequity has a tendency to create power imbalance. This chapter has suggested that power difference and the potential power imbalance begins with genetics, and therefore, the effects are hard to battle. As we move toward gender equity, it would stand to reason that the inner life of families would strengthen, become enriched, and become a source of great power. It is clear that inequity in relationships creates disharmony. A mistaken idea is that inequity is the same as equality. Inequity is not about equality and perfect role sharing. Instead, inequity is about fairness of role distribution, resources, and interpersonal caring (meaning when there is equity, we care for one another in ways that are fair and well distributed). When there is inequity, interpersonal care favors the one with the most power and demand capability.

☐ Study Questions

1. What is the Human Genome Project and why was it featured in this chapter?
2. In the study by Booth et al. (2005) reported in this chapter, they thought that when men had higher levels of testosterone they would be more aggressive. What did they actually find and why is this finding important?
3. Reread Principle 5.1 and restate this in your own words. What is the importance of knowing about genetics in family life?
4. In the personality section of the chapter it was stated that we will be more effective in relationships when we understand another person instead of trying to change them. Comment on this message and provide a personal example of how that could work in your life.
5. What are the different personality attributes signified by the OCEAN model suggested in your text?
6. How do parents treat their children in gendered ways?
7. How is gender related to power in families? What is the primary connection?
8. What are the key effects of power imbalance in family life?
9. Define social capital and explain why it was introduced in the section on power in families.

☐ Key Terms

Personality
Gender
Genes
Human Genome Project
DNA
Behavioral genetics
Genetic heritage
Openness
Conscientiousness
Extrovert
Introvert
Agreeableness
Neuroticism
Gender
Sex
Economic dependence theory
Reciprocal obligation
Power
Power dependency theory
Social capital

☐ Suggested Readings

Aspinwall, L. G., & Staundinger, U. M. (2003). *A psychology of human strengths: Fundamental questions and future directions for a positive psychology.* Washington, DC: American Psychological Association.

Glazer-Malbin, N., Waehrer, H., & Youngelson, Y. (Eds.). (1973). *Woman in a man-made world: A socioeconomic handbook.* New York: Rand McNally.

Mikulinger, M., & Shaver, P. (2007). *Attachment in adulthood: Structure, dynamics, and change.* New York: Guilford.

Reiss, D., Neiderhiser, J., Hetherington, M., & Plomin, R. (2000). *The relationship code.* Cambridge, MA: Harvard University Press.

☐ Endnotes

[1] Deoxyribonucleic Acid is the chemical formula that spells out the exact instructions required to create a particular human or other organism. Protein elements are linked together into 24 distinct chromosomes comprised of as many as 250 million different pairs of protein bases. Sometimes the pairs break, or are translocated, or even joined wrong, creating genetic anomalies in the organism. The genes encode the instructions of heredity and are passed.

6

CHAPTER

Fixed Family Relationships

Generations in Family Life

☐ Chapter Preview

In this chapter, readers will learn:

- That some relationships in life are fixed and inalienable.
- How fixed relationships within families are very difficult to untie.
- That the birth of children is one of the most commonly experienced events of all humankind.
- How the birth of a child usually represents connections to a larger family group.
- How the socio-generational principle tells us that social connections between generations matter in family life.
- About the generational alliance principle that helps us understand that it is important to have clear-cut generational boundaries.
- That the generational transmission principle speaks to the idea that families tend to transmit their style of life to each new generation.
- That learning how to build a genogram is a useful tool for intervening with families.

☐ Introduction

The very best reason parents are so special . . . is because we are the holders of a priceless gift, a gift we received from countless generations we never knew, a gift that only we now possess and only we can give to our children. That unique gift, of course is the gift of ourselves. Whatever we can do to give that gift and to help others receive it, is worth the challenge of all our human endeavor. (Fred Rogers, Mister Rogers Talks With Parents, 1983)

When a child is born into a family we typically rejoice and celebrate. As it turns out, this type of rejoicing and celebrating goes on around the clock and around the world: Throughout the world, about 150 children are born every minute. Imagine three soda machines side by side. Every second of every day each of those machines dispenses a can: It falls to the open slot and the happy customer grabs it just as the next can falls. At that rate, there are about 80 million children born each year in the world, or about 219,000 per day. By contrast there are about 100 deaths per minute worldwide for a net increase in worldwide population growth of about 50 people per minute. Therefore, every year the world has a net growth of about 72,000 people per day, which totals 26,280,000 per year. That means the population of a city about the size of greater Mexico City (28 million) is added to the world each year. All of the members of that newly formed city of babies need food, water, heat, and education services. In their lifetime, each of these people will probably be involved in bearing a child or two. That is a challenge for our worldwide community. As we create this new city of babies each year, we need better answers about what to do and how to approach the enormity of that social problem. A good place to begin is strengthening the homes within which each of those children resides.

Broaden your thinking and picture the parents of those 80 million children. By nature's law, the vast majority of those children were conceived in an act of intimacy that led to that eventual birth; in most cases these children are born into a household within which a mother and a father have a vested interest in the birth and survival of that child. Once we begin to consider the parents of the child, we include an additional 160 million people, realizing, of course, that several million of those children will not know their fathers and perhaps hundreds of thousands of them might not know their mothers. Let's speculate that for the majority of those children there are also other kin who are interested, caring, loving relatives who are also focused on seeing that the child thrives and survives. If we made a guess that the birth of the average child around the world involves on average about four relatives per child, we could add an additional 320 million people to our birth celebration by considering the grandparents, aunts, uncles, and siblings of the newborn. Therefore, each day of every year, 560 million people (including the child) are involved in the birth of a child.

Unfortunately, about 83 out of every 1,000 of those children, worldwide, will not live past their first year: Therefore, each year of the 80 million children born we expect about 8% will die within 12 months (about 6.5 million). That also equals 13 million caring parents who will be very sad about the loss of that child and perhaps another 26 million grandparents, aunts, uncles, and siblings that will experience the loss.

The point is that each day throughout the world there are millions of family members who are focused on the birth and survival of children. Moreover, during the course of the year, millions of those parents will be affected by the loss of one of those children. This childbirth and death process is probably one of the most common experiences of human-kind and highlights the central human theme of generational connection.

This chapter is about the social connection that is initiated with birth. The social (and biological) heritage of a child plays a key role in the development of most children around the world. That we have mothers and fathers, grandparents, aunts and uncles, and other extended kin and caring kin-like family members is probably the most ubiquitous experience of all humankind. This chapter introduces the idea that these relatively **fixed biological and social connections** matter. The previous generation of parents and extended family teach, nurture, protect, and provide for the new generation.

☐ Why the Study of Generations Is Important

The birth of each of the 80 million children born in the world within one year is (for the most part) a special and cherished event. We commonly believe that children are the world's most valuable resource. Parents sacrifice for, protect, and nurture their children and many would be willing to even sacrifice their own life to protect their child. Why is that so? One reason is that all of us in the animal kingdom are genetically hard-wired to protect and care for the next generation because they represent the continuation of humankind.

From a social and emotional view, as the generational link is built, the previous generation seeks to pass on key knowledge, strategies for survival, financial inheritance, and whatever resources are available to the next generation. The previous generation purposively and specifically spends valuable time and treasure in that investment. For the parents and grandparents, new roles and responsibilities are created for those connected to the child. In most situations, parents care for and protect the child, often the role of grandparent is invoked, and the brothers and sisters of the parents and grandparents are automatically designated as aunts and uncles. Society assures that those who can potentially assist in the job of next-generation survival surround the child. In like manner, the child automatically becomes a niece or nephew, grandchild, sibling, and possibly even a great-grandchild. All of this activity is focused on connecting to the child and increasing the chances of that next generation surviving. For the most part, these assignments to kin are not negotiated in a special meeting, there is no specially appointed community-elected committee to adjudicate these relationships, nor does the person being assigned (the newborn) have much to say about the assignments. As a human society we have, collectively, figured out that connecting in these primal kin ways is what is needed and what must happen.

In addition to the biological connections that are so powerful, survival is also connected to the family unit's ability to transmit ideas, beliefs, rituals, problem-solving strategies, and other key elements of everyday life that can help the child prosper and grow into adulthood. The dual punch of an inalienable biological connection plus the possibility of the familial unit passing on the knowledge and patterns from the previous generations helps ensure that there will be children who survive during the next generation.

☐ Generational Processes Are a Basic Key of Family Life

The Human Example of Generational Connection Is Unusual

As suggested earlier, generational connections are a key building block of the family realm. Survival and the ability to do well rely on our skill at transmitting our acquired knowledge and abilities to the next generation. This type of close attention to the next **generation** within an organization is unusual and, for the most part, only happens in family life. When we speak of generations in the public sector we usually mean something different: For example, we could speak of another generation of the new Chevy Corvettes. Alternatively, we could plan our training for the next generation of workers in a large factory; the supervisors care about the outcome, but only to a point. It would be rare to hear of a McDonald's shift manager giving her life savings to her employees so they could go to college, or inviting them to stay at her house for weeks at a time during vacation, or including her workers in her will. She might be interested in the birth of a child of one her employees and might even give a packet of Big Mac coupons to the happy parent, but it would be unusual for her to ask to be in the delivery room with the mother or to spend her vacation time helping the new mother make the transition to motherhood by staying at her house, cleaning and cooking, and getting up at night with the new child.

Dedicated activities such as staying with the new mother, helping with chores, and taking care of the house are generally taken care of only within the family (at least on a consistent and regular basis). And, as I am sure you would agree, it is wonderful that many families in the world have relatives (or even close friends who act as kin) who will dedicate time, resources, and focused caring to help them with the next generation of children. Let's take a look at the effects of that caring. While we are doing so, keep one important caveat in mind: Not all families care for their children in the same way. Sometimes the connection is dysfunctional, disastrous, and even deadly. For the most part, however, the large majority of family connections are positive. We should not make the mistake, though, of overgeneralizing and assuming that all family situations are effective in achieving generally desirable goals.

Human Generational Connections Are a Special Resource

The human generational connection provides the structure and mechanism to help the new child thrive, survive, and emerge from childhood. These connected individuals are generally more likely to have access to the child and, therefore, have the ability to influence how the child thinks about the world, what the child believes in, how the newborn and toddler build relationships with those outside the family realm, and the child's worldview about what is important and unimportant or whether the child believes the world is a friendly or unfriendly place. Our grandparents and parents also can influence our aspirations, our values, how we approach the struggles of life, and our resourcefulness. Family members can also influence and shape how we care for others, treat the property of others, and respect nature. We might also watch and learn from them about more subtle elements of daily living, such as how to solve problems, resolve conflict, manage intimacy and respond to the anger of others; how to receive and express love; and even how to hate or disregard the sacredness of life.

Generational Connections Are Relatively Fixed

A key reason why these extended relationships are so powerful is that many of these connections are **fixed** and **inalienable.** The word *inalienable* (when used in the context of relationships) means that we cannot annul, escape, or cancel the relationship: We cannot annul, escape, or cancel who our mother and father are. As an old saying goes, we can choose our friends but not our relatives. Our connections with relatives remain in place unless we work very hard to change them, and some of the connections are actually impossible to change at the most fundamental level. For example, a parent cannot decide to erase his or her biological connection with a child: Children cannot decide to have a different set of biological parents.

We can make changes in living arrangements through legal processes (e.g., divorce, adoption, and custody), but these changes can never erase the biological connection. Even though some parts of these connections can be changed, it is very difficult to change them, and most of us do not. We just live with them as they are. We either do not want to change them, we do not know how to change them, or it does not occur to us to try to change them. Even when we would like to change them, most of us do not have the resources or willpower to change them, or we do not want to pay the emotional and interpersonal price we would have to pay to change them.

Early Influence

In addition, generational processes are influential because they start making a difference at the earliest stages of our lives, when we are infants and small children dependent on the older generation. The influence of our parents, grandparents, aunts, uncles, and cousins is the most powerful when we are the most impressionable. The key people in our life sculpt and form our deepest sense of who we are, our connections to community, and what is important.

Social Capital

Coleman (1988, 1990) theorized that within and between relationships, we find a special kind of capital. Capital is another term for a strong and focused resource that one can possess. Financial capital is the kind of capital we most often think of in this context. When we acquire financial capital we are able to buy what we need and invest in life's financial opportunities. **Social capital** is not as tangible and resides within relationships. Of course, when life's problems arise we turn to all kinds of resources for solutions. Financial capital might be the easiest to imagine but the social capital found within generational connections might be among our most valuable.

Imagine Bernice trying to secure a job. She asks her mother if she can help or knows anyone who needs a worker. Her mother indicates that her friend Marge operates a local convenience store and that she knows that Marge is looking for helpers. Bernice makes an appointment with Marge, the interview goes well, and Bernice gets the job. Although this exchange could have happened as the result of a close friendship, for most people, family members are a ready source of social capital. Friends come and go, but one is much more likely to have a constant source of social capital within one's kinship network than from within one's friendship network. It is also important to remember that social capital transcends just knowing someone who has a job; it is much more powerful than that. High levels of social capital also contain elements of trust, reliability, history, and even affection.

Coleman's (1988) ground-breaking book on social capital provided an example of a family in New York City who sold diamonds. The father maintained a central repository of hundreds of diamonds worth millions of dollars. As the story goes, his children and siblings who worked with him would come to the central office and were able to take diamonds out of the store and travel worldwide to meet customers who would then purchase their stones. Because the trust was high and the father knew his family members, there was no need to sign protective legal documents, leave financial deposits, or provide background information. The high levels of trust and long-term experience with them provided another kind of capital in "the bank." The "money" in this type of bank had significant payoff. The result was that significant amounts of time, personnel, and paperwork expense were unnecessary: The need for fewer staff and lower overhead cost to their business was substantial. And, of course, the company ran smoother and more efficient.

Of course, if just one family member betrayed that trust, the social capital would be crushed. However, in such situations, as long as the social capital continues to build, the business financially benefits from the resulting repository of social capital. In short, families are much more likely to be the source of rich social capital, which, in turn, boosts the quality of family members' lives. These close generational relationships represent connections with those who mean the most to us and with whom we usually have the greatest responsibility.

Constructive social-generational connections help us have a sense of bonding without bondage, closeness without suffocation, and identity without overidentification. Many families have deep ideological goals about work, education, religion, and love that they wish to transmit to the next generation. Through our connection to parents, grandparents, and others in our kinship network our sense of who we are is created, identities are formed, strong social capital is created, and our places in the community and the world are shaped. Back to our original theme, the inherent social capital in these relationships does not ensure the success of the next generation, but it does enhance the probability of success and increase the chance that the children of the next generation will live well and prosper.

Unhealthy Generational Connections

On the other hand, unhealthy generational processes can be very destructive. They can ruin family relationships, crush generational social capital, destroy trust, and suppress the transmission of the powerful and positive elements of family life. For example, many forms of abuse can be transmitted from one generation to another. These abusive patterns of interaction can interfere with mental health, ruin marriages, and interfere with the healthy development of children in many ways. Examples of this type of potential destruction are presented later.

The socio-generational principle summarizes the power of kinship and social connections with our family members.

PRINCIPLE 6.1   THE SOCIO-GENERATIONAL PRINCIPLE

Close family members of the previous generation (mother, father, grandparents, etc.) significantly influence how children approach their social world and develop ideological orientations, understand and respond to emotions, develop and use their intellect, and learn to navigate interpersonal relationships.

☐ Two Kinds of Generational Processes

This section introduces two key generational processes. Once we understand that generational connections are important, we can begin to think about how those connections work or do not work to promote healthy family functioning. The generational alliance principle alerts us to the idea that it can be problematic to form strong emotional alliances across generations (e.g., a mother forms an unusually strong alliance with her daughter that, for the most part, excludes the father). The generational transmission principle captures the idea that certain healthy and unhealthy patterns of interactions and beliefs can and usually are transmitted to the next generation.

Generational Alliances

If there is a fundamental rule of social organization, it is that an organization is in trouble when coalitions occur across levels of a hierarchy, particularly when these coalitions are secret (Haley, 1976, p. 104). As one research study has shown, "The close alliance between mother and child is then implicated as a problem factor in the substance abuse" (Bartle & Sabatelli, 1989, p. 264).

Definition

The term *alliance* refers to the connections and the boundaries among subsystems in a family system. An alliance is when two or more individuals in a family become unusually close or align themselves together so they are a clique or a semi-unique unit in the family. As they do this, they change the boundaries in the family system. The boundaries in a family system are the barriers between parts of a system or between the system and its environment. What people do when they create an alliance is reduce the boundaries, or make the boundaries more permeable, between the individuals in the alliance and increase the rigidity or closedness of the boundaries between them and the others in the family.

One of the important and healthy alliances in families is to have a fairly clear parental alliance while the children are being raised. This means the parents form an alliance with each other in their relationships with their children. In ideal situations, this means the parents are a cohesive, integrated, and coordinated team. They are supportive of each other and unified in the way they relate to their children, and the boundaries between the parents are few and permeable. At the same time, there are a number of more rigid or impermeable boundaries between the parental alliance and the children. For example, the parental alliance is "in charge" in the family, and the parents set limits and guidelines for the children. The parental alliance becomes the executive subsystem in the family, and it is responsible for disciplining, correcting, and teaching the children.

Unhealthy Alliances

There are many ways families can form unhealthy alliances. One fairly common way is where there is unresolved conflict or tension between the parents and one of the parents forms an alliance or coalition with a child. For example, if one parent is an alcoholic and has difficulty being an effective parent, the other parent might turn to a child for help in running the home, disciplining the children, solace, and companionship. A common example of this is when a father cannot keep a job, or is distant emotionally from the family and the mother creates an alliance with one of the sons by having the son be a substitute husband in a variety of ways.

These **cross-generational alliances** or **intergenerational alliances** (I use these terms interchangeably) place the oldest child in an awkward position because the child is, in a sense, a member of two different generations. These intergenerational alliances often lead to emotional and interpersonal problems for the parents, the oldest child, and sometimes for some of the other children.

The Generational Alliance Principle

The principle that describes these important process is called the generational alliance principle.

PRINCIPLE 6.2   GENERATIONAL ALLIANCE PRINCIPLE

It is helpful in family systems to have clear-cut generational boundaries about such things as leadership, responsibility, support, and emotional feelings. When the boundaries are relatively clear, it helps the adults and children develop in healthy ways, and when cross-generational alliances and coalitions occur, it tends to lead to emotional and interpersonal difficulties for the adults and children.

The following family situation illustrates several different types of generational alliances. Some of them are simple, overt, and desirable. Other patterns in family alliances are destructive and harmful. For example, the following situation illustrates a family that had healthy generational alliances most of the time, but the boundaries between the generations became blurred temporarily to cope with a unique situation. In this situation, the unique demands and the temporary nature of the cross-generational alliance kept it from being unhealthy.

The Williams Family

In my family, the boundaries between the parents and children have for the most part been observed and followed. There was a time though, when I was required to cross the boundary and take on adult responsibilities for a time. My mother had just had my younger sister who is the last child of our family. Both my mother and sister about died during birth. This was the hard beginning to a very long 3 years. Kami (my sister) was sick constantly as a baby and came close to death two or three times. She cried constantly both day and night, which slowly exhausted my mother's strength. This caused me to have to cross the boundary between being a young teenager to that of being a part-time mother. Almost every day I would come home from school and take the baby for 3 or 4 hours so that mom could rest. My father had to travel a lot, so when he was gone, many times I would even get up with Kami in the night so that my mom could have a break. It was a hard time for my family and often times I felt a lot of stress and discouragement. But crossing the boundary between my mother and I was a necessary step for the health of my mom. It was not exactly easy to do and many times I would feel overwhelmed by the responsibility, but now as I look back on it I see that it did a lot of good for me, too.

The term *coalition* means a process of joint action against a third person. This idea is in contrast to an *alliance* where two people might share a common interest not shared by the third person (Haley, 1976). The most problematic coalitions in families (Palazzoli, 1988) occur when one parent reaches down and makes an emotional bond or coalition with a member of the next generation (usually a child) and in the process cuts out the natural alliance that should exist between the members of the executive subsystem (usually the two parents). As the generational alliance principle suggests, the boundaries are crossed in ways that create significant inefficiencies. Loyalty to the original executive subsystem is shattered and trust is diminished.

Many family therapists also have found this principle helpful in practicing family therapy. Palazzoli and her coworkers in Italy wrote extensively about this principle and used it to work with families who had a severely anorexic child (Palazzoli, 1988; Palazzoli, Boscolo, Cecchin, & Prata, 1978). In counseling these families whose children (and sometimes parents) displayed psychotic problems, they used this principle to intervene. During the first part of their treatment program they would attempt to strengthen the parental alliance. They developed a number of ingenious strategies to increase the cohesion between the parents and increase the status and influences of the parents in the home. For example, in one strategy, the parents are taught the power of unhealthy alliances and coached to actually keep secrets from the children. Then as a second stage, the therapists instruct the parents to plan and leave on unannounced excursions that exclude the "problem" child. In this way, the family alliance system is reconfigured and members are shown how to cope with a new and stronger alliance system that centers on the executive subsystem, and do many other things to help families strengthen the parental alliance. They found that this strategy helped the families cope with their challenges much more effectively.

Generational Transmission

Scholars in a number of different disciplines have researched the process of generational transmission in recent years. Generational transmission is the process of transmitting information, beliefs, traditions, and communication styles from one generation to the next. The main principle the researchers have developed is the generational transmission principle.

PRINCIPLE 6.3   GENERATIONAL TRANSMISSION PRINCIPLE

Families with more functional, healthy generational processes tend to transmit those family styles to their children and those children are more likely to develop a functional, healthy family life.

There are many qualifications that influence when and how this principle operates. For example, it seems to be more powerful for characteristics of the family realm than characteristics of the public realm. This means that there is more generational transmission with regard to ways of loving and maintaining intimate relationships than such things as political ideas, careers, leisure interests, social class behavior, and even marital instability (D'Onofrio et al., 2007).

One aspect of this principle is that it reinforces the idea that family life is "the best of times and the worst of times." For example, when families have patterns of relating in kind, loving, empathic, intimate, understanding, and facilitating ways, these patterns are passed on to new generations of children. When families interact harmoniously with each other and cope with life's challenges in helpful, creative, and humane ways, these patterns are passed from parents to children and it helps the children become well-rounded, creative, constructive, resourceful people who can accomplish their goals and establish and maintain intimate, beautiful, peaceful, loving, harmonious relationships with others.

Unfortunately, the "worst of times" part of generational transmission is also very real, and it has so much effect in our society that we cannot escape it. When families have traditions of unwholesome, harmful, abusive, and disastrous patterns, these too are passed from parents to children (Pears, Capalidi, and Owen, 2001). We call this **intergenerational transmission**. The worst forms of human abuse, exploitation, discrimination, prejudice, hate, vengeance, and animosity occur in families, and frequently they are also passed from one generation to the next.

Ironically, the privacy that is so important for the positive and constructive dimensions of human growth, intimacy, and wholesome bonds also tends to allow, protect, hide, and preserve the heinous parts. The fact that most of what happens in families is "behind closed doors," in the privacy of the home, or in the hidden part of the iceberg means that the unfortunate parts of the human experience can be perpetuated in ways that are mostly invisible to outside observers.

☐ The Genogram: A Tool for Understanding Family Processes

Thus far this chapter has demonstrated that generational alliances and generational transmission are two important parts of all our lives. With these insights as givens, we can then move to the next concern that is important to family scientists: How can we use these ideas to help families and individuals better attain their goals?

A group of scholars have developed a technique that can help us use these ideas to help others. It is called the **genogram**. Genograms are a method of identifying and measuring intergenerational characteristics of families, and they can be used by individuals, families, educators, ministers, therapists, and counselors.

Genograms are charts or graphs that diagram the biological and interpersonal relationships of people across several generations. They also identify significant events in intergenerational relationships that can have an influence on the families and individuals.

Genograms can be helpful in several ways. Each of us can make a genogram for our own family, and they can help us better understand the desirable and the undesirable influences that earlier generations have had on us. This can help us enjoy and appreciate the desirable effects, and sometimes find ways to minimize and change some of the undesirable effects. We can also use genograms as family scientists to help others better understand their lives, their families, and the options they have to grow and improve their lives.

How to Make a Genogram

There are four parts to a genogram. The first part is the chart or diagram. A simple chart is shown in Figure 6.1. McGoldrick and Gerson (1989) developed a set of standardized symbols and methods for constructing these charts, and many of their conventions are used in this chapter. Figure 6.1 shows a fairly simple genogram for the family of a person I have named Sandra Jones, and this figure illustrates how to diagram some of the basic parts of a genogram.

Each family member is represented by a box or circle. The boxes are used to indicate males and circles show females. A genogram chart is usually created to understand a particular person, and that person is known as the index person. Double lines are used for that person: Notice Sandra Jones has a double circle, indicating she is the index person. If you were doing a genogram of yourself (possibly as an assignment) you would show yourself as a double circle (or box) in the same way. It is helpful to put names and years of birth and death on a genogram, and the best method I have seen is to put them just below the box or circle. If there is just one year shown, it is the birth year, which means the person is still living at the time the genogram is made.

The children are arranged with the oldest child on the left and youngest child on the right. Thus, in Sandra's family, she is the oldest child. Her younger brother Mark was born in 1969, and the youngest child, Kyle, was born in 1970. The dotted line above Kyle shows

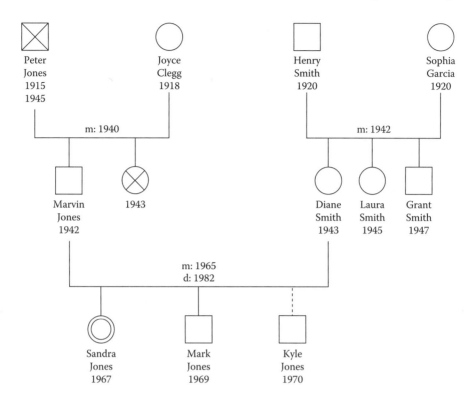

FIGURE 6.1   This is a simple three-generation genogram of the Sandra Jones family.

that he was adopted. Sandra's parents were married in 1965 and the marriage is shown with the horizontal line connecting them. Sandra's father, Marvin, was born in 1942 to Peter and Joyce Jones, who were married in 1940. Peter Jones died in 1945, and Joyce did not remarry, so the genogram shows that Joyce raised her son as a single parent. The other aspect of their family that is shown is that they had a stillborn child in 1943. The X inside a box or circle indicates a person died.

Figure 6.1 shows that Sandra's mother was the oldest of three children. Her parents were the same age, as both of them were born the same year, and they were married in 1942.

Families are seldom as simple as the information in Figure 6.1 shows. They usually have a number of complications, and the method of diagramming some of the complications that can occur is illustrated in Figure 6.2. This figure shows the same family 5 years later. Sandra's parents were divorced in 1982, and the year of their divorce is placed just below the year of their marriage. Marvin, Sandra's father, remarried quickly, as he was married to Leanne Brady in 1982. Sandra's mother, Diane, was married in 1983 to Phillip Page.

The dotted lines show the residential patterns of the stepfamilies. Sandra and her youngest brother Kyle live with her mother and her stepfather. Sandra's brother Mark lives with his father and stepmother.

Figure 6.3 shows how to diagram a number of additional complications that can occur in families. In this diagram, the stepfamily residential patterns are not shown because Sandra and her surviving brother are now married and have their own families. Sandra's brother, Mark, died in 1987, and because he died an X is placed in the square.

Sandra was married to Jeff Brown in 1987, and they have given birth to two sets of twins. The older twins are fraternal twins, and one of them, Janet, died as an infant. The younger set of twins, Aimee and Nicole, are identical twins.

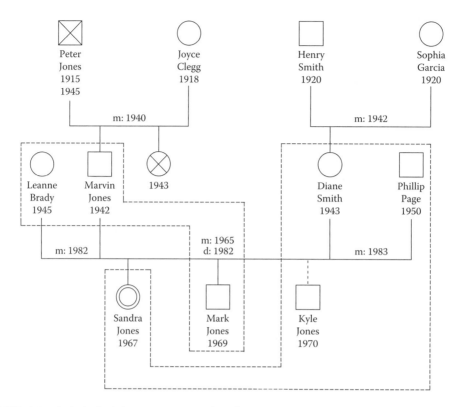

FIGURE 6.2 It is helpful to put as much information on a genogram as possible. The information can vary depending on the genogram's purpose.

Figure 6.3 also shows how to diagram relationships where two individuals are a "couple" but they are not legally married. Sandra's youngest brother, Kyle, had a relationship with Lori Rice. They met in 1987 and separated in 1989. Lori had an abortion in 1987, and it is shown with a vertical line and small "x." Later, Kyle was married to Brenda Strong in 1991, and Brenda experienced a miscarriage in 1992.

Figure 6.3 also shows that Sandra's stepfather Phillip Page died in 1987, and her mother married Bradley Derrick, a man who was 20 years older than she was in 1989. This marriage was Bradley Derrick's third marriage. He was married to his first wife, Ruth Dietzel, for a very short time, and they had a daughter named Jill in 1945. Bradley's second marriage was to Deborah King in 1948, and they had a son named Scott. Thus, Jill and Scott are stepsiblings, half-brother and sister. Jill was married to Harvey Zinn in 1966 and they had a son in 1969. Thus, when Sandra's mother, Diane, married Bradley in 1989 it created some unusual family relationships. In addition to getting a stepfather, Bradley, the remarriage also gave Sandra a stepsister named Jill who is 20 years older than she is, and she has a nephew, Kenneth Zinn, who is 1 year older than she is. Another unique aspect of these relationships is that they did not begin until the year after Sandra was married.

On the other side of Sandra's family, Figure 6.3 shows that her father was divorced again in 1986 and married Paula Kersten who was 19 at the time, the same age as Sandra. Thus, Sandra then had a stepmother who was the same age she was. Also, Sandra's paternal grandmother, Joyce, remarried at the age of 68. Her new husband, and Sandra's new stepgrandfather, was Donald Todd. The genogram also shows that Sandra's maternal grandparents died in 1987 and 1988. Genogram charts are sometimes helpful in giving us insights about what is happening in the lives of individuals and families, and they can

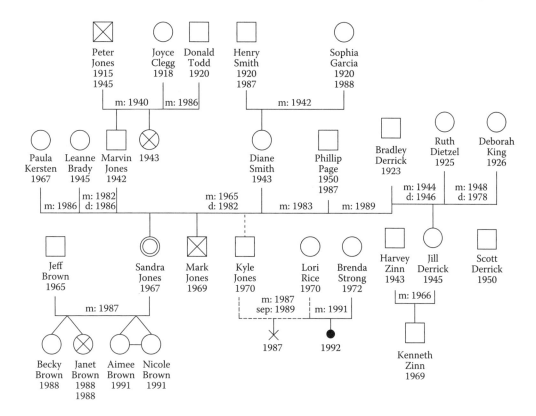

FIGURE 6.3   As life progresses, the genogram usually gets more complicated.

help us find ways to cope and adjust to many of life's challenges. For example, we would expect that the period between 1986 and 1988 was a challenging time for Sandra and her family. During this period of time her 18-year-old brother died, two grandparents died, and her stepfather died. Her youngest brother had a temporary relationship that included an abortion, and her father was divorced for the second time and married a woman the same age as Sandra. Shortly after this marriage Sandra was married. With that many dramatic events happening in Sandra's family situation, it would be likely that she would have a number of emotional reactions that she and her new husband would find themselves dealing with. Many people find a genogram chart such as this helpful in putting these events in perspective, understanding the emotional reactions, and working though the many feelings that would be occurring.

How to Make a Family Chronology

The second part of a genogram is a family chronology. This is a chronological listing of major events experienced in a family. A family chronology should include desirable and unfortunate events. For example, events such as graduations, serious illnesses, moves, changes in careers, changes in family composition such as a grandparent or other relative moving in or out, periods of drinking or other substance abuse problems, runaways, special honors or awards, times when a parent is gone for extended periods of time, times of financial affluence or difficulty, accidents, and periods of unusual closeness and love would usually be important events if they were to occur in families, and they should be included.

Many families experience unfortunate events such as a family member being in prison or a mental hospital, serious illnesses such as cancer and incapacitating strokes, affairs, suicides, physical abuse, sexual abuse or incest, and homes burning. These events have an important effect on individuals and families, and they should be identified. Care should be taken in describing them to be sure that confidences are not breached, and sometimes it is best to describe some of them in general terms. For example, saying something like "Paul and Sarah not close" could mean many things to the person making the genogram, and that is what is important.

Sometimes there is a tendency to focus on the tragic and traumatic events in writing the chronology of family events, but this tendency should be avoided. Unusual positive events should also be described because they influence families and the individuals in them. Some examples of these are such events as a member of the family being on a championship team, getting special awards or recognitions, developing unusually meaningful friendships, having a special musical or artistic performance, special trips or vacations that are memorable, or being elected to a high office.

The following family chronology for Sandra Jones lists some of the information from her family life to show how a family chronology is written.

A Chronology of the Jones Family

1915—Peter Jones born.
1918—Joyce Clegg born.
1920—Henry Smith born. Sophia Garcia born.
1939—Henry Smith moved to Mexico.
1940—Peter Jones and Joyce Clegg married.
1942—Marvin Jones born. Henry Smith and Sophia Garcia married.
1943—Diane Smith born. Stillborn child born to Peter Jones and Joyce Clegg.
1944—Peter Jones has a severe stroke.
1945—Peter Jones died.
1952—Henry and Sophia Smith move from Mexico to South Carolina.
1965—Marvin Jones and Diane Smith married.
1967—Sandra Jones born.
1969—Mark Jones born.
1970—Kyle Jones born and adopted by Marvin and Diane Jones.
1982—Marvin Jones and Diane Smith divorced. Marvin Jones and Leanne Brady married.
1983—Diane Smith and Phillip Page married.
1986—Marvin Jones and Leanne Brady divorced. Marvin Jones and Paula Kersten married.
1987—Sandra Jones and Jeff Brown married. Mark Jones died at the age of 18. Phillip Page died. Henry Smith died. Kyle has affair with Lori Rice. Lori Rice has an abortion.
1988—Diane Jones has mental breakdown. Sophia Garcia Smith died. Twins, Becky and Janet Brown, born. Janet died.
1989—Kyle and Lori break up.
1991—Twins, Aimee and Nicole Brown, born.
1991— Kyle Jones and Brenda Strong married.
1992—Kyle and Brenda Jones have a miscarriage.
1996— Kyle graduates from local college and finds first job in construction industry
2000— Brenda and Kyle have first child. It is a girl (Keensha); she has a serious eye defect.
2001— Keensha has a series of operations on her eyes. She will see, but the vision is limited.

2005— Keensha begins school and is placed in a special program for vision-impaired children.

2006—A second child is born to Brenda and Kyle. His name is Brandon.

2007—Brenda begins home business as a day care provider. Finds it fulfilling.

A thorough family chronology involves events from at least three different generations, and it usually has more than 50 items. The preceding list has only a few to illustrate how a family chronology is made, but it does not include many events that would be important in the family life of Sandra Jones and her extended family. A rich family chronology can be an excellent starting point for building an extensive family history.

Describing Family Relationships

The third part of a genogram is a description of the relationships among family members. These are usually fairly simple and straightforward descriptions, and some of them can be drawn on a genogram chart with the symbols shown in Figure 6.4. Usually it is not possible to diagram all of the important information about relationships on a chart because it becomes too complicated and confusing. Therefore, most of the time it is necessary to write the information about relationships on a few additional pages of paper.

Another way to describe relationship information is to make the basic chart and then make several photocopies of the chart. It is then possible to diagram some of the relationship information on the duplicate copies. Also, sometimes it is helpful to show the relationships at several different time periods in a family life cycle.

The following list of questions illustrates the kind of information that is usually included in the relationships part of a genogram:

1. Who was close to whom?
2. Which individuals had conflicted relationships?
3. Which individuals were "left out"?
4. Who tended to be the family scapegoat if there was one?
5. If there was a "favorite" child of a parent or grandparent, who were they?
6. Who were the leaders? Who were the followers?

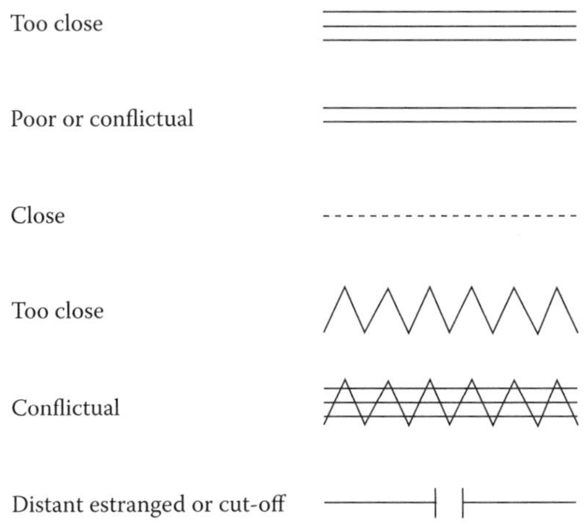

FIGURE 6.4   Genogram symbols.

7. Who was the family peacemaker? Who was the troublemaker?
8. Who was distant from the family?
9. Were there intergenerational alliances? If so, how did those alliances influence family functioning?
10. Who was "overfunctioning" or "underfunctioning?" Overfunctioning individuals take on an excessive amount of responsibility to make sure the rights things get done. Underfunctioning individuals take little responsibility and initiative as they let others get things done.

Describing Family Processes

The fourth part of a genogram is a description of circumstances or processes that can help us understand how generational relationships influence a family and the people in it. Several examples of processes that can be helpful are things such as cliques, alliances, and coalitions in families; ways children are treated differently by the parents; favorite relatives; conflicts that are not resolved; ways of solving problems; in-law pressures; marital harmony or difficulties; feuds among family members; determining who helps out when help is needed; and difficulties coping with life's challenges. The following list of questions helps identify some of these processes:

1. How did the family react when a particular family member was born or died? Who took it the hardest? The easiest?
2. Have there been any job changes that influenced the family? How do people feel about their jobs?
3. How do people in the family get along with relatives? Are some relatives especially difficult, close, or helpful?
4. Have any members of the family had a drinking problem? What about trouble with medications or other substances?
5. Who is supportive or helpful of other family members? Who is unselfish, and who is selfish?
6. In what does the family take pride?
7. What are the leisure time and recreation patterns in the home, and how do the various members feel about them?
8. Were any individuals especially successful in school? Did any have problems?
9. What are the talents and special gifts that members of the family have?
10. Did the family have any special "program" or "plans" for a particular child?
11. Did sibling positions or relationships influence any of the children?
12. How involved was the family with churches, clubs, fraternities, or other organizations?
13. Were any life cycle transitions (births, deaths, moving away from home, marriages, etc.) especially gratifying or difficult?
14. Did any members of the family have unusual ways of gaining recognition or success?
15. What were the successes, failures, traumas, satisfactions, and themes in the home?
16. Were there any coincidences of life events?
17. Did any economic or political events such as economic depressions or wars influence the family?
18. Were there any triangles inside or outside the family that had an effect on people?
19. Were there any "black sheep" or "family skeletons?"
20. Were there any resources such as inheritances or unusual brilliance or beauty that influenced the family?

Another helpful strategy in completing a genogram is to have the index person tactfully do "research" about his or her own family history by interacting selectively with relatives. Many people find it helpful to get more "involved" with their extended family by attending reunions, weddings, funerals, and other family gatherings and by observing others and their own emotional reactions to what they experience. It is especially informing to be around extended families when important emotional feelings are occurring, such as at a birth, a marriage, a death, a special achievement, a crisis, or an illness. It usually is not very helpful to get involved with relatives to try to "straighten them out."

Interpreting a Genogram

You are encouraged to make a genogram for your own family. Making one for your own family provides an "experiential" type of learning that does not occur in any other way. You learn to better understand some of the interesting, informative, and subtle aspects of your own family situation. You can also learn in a firsthand way how your generational connections have an influence on you, and how you can influence your posterity. It takes several hours to make a good genogram, but many of my former students and colleagues who have made genograms for their own families have found that it is an interesting, helpful, and useful learning experience. None of us should try to use a genogram to help someone else until we have made one for our own family first.

The payoff with a genogram is that it usually gives us a lot of new information. When we are making a genogram of our own family, it usually helps us better understand why we have some of the feelings we have, why we believe some of the things we do, why we have some attitudes, and why we relate to people the way we do.

This information often helps us and others become more effective in managing our lives, and it might help us cope more effectively with life's challenges and difficulties. The insights we get from genograms often help us better attain the things that most of us want in family life: closeness, understanding, love, richness, fulfillment, commitment, healthy development, support, communication, empathy, and intimacy.

If we are using a genogram as an educator or therapist to try to help someone else learn and grow, it can have the same effects. The other people often gain insights about why they feel, act, relate, and think the way they do, and they can then use their new insights to better attain their goals.

My experience with genograms has identified several strategies that are helpful for interpreting them. One strategy that usually helps is to try to identify some positive things first. This can be done by looking for events, patterns, relationships, and processes that have helped create strengths or things that are valued and desired. All individuals and all families have some strengths, good aspects, and admirable characteristics, and finding some of them builds morale and motivation. Even the most troubled and problem-ridden families have assets. In fact, sometimes the individuals and families that have had the most challenges have an unusual number of strengths.

Another strategy that is usually helpful is to be tentative and hypothetical when trying to understand what a genogram means. This means it is wise to state ideas as hypotheses or guesses about the effects of various relationships or processes. Some examples of this are: "It may be that . . . ," "It's possible that . . . ," "It could be that . . . ," and "Maybe . . . ."

There are a few cautions that are helpful when we try to use a genogram to help someone else. Some people have very painful experiences in their families, and the strategies they have used to cope with some of their experiences are sometimes to forget and avoid them. In some of these situations, they might be very uncomfortable when they begin to think about their earlier experiences, and forcing them to think about them could do more harm than good. Therefore, people's feelings, desires, and wishes should be respected, and they should never be forced or coerced to face or deal with aspects of their family life they are not ready to deal with. Their personal wishes and desires should determine what they do, and only when they are emotionally ready should they try to think about or understand how their earlier family experiences have influenced them.

☐ Using Knowledge About Generational Processes to Help People

Even though the study of generational processes is only a few decades old, family scientists have begun to discover ways to use some of the new ideas to help people attain their goals. We can use these ideas in our own family situations, and we can use them in a number of professional and vocational settings. For example, family therapists, family life educators, social workers, medical doctors, lawyers, and the clergy can use these ideas.

Liberating Families From Undesirable Generational Effects

Conservatism is the process of trying to protect ideas and practices people think are valuable. It attempts to protect and maintain traditional ways of doing things people think are worth keeping. Liberalism is the opposite, trying to liberate people from conventions, practices, and ways of doing things that are oppressive and undesirable. We usually think of liberalizing as liberating people from political and economic oppression. When we think about events such as the civil rights movement and the women's movement we should also realize that the family realm can be excessively dominating and oppressive. One goal of family scientists should be to help liberate people from the undesirable bondage and oppression that can occur in families. When desirable patterns are being passed from one generation to another, there is a technique that can help liberate families from these patterns. This technique is to be a transitional character.

Transitional Character

A transitional character is one who, in a single generation, changes the entire course of a lineage. The individuals who grow up in an abusive, emotionally destructive environment and who somehow find ways to metabolize the poison and not pass it on to their children. They break the mold. For example, they refute the observation that abused children become abusive parents. Or, they might turn the corner and turn away from alcohol. Their contribution to humanity is to filter the destructiveness out of their own lineage so that the generations downstream will have a supportive foundation on which to build productive lives.

There are many things people can do to help themselves be transitional characters. Eight of these things are deliberateness, distinctive family rituals, maintaining emotional distance, marrying later than average, reading good books about family life, joining organizations that can help, getting an education, and getting a philosophy of life.

Deliberateness

A group of researchers at George Washington University have discovered that deliberateness can influence generational transmission (Bennett, Wolin, Reiss, & Teitelbaum, 1987). They conducted a series of studies of the transmission of alcoholism in families, and one of the factors they found to be important is the amount people deliberately try to plan their own family identity, rituals, and ways of living.

In one of their studies they included 12 couples who had a high level of deliberateness; 75% of them were able to be transitional couples by interrupting the transmission of alcohol problems. Of the 31 couples who were low on deliberateness, 77% of them transmitted from their parents the pattern of having alcohol problems (Bennett et al., 1987).

Distinctive Family Rituals

A second idea (Fiese, 2007) has to do with family rituals, traditions, and routines. Researchers have discovered that families who do not allow a parent's alcohol abuse to disrupt important family rituals are less likely to pass their severe drinking problems to their offspring.

They found that when alcoholism becomes intertwined with family rituals and traditions such as birthday parties, dinners, family reunions, and holidays, the alcoholism tended to be transmitted to the next generations. However, when the alcohol problems were kept separate from the family traditions and rituals, the alcoholism did not tend to be transmitted to the next generation. They called this process the distinctiveness of rituals because families that were able to keep their family rituals and traditions "distinctive" from the problems they were having with alcohol were able to disrupt the transmission processes.

Maintain Emotional Distance

Research about generational transmission has revealed that the emotional distance between people in families also tends to influence the transmission process. If the individuals in the child generation of a family remain emotionally intertwined with their parental generation there tends to be more transmission, but if the children create a certain amount of emotional "distance" from their parents there is less transmission.

This idea is well documented in several of the studies in the George Washington research program (Steinglass, Bennett, Wolin, & Reiss, 1987). They summarize the point in the following way:

> Couples with an alcoholic legacy are relatively more protected from transmission if they take certain measures regarding their family attachments. Ideally, contact with the child's alcoholic origin family is not high, although it may remain moderate with no strongly adverse effects. (Bennett et al., 1987, p. 128)

Thus, the best research evidence suggests it is not necessary to completely sever emotional attachments and visiting patterns with the parent generation. Apparently, there can be a "moderate" amount of emotional attachment and interaction when someone is trying to be a transitional character, but if adult children are highly involved with their parents it is more difficult to disrupt the transmission of such things as values, traditions, rituals, attitudes, and behaviors from one generation to the next.

☐ Preserving Desirable Generational Processes

Many of the things that are transmitted across generations are very desirable. For example, many people grow up in healthy families, and they learn the subtle values, goals, feelings, and attitudes that give meaning, purpose, and a sense of direction to their life. They learn ways of trusting, loving, being close, serving, supporting, communicating at the deepest and most meaningful levels, and helping infants and elderly in ways that give purpose and joy to their lives.

Many people acquire a set of bonds in their family that are multifaceted and strong and provide loving, intimate, close relationships that are of infinite value. They form lifelong connections with their siblings, parents, grandparents, and their own children and their children. These kinds of connections involve many feelings that are so complicated, deep, and fundamental to a healthy life that they provide a richness and beauty that is difficult to describe.

Even those who grow up in families where they want to do some things differently than their parents learn many things from their parents that they want to continue in their own lives. They also, except in extreme situations, have bonds and feelings for their family that last their whole lives.

Some of the research about factors that help people disrupt generational transmissions can also help people create healthy generational processes. For example, the ideas about deliberateness and distinctiveness of rituals can be used to create healthy patterns. People who deliberately try to create healthy traditions, beliefs, rules, and patterns of relating will undoubtedly be more effective than people who never bother to think about these processes. Families who integrate their rituals, traditions, and routines with healthy and desirable ways of behaving are undoubtedly increasing the likelihood that the desirable patterns will be passed on to succeeding generations.

The management of emotional closeness also, undoubtedly, goes both ways. Families who create emotional distance between the generations decrease transmission from one generation to the other, and families that create emotional closeness between the generations increase what is transmitted. Therefore, families who want to enhance or perpetuate desirable patterns should try to cultivate emotional closeness.

☐ Creating Healthy Generational Alliances

There are a number of strategies that can be used to create healthy generational alliances. Some of these strategies are simple things. For example, the parents in a family can help the parental subsystem be the executive subsystem in a family by periodically having "planning sessions." These sessions would help them be a board of directors of the family or an executive committee. The small children would not attend these sessions, and in them the parents could discuss the ways they are relating to the children, ways they are disciplining them, what is going well, and what needs to be changed. Sessions such as these can help them make plans together so they are a coordinated team. If they have disagreements about how to structure the family or relate to the children, they can use sessions such as these to try to find common ground and compromise. As the children mature, the family system can gradually change so the older children have increasing access to the executive subsystem and influence it an increasing amount.

Another idea that can help families create healthy generational alliances is for the parents to have a "social life" as a couple in addition to the social activities of the family. This can include "dates" with each other, vacations as a couple, and joining social organizations together. These activities can help tie bonds in the marital relationship by showing how the couple subsystem is a unique and important unit in the family.

Another concept that can help families deal with generational processes in healthy ways is called unfinished business. Unfinished business refers to the need to deal with unresolved issues, feelings, injustices, and conflicting loyalties in a family.

A book titled *Invisible Loyalties* by Boszormenyi-Nagy and Spark (1973) helped the family science field begin to understand the role generational loyalties have in the healthy and unhealthy development of individuals and families. According to Boszormenyi-Nagy and Spark, each generation has ethical obligations and loyalties to the generations that preceded it and to the generation that follows it. For example, parents have ethical obligations to their children to provide affection, care, and nurturance. They also owe their children a secure and loving home, economic support, and security while the children are small and dependent. These obligations create a complex web of **invisible loyalties** and obligations.

A set of invisible loyalties and obligations exists from children to parents. When parents fulfill their obligations to their children, it creates an obligation in the child generation to be appreciative for the valuable and essential things they receive from their families. It also creates invisible loyalties that children feel toward their parents and they develop feelings of appreciation, respect, bonds, closeness, and admiration for their parents.

Boszormenyi-Nagy and his colleagues believe that the network of intergenerational loyalties in family systems is not something created by cultures or societies. It is a "natural" part of the family realm that exists because the generations are so intricately intertwined emotionally, mentally, and experientially (Boszormenyi-Nagy & Spark, 1986). Cultures and societies, however, influence and shape some of the ways these networks appear and whether they are healthy or unhealthy.

The research of Boszormenyi-Nagy and his colleagues helps us realize that these patterns of invisible loyalties in the family realm deal with deep feelings and emotions, and they are extremely important to most people. Therefore, when families have healthy patterns in their web of invisible loyalties across generations it provides a helpful reservoir of emotional stability. It also provides emotional and interpersonal bonds that help people deal effectively with the challenges and obstacles of life, and it provides a deeply experienced sense of meaning, purpose, and lineage consciousness that extends across the generations.

Another aspect of these invisible loyalties is that they gradually evolve and change as the family progresses over time and the family members mature and move to new stages of life. For example, young adults gradually shift their primary family loyalties from their parental family toward their spouse and the children they want to create and raise with their partner. As they make these shifts, they develop new loyalties and some of their old loyalties change and become less important. The old loyalties that diminish deal with obedience, reverence, allegiance, and indebtedness, and the new loyalties deal with subtle, invisible, and intangible, but extremely important things such as emotional dependence, connectedness, fidelity, nurturance, and creating together a sense of home, meaning, growth, and rootedness.

In some family situations, the disruption in the ledger of invisible loyalties becomes difficult and tragic. For example, when serious misbehavior occurs such as child abuse, incest, negligence, alcoholism, violence, manipulation, exploitation, and substance abuse, these destructive behaviors create serious disruptions in the invisible loyalties in a family system. In these situations it takes a long time for the members of a family to find ways to balance the ledgers and help the individuals and families become free of the hurts, fears, and resentments. Fortunately, many of the people who have experienced these tragedies in their families are able to face their feelings and they eventually work through their emotional responses in ways that are productive and enabling.

Many families do not have these serious tragedies, but most families, and maybe all of them, find it necessary to deal with unfinished generational business at certain stages of their life. For example, it is fairly typical for ledgers to become imbalanced during the launching stage of the family life cycle. It is natural for the younger generation to be striving to gain freedom and control over their lives and for the older generation to be hesitant to let the younger generation have control because they are aware of the limitations in their judgment and experience. The result is often that there is considerable conflict during this period of the life cycle and the invisible loyalties get trampled, twisted, and out of balance.

When this occurs in family systems, they have unfinished business, and they would be wise to try to deal with it. The unfinished business is that there are resentments, frustrations, and animosities at the same time that there are feelings of connection, loyalty, and love. When this occurs it is helpful for families to try to find ways to work through the negative feelings and inequities so they do not interfere with the ability of the individuals to move on to their new stages of life and new responsibilities. When young adults have deep resentments and conflicting loyalties in their relationships with their parental family it is difficult for them to begin their own family without the scars from the earlier family system interfering with the new family. Thus, it is helpful to find some way to take care of the unfinished business.

There are many ways that the younger generation or the older generation can take care of unfinished generational business. Sometimes it helps to try to talk about the feelings with parents, children, or siblings. In other situations it is neither possible nor wise to talk directly with the people who have been unjust because it would just make the situation worse. In these situations it sometimes helps to think about the unique circumstances that helped make it difficult for the parental generation to be as wise or fair as desirable. This sometimes helps people cope at least somewhat with their negative feelings. It also helps in some situations to accept the fact that the parents are also frail and limited in their humanness and they might need acceptance and understanding, or in some circumstances tolerance and even pity. Sometimes it is helpful to adopt a forgiving attitude and conclude that the parents probably had reasons for what they did and it will not be helpful to continue to feel resentful. Sometimes it is helpful to get professional help to work through these types of unfinished business.

☐ Summary

This chapter described how generational processes influence families and people. Two principles were introduced. The generational alliance principle states that there are several boundaries between parent and child generations that are natural and desirable. When families maintain these boundaries it contributes to the healthy development of the members of the family. Conversely, when these boundaries become blurred it interferes with healthy development.

The generational transmission principle states that aspects of the family realm are transmitted from one generation to the next, and this includes the good, the bad, and the ugly. Three areas where there is considerable evidence that transmission occurs are marital stability and instability, abusive and nonabusive behaviors, and mental health and illness. The chapter described how to make and interpret a genogram, and then described strategies that can be used to conserve desirable generational ties and transmissions and liberate people from undesirable generational ties and transmissions. Readers were encouraged to make a genogram for their own family because learning how to make and interpret genograms can help them deal effectively with their personal lives and learn an effective method of helping others to cope wisely with their generational processes.

☐ Study Questions

1. Define the term *fixed biological connection*.
2. What is the genogram symbol for divorce?
3. What is the symbol in a genogram that tells the reader who the person of focus is?
4. Name four ways a genogram might be used in clinical or counseling settings.
5. Define the term *generational transmission*.
6. What is the definition of a generational alliance?
7. Why do we care about cross-generational alliances?
8. In your own words, why is the study of generations important?
9. Why are generational alliances so problematic?

☐ Key Terms

Fixed biological and social connections
Genogram
Cross-generational (or intergenerational) alliances
Generations
Fixed
Inalienable
Social capital
Intergenerational transmission
Invisible loyalties

☐ Suggested Readings

Beavers, W. R. (1985). *Successful marriage.* New York: Norton.
Carter, B., & McGoldrick, M. (Eds.). (1989). *The changing family life cycle: A framework for family therapy* (2nd ed.). New York: Allyn & Bacon.
DeMaria, R., Weeks, G., & Hof, L. (1999). *Focused genograms.* Philadelphia: Brunner/Mazel.
Elkind, D. (1988). *The hurried child.* Reading, MA: Perseus Books.

7

Chosen Relationships and the Roots of Mature Love

☐ Chapter Preview

In this chapter, readers will learn:

- That courtship practices around the world vary greatly. Most cultures have some form of family-involved mate selection, but others (mostly in Western cultures) have moved to love-based selection.
- That dating practices found in U.S. culture are the normative premarriage behavior around the world.
- That over the last few decades several cultures have changed from family-involved mate selection to love-based mate selection.
- About how current love-based mate selection reflects our movement toward individualistic thinking and away from familial-kinship and community values-based thinking.
- That mature couple love has three elements: intimacy, commitment, and passion.

☐ Introduction

The purpose of this first section is to explore how one's dating and mate selection activities direct who we chose to marry and set the foundational rules about that relationship. In particular, styles of partner selection speak to issues of commitment, intimacy, passion, loyalty, devotion, romantic love, and other core ideological themes that can shape future relationships. The overall purpose of this chapter is to show how the way we select a partner influences family processes and patterns throughout the life cycle. Additionally, we explore the idea that mature couple love is built on intimacy, commitment, and passion.

Courtship Around the World

Most people living in the United States and Western Europe understand the practice of self-choice in dating and partner selection. In our culture, this process generally focuses on personal choice. Usually young men and women do not rely on or might not even want their parents to be closely involved in the dating and selection process. Most of us hope our parents will approve of the choices we make, but we typically find a partner on our own and then seek approval. That simple process is not found in much of the rest of the world.

In fact, the concept of dating is relatively new and is culturally located in the United States, Canada, most of Western Europe, and Australia and New Zealand. It is rare in other countries: For example, Egypt, India, and China have more than half of the world's population and dating and courtship is uncommon at best. In Korea, Japan, and other Asian countries, Western-style dating is only just starting to emerge. In most Muslim countries, dating is not only forbidden, but self-initiated courtship activities done without family sanction can carry serious consequences. Because marriage is at the heart of Muslim cultural and family life (Sherif, 1999), most Muslim men and women are expected to marry; marry with family direction, approval, and supervision; and are expected to remain sexually pure and monogamous. Also, Baron (1991) and Tucker (1991) indicated that if a person chooses to not marry in the Muslim culture, family anxiety and pressure increases dramatically with each passing year. In addition, cultural norms not only limit but actually exclude a person from living alone: Unmarried children live at home with parents, and few exceptions are allowed.

However, even with that pressure, cultural norms proscribe a young unmarried man from simply "picking up" a date from the workplace or a nightclub. In fact, it is forbidden in Muslim culture for an unmarried woman to even be alone with an unmarried man. If such an encounter becomes known, it could greatly reduce her marriage desirability (Sherif, 1999). Even an engaged couple is never left alone but always chaperoned: A lingering look or eyes meeting in a gaze can be considered a violation of moral purity. The virginity and moral virtue of women (and men to a lesser degree) is extremely valued and protected.

So, how do young people in these cultural systems get acquainted? How do they "hook up," to use today's vernacular? What can we learn from dating and mating practices around that world that can inform family process practices in the United States?

FIGURE 7.1 In many cultures, even casual contact with the opposite sex is closely monitored and it is inappropriate to have "office flirtations."

☐ **Family-Involved Mate Selection**

In Egypt, prior to the 1950s, marriages were almost exclusively arranged using match-makers or through direct family contacts. In other highly traditional societies such as China, choosing a partner is a **family-involved mate selection** (FIMS) process. Selection criteria are centered on social class and position. Typically, fathers and mothers warn children about playing with other children from another class, and, at a very early age, parents begin the search for a suitable marriage partner for their child. According to Sherif (1999), more recently, dating situations are slowly changing: Young people are now permitted to meet potential marital partners through work or other social situations. However, in a FIMS system there is a strong push by family members, teachers, and even matchmakers to pick partners within one's own social class and economic status.

Perhaps you have seen the movie or musical *Fiddler on the Roof*. In this poignant story, the rural Jewish father (circa 1900) of four marriage-aged young women tries to find partners in several different ways—each one challenging the FIMS system of rural and agricultural Jewish communities in Europe of only a few decades ago. Tevya, the local milkman and father, is faced with finding his daughters good Jewish homes. In one scene, the daughters sing a lament about the capricious process of finding a husband through the local match-maker. As they sing, it is clear that they could find themselves married to people who really do not know or care about them. In the United States and Western culture, it is hard for us to have even a vague understanding of the idea that a young girl is betrothed to a man she might not even know.

"Helpers" or matchmakers assist in making sure the family (and the young person) does not make a poor choice. To reiterate, most couples worldwide do not secure a marriage partner in the regular American way: See someone attractive, give him or her a call on the phone, ask for a date, and go to a movie—and then see what evolves from there. Instead, in most Asian and Muslim cultures, someone expresses interest in a person, a host of gate-keeper relatives and friends consider the bid, families potentially gather and introduce the young people and they (while not looking directly at each other) "court" in the presence of on-looking relatives.

Back to our Egyptian example, the courting process usually involves an element of family negotiation. That is, the man requests the hand of a woman through very formal channels (Nasir, 1990; Sherif, 1999). Sometime during these negotiations (and well before the potential couple have really spoken in depth with each other) the man will approach the woman's family and the inquiries begin. Both families seek to find out as much as they can about the status of the family, position in the community, and potential for future status attainment.

At some point, when the negotiations seem to be going well, the man will consult with his mother, sisters, and friends as he considers the purchase of a *shabka*. The shabka is a gift given to the prospective bride and usually is of the highest quality and price the man can afford. In wealthier families, this is usually a fine piece of jewelry (Sherif, 1999). During the next phase of this very structured courtship or *khutba,* either party can bow out of the pre-liminary contract. It is during this time that the couple gets to know one another and can talk together. However, this getting-to-know-you phase is very structured. Families get together for dinners, outings might be planned, and the two families begin to intertwine. If all goes well, the families negotiate a contract for marriage. The contract is signed, often long before the actual marriage, but the contract is very formal and binding.

> **PRINCIPLE 7.1   FAMILY-INVOLVED MATE SELECTION**
>
> Families have historically been very interested, involved, and even demanding about whom their children marry. This pattern is generally changing around the world.

In Activity 7.1 in your workbook, you are asked to comment on the effects of arranged or carefully monitored dating and mate selection practices. In other words, when couples are brought together in the ways just described would you expect more loyalty (or less) to the relationship? Why or why not? What other core ideologies might be formed when others have so much to say about future family members?

Scandinavian countries are at the other end of the spectrum. Any semblance of a family-based marriage system has long since disappeared from the social relations landscape. Sweden, in particular, has led the way in promoting the most liberal marriage, dating, and courtship customs found anywhere. **Cohabitation** is the norm in these countries and has been for several decades. The nearly universal practice of cohabiting has become something of a national mandate. It is a cultural norm so strong that only a small fraction (fewer than 10%) of marriages are not preceded by living together first in Sweden. The decision to connect and live together is nearly completely regulated by individuals and not the extended or even immediate family members. One result of this type of less formal, individual choice-making system is that more than half of all children born in Sweden are born to unmarried parents (Duvander & Andersson, 2006). There is little, if any, stigma or social concern about a child being born to a couple that is not formally wed. In these countries, the need for religiously sanctioned or community-regulated relationship pairing (and even childbearing) has all but disappeared.

☐ Love-Based Mate Selection

The differences in these mating and courtship styles are stark. Again, reflect on what this type of courtship practice might mean for the quality, durability, and strength of the future relationship. The type of dating and mate selection system we find in places like Sweden could be labeled **love-based mate selection** (LBMS). LBMS, based primarily on individual choice and personal attraction, continues to grow in popularity across the world. These relationships might or might not result in marriage, per se. In many Western cultures, cohabitation rates are very high, with individuals experiencing several premarriage partners before a marriage choice is made. Again, it is important to note that general cultural stigma about this type of system is faint at best. In these countries, the cultures have decided that the individual choice trumps religious, extended familial, or other community concerns or needs.

> **PRINCIPLE 7.2   LOVE-BASED MATE SELECTION**
>
> In most Western, modern, and industrialized countries, young people are more likely to have the final say about who they marry. This is a new and emerging world trend.

These types of love-based unions have spread rapidly in the 20th century as the ideals of Western-style individualism have spread. Consequently, highly religious (e.g., Muslim), traditional, and conservative cultures that still embrace the ideal of FIMS see themselves as being in a desperate fight to keep their cultures from drifting toward Western ideas of individual choice and the rejection of historic and traditional ideas about marital union. These cultures hope to keep young people free from the emergent Western-style morality. Many of these cultures view this type of individual choice and self-chosen sexual contact as the very definition of evil and offense to God (or Allah).

Largely, Western-style individualism has brought with it the notion that marriage and sexual activity are not as connected as they once were. Societies that move toward decreased religious orientations and increased liberal and individualistic ideologies are more likely to adopt the idea of LBMS, within which the individual should have first and final say about personal choice in such matters of the heart. This type of individual choice also brings with it—or can bring with it—the choice to choose and act on sexual desire outside of religious or family sanction. One of the keys to understanding this move toward LBMS is the advent and worldwide acceptance of birth control and the general liberalization of abortion practice. With these two widely accepted practices in hand, the cultural idea of sex for recreation has been allowed to flourish. One can, in a purely LBMS system (devoid of religiously proscribed sexual activity) choose to have multiple sexual partners with impunity and with decreased worry about unintended pregnancy (more on this topic appears later).

As can be imagined, when cultures shift from FIMS dating to LBMS individual-based decision making, that shift has an impact on the general kinship family system. The following are several changes that occur with a shift from FIMS-based marriage decisions to an LBMS decision format:

1. In an LBMS, there is not as much pressure to adopt the family system patterns of daily living from the previous generation. Couples feel far less pressure to do their daily life routines in the ways done by their parents and have more freedom to choose their own style of relationships and patterns of family life.
2. In FIMS, the generation-one parents have much more power over who does what and how resources are spent. They have been heavily involved in the selection of the new family member and might have chosen him or her for economic reasons. It is also likely in FIMS that there is a built-in expectation that the newlywed couple will be a part of the farm, business, or family enterprise.
3. In FIMS, the connection and value of kinship is enhanced. Once your family has been deeply involved in the marriage choice, they are also more likely to feel a connection and investment in the outcome of that relationship, the number of children born, what the children's names are, who the godparents are, and even how far you live from the epicenter of family life.
4. On the other hand, in LBMS, the wants and wishes of the individuals are enhanced. If they choose to not have children, or name the child for a popular rock star, or even move to a faraway country, the kinship wishes and wants become secondary to the couple's wishes.
5. In LBMS, relationship dissolution is the purview of the couple—not the family. Conversely, in FIMS one would expect the larger kinship system, the church or religion, and even the government to have a say. After all, they had a say in the formation of the relationship, they have a keen investment in the family connections created through the contractual negotiation and, therefore, will probably have a lot to say and pressures to bear when things are not going well for the couple. In more

religious and traditional societies one would expect the couple to be reminded of religious covenants, promises, and mandates that govern marriage. Government agencies would want to regulate these activities if informal unions pay different tax amounts or require different provisions for health care and social safety net benefits.

6. In FIMS, it is much more likely that having and rearing children will take on greater importance. Children represent family continuity, name transfer, and inheritance perpetuation. The government always has interest in future workers, future soldiers, and the well-being of future taxpayers. All of those values center on the maintenance and enhancement of family prestige, power, and status.

PRINCIPLE 7.3   LBMS INFLUENCES CULTURE

Not only has culture shaped how we choose marriage partners, but our partner-choosing folkways influence culture. Cultures have historically moved from family-based mate selection (FIMS) to love-based marriages (LBMS). This change has direct impacts on the goals, themes, loyalties, and general family functioning of the forthcoming generations. This change also has a direct impact on community and larger governmental plans and programs.

☐ Dating in the United States

We can see the change and emergence of these principles clearly when we examine the changes in courtship and mate selection practices in the United States over the last 60 to 100 years. During the 1950s in the United States, the courtship process was in transition. Prior to this time, religious values were much more prevalent and courtship much more reflective of an FIMS as described earlier. Young people were much more likely to be supervised by parents and dating was done under the watchful eye of one's elders. Even the architecture of homes built prior to the 1930s reflects this value. Imagine a large farmhouse or family dwelling that was built prior to the 1930s and has not been remodeled.

One striking feature common to most of the homes during this era was the parlor. Parlors were large rooms, usually in the front of the house near the front door. They had three key family functions. First, they were a place to receive special guests such as a visiting neighbor or the local minister. Second, these rooms played a special role during the death of a family member. The deceased was placed in a casket for viewing in the parlor, hence the need for large sliding doors often found in the parlors of larger older homes. Today we have funeral parlors instead of home-based parlors to take care of this function.

Third, home parlors were the space allocated for couple courtship interaction. Couples were regulated and watched over as they journeyed through the courtship process. They were allowed to interact when a prospective mate (usually the man) would come "a-courtin'." He would be ushered into the home and given a place of honor to sit in the parlor. In more well-to-do homes, there might be a piano available and the woman being courted might play for the visitor or the group might engage in singing or parlor games. Typical of this era, the couple would play clever word games, have card parties, and engage in storytelling. This type of highly structured, supervised courting was very popular during the Victorian and Edwardian eras in the United Kingdom and the United States. It was usually punctuated by witty conversation and the evening would often include the presentation of special cakes and cookies created by the woman being courted so she could demonstrate her domestic abilities. Conversation was carefully crafted, touching and even long gazes carefully monitored, and watchful adult supervision was always within earshot.

The early 20th century brought several dramatic cultural changes that impacted this type of FIMS system. The Industrial Revolution moved people away from small community agrarian society. In agrarian societies, families had more control because children were a part of the enterprise and there was a chance that through obedience to family and perhaps religious traditions they would be eligible for inheritance and access to the family's collected wealth. However, as we collectively moved toward more urban, factory-based economies and began to embrace more secular, individualistic cultural systems, young men and even women began to find jobs not connected to family farms and, therefore, family control decreased. Increased numbers of nonfarm jobs that were unconnected to one's family business became the norm. These opportunities increased personal wealth (as opposed to family or kinship wealth) and mobility.

Additionally, cultural observers often cite the rise of the automobile as a prominent reason for movement toward LBMS and away from FIBS. With the auto, couples could escape the watchful eye of the parlor. This one invention and a willingness to change the existing courtship practices at the time led to the evolution of dating as we know it today.

The decision to date was shifted from a family-involved process to a love-based, person-initiated process away from the scrutiny of family members. With that change came the ability to initiate a date, take that date to a nonfamily setting, and even engage in unsupervised sexual behavior. These changes brought about a significant shift in power. In an FIMS process, family members are the gatekeepers and are very powerful as they direct mate choice outcomes. In an LBMS, independence is enhanced in the person and he or she takes the reins of power about partner selection. Initially, however, the power did not go to both men and women equally. Until very recently, it was considered improper, gauche, and forward for a young lady to ask a man out for a date. Men were expected to initiate, make good choices, pay for the date, drive the car, and carry with them the rules and expectations of parents into the dating situation. Women were to wait at home by the phone and not be too eager about answering the phone nor about accepting last-minute dates (a sign that the young woman had not been chosen and was desperate; Seccomb, 2008). This gaming strategy became a well-defined and well-oiled system within which the process headed in the direction of a true LBMS process, yet it was still regulated and structured with remnants of an FIMS.

The scripts of the dating scene in the United States from the 1920s until the 1990s were well-defined, culturally normed, explicit, and sanctioned. First, the man picked a young woman (same-sex attraction was usually forbidden, hidden, and not sanctioned) he was attracted to and asked her out on a date. If mutual interest emerged, they would continue dating and eventually promises would be made about monogamy. At some point, the guy would present the lucky girl with a special ring (sometimes a high school, fraternity, or college ring) to signify that they were now "going steady." Going steady meant you were monogamous (not dating someone else) and that this girl (from the guy's view) was tagged property—she was wearing his special fraternity pin, ring, or letterman's jacket. If that relationship continued, the couple would begin talking of marriage.

Commitment and Sexuality

Until recently in the United States, very few of these couples would actually live together; sexual activity was not uncommon, but was largely hidden from public view. In the later stages of the process it would usually be expected that the man would surrender more and more devotion and commitment, and the woman would yield more willingness to be sexually available. This **sex–commitment connection** was thought to be part of the deal and especially important (from her point of view) if she were to allow sexual intercourse, she had the most to risk in a pre-birth-control environment. In the pre-1960 world before birth control pills were invented and distributed, the woman was much more of a gatekeeper with regard to sexuality and was less likely to agree to sexual intercourse if there were not some kind of formal or informal commitment assurances. If she were to become pregnant before marriage, a woman's dating and mate-attracting possibilities would plummet. Of course, having a child without a provider and committed husband or someone to chop the firewood, was also among her worst fears. So, the usual script was for her to bargain hard for commitment and for him to bargain hard for sex. Sex was, therefore, for many women, not about pleasure or experience but about danger, childbearing, and responsibility.

PRINCIPLE 7.4   COMMITMENT AND SEX DISCONNECTED

In recent years, Western culture generally has moved away from having sexual intimacy connected to relationship commitment. This movement has had some impact on fertility and marriage rates in the United States.

As we approached and passed the millennial marker, many of those kinds of cultural scripts and processes about dating and courtship seem to have passed into history. Today's coupling process is much more of a free-for-all. Young people group together, women are not nearly as likely as before to hesitate to ask someone to participate in an activity. Formal dating still exists, but is usually reserved for relationships that show more promise and are being considered as something "serious." Smith (2005), in his ground-breaking book *Soul Searching*, describes the teen years (a rather small U.S. sample) as a time when many teens experiment with various ideologies and styles of life. Many of them adhere to religious and parental directives. Although many of them are quick to assert that they believe in God, many (one in five) by age 17 have had about four sexual partners. The national averages indicate that about 64% of 12th-grade boys and 62% of 12th-grade young women in the United States report having had sexual intercourse (*http://www.thenationalcampaign.org/national-data/pdf/TeenSexActivityOnePagerJune06. pdf*).

One obvious difference is that the risk of pregnancy is decreased if the couple uses preventive measures. Additionally, they might elect to be involved in protected sex because of the HIV/AIDS risk. Today, the age of first marriage is much later than it was just a few years ago, so young people feel much less pressure to lock someone into a serious relationship. In much of the United States and Western Europe, religion and spiritual values play only a minor role. Generally, the use of birth control is nonstigmatized and is rarely blocked by parents. It is easily available, with the result being that very young women and men are acting much more freely on sexual passion.

Buss, Shackelford, Kirkpatrick, and Larsen (2001) help us understand some of the more dramatic shifts in ideas and practices over the last 80 years. They gathered data about mate preference across six decades (1939–1996). These researchers assessed 18 characteristics or ideas that were asked of men and women as they thought about people they would like to marry. Some of the preferences for these characteristics have changed dramatically in the last 80 years and some have stayed fairly constant.

The first one listed was dependable character. This idea about partner character does not seem to have changed much. Both men and women expect a partner to be dependable, reliable, and committed to the relationship. At the other end of the spectrum, having a similar political background was not very important in 1939 and still is not.

Some of the characteristics, however, have made significant shifts. Chastity is the most notable. In 1939, men ranked this attribute as number 10, ahead of education and even good looks. By 1996, men rated chastity 16th on their list of desirable characteristics behind such things as good health, refinement and neatness, education, and good looks. The men of our day are much more interested in a woman who is healthy, neat, educated, and good looking and care very little if she has had other sexual partners.

On the other hand, women in our day prefer to be with a man who is in love with them, emotionally stable, has a pleasing disposition, is educated, and has a good strong desire to have children and provide a home. Interestingly, most (in this survey) cared very little about his previous sexual behavior. That represents a dramatic change from the 1939 data.

In short, it would appear that over the last 70 to 80 years our mate selection process has moved away from an FIMS system to a more love-based system. That system reflects the growing idea that young people do not want to rely, nor do they have to rely, on family and parents for support and decision making about such things as future partners.

The fully developed individualistic ideology of Western civilization (see Chapter 1) has had a substantial impact on relationship selection, sexuality, and decisions to have children. With that shift has come a dramatic shift in power of procreation that once resided within the walls of the home and has traversed to the apartment of the independent young person. In like manner, we have seen the decline and, in some cases, the demise of religious and other community institutions that used to direct, sanction, proscribe, and regulate the sexuality and mate selection process of young people. Although many in the United States still declare allegiance to a church and belief in God, the trends clearly show a movement away from that allegiance as a source of direction for mate choice as a family or spiritual-based decision. Of course, there are plenty of exceptions to that general trend. However, one only has to turn to the trajectory of countries like Sweden and the United Kingdom to anticipate the direction of changes that seem to coming.

☐ Love: Commitment, Passion, and Intimacy

My boyfriend used to ask his mother, "How can I find the right woman for me?" and she would answer, "Don't worry about finding the right woman—concentrate on becoming the right man." (Anonymous)

Love seems the swiftest, but it is the slowest of all growths. No man or woman really knows what perfect love is until they have been married a quarter of a century. (Mark Twain)

I didn't marry you because you were perfect. I didn't even marry you because I loved you. I married you because you gave me a promise. That promise made up for your faults. And the promise I gave you made up for mine. Two imperfect people got married and it was the promise that made the marriage. And when our children were growing up, it wasn't a house that protected them; and it wasn't our love that protected them—it was that promise. (Thornton Wilder, The Skin of Our Teeth)

The study of romantic love is fairly new. It is only within the last 30 to 40 years that social scientists have tried to put this elusive and controversial topic under the microscope. There is not much agreement among scholars about how to define love within the purview close relationship. Berscheid (2006) indicated that if forced to choose among the variety of definitions and ideas about love, she would have to go with the notion that, for young people at least, we often mix sexual desire with love. In the movie *When Harry Met Sally*, the philospher and protangonist of the movie (Harry) comes to the same conclusion, that men (in particular) cannot actually be friends with members of the opposite sex without it having sexual overtones. However, notice the preceding Mark Twain quote. It suggests that there is another type of appreciation, emotional connection, and feeling that occurs only through years of being together that perhaps transcends the sexual attraction element.

As mentioned in the last section, we have shifted over the last 100 years or so from marriages as partnerships to marriages that demand an element of romantic love. It was not until the modern era that romantic love was even a part of the equation. But what it is about love—or what is it *within* loving relationships—that informs, builds, strengthens, and potentially enhances the quality of family life? Instead of reciting the voluminous ways in which love has been discussed, our focus here is on one theoretical formulation that helps us understand love as a pillar of strong and effective family life.

☐ The Triangular Theory of Love

Sternburg (1986) proposed that love is built on three key elements: **intimacy**, **passion**, and **commitment**. One of the reasons it makes sense to talk about this approach to love is that those three elements of relationships can be measured and combinations of them seem to make sense when thinking of a couple coming together, having children, and building an effective home environment.

To grasp the idea behind the **triangular theory of love**, examine the single triangle in Figure 7.2. This is a replication of Sternburg's (1986) formulation. As you read the following examples, imagine that the elements mentioned become bold representing the specific configuration discussed. For example, the first kind of configuration Sternburg mentions is liking. In a liking situation, the element of the triangle that becomes bold is intimacy. Although this type of interpersonal connection is a powerful element of effective close relationships, by itself it does not carry much punch. If a couple were to marry only because they liked each other, this theory would say that their relationship would not be as strong as some of the other configurations. You might have examples in your life where you had a friend of the same or opposite sex that was a good friend, confidant, and close associate, but you did not feel moved to marry that person or even pursue a more in-depth close relationship. Intimacy is a key element in friendship: We confide in the other, share secrets, reveal the past, and contemplate the future. However, those activities are necessary but not sufficient for a lasting relationship that will endure the stress and trouble we experience during life.

In like manner, one could encounter a situation within which the passion leg of the triangle is bold and pronounced, but the other two dimensions (intimacy and commitment) are lacking. In today's world, young people often report that they "hook up" with someone at a party and experience sexual or passionate interaction with that person, but, in fact, they do not know much about the person or about his or her wants, wishes, desires, or life goals. There is no exchange between commitment and sexual contact (see earlier); there is no one gatekeeping with regard to the negotiation between commitment and intimacy.

FIGURE 7.2 Sternburg's triangular theory of love features three elements of love and describes what happens if one or more of these is lacking or weaker than another.

Sternburg refers to this type of relationship as *infatuated love*. The passion runs high, but the thinking or even moral value of the relationship is disregarded. Imagine if a couple decided to drive to Las Vegas and be married at the Elvis Drive Through Marriage Parlor based on passion only. Sternberg and associates would claim that these types of relationships either grow to include some of the other elements, or they languish as the passion element becomes routine.

Next, one could be in a relationship that was based only on commitment. Think again of the arranged marriage situations. This person feels the heat from the family commitment, the pressure from the cultural norms and traditions to stay in the relationship even if there is no passion or intimacy. There are many stories and examples of arranged marriages within which intimacy and even passion grow through the years. However, there are also volumes of examples in which the wife and husband are utilitarian partners not sharing much passion or even confiding in the other. Most of the readers of this text would frown at the prospect of being told whom to marry in a situation where commitment was the predominant factor and there was little or no passion or intimacy.

Romantic Love

Romantic love, according to Sternburg, invites the couple to embrace both intimacy and passion. In this case, the couple shares deep feelings, they are confidants to one another, and, at the same time, they feel sexual attraction, passion, and physical connection. What is lacking, of course, is a strong sense of commitment. Some researchers suggest that in today's world of high cohabitation rates, couples might feel a deep sense of passion and even see the partner as a true confidant—and that is enough to decide that living together is a viable option. They might be only partially committed: The woman probably does not feel the need to bargain for long-term protection and provision. In today's world, chances are she is working at her own job, financially independent, and would move to another close relationship if she found one. In this hypothetical case, she (and perhaps he) is using birth control to prevent the addition of children to the situation. If there is a break-up, the couple does not go through the pain of divorce. They might believe they are capturing the best of all worlds.

Cohabitation

Researchers suggest that, in fact, cohabitation is not a substitute for marriage (Bumpass & Lu, 2000). If cohabitation were a marriage substitute, one would expect to see these unions lasting longer. In fact, according to Bumpass and Lu (2000), half of cohabiting relationships last a year or less and only 1 out of 10 lasts longer than 5 years. In addition, in cohabiting relationships, if the woman becomes pregnant, a majority marry the cohabiting partner. Again, the rise of the use of birth control, the ready access to abortion, the financial independence of women, and the nearly total acceptance of sex outside of marriage have conspired to make cohabitation an attractive alternative to many couples.

Does cohabitation (passion and intimacy without strong public commitment) increase one's chances for a strong marriage later on? The answer is probably no. That is especially true for those who do not intend on marrying the live-in partner. Although the majority of marriages today begin with some form of cohabitation (Seltzer, 2004), our ideas about what that means might be changing. It is often thought that living with someone is good practice to assess compatibility. The bad news is that cohabitation before marriage strongly predicts future divorce (Phillips & Sweeney, 2005). Additionally, cohabitation following divorce is significantly associated with reductions in marital satisfaction and general well-being in subsequent marriages (Xu, Hudspeth, & Bartkowski, 2006). Although there might be some selection bias in these statistics (those cohabiting and divorcing are not as likely to experience marital satisfaction in any case), there is a strong possibility that cohabitation promotes independence in finances, decision making, and educational choice (Landale, 2002).

Companionate Love

The next type of relationship configuration is called *companionate love*. In this case, the couple has a high level of commitment and intimacy but little passion. Imagine, for a moment, marrying someone with whom you were best of friends, to whom you felt committed, and wanted to be with forever, but there was (for whatever reason) a weaker sense of passion or physical interaction. One would expect these relationships to be fairly strong and durable but the partner(s) might feel a deep sense of loss when considering the loss of deep physical passion.

Consummate Love

The final type to be mentioned here is called *consummate love*. In this situation, the lucky couple has the advantage of experiencing all three components. Commitment is high: They have made their relationship public and have vowed to be with one another for life. They feel a strong sense of sexual passion and physical need that is reciprocal and filled with desire that is not exploitive, and they experience a deep sense of camaraderie and view the partner as the primary person with whom to share their deep feelings and secrets of life.

With regard to these types of loving relationships, we can call on a principle from Chapter 2, the epigenesis principle, which states that what happens early on in one's life affects outcomes in later life. That idea is extended here and suggests that the type of relationship one designs early on builds the foundation for the relationship later on.

PRINCIPLE 7.5   EPIGENSIS IN RELATIONSHIP STYLES

The type and style of relationship one adopts early in the relationship defines and directs the the relationship as it emerges and matures over time. For example, if the relationship lacks commitment early on, it will be more difficult to generate commitment later on. Further, those relationships that are passionate, intimate, and committed should produce relationships that are more efficient in solving problems and better at fending off crises, and the couple will make more effective decisions.

☐ Summary

In sum, the way we date and mate around the world has changed in the last 100 years. For the most part, many cultures are moving away from family-based involvement in mate selection and toward love-based selection. This shift has many implications for how we view marriage and marriage-like relationships (e.g., long-term cohabitation). In addition to changes in the selection process, we have also experienced a dramatic shift away from the connection of relationship commitment and sexual intimacy. Very quickly, many young people today have disconnected those two ideas. That disconnection has had a significant impact on such issues as abortion, age at marriage, the divorce rate, and the overall meaning of marriage today.

A major shift has also occurred in how we view love. This chapter presented the view of Sternburg (1986), who suggested that love has three important components and that the most long-lasting type of relationship is built on strong commitment, a strong feeling of intimacy, and passion. The type of love style that emerges is reflected in the combination of those three elements.

Finally, the dramatic rise in cohabitation was addressed. As the mores and folkways surrounding mating change and alter, the culture seems to be experimenting with different forms of relationships and patterns of pairing.

☐ Study Questions

1. How would the Egyptian form of courtship have an impact on future family processes?
2. Explain what is meant by family-involved mate selection in courtship.
3. Comment on your world: How do the young people you know (or even the older ones) seem to be hooking up, dating, and choosing partners? Does the analysis in this chapter support what you are seeing around you?
4. What are the components of love according to Sternburg as explained in your text?
5. Which of the love styles (according to Sternburg's suggestions) do you think would be the strongest relationships and which would be the weakest?
6. Would you ever consider (or have you ever considered) living with someone before marriage? Explain your views in this regard: Why would you (or wouldn't you) entertain that as a possibility?

☐ Key Terms

Family-involved mate selection
Love-based mate selection
Commitment
Intimacy
Passion
Cohabitation
Sex–commitment connection
Triangular theory of love

☐ Suggested Readings

Berscheid, E. (2006). *Dynamics of romantic love: Attachment, caregiving, and sex*. New York: Guilford.
Crouter, A., & Booth, A. (Eds.). (2006). *Romance and sex in adolescence and emerging adulthood: Risks and opportunities*. Mahwah, NJ: Lawrence Erlbaum Associates.
England, P., & Edin, K. (Eds.). (2007). *Unmarried couples with children*. New York: Russell Sage.

The Core of Family Life

Family Paradigms, Themes, and Ideologies

☐ Chapter Preview

In this chapter, readers will learn:

- That an *ideology* is a set of ideas or beliefs. The ideological part of family systems is different from the generational and emotional parts, and all three are important.
- How some aspects of family ideology are more abstract than other aspects. Three levels of abstraction are explained.
- That family paradigms are an important part of families and are the enduring, fundamental, shared, and general assumptions families develop about the nature and meaning of life, what is important, and how to cope with the world they live in.
- About four general types of family paradigms: open, closed, random, and synchronous.
- About the ideology principle, which teaches us that many of the other elements of family processes are built on the themes, paradigms, and shared fundamental beliefs found in the family's ideological core.
- That the exaggeration principle helps us understand that when families encounter stress they have a natural tendency toward exaggeration of the processes created by their paradigmatic beliefs.

☐ Introduction

This chapter deals with a fundamental and important part of family systems—their **ideology**. Before we can understand the role of ideology in families, we need to understand what this term means. The root of the word *ideology* comes from the Greek term *ide*, which means *idea*. Therefore, ideology refers to the body or group of ideas that exist in a group, society, or social movement. Thus, when we focus on family ideology we are focusing on the cognitive or intellectual aspect of family systems that is reflected in their beliefs, thoughts, myths, symbols, ideals, aspirations, values, worldviews, philosophy of life, or doctrines.

It is helpful to realize that the ideological aspect of a family is different from the generational and emotional aspects. One difference is the emotional part is experienced as sensations or emotions rather than thoughts. It is not as much an intellectual process as it is an affective, emotional, or somatic process. Also, the generational processes discussed in Chapter 6 are not part of the "idea" part of family systems. They are connections, continuities, discontinuities, and other processes that occur between parents and children—even when families are not aware of them intellectually. When families develop ideas or beliefs about their emotions or their generational processes, these ideas are part of their ideology, but the emotions and generational processes themselves are fundamentally different, as they are not ideological.

☐ Understanding the Continuum of Abstraction: A Key Thinking Tool

The following discussion is presented as a general thinking tool. It can be used in thinking about family science, but is useful in more than just the study of social sciences. A key element of beginning to think academically and logically is the ability think in terms of a **continuum of abstraction**. Younger children do not have this ability and it only begins to emerge as a feature of young adulthood. Because it is a central notion in understanding the **paradigms** found in family life, a few paragraphs are devoted here to explaining this key tool to cognitive ability.

The Continuum of Abstraction

To understand the concept of **levels of abstraction**, we first need to clarify what we mean here by abstraction. Abstraction refers to whether something is relatively specific, tangible, and concrete. The opposite of abstract is when an idea is relatively general, intangible, obscure, and unspecific. For example, there is a difference between thinking about our own personal experience in family life and imagining family in general. Our own version of family life is a specific and concrete example. On the other hand, when we think of family life, generally, we imagine a wide-ranging way of organizing humans. Frequently we make the mistake of jumping from one level of abstraction and of generalizing that experience to a broader, less concrete feature of the same experience. For example, if you were to assume that your version of family life or the example of family within which you were raised is the norm, the typical, or even the ideal, you could run into a host of problems.

Here is another example. The idea of a democracy is at the far end of the scale of abstraction. It is not very concrete in its ideal form. It is more of a philosophy than a set of laws or suggestions. Moving down the scale of abstraction toward something more concrete is the U.S. Constitution: It is a collection of principles that are more specific than the idea of democracy, but the principles still can be vague and almost philosophical. The result is that those statements, like "promote the general welfare," can be interpreted in a variety of ways—hence the 200-year history of the U.S. Supreme Court.

From the general articles and statements of the Constitution come more specific laws. For example, there have been many attempts in the Congress to ensure the welfare of families. During the 1930s, Congress passed a series of initiatives that were very specific and aimed at relieving the suffering brought on by the Great Depression. These are generally referred to as the New Deal. In turn, and as a much more specific example, the New Deal spawned the Works Progress Administration (WPA). This was a very specific program designed to assist rural and western mountain citizens who were on the brink of poverty and starvation. This program built public buildings, dams, roads, and schools.

In the small town of Bluejacket in northeastern Oklahoma, the Ralph Day family lived in near poverty conditions. Ralph had four children, was a World War I veteran, a skilled leader, brick mason, stone craftsman, and engineer. He was, however, without employment. In the fall and winter of 1938, this family (the author's grandparents) had nothing to eat except 200 pounds of rice and a shelf of canned blackberries picked from the roadside that fall. Times were tough. In the summer of 1939, Ralph was chosen to lead a group of local townspeople and commissioned to build a local school using funds created by the WPA. The project lasted nearly a year and employed dozens of local workers and their families. The school stands today as an example of how a vague concept like democracy can be converted into a more specific idea like a constitution that indicates that the role of government is to assist and provide help so that the general welfare of the group is maintained. That less abstract idea of the general welfare is then converted into specific action in the form of bills, laws, and ordinances; and subsequently real money is transferred to a bank, workers are hired, and a school emerges.

Therefore, the idea of abstraction is a continuum that varies between the two extremes of highly abstract (philosophy, ideal, idea, and thought) and concrete (specific, tangible, measurable, observable).

Applying the Continuum of Abstraction to Family Paradigms

Family scientists in the 1970s began talking about different levels of functioning in family processes (Broderick, 1993; Hess & Handel, 1959; Kantor & Lehr, 1975). They decided that family interaction centers around two levels or types of family tasks (Watzlawick, Weakland, & Fisch, 1974). These two levels, it was thought, operated at different levels of abstraction, as previously explained. Further, they suggested that these tasks (tasks at different levels of abstraction) were functions or daily life activities that the family must manage, control, and negotiate. Also, they suggested that to understand family life we needed to realize that the key to understanding each unique family resided in understanding how families approached each of these tasks or functions. Researchers suggested that like snowflakes, no two families have the same way of organizing their lives, managing rules, negotiating role divisions, and establishing boundaries. For our discussion here, these tasks have been divided into three levels. The first are at the least abstract level, called *first-order tasks*. On the scale of abstraction, they are very specific and concrete.

First-Order Processes

First-order processes are visible, noticeable, and apparent to anyone in and around a given family. These processes are not very abstract, but they might be markers of something much more complicated and fundamental to a given family. First-order processes center on patterns of daily living: solving daily problems, getting decisions made, and keeping the daily business of the family humming. If we were observing family interaction and taking notes about first-order processes, we would want to know what families members are talking about and with whom they communicate. We would try to assess if their communication styles were effective. We might take note about how they solved a financial problem, celebrated a special holiday, and managed to get a room in the house painted.

Additionally, we would take notes on family boundaries. Families have a first-order task of deciding who belongs in the family, who is not in the family, and how far from home family members should roam. Each family also has the first-order task of role allocation. That is, they have to decide who performs which roles, and they have to negotiate the sequences of daily practices (e.g., when children rise in the morning, when the lawn is mowed and who is in charge).

These first-order processes or ways of thinking about family life are simple, fairly visible skills and contain rules that are, for the most part, more specific, observable, and concrete. Most of the rules and skills families have fall in this category. Notice that the rest of the chapters in this text could be organized around first-order elements of family life. Only this chapter focuses on the more complex and invisible second-order layer of family functioning.

Most of the research about family life focuses on first-order elements. For example, there is an emerging line of research about how family rules emerge. Researchers ask questions about how families make rules, negotiate rule behavior, and handle rule violations.

A typical family system has thousands of these specific "ideas" about how family systems should operate. For example, most families think they should put beds in bedrooms rather than in living rooms, and they think it is okay to show physical affection to each other—as long as it is appropriate. Of course, families differ in what they think is appropriate. Some families express affection a great deal and others express it less. Most families have ideas about where people should and should not eat, and how family members should dress. They also believe that lawn mowers and garden tools should not be left in driveways, electrical appliances should be kept safe, and toys should not be left on stairs.

Another first-order task in family life is the development of life skills that help define personal competence (Beavers, 1985). Well-being in family life is, in part, a function of how competently family members can make decisions, solve problems, take leadership, and make desired goals happen. According to Gontang and Erickson (1996), family well-being can be assessed by examining the ability families have to perform skills that are crucial as families choose between individual needs and group needs. On the one hand, family members experience individual wants and needs. We all feel the pressure to take from the group what we want. Stronger families, according to these authors, can balance the needs and wishes of the individual with the needs and wants of other family members. The group agenda is considered along with the needs of the individual. For example, a family might need a new or different car to meet the group needs of transportation. Stronger families can balance that general group need with the need of the individual family member who is pushing the group to spend extra funds on a personal want.

Another aspect of observing families from a first-order view is observing how skillful they are at implementing the choice. Families that are more competent and experience better outcomes are more balanced and flexible in solving first-order processes. In this case, they find ways of successfully balancing the needs of the child and the larger needs of the family group. They know how to both be flexible and show concern for the needs of the weakest or youngest in the group.

Some family processes are more subtle and unspoken. Sometimes (think now of the continuum of abstraction), even first-order family processes start to slip from obvious view and are hidden even from the family. These patterns of acting or task-oriented behaviors are subtle, implicit, and often unknown even to the family. For example, a family might have an implicit idea that "Dad can criticize other members of the family but the other members cannot criticize Dad." Or, some members of a family might think that "Stephen is the mother's favorite child," but the mother might think she has no favorites. More competent families have skills that promote openness, emphasize generosity, and communicate caring. Families who struggle are more likely to be rigid, less caring, and more authoritarian about interactions.

It is interesting that by observing the skills and rules families adopt to solve daily problems, we can begin to get some idea about deeper, strongly held ideologies to which they subscribe. These much less visible, abstract, and vague elements of family life are rarely measureable; however, the more visible first-order processes and strategies for completion are bread crumbs along the trail. We observe what we can and use those data to extrapolate about the secret inner life that is usually inaccessible.

Second-Order Family Processes

By contrast, *second-order processes* identify the deeper inner patterns and beliefs that are held by the collective family group. Second-order processes include the themes that bind the family together, the beliefs they share, and the patterns of daily living. For a more detailed look at the patterns and rules of daily life, see Chapter 9, which speaks directly to the notion of the patterns and rules of daily living. Pay particular attention in that chapter to the concept of rule sequences.

The rest of this chapter focuses more on abstract and fundamental elements of family construction, sometimes called second-order family processes. Second-order family processes center on how the family negotiates and subscribes to (or decides not to subscribe to) key themes, ideologies, and core beliefs. It is from these core themes and ideologies that much of what is family arises. Family paradigms inform much that is done in family life and we assume that the core beliefs held by family members direct behavior. For example, if parents believe that the development of a love for learning is a key aspect of family life, the daily behaviors chosen by those parents should, for the most part, reflect what they truly believe. If educational pursuits are at the core, they will find a way to allocate time, money, space, and personal energy to that end.

It is important to introduce the term *schema* at this point. *Schema* is a Greek word that means shape or plan. In the social sciences, the most prominent use of this term comes from the work of Piaget, a Swiss philosopher considered to be the father of developmental psychology. The plural form of schema is *schemata*. Schemata are the mental structures that represent one's understanding of how things are organized, shaped, and linked. Family members, especially as each one passes the age of 12 or so, build mental schemata about their personal world; part of that construction is very vague, deeply held, and core to their worldview. This core belief structure or schemata we label ideology.

These more abstract family ideological elements are very abstract, vague, and certainly influenced by other family members. However, when we are talking about this kind of deeply held, abstract, and vague schemata, we probably cannot identify a certain moment when those elements of our being were formed, who shaped them, and why we adopted them. Ideological schemata are not usually openly negotiated by family members; they are very general ideas basic to the way we think and believe.

Sometimes the deep ideological schemata found in family members represents general summaries that shadow the things a person believes about the world. For example, some family members might believe that the world is a hostile place to be feared, whereas others might believe that the world is a garden of opportunities to be experienced and embraced. Other core ideological schemata deal with values such as the nature of reality and how to cope with it. Some might believe the world is basically simple, black and white; others believe it is complex, complicated, and intricate. Some might believe they have control over their destiny and others think they have little control over what happens to them.

Abstract ideas are difficult to articulate and define clearly because they are, by their very nature, general and diffused rather than specific and concrete. Nevertheless they are an important part of family systems. People's abstract beliefs influence their major goals in life, the ways they try to attain their goals, and how they behave.

It is also important to note that families have a difficult time changing these deep beliefs. Sometimes in a severe crisis they might rethink whether or not there is a God, or really examine who they are, but most us rarely even think about these deeply held ideas that direct our lives.

To Summarize

It is helpful to think about three different levels of abstraction in family systems. First-order processes refer to specific and concrete ways of behaving and organizing family life. Second-order processes are highly abstract schemata residing within family individuals, probably shared, but rarely discussed. Some of the ideological schemata we hold come from the training and years of exposure to our families of origin. Other schemata come as the result of our own experience and others are formed deliberately as we make decisions about the meaning of life.

☐ Family Paradigms

This section speaks in greater depth about the nature and fabric of our deeply held beliefs and asks readers to reflect on the ideological orientation of their families of origin and families of procreation.

Paradigm

Only in recent years has the word *paradigm* been used widely. In his landmark book, *The Structure of Scientific Revolutions*, Kuhn (1969) wrote about the changing ways the science community approached what is science and how it is studied. He asserted that the science community could possess what he labeled a paradigm. In the 1969 edition of his top-selling book, he clarified what he meant by a paradigm: A paradigm was an entire constellation of beliefs, values, and techniques, and so on, shared by the members of a given community (Kuhn, 1969, p. 34). With the term *paradigm* we move beyond schemata. When taken together, the constellation of collected schemata about beliefs, values, and viewpoints, when shared by a community becomes a paradigm. The community of interest here is a family.

Like any community collection, family members can and do share schemata about beliefs, values, and viewpoints. Schemata, therefore, reside within the individual, whereas paradigms are properties of communities. You might have heard the term **paradigm shift**. If one is using the definition proffered by Kuhn and his scientific community, an individual cannot experience a paradigm shift, per se. A change in ideological orientation or a reevaluation of one's personal ideological schemata should, in proper terms, be labeled an ideological schemata shift. That sounds a bit awkward, but it makes two important points. First, individuals create and maintain ideological schemata about how the world is constructed. Those collected views can (and often do) change. However, changes in one family member's worldview are not the same as a community change. The second point, therefore, is that a community of individuals can share viewpoints, beliefs, and values. Those shared beliefs can (and sometimes do) change and when they change we call that a paradigm shift. We return to this discussion in Chapter 13 when we talk about coping with change and crises.

Family Paradigms

Noted family therapist and researcher David Reiss (1981) wrote a book called *The Family's Construction of Reality*. In this well-known scholarly book, he developed a concept that helps us understand how the ideological schemata of family members can be shared; he called the sharing of values, beliefs, and viewpoints *family paradigms*. By way of definition, a family paradigm (or deeply held family ideology) is the shared, enduring, fundamental, and general assumptions or beliefs to which family members subscribe about the nature and meaning of life, what is important, and how to cope with the world they live in (Reiss, 1981). He even demonstrated that family members constructed and shared ideological schemata in spite of disagreements, conflicts, and differences. Indeed, the core of an individual's membership in his or her own family is acceptance of, belief in, and creative elaboration of these abiding assumptions (Reiss, 1981, p. 1).

Awareness of Family Paradigms

Family paradigms are rarely explicit or conscious in families. Also, paradigms are the fountainhead from which the rest of family life seems to emanate. When we believe the world exists in a certain way, we organize the rest of our life's activities to reflect that notion. For example, if a family believes the world is a hostile place, they would have more strict boundaries, have tighter rules about daily events, and take more care about activities outside the safety of the home.

There are a few times when family paradigms are more likely to surface in family life and become known to family members. For example, they are much more likely to appear and be noticed during times of extreme crisis, including major transitions like divorce or remarriage. In times of crisis, the very existence of the family can be threatened and family members turn to their most basic shared beliefs to help them manage their way through the crisis. When these periods of crisis are resolved, the basic beliefs recede into the assumed foundation of daily life, and attention can again be given to everyday and routine challenges.

Visibility

Family paradigms are like an iceberg beneath the surface, hidden from the view of outsiders and, at least most of the time, from the families themselves. We see only a small fraction of the total; the rest of the ideological core is usually hidden from observers and even the family members have difficulty identifying their own paradigms. Constantine (1986) noticed this phenomenon and suggested that invisibility of family paradigms is so complete that usually families never become aware of them. He did note, however, that even though invisible, this deeply held ideological core is so pervasive and powerful that it becomes a template for the actions, decisions, and strategies families use to attain goals (Constantine, 1986, p. 16).

How Do Families Construct Paradigms?

We are just beginning to learn about how families construct, modify, and maintain their deeply held beliefs. The first element of a family paradigm are the individual ideological schemata. The schemata we bring with us into relationships have been under construction for many years. It is shaped by our family life experience, subsequent life experiences, images we incorporate from media, and from ideas we consciously adopt. As we initiate relationships with others, our core ideological schemata bump into theirs, so to speak. When we notice ideological differences, one of two processes (or a combination of two processes) occurs: assimilation or accommodation. These terms also come from the field of human development, especially within the area of cognitive development. Assimilation means that we adopt the difference and accommodation implies that we actually reorder our internal schema to make room for a new idea—a new addition to our existing "house of ideas."

Suppose a young man is talking with a young woman and they are mutually attracted. During their conversation the topic of sports comes up. She, it turns out, is an avid Boston Red Sox fan and would not miss a game. He, on the other hand, is a true blue, dyed-in-the-wool New York Yankees fan. Let's pick up this process from his point of view. His personal ideological schemata (values and beliefs) dictate to him that the Yankees are the most important baseball team to have ever played the game. As he listens to her rave about the Red Sox, we would want to know if he assimilates or accommodates during this exchange. Someone who assimilates, in his case, would have a place within his existing schemata structures for "weirdoes and kooks" who do not really understand baseball. Her rantings do not move him to change his worldview—instead, he takes what she is saying and tucks it away into the worldview he already has shaped.

On the other hand, someone who accommodates during these types of exchanges might listen carefully to her stories about the Red Sox and the path to glory during the 2004 World Series as they swept past the hapless Cardinals to take their place in baseball history. He pauses; he reflects. He builds a slightly different view and begins to realize that he has not taken this earth-shattering event seriously. Accommodation is about change in schemata, whereas assimilation is about finding room for an idea to reside within a schema that already exists. An earth-shattering event like this could, in fact, create an ideological schemata shift, in which case, he would realize the sports faux pas of his whole life and toss out his ill-conceived previous worldview about the New York Yankees.

In this facetious example, one can easily see how the individual schemata are shaped and changed as we go through life. As we enter into close relationships, the process is more serious. There is probably nothing more important in courtship and partner selection than finding out about the other's core ideological schemata and finding out if the ideological core of two individuals matches, can merge, and somehow combine into a solid family paradigm that is compatible for both individuals. A clear application of this information is that relationship formation is best achieved when one pays close attention to ideological differences but also (and maybe even more important) to how each partner deals with assimilating or accommodating to differences. If, for example, one partner is pushed to change and accommodate or even reject a deeply held belief, one would expect relationship trouble to emerge. However, one would expect greater success when there is a comfortable fit of important ideological values and worldviews. We would also expect future family systems to be more efficient when the key adults in those systems know how to negotiate ideological differences effectively.

Formative Period

To follow the preceding idea, when a couple comes together in a relationship, one of their relationship tasks is to decide, consciously or unconsciously, what their new family will be like. In most situations the two individuals grew up in a family that had been through its formative period and constructed its basic ideology or paradigms. As they grew up, the beliefs their parents held were assumed to be the "normal" way of viewing the world. If the individuals who are beginning to form a close relationship ignore this vital topic and superficially adapt for a temporary fix, we would expect to see relationship problems later on. Most couples go through a formation stage that can last for several months. During this time they talk with each other at great length. These discussions are usually exciting and filled with discovery. Somewhere along the way, a couple bonds and joins their thoughts. The two individuals discover what they share as common. They might also redefine who they are as they attempt to create something new.

This sense of richness and depth that is almost universally experienced probably is partly because each couple goes through a process of constructing their unique set of meaningful and basic assumptions about what the world "really is" like for them. This process is a combination of consciously and unconsciously selecting some aspects from the family each person grew up in and from other families that are respected, and developing some entirely new assumptions and beliefs (Steinglass et al., 1987, p. 308).

Family scientists believe that the first paradigms of a new family are borrowed and invented. As various aspects of the relationship are identified, talked about, tested, and revised, they come and go in consciousness. They remain conscious as long as there is uncertainty, ambiguity, and conflict, and when they are resolved they slip into the implicit, implied, unconscious part of the gradually growing family paradigm.

Changing Established Paradigms

Reiss devoted much of his research and a book to showing the ways family crises influence paradigmatic beliefs. He found that the strategies that families use to recover from crisis are found in the collective part of the family paradigm. That is, the individuals in a family share some idea about how best to solve the problems they encounter. They interact in certain ways that they believe will be effective in resolving their crisis. When the crisis is very severe, the family sometimes changes. They might even have to change the foundational, core ideologies they have to get through a crisis situation.

When family life is uncomplicated, there is little reason to even think about one's beliefs. Instead, the paradigms provide a sense of meaning and order, and they are used as the guiding beliefs in selecting goals, making decisions, and managing resources. However, in times of crisis, the typical pattern is for families to begin to question old ways of thinking and doing things and to construct new ways of defining the stressful situation and new strategies for trying to cope with the stress.

Apparently, the usual pattern is that the longer a family experiences difficulty in coping with a stressful situation, the more the parts of their ideology are called into question, eliminated, or revised, and new definitions and perceptions emerge. If the new constructs are effective in coping with the stress, the general and abstract parts of the new beliefs are assimilated into the family paradigm. We visit this discussion again in Chapter 13.

Unfortunately, there is also a "worst of times" aspect to these processes. Some families are rigidly attached to some of the ideas they hold and they do not have the flexibility, creativity, or other resources to change. This inability to change can keep a family in a state of chronic difficulty until they can get outside help.

☐ The Role of Family Paradigms

Family paradigms play a key role in the managing processes. You will remember from earlier chapters that families have goals. Simply put, the ideology a family creates either helps or detracts from their ability to attain the goals. This idea is reflected in the Principle 8.1.

PRINCIPLE 8.1   FAMILY IDEOLOGY

Deeply held family ideologies have the power to either assist or detract from a family's ability to attain the goals they seek.

Several analogies illustrate the role of family paradigms. A family paradigm is like the north star in a family's attempts to navigate a complicated world. Another way to describe the power of a paradigm is to imagine it as the family's constitution that is used to govern itself. Reiss (1981) described this role by saying that family paradigms are the "central organizer" that does the "shaping," "fashioning," and "guiding" of what families do when they regulate, order, and transact with their environment.

☐ Types of Family Paradigms

The concept of family paradigms is so new that scholars have not conducted much research about them. One of the reasons is that they are very hard to measure and discover. A few scholars, however, have begun this process, and their ideas are helpful. For example, Kantor and Lehr (1975) and Constantine (1986) described four kinds of family paradigms that seem to appear repeatedly when counselors and therapists work with families. They labeled these four paradigms closed, open, random, and synchronous families.

Closed Families

A *closed family paradigm* is when a family has a cluster of fundamental beliefs that emphasize continuity, steadiness, and conventional ways of doing things. They believe that security and belonging are very important. They prefer stability whenever possible and are concerned about deviations from what they believe are the "right" ways to do things. The motto in closed families could be described as "stability through tradition and loyalty" (Constantine, 1986, p. 20).

FIGURE 8.1   The closed family: Some families organize boundaries in such a way that the family seems like it is a castle—surrounded by a moat, with doors and windows that do not allow much to come or go.

When families have a closed paradigm it leads them to adopt well-defined goals with clear boundaries. For example, when a family adopts a closed ideology, the parents are more likely to be concerned about their children's friends, and there are many more locked doors, careful scrutiny of strangers in the neighborhood, parental control over the media, and supervised excursions (Kantor & Lehr, 1975, p. 121).

Families with this paradigm tend to organize their time so it is predictable and stable. They pay attention to the past and to the future, frequently seeking to preserve or restore something that was, or attain or achieve something that has not been accomplished. They tend to have a well-understood pattern in using time, and the individuals tend to fit their schedules to the family pattern.

The method of making decisions in closed families tends to be relatively authoritarian. Tradition or aspirations are important, and what the parents think is important. These two qualities tend to create a more authoritarian power system and method of government than exists in open and random families.

Open Families

When families have an *open family paradigm* they believe in a style of life that emphasizes dialogue, communication, patience, and a willingness to change. These families believe in adaptability and innovation and they are looking for new ways to do things. They believe in negotiation and collaboration as the fundamental ways to live and cope.

Space in open families is more movable and flexible than in closed families, and the individuals have more freedom in what they can do. They are allowed to self-regulate and they are more free to choose their own destinations as long as they do not interfere with the rights and space of others. Frequent guests, unlocked doors, and lower levels of monitoring typify these families. The parents are much less likely to be intrusively involved in keeping track of family members' movement.

The method of governance that is more consistent with this style of life is less authoritarian than the closed type. Therefore, there is usually more discussion, sharing of ideas, democracy, and flexibility. The approach tends to be to try to find consensus rather than to try to find what is "right" or proper.

FIGURE 8.2 The open family organizes itself around the notion that people, ideas, and information can come and go pretty freely.

Random Families

When families have a *random family paradigm* their core ideology emphasizes discontinuity and they maximize change in a radical focus on the present. In the random paradigm, the guiding images are novelty, creativity, and individuality. The motto of a random paradigm family might be "variety through innovation and individuality" (Constantine, 1986, p. 20). Random families are flexible with regard to traditions and established ways of doing things, but they tend to be fairly rigid in emphasizing individuality, little restraint, and high levels of freedom.

FIGURE 8.3 The random family is organized around the idea that routines, boundaries, and expectations are ever changing and malleable.

These abstract beliefs are used to manage family resources in ways that are quite different from closed and open families. The use of space has some predictability, but less so than with closed or open families. For example, eating and sleeping can occur in many places. Expressions of anger, affection, and joy might occur in the street as well as behind the closed doors of the home.

The method of making decisions and governing tends to emphasize individuality. The family interests are considered, but what is important to the family is that the individuals are free to fulfill their needs and goals. Therefore, the individuals are quite free to "do their own thing," make their connections, set their goals, and arrange their schedules.

Time is irregular, and can be used and viewed very differently at different times and by different individuals or groups in the family. The preference is for evolving and spontaneous patterns that emerge from and out of what happens rather than because it is part of a plan or structure.

Patterns of getting energy are fluctuating and changing. Family members might engage in fueling operations singly or in groups, and they have great freedom to seek the type of fueling they want. Foods tend to be prepared more individually. Music and entertainment is more spontaneous and varied.

Synchronous Families

The *synchronous family paradigm* emphasizes harmony, tranquility, and mutual identification. When families have this paradigm they believe they will be able to move through life with little conflict and they will be able to easily resolve the conflict that does occur. These families depend on family members thinking alike, not to control, but to avoid conflict. Many of these family decisions will be based on *consentience* (the root word here is consent and the word means a nonintellectual sense of unity) and they will try to function with consentaneity and try to act in harmonious agreement. Some have commented that families who adopt this ideology have a distinctly utopian, mystical, or magical flavor to their family climate. The motto of synchrony might be "harmony through perfection and identification" (Constantine, 1986, pp. 20–21).

Other Paradigms

The four paradigms already discussed are only the beginning of the many deeply held beliefs that families can have. For example, in the many years I have taught the course associated with this text, I have heard hundreds of hours of discussion by students about the themes, beliefs, and deeply held paradigms their families hold. Some of these include such ideas as "education is to be revered above all"; "our family will succeed in business"; "we will do everything we can to assure that our children make it to heaven"; and "our family members will prove themselves at sports at all costs."

The last one mentioned is particularly interesting. Not long ago in a class using this text, a young woman took about 10 minutes of class time explaining how her family was a water-skiing family. At first, I did not believe that what she was saying was really an explanation of how paradigms work in families. But, after a few minutes I began to see her point.

From an early age, her father had decided that she was going to be a world-class water skier. She explained the deep core ideology was about success and winning. She went on to say that attached to that winning notion was a very closed family ideal. She was not allowed to have friends unless the friends were willing to help with the water-skiing work-outs. The only magazines found in the house were about fitness and water-skiing-related topics. Schoolwork was even scheduled around practices. Meals in the home were designed for fitness and energy and every part of her life was regulated around ski meets, winning certain events, and progressing to the championship.

Additionally, the family finances were organized around this one idea (ideology, ideal, and paradigm). The family lived in Seattle and they purchased a home next to a lake that included a dock so that travel time for practice would be minimized. The mother took an extra job to make payments on a very expensive state-of-the-art ski boat. The family vehicle had to be one that could pull the boat and take the family on weekly ski trips.

Although this is an extreme example of a family paradigm, it does illustrate how the principle works. Imagine for a minute if the girl was diagnosed with cancer and could no longer water ski. Or—and this was part of the story—imagine if one day she said, "That's enough" and refused to ski. The **exaggeration principle** (presented next) would suggest that instead of finding a new deep purpose or ideology, they would, instead turn up the volume of the old one and try to make it work. That is exactly what they did; there was a younger sister that became the next family skier. The young woman related how her family thought of her as a traitor and she was barely allowed to visit her home. The story was obviously a painful and traumatic one for her. Until she read the material for class, she really had not realized what had happened. What would you do to comfort her?

☐ The Exaggeration Principle

When confronted by problems, families do the best they can to solve the issues at hand. Again, they maximize their resources and try the best strategy they know to survive and attain the goals they have at their core. One strategy that most families try when something goes wrong is to try harder. "Trying harder" is itself defined paradigmatically: Families try harder by doing more of the same. Instead of changing strategies or changing their ideology, they turn up the volume of the strategy they already use. Thus, by using the available resources, each family under stress has a natural tendency toward exaggeration of its own special character.

PRINCIPLE 8.2   EXAGGERATION UNDER STRESS

When families are under stress there is a tendency to exaggerate the family ideologies (paradigms). In other words, under stress families usually do not change strategies or ideologies; they exaggerate the one they are most used to.

A family paradigm represents a commitment to certain priorities that direct family action in one direction or another as they seek to overcome difficulties. A family's methods of managing its resources consist of essentially stable structures maintaining coordinated family processes. The regime is resilient and not likely to change fundamentally in response to stress, especially as it is guided by the family's paradigm.

The stability of a paradigm can be appreciated if it is remembered that a family paradigm is the family's way of perceiving the world, including their problems, as well as their way of approaching and solving problems. Thus, the most likely response to any challenge from within or without is for a family to respond in a manner consistent with its paradigm and organization. The more difficult and intractable the situation, the more extreme are the measures that will be taken; extreme, that is, in a way consistent with the family paradigm. The longer an impasse is sustained, the greater the degree of typical exaggeration.

The closed family confronted by problems relies on tradition, authority, and loyalty to solve them. The more difficult the problem proves to be, the stronger are the attempts to control, to pull the family into line, and to maintain consistency against a threatening world. Thus closed families tend to become more isolated from the world, more strongly and intensely connected internally, and more rigid as they become increasingly disabled. The rallying cry is essentially "Fall in! Toe the line!"

The random family relies on spontaneity and creative individuality to find solutions to problems. As members work with increasing independence to find more creative solutions, family process becomes more chaotic and less coordinated. The random family tends toward greater separateness and chaos as it becomes more disabled. In the random family, the appeal is "Be more creative. Find something new" (which, it must be noted, does not imply a change of basic tactics; finding something new is what the random family does normally).

When initial attempts fail, the open family hangs in there, trying to hammer out a consensual solution. They gather more and more information and try harder to communicate. They become inundated with information and overwhelmed by hashing things through. As they question more and more of their basic rules, less and less is clearly known. They go around in circles. If problems remain they become more and more enmeshed in a process that generates chaos. Their rallying cry is "We've got to work this out. We'll talk it through again and consider it more thoroughly!"

The synchronous family relies on its essential agreement to enable it to solve problems in a coordinated way while acting independently. When this consentaneity breaks down, the family moves toward greater separateness. To remain coordinated and true to its paradigm, it narrows its scope and restricts its actions to those on which there is the closest agreement. Thus it becomes more rigid and stereotyped in its behavior while also becoming less connected. As synchronous families are based on similarity and do not deal as well with difference, which would contradict their synchrony, it becomes increasingly necessary to deny differences and problems, hiding these under a veneer of agreement and competence. As it becomes disabled, the synchronous family attempts to continue "business as usual" and insists, "There is no real problem. As always, we are really in agreement about this." Less and less happens as they become increasingly "dead" as a family or increasingly disconnected from their real problems (Constantine, 1986, pp. 182–183).

According to Constantine's ideas, most of the time when families become disabled it is not the family paradigms that are the root of the problem. The family paradigms are the abstract beliefs, and most families have defensible, coherent, and healthy basic assumptions. It is the less abstract processes that occur at the first two levels that become disabled. In other words, it tends to be the management that becomes disabled rather than the ideology that guides the system. It is the family's strategies for clarifying goals, making effective decisions, and managing resources that become dysfunctional.

When families find themselves in deep trouble, they tend to seek help. Closed families are more cautious about whom they turn to and how they do it, but closed, open, and random families all seek help in their own ways. They turn to books, friends, relatives, educators, therapists, ministers, Ann Landers, psychiatrists, social workers, and so on.

The strategy for using the exaggeration under stress principle to help families is to help them learn how to "borrow" management strategies from another type. It is usually easier for a closed family to use open strategies than random strategies. It is usually easier for random families to use open strategies than closed strategies.

☐ Summary

This chapter focused on what Reiss called family paradigms. Family ideologies or paradigms are the fundamental, general, abstract, and guiding beliefs families construct about their world. It was suggested that an individual develops a private schema about how the world is organized, but that families have a collective, communal notion about how it should operate. This familial view is called a family paradigm. Further, it was suggested that families can have an open, closed, random, or synchronous family paradigm. They can also have identified themes that drive family behavior and choices. Having this concept helps us better understand how family systems work and how we can help families regardless of the stage of life cycle.

A key idea in this chapter was that some parts of family paradigms are more abstract, central, and fundamental than other parts of paradigms. This idea helps us realize there is great flexibility in the way families can organize themselves and be successful. It is not usually helpful to think that families need to conform to one particular mold or style of life if they are to be successful. There are plenty of examples of successful families who are close, open, cautious, frugal, religious, adventurous, or whatever the overall core belief is. A real problem occurs if an ideology becomes too extreme in any of the many directions it could take.

This chapter also explored the idea that problems also arise when families get stuck in ways of doing things that are too narrow and restricted, because their way of behaving can interfere with their ability to cope with new developmental, cultural, or technological changes. This can happen when family members are assigned roles that fit some predetermined ideal and there is a belief that to change how activities are done would be to damage the family.

Sometimes when we try to help families we wish they would change easily and quickly. We naively want our therapy, advice, or educational programs to make big differences in families. However, when we realize how earlier generations are involved in family paradigms, how slowly and gradually they are initially formed in courtship and early marriage, how they are intricately tied up with deeply experienced affective states, and how they are probably changed only by severe crises, it helps us realize that these basic assumptions are not fleeting and flexible ideas that can change easily. They are the most fundamental rudders in the ship of life, and once they are formed they only change slowly and only when there are very unusual circumstances.

Once we understand the nature of family paradigms and the role they have in family life, we can better understand what families are going through when they are experiencing enough stress that they are changing their paradigms. Also, we can adapt our attempts to help them so we focus on the parts of their systems that can change.

☐ Study Questions

1. Name all four types of family paradigms, give the definition of each, and provide an example of what each of those family styles would be like.
2. What is meant by the idea of subscription rate in regard to family ideology?
3. What is the continuum of abstraction? Provide your own example that helps explain this idea.
4. Explain why most of us never really think about family paradigms.

5. Provide four clear examples of how you could apply the principles in this chapter to make family life stronger.
6. Is an ideology different than a paradigm? Explain.
7. Why do you suppose that families exaggerate the core family ideology when they are under stress?

☐ Key Terms

Paradigms
Levels of abstraction
Exaggeration principle
Ideology
Continuum of abstraction
Paradigm shift

☐ Suggested Readings

Boszormenyi-Nagy, I., & Spark, G. (1973). *Invisible loyalties.* Levittown, PA: Harper & Row.
Hess, R. D., & Handel, G. (1959). *Family worlds.* Chicago: University of Chicago Press.
Kantor, D., & Lehr, W. (1975). *Inside the family.* San Francisco: Jossey-Bass.
Reiss, D. (1981). *The family's construction of reality.* Cambridge, MA: Harvard University Press.

CHAPTER

Rules and Rule Sequences

☐ Chapter Preview

In this chapter, readers will learn:

- The difference between mores and folkways.
- That social norms and family rules are similar terms but have slightly different meanings.
- How rules emerge and take shape in family life.
- That rules and rule systems are a part of the paradigmatic orientation found in families.
- That rules have distinct purposes including helping with family member accountability, boundary maintenance, distance regulation, and resource allocation.
- The difference between explicit and implicit rules in families.
- The power of rule sequences and how those sequences can create family growth or family dysfunction.
- How to manage rule sequence effectively.

☐ Introduction

Most families have thousands of formal and informal **rules** that regulate and direct family life. For example, think of the mail each family receives every day. We might take notes about who goes to the mailbox and retrieves the mail. Where is it placed? Is it sorted and delivered to each person's room? Can anyone in your family open the "junk" mail? Can parents open the children's mail? Are there certain types of letters that do not have to be shared at all? Most of the rules that govern these processes emerge without any fanfare or even much negotiation, but they have the power to direct and dictate much of what we do. They might direct where one sits at dinner, what is watched on television, and when homework is done (if at all). The family rule system can also specify which towels to use in the bathroom, where to store holiday decorations, and who should replace the empty toilet paper roll.

In the following discussion, we explore where the idea of rules comes from, how they influence family life, and how rules can change. For example, sometimes we think of family rules as **social norms**. Some of these rules come from accepted ways of doing things that we adopt from our culture, some are created as family life emerges, and some are developed in response to specific events in everyday life as we raise children and become involved in other complicated family activities. Other times family rules are created in ways that do not represent standard social norms. In this chapter, you explore how rules are formed, what their purposes are, and learn the difference between **implicit** and **explicit rules**. In the second part of the chapter, the concept of rule sequences is explored. These rules are much more abstract than the daily rule structures about the ordinary events of life. Instead, **rule sequences** are about the patterns of interactive behavior that seem much like a play: She says "X"; then dad says "Y"; then Billy says "Y-not"; then she says "X"—and the pattern begins again. A key element of this part of the chapter is about how to identify and manage rule sequences.

☐ Rules as Social Norms

Over the past 100 years, sociologists have been helpful in showing how social norms are created and how they influence people. Social norms are beliefs that exist in a culture that prescribe certain behaviors and proscribe others. Thus, they deal with "shoulds" and "shouldn'ts" that get communicated to us by the groups of people we are around each day.

Social norms can apply to minor acts, like what utensil one uses at the dinner table, or to more major occurrences, like who should be chosen as a sexual partner. Sociologists have developed several concepts that help us tell the difference between norms that deal with serious matters (those rules that become formalized over time are called laws) and those that deal with less serious behavior. They refer to norms dealing with behaviors considered especially important as **mores**, and behaviors that are preferred but more or less optional are called **folkways**.

PRINCIPLE 9.1   FOLKWAYS AND MORES

Folkways and mores are different. Mores (usually pronounced "morays") focus on the ideal, whereas folkways focus on the behaviors that emanate from mores.

For example, in the state in which I live, there are many fathers who feel a strong pressure to take their children fishing and hunting. It is part of the news, frequently mentioned in conversation, and one often sees boats and fishing gear in people's yards. This is a folkway, or, in other words, it is a way "folks do things here."

Mores are customs or conventions that are essential to the maintenance of community life. They are a bit stronger than a folkway. An example of a mores can be found in the choice and timing of dating behavior. From folkways and mores we learn who we are and how we fit into society. Folkways and laws have a powerful influence with regard to how we manage family business. In contrast, there are also explicit laws that govern what we do. Laws tell us it is not acceptable to discipline children with abusive strategies. On the other hand, mores dictate an ideal about parent–child behavior within a culture. Folkways are more specific behavioral expectations that might pressure us to dress our children in certain ways and speak to our spouses in particular ways, for example. Imagine the law:

Don't kill your children or you will be arrested; think now of the mores in the Amish culture about dress and behavior that exemplify modesty and avoiding the appearance of being connected to worldly pressure; and think of the folkway that specifies the wearing of a certain kind of dark dress and bonnet.

Children in their parental family learn many social norms that deal with the family realm, and the family of origin of a newly married couple has an enormous impact on what they adopt as the normative elements of their family life.

Additionally, family behavior can be greatly influenced by where the parents work, their religious orientation, and even the neighborhood in which they live. Every affiliation, and to some degree every past affiliation of a family member has an influence on the norms that a family consciously and explicitly accepts as well as the tacit or "hidden" understandings, the "taken-for-granted" definitions that often are brought to light only when violated.

Because social norms are an important part of family processes, it is important to consider how families teach, adopt, and change the norms they use. Additionally, understanding the nature of social norms helps us understand some of the sources of stress in families. For example, teenagers might learn something new from their peers and try to introduce that idea into their own family.

There is one distinct property that clearly identifies the nature of a social norm or rule: They are simple. In other words, normative social rules are not complex. They do not describe behavior sequences, nor do they necessarily rely on other rules as a requirement for their existence.

☐ How Rules Emerge in Families

There are many ways rules find their way into family systems. Some are copied from the family of origin and are brought into the new relationship by either the husband or the wife. From the time of birth we assimilate and learn the rules we need to follow to live successfully within our families. In Chapter 8, we discussed the idea of inner schemata that form together to define and circumscribe one's world. In addition to the values, beliefs, and ideals that were discussed in Chapter 8, one also collects and builds schemata about managing and surviving daily family life (and nonfamily life as well). As we gain experience in family life, we slowly acquire, moderate, build, tweak, and shape a family rule schemata (for our own point of view). This collection of rules first resides in the mind of the couple when forming a relationship. They bring with them ideas and history about who should do the dishes, make beds, discipline children, clean the windows, and paint and repair the broken door.

Sometimes the old, well-used family rules follow us into our new relationships. These old schemata reside within us, planted there by years of watching the adults in our life as we grew up. It is inevitable that when a partnership is forming and two people are merging their worlds, that there will be some disconnect about how the two competing rule schemata (one from each partner) should come together, a clash can occur. One of the purposes of courtship is to begin the process of rule discovery, negotiation, and creation. It is during this time that partners begin to adopt some rules from one person's family of origin, some from another, and discover they have some rules in common. This process of assimilation and accommodation (see Chapter 8) is critical. As we saw in Chapter 5, power imbalance is a key to understanding strength and efficiency in family life. If, during the formation of the relationship, one partner dominates and only assimilates—expecting

FIGURE 9.1 Newly formed families construct family life and it emerges as a new creation day by day. The rules, routines, and rituals they build create the "frame" of the home they construct.

the other partner to accommodate, change, and adapt—trouble will probably not be far behind. Each of us, by definition, comes with elaborate family rule schemata in place about how "things" should be done. When we enter a new relationship and assume our rule collection is the "right and true" way of doing things, we will tend only to expect minor assimilation for ourselves. But, we probably expect the other person to see the light and to change, accommodate, get on board, and adopt the better way of doing things from our point of view.

We not only acquire rules schemata from the culture in which we live; we can also adopt by choice or simply accommodate beliefs and rules from external influences. For example, movies and television are sources of influence from which we might adopt bits and pieces of how to act in family life. This is a risky strategy because typically family life in such venues can be represented in ways that are unrealistic, oversimplified, and even inaccurately portrayed.

PRINCIPLE 9.2   RULES CAN COME FROM MANY SOURCES

We learn rules and rule patterns from our culture, family, friends, and media. Sometimes the rules we learn in one place conflict with expectations or rules we learn in another place.

A good example of this is the often-used portrayal of family life in shows that emerged during the 1950s and 1960s. Programs like *Leave It to Beaver* and *The Donna Reed Show* portrayed family life in ways that represented ideals rather than anyone's reality. People watched these programs and thought of their own lives as deficient because they were not living up to a fantasy portrayal of what someone thought family life "should" be like.

Another excellent example of this type of inaccurate portrayal can be found in *The Cosby Show* of the late 1980s and 1990s. Although it was certainly an amusing program, I would often find myself saying, "How can he solve all of these problems in a half-hour show?" or, "How is it his children have only superficial problems?" In that particular program, it was also inaccurate to portray this family, with a beautiful house and low stress, when the father was a pediatrician and the mother an attorney. Parents were rarely seen struggling with work or competing family and work roles. Of course problems arise when a young couple believes that *The Cosby Show* family in fantasy is how their life should be emerging in the harsh flurry of daily reality.

Third, family members adopt rules of daily life by negotiation. This process can include discussion about such mundane issues as who sleeps on which side of the bed, who sits where at the table, who puts their clothes in what closet, and whether to squeeze the toothpaste in the middle or at the end of the tube. Negotiation also is used for rules about deeper issues like who controls the money, the distribution of other resources, and the division of labor.

Multiple Interactions

Many rules also appear through a series of multiple interactions (Galvin & Brommel, 1991; Haley, 1963). Through the processes of trial, struggle, error, conflict, and resolution, family members adopt what seems to work for them. By "work for them," I mean the processes that families find helpful in keeping the system in balance, free from chaos, and working in harmony. Eventually, they learn, adapt, assimilate, and accommodate. Not everything chosen is best for all members. Those within the system believe what they are doing is necessary to keep the system in working order. The process begins with the couple meeting for the first time, and continues on as a developmental process. They cannot avoid the process as it occurs with or without their approval or knowledge. Every transaction results in the creation, modification, or support of rules.

If your family was like most, you had a plethora of informal "rules" about each of these areas. In fact most families construct hundreds of rules about how to manage their daily lives. Most of these rules emerge without fanfare or proclamation, and they have a curious power to direct and dictate how we act toward one another, how we come and go, and what we say or do not say. Additionally, they become the "bag" of internalized mental schemata representing a personal worldview about how family should be done.

☐ Family Rules Paradigm

In Chapter 8, it was noted that the term *paradigm* invokes the idea of a collected worldview held by a community or specified group of individuals. This, as you will remember, implies a subscription rate. That is, a paradigm only exists when the group members buy into or share certain ideals, beliefs, and views. A part of the family paradigm extends beyond the shared view about values and beliefs (as discussed in Chapter 8). It also includes the negotiated, collected, and shared view family members have about rules. Of course, a mother could have in her head that it is terrible for other family members to be unkind to one another. But that personal ideological schema does not transcend into a family paradigm unless it is a rule that is adopted and shared by the group. Unfortunately, this is one of those areas of research in family life about which we have little knowledge. The research agenda for this topic would need to include a careful cataloging of shared and nonshared family rules. One would expect that some families experience high levels of consensus about rules, rule implementation, and what to do when rules are violated. We would expect that a key to creating an effective family would be the ability to adapt rule structures as group membership matures and changes; the creation and careful maintenance of clear and equitable rules; and, the ability to discard rules that are simply historical and have little real utility.

☐ Rule Purposes

Accountability

Rules hold system members accountable for actions within and outside of the system (Cronen, Pearce, & Harris, 1979). In Chapter 8, we learned that families have expectations and usually create a family paradigm that speaks to group values, desired outcomes, preferred activities, and common goals. From a family paradigm, simple family rules become a mechanism and useful tool for performing in ways that meet those generalized expectations.

Boundaries

Family rules also help family members know the boundaries (see Chapter 3) that exist between a family and its environment. Each family exists in a complex network of other family systems and external systems, and it has to maintain a certain amount of uniqueness and distance from the others or its own existence fades. Therefore, norms are developed to define the boundaries that represent the interface between each family and its environmental systems. Boundary rules dictate how permeable the family and subsystem boundaries can be and specify limitations of individual family member freedom to roam beyond the immediate limits of the system.

For example, if the adults in a family are having a serious conversation and the bedroom door is closed, rules about boundaries specify to other family members about when (if at all) they can interrupt that conversation. When the group is in a public setting, boundary rules can also specify the limits of conversation and disclosure. For example, the rules might specify that it is inappropriate to speak of a forthcoming pregnancy. Boundary rules also can spill over into rules about visitors. Our family rule schemata usually dictate the limits of knowing when (or if) it is appropriate to bring outsiders home.

These types of rules maintain system boundaries. Families are more effective when the group members know the rules and are willing to abide by them. Without implicit knowledge of boundary rules it is very difficult for the family system to be a system at all.

It is important, however, to note that when family rules begin to be questioned and challenged, often it is the rules about boundaries that are being questioned. A healthy family system has effectively created functional and healthy rule systems that tell family members where the system begins and ends, where they can and cannot go, and what they can and cannot do. This is assuming, of course, that the system has created a flexible and nondestructive rule system.

Distance Regulation

One specific purpose of simple rules is that they regulate distance or the amount of closeness (see Chapter 11 for a discussion of this idea). Maintaining appropriate **distance regulation** means that the group has learned how to manage a pattern of separateness and connectedness (Day et al., 2001; Gavazzi, Anderson, & Sabatelli, 1993; Hess & Handel, 1959; Kantor & Lehr, 1975; Minuchin, 1996; Olson & McCubbin, 1982). Family rules tell us how and when we should be close and when we should be separate. Rules also help us to know how to disengage when there is too much closeness.

Resource Allocation

Another purpose of rules is to regulate how families allocate and exchange resources. These rules govern how scarce resources should be divided up within the system. This includes how family money should be spent, rules about living space, and rules about intangibles like time and affection. For example, if there is extra cash, a father might have first choice about whether he will spend it on a new tractor part or a mother might have first choice about whether she will invest it.

Rules of Responsibility

Rules of designated authority are rules about division of responsibility. Mother might be in charge of anyone who feels blue. An older grandparent living with the family might be in charge of relieving tension when the pressure of an argument gets too intense. A father might be charged with the responsibility of the first reaction in times of emergency. At times of divorce or death, rule and role reallocation might occur to fill the void created by the absent family member.

Implementation

Many of the rules we have in private life have to do with implementation. Rules of implementation exist for the purpose of implementing other rules and expectations. A family might have a series of rules about a topic (how much schoolwork), but they also have a series of rules that designate how they go about getting the work done. For example, suppose one's family paradigm centers on achieving educational excellence. The rules that become part of that family paradigm would probably include rules about grade performance, studying, and allocating group resources to make that happen. That particular family would, no doubt, develop a series of implicit and explicit rules that direct the system to assist children in fulfilling the established goal.

Exceptions

Families can also have rules about exceptions. The exceptions allow the system to deal with the unexpected and regulate necessary behavior even when an important family rule cannot be followed. In the schoolwork example, an exception might go like this: "Jill is very athletic and we believe personal talents should be enhanced. But we also believe everyone needs to get better grades." In Jill's case, both of these things are not going to happen, so the rule exception in these types of cases emerges as: "We will let her choose where she will put the emphasis of her time."

Violation

Another category of family rules is rules about violation. What happens in a family when a member gets bad grades and has violated the rule about good grades and achievement? What happens when someone does talk about death or negative ideas when the family has proscribed that kind of interaction? These actions will trigger another type of rule that specifies what is to be done following violation.

☐ Explicit and Implicit Rules

Some of the rules in families are explicit and some are implicit (Satir, 1972). Explicit rules are the beliefs that are recognized, acknowledged, and known by a family, and often they can be overtly talked about (Larson, Parks, Harper, & Heath 2001). Explicit rules are usually more formalized because they are made visible. An example of an explicit family rule is one that is made by decree: "All children who go on dates have to be home by 12:30 p.m.," or "Before a visit to your father, you must have your room clean." Such rules are a little different than daily requests that require a specific and perhaps a one-time response. They take on the form of regulating behavior over time, as a generalized guideline, meant to be in force "forever" or "until altered."

Another example of an explicit rule is, "Your grandmother and I have decided that all children should get some type of allowance, on a weekly basis." This type of rule has the necessary components. First, it implies that two or more people have discussed the need openly. Second, it has a long-term element to it, prescribing an action over time. Third, it is meant to regulate the flow of resources within the system or perform some other function. Also, it helps to maintain order and prevent debilitating chaos.

The members of a family do not recognize some rules and these we call the implicit rules. Implicit rules remain hidden and submerged from view. They are not discussed, and they have not been thought of or labeled by family members. This invisibility makes them very powerful. As invisible simple rules, they take on the status of something never questioned, or even considered as changeable. They are the way "things are."

An example of an implicit rule can be found in the way family members greet each other after a long absence. Do they hug, do they shake hands, or do they just smile? In this example, the norm reflects what the family has decided is appropriate about distance regulation: how close and affectionate family members should be.

Many families have implicit rules against sharing special feelings. They might go to great lengths to "help" family members learn ways to express or suppress how they feel. Suppose a family has an implicit rule that only good topics and feelings should be discussed. The belief might be that to talk about negative parts of life is a destructive process. The negative feelings and experiences could go unexpressed. The negative feelings remain unspoken, but probably not unfelt. It could be very dangerous for a family to create a system in which significant and important feelings cannot be discussed.

☐ Rule Sequences in Family Life

In the 1950s a group of family scientists led by Jackson and Bateson discovered that family systems have rules that are different from the rules families get from society or invent themselves (Jackson, 1957, 1965). These rules are patterns of behavior in family systems that are repeated so regularly that they are a governing or regulating part of the structure of the family systems.

The family scientists who discovered these rules found that usually the rules "tend to be implicit and they are rarely, if ever, explicit or written down" (Ford, 1983, p. 135).

Therefore, the only way to identify the family rules is to infer them from the repeated or redundant patterns in the behavior in a family (Larson et al., 2001). Clinicians have long recognized the value of understanding the deeply held rule patterns within families (Constantine, 1986; Ford, 1983; Satir, 1972). They would make the claim that one, especially a clinician, cannot begin to intervene or even really understand a family until one understands the rule patterns that lie beneath the surface. According to this line of research, the rule patterns regulate and govern family interaction (Larson et al., 2001). Further, they would claim that these rule systems either promote growth and strength in family life or they perpetuate dysfunction and instability. These rule sequences can empower families to attain goals and create patterns of efficiency. On the dark side, rule patterns can create communication problems, cause low self-esteem, internalize shame and guilt, and even disrupt intimacy in young adults (Ford, 1983).

An example of an implicit rule sequence is found in the writing of Jackson and Yalom (1965). They presented a real family case within which the family had a pattern that the only time the parents were able to act together was when they teamed up against a rebellious child. The parents rarely went out together and they maintained a pattern of discord most of the time. The father was not generally in charge of the family, but he gained control with occasional violent outbursts. These researchers claimed that in this family system, we could infer that "it seems as if" the family has some rules that discord must be maintained at all costs, the parents shall not cooperate unless it is to gang up on the child, and the father shall gain power only by violent outbursts (Jackson & Yalom, 1965).

Another interesting example of a family rule sequence is found in a book by Caine, *The Personal Crisis of a Widow in America* (1974). Her husband is dying of cancer and as the story unfolds he is dealing with the devastating feelings of knowing his life is about to end. Caine describes how this crisis debilitated their relationship. A source of major stress in her situation was a hidden rule sequence that the subject of the husband's death could not be overtly talked about. The sequence developed slowly and informally. In this story, you do not see anyone declaring a rule prohibiting talking about death. Instead, the power of this story is about how skillful the family members become at learning and reinforcing the rule sequence designed to avoid the topic of death. If the topic of dying starts to arise, someone steps in and offers a diversion or finds a way to take the conversation somewhere else. In a very poignant and depressing part of this story, the author shares her deep and troubled feelings following the death of her husband. She reports how much she wished she would have changed the rule sequence (our term here) and talked to him about the end of his life and the hundreds of issues that needed to be resolved. However, the rule sequence had prevailed at the cost of never discussing what was uppermost on their minds.

Rules sequences like these regulate what can and cannot be talked about. The point of this story is that sometimes the rule sequence can prevent us from being as effective in family life as we would wish.

Haley (1976) was another researcher and therapist who helped develop the idea of rule sequences. He indicated that a rule sequence occurs when there is a connected series of rules that govern a complex pattern in the behavior of several individuals in a family system. He further suggested that these sequences tend to have a cyclic pattern to them. When they deal with negative or disabling patterns we often refer to them as *vicious cycles*.

Here is an example of the kind of rule sequence he spoke of:

1. When one parent has a bad day at the office, he or she comes home and is critical of the other parent.
2. The second parent takes the anger out on a child.
3. The child picks a fight with another sibling or kicks the dog.

On the other hand, many rule sequences in families are healthy and enabling. For example, a family might have a pattern of the parents getting up a few minutes earlier than they would need to so they can visit for a minute with their child and express affection before beginning the daily routines. When the parents conform to this rule it can tend to begin a cycle of other rule-bound behaviors in the family such as the children and adults being more pleasant, listening to each other, doing favors for each other, and so on. When the parents do not follow this pattern (family rule), a different cycle can usually be precipitated in the family, such as the children and adults being less patient, more irritable, more short-tempered, or more critical as they begin the day.

Most families have many healthy rule-bound sequences covering such activities as time management, allocation of scarce family resources (i.e., space, money, affection), interaction with those outside of the kin system, and every aspect of general family functioning.

Some rule sequences are disabling and destructive. For example, the following story illustrates an oversimplified situation where there is a father, mother, and child, and each of them is either competent or incompetent. Because these sequences tend to be cyclic, there is a series of steps that lead to the next and they eventually lead back to the beginning again. We could start the description at any point in the cycle.

Step 1. *Father—ineffective.* The father behaves in an upset or depressed way, not functioning to his capacity.

Step 2. *Child—misbehaving.* The child begins to get out of control or express symptoms.

Step 3. *Mother—ineffective.* The mother ineffectually tries to deal with the child and cannot, and the father becomes involved.

Step 4. *Father—competent.* The father deals with the child effectively and recovers from his state of incompetency.

Step 5. *Child-behaving.* The child regains his composure and behaves properly or is defined as normal.

Step 6. *Mother—competent.* The mother becomes more capable and deals with the child and father in a more competent way, expecting more from them.

Step 7. *Father—ineffective.* The father behaves in an upset or depressed way, not functioning to his capacity, and the cycle begins again (Haley, 1987, p. 113).

PRINCIPLE 9.3   RULE SEQUENCES ARE POWERFUL

The rule sequences families create and maintain can create great efficiencies, but can also generate dysfunction. Harmful rule patterns are very powerful, potentially destructive, and extremely difficult to change in families.

There are several elements of this sequence that illustrate how rule sequences usually operate. First, the steps seem to occur in a cyclic pattern, and the pattern repeats itself over and over. Second, it is quite arbitrary where the cycle begins because it can begin with several of the steps. Punctuation is an attempt to identify where complex patterns begin and end, but it usually distorts the cyclic reality of these patterns.

Third, the strategy the mother uses to "change" the husband and child by increasing her expectations actually has the opposite effect. The more she tries to get them to improve the more they go in the opposite direction. This points out how these repetitious rules can be painfully obscured from the vision of those who participate in them. A major

FIGURE 9.2   Sometimes the rule sequences in families are not helpful and can lead to a fracture in the fundamental relationship strength.

element of family interaction patterns is that most of them are hidden from immediate view. Often, only an outside observer or a person trained to focus on systemic processes can piece them together.

Fourth, the details of the behavior might change in different situations, but when the pattern in the cycle is rule-governed it will reappear over and over again in different forms. It is critical to remember, however, that most of the time the family members are unaware they are choosing behaviors that are rule-governed or pattern-like. Most people are surprised when such rules are brought to light in counseling sessions or by a skillful observer.

These patterns help us understand more about a family's paradigm and what they really believe is important. The individuals are tied together and try to solve problems using rules of interaction that have somehow emerged over time, which might have worked in the past, and are now reemployed to respond to life's changes and challenges. By solving problems and allocating resources, we begin to understand what kinds of beliefs, values, and viewpoints are the most important to the group. Therefore, one way to see into a family's paradigmatic world is to take careful note of the rule sequences that emerge over time.

These rule sequences also help us understand the way different perspectives influence how we try to help families. A common approach to assisting families with problems is to focus on the individuals rather than the family system. In the preceding situation, a therapist with an individualistic orientation might encourage the mother to be more assertive or let the child "solve her own problems." The therapist might tell the parents to let the individual consequences of individual behavior take over. A therapist with a family process approach in mind might, instead, try to identify problematic rule sequences and then help the group interrupt those sequences that were destructive.

Generational Rule Sequences

Sometimes rule sequences involve three generations. The following example is a case study presented by Haley (1987, p. 117) in which a single parent has returned to live with her mother after a divorce. Think of the principles found in Chapter 6 as you read the following. In particular, note how the following is an example of cross-generational alliance.

Step 1. Grandmother takes care of grandchild while protesting that mother is irresponsible and does not take care of the child properly. In this way the grandmother is siding with the child against the mother in a coalition across generation lines.

Step 2. Mother withdraws, letting grandmother care for the child.

Step 3. The child misbehaves or expresses symptomatic behavior.

Step 4. Grandmother protests that she should not have to take care of the child and discipline him. She has raised her children, and the mother should take care of her own child.

Step 5. Mother begins to take care of her own child.

Step 6. Grandmother protests that the mother does not know how to take care of the child properly and is being irresponsible. She takes over the care of the grandchild to save the child from the mother.

Step 7. Mother withdraws, letting the grandmother care for the child.

Step 8. The child misbehaves or expresses symptomatic behavior.

It is impossible to identify the beginning or the "causes" of the problems in these situations because they are ongoing cycles that have no beginning and no end. A systems theory perspective, however, suggests it is helpful to view these situations as rule-governed cycles. When we think of them this way it reduces defensiveness, helps us better understand the system characteristics that help maintain problems, and opens up several possibilities for improving the family system.

Strategies for Managing Rules in Family Life

There are a number of important strategies that can help family members manage the rule parts of their family systems. Among them are developing a clear understanding of how and when to be adaptable, understanding developmentally appropriate rules, avoiding rule rigidity, and learning to avoid disabling rules.

Adaptability Is Helpful

The idea of change is an important idea. When family rules are too rigid, the family could break instead of bend when the winds of stress come their way (Haley, 1976). If families are willing to be flexible or adaptable in their rules it is very helpful. An example of little adaptability is seen in what occurred after a mother died. Before her death the rules of family functioning were clear. Everyone knew the goals how to accomplish what needed to get done. When this mother died suddenly, the system went into almost complete shutdown because there was no provision for flexibility. Therefore, when she died, there were great gaps left in the system's ability to function.

Before her death, she had taken care of the bills, managed money matters, run the household, maintained connections with other relatives, and made many of the decisions about the growing children. It was months before this family could reorganize, change the rules, reallocate responsibilities, and begin functioning again. The vitality of systems lies in a balance between the chaos of undefined competing rules and the rigidity of inflexible and less adaptable rules. As Haley (1987) suggested, "it is the rigid, repetitive sequence of a narrow range that defines pathology" (p. 112).

The rule part of families can develop several different kinds of problems that need adaptability. Some of these problems are that rules can become developmentally inappropriate, rigid, or disabling. When problems such as these occur, flexibility and adaptability are important, especially as developmental changes occur.

Developmentally Inappropriate Rules

Families sometimes create rules and rule sequences that are effective for a developmental stage, and they find it difficult to change as developmental changes occur. An example of this is a family that creates a group of rules that the children must obey their parents. The rules could be appropriate when the children are young and immature, but as the children mature they increase in their ability to think for themselves, and it is developmentally appropriate to gradually let the children have increasing amounts of autonomy and control over their lives. As they mature in these ways, the rules that they must obey become less and less useful and more and more inappropriate.

Another example of a rule that is developmentally appropriate at one stage and inappropriate at another is a rule that children should go to bed at 8:30 p.m. The rule might emerge for several reasons when the children were young: Children need a lot of sleep when they are in grade school, parents need free time in the evening, and having a set time allows for easy planning and makes the day orderly. However, if the parents were still trying to make the children go to bed at 8:30 when they are in high school, it would be unreasonable and developmentally inappropriate.

There are several situations in which it can be difficult for parents to change rules about obedience. One situation is when the rules about obedience are tied in with emotional fusion or chronic emotional tensions in the family system. In these situations, the emotionality in the family system might be so powerful that it interferes with the ability of the parents to understand that the rules are becoming inappropriate, and they might put extreme pressure on mature children to continue to be obedient.

Another situation in which it can be difficult for parents to change rules about obedience is when the rules are closely tied to family ideologies. When the parents in a family place a high value on obedience and conformity, they might be unwilling to let the system change so the children can become autonomous and independent.

A third situation in which it can be difficult to change rules about obedience is when parents have high standards for their children and they have a child that is not meeting their standards. For example, if a child is rebellious or independent, or if a child gets into trouble often, the parents might be inclined to try to help the child by trying to enforce rules about obedience long after they are developmentally appropriate.

Developmental changes are continually occurring, so it is wise to expect that rules in family systems will always be in a state of flux. Much of the time the rules evolve and change gradually without anyone paying attention to them, but in some situations it is helpful to consciously make adjustments and modifications.

Rule Rigidity

Rule rigidity occurs when families do not have enough flexibility in rules or they are resistant to change. Sometimes rule rigidity occurs when rules are appropriate in some situations but not in others. The following story is an example of this type of rule rigidity. A young newlywed is preparing Sunday dinner. He was preparing the roast when, to the surprise of his wife, he cut the end off of the roast, wrapped it up, and put it in the refrig-

FIGURE 9.3 Sometimes rules are like an unsolvable puzzle; they are too rigid, and family members might not know how to change the rule or cope with the effects of the rules that are in place.

erator. His astounded wife asked him why. "I don't know," he replied, "that's the way my mom does it. I guess it's good to have a little left over."

When the puzzled wife was visiting the mother-in-law, she asked her the same question, and got the same answer. Later, during a holiday, they all were at the grandmother's house, having a roast, and to the wife's amazement, the grandmother cut off the end of the roast, wrapped it, and continued on with preparations. "Could you tell me why you just did that?" asked the wife. "Well," the grandmother said, "I bought this roasting pan many years ago, and as you can see it is quite small. There is hardly a roast I buy that fits."

Of course, the point of this apocryphal story is that sometimes rules and rules sequences persist long after we know why they were initiated. The rule rigidity element of this story is that even though the principle actors did not seem to have a clue why they were cutting the roast, they continued doing so. Any suggestions to change that would probably be met with some (if not strong) resistance.

The rule emerged, and it was necessary at a period of time. Later, it became obsolete, but it remained as an unexamined, submerged family rule. So are many of the rules families sustain. They have lost their purpose, but they continue on, as if breaking or changing them would be harmful. Sometimes families act as if changing a rule means destruction. In actual fact, to not change and adapt creates a better chance for destruction than holding on to outdated and useless rules.

Disabling Rules

Another problem that occurs in some family systems is that some of the rules are disabling. This means that rules can cause family members to interact in unhealthy and damaging ways, and this interferes with families accomplishing their goals. Also, when rules are disabling, energy and a sense of direction dissipate.

Examples of ineffective or disabling rules are those that result in abuse to system members. A family could have a rule legitimizing the hitting of family members by those who are bigger and stronger when someone violates a boundary. Another type of ineffective rule is one that labels individuals as having little value to the system. The rules might eliminate a person from important decisions, important conversation, and problem-solving processes. Unfortunately, other family members often might not realize that they have established simple rules at the expense of one of the system members. Unintended results can abound.

Some rules limit expression and keep family members from disagreeing openly, without reprisal (Satir, 1972). Such rules can limit freedom and squash individual growth and expression. They exclude individuals and make them feel like outsiders in their own family system.

One type of family rule that is destructive is to have rules that communicate mistrust (Lidz, 1963). In these situations a child might be taught to mistrust everything and everyone. Rules also might exist that prohibit family members from testing ideas in the outside world. The "facts" of the world are distorted to meet the needs of family members. Consequently, the children might not learn to test reality, but are trained to accept the particular brand of irrationality constructed by the family as reality.

Some ineffective family rules might suggest two rather powerful, yet contradictory, behaviors. For example, a family might have consciously selected a democratic parenting style, encouraging individual expression and growth, but at the same time censuring family members for seeking a life outside the family. They construct two competing rules: (a) we are an open and accepting family; and (b) we accept only certain types of choices about really important life decisions. In an extreme case, the family might be filled with a milieu of inconsistencies and contradictions. The result can be people acting in inconsistent and unpredictable ways.

When families have rules that are disabling, it is helpful to have enough adaptability and creativity that the old rules can be adjusted or new ones invented. In these situations honesty, openness, and willingness to compromise and try new ways of doing things can make the difference between a family being enabling and helpful in achieving personal and family goals or disabling and destructive. When there is adaptability, the rule part of families can serve as a generative mechanism that is capable of creating regularity out of chaos.

☐ Implicitness Is Desirable

Reiss (1981) developed an idea about what happens in families when they find attention is focused on the rules that are usually **implicit**. He reasoned that:

> The first sign of a disorganizing family is the falling away of implicit regulation and coordination. In a smoothly running family, shared objectives, understandings, role allocations, and norms do not often have to be stated. Even when they are, limit-setting messages can be very brief and can often be conveyed as gestures. When a family finds it is engaged in laying out verbally explicit rules of itself, it is already in the midst of a stressful situation—although it may still be far from a full-blown crisis. (Reiss, 1981, pp. 179–180)

Apparently, when a family encounters a situation that is so unusual or stressful that its normal rules do not adequately deal with the situation, the family's attention is diverted to the rules it uses to manage. As a typical consequence, old rules are modified, new ones are invented, or both. Many times these situations are handled without disrupting the normal operation of the family system, and the new version of family rules recedes into the implicit. However, when families are not able to devise a system of rules that cope with the new situation, a disorganizing cycle tends to occur.

The disorganizing cycle is that when greater attention is given to rules, more of them are made **explicit**, and the family becomes more disorganized. The disorganization apparently occurs for several reasons. As a family's attention is diverted to its rules, members' concentration on coping with other aspects of life decreases. This results in chores not getting done, missing work, meals being disrupted, and so on. Also, the family realm has such complicated and yet intimate systems that they bog down when attempts are made to explicate very many rules. In the public spheres where relationships are more limited, rational, and efficiency oriented, it is helpful to bureaucratize and formalize laws, rules, and policies. In the family realm, however, this strategy is the "kiss of death." Families can only operate when the majority of the beliefs they use to govern themselves are shared, implicit, and affectively comfortable.

Thus, Reiss's idea is that when families find it necessary to divert a substantial amount of their attention to explicating rules, it tends to disable them from doing other things, and these processes frequently become parts of a vicious cycle.

PRINCIPLE 9.4   IMPLICITNESS IN SOME FAMILY RULES IS DESIRABLE

When families frequently divert energy and attention to rule making, maintaining, and explicating, they tend to be less efficient and more likely to fail at essential goal attainment.

This idea is helpful in understanding many disabling cycles in families. For example, many families have a difficult time adapting their implicit rule structure in a comfortable way during the teenage years. Parents and teens try to solve this problem by developing long lists of elaborate rules about what the teens can do and cannot do, and the rules become part of the problem. Also, when one member of a family begins to deviate from the behaviors that have traditionally been acceptable in a family, a typical response is to "lay down" rules about what is appropriate and acceptable, but the rules seldom help. It does not matter whether the "deviant" behavior is alcoholism, using prohibited drugs, or a religious conversion; explicating rules tends to set up disabling cycles.

There are several stages of the family life cycle that might be exceptions to the generalization that families are functioning the best when rules are implicit. One exception is during the formative stage of a family. When couples are engaged or newly married they find it enjoyable and helpful to focus a great deal of their attention on defining their rules and beliefs. At this stage of family life it is enabling to focus on their values and rules as it helps them lay the foundations of their family system. Gradually, as they construct rules they can live with comfortably, they move beyond this stage and the rule part of their system becomes implicit.

The same process can also occur somewhat when families encounter major transitions in the family life cycle. For example, when a new child is born, children reach adolescence, children start leaving home, retirement is near, or a death occurs, families seem to find it helpful to spend some time defining and redefining their rules. Usually, however, this occurs without the cycle escalating excessively, and the family is gradually able to let their new "understandings" recede into the realm of the implicit.

Focusing on Metarules

The word *meta* means about. Therefore, **metarules** are rules about rules. The metarules that family scientists focus most of their attention on are metarules about how to create new rules, how to eliminate old rules, or how to change rules. Laing (1972) referred to metarules in his comment that sometimes "there are rules against seeing the rules, and hence against seeing all the issues that arise from complying with or breaking them" (p. 106).

There are many examples of metarules. When families have young children it is common to have a metarule that it is parents and not children who make and change the family rules. A metarule that qualifies this could be that if the children want a rule changed, they can ask the parents, and even express their desires, but the parents decide. As the children in families mature, the metarules usually change. For example, a typical metarule when the children are teenagers could be that the ones who are the most upset by old rules and make the biggest scene determine the rules.

Hopefully, families have a metarule structure that assists them when rules no longer work. This issue is closely tied to the ideas of adaptability. As rules become obsolete, an adaptable family will have a viable metarule structure that allows them to replace, alter, and negotiate new rules that might be more appropriate for the situation. Some families do not have an adequate set of metarules about how to change their rules. When this occurs, families tend to become "stuck" in ways of doing things that were appropriate for earlier stages of development, and they have difficulty making the transitions into new stages of development.

One of the important ways family therapists help families is to help them develop metarules that help them change and grow. As Greenberg (1977) observed in his analysis of one of the main schools of thought in family therapy, "It was postulated that a central function of the therapist entailed the facilitation and the development of rules for change" (p. 396).

When families try to take a step back and think about their metarules, they can gain great insight. For example, assume a young man is studying family science, and after he studies these ideas he realizes that he has been locked into a Level I struggle with his parents about rules. He realizes the struggle is a standoff and he is not getting anywhere. He wants to have the freedom to decide what to study at the university, where to work, who to associate with, and so on. His parents, however, want to have considerable say in his life. He now realizes he and his parents have been only dealing with Level I processes when they were putting pressure on each other and trying to talk the other into agreeing with them. He now wants to talk about the metarules to see if they can find a better way to change the family rules. He could initiate this type of conversation by saying things like this: "Mom and Dad, I'd like to see us change some of the ways we do things in our family, but I don't know how to do it. What should one of us do if we want to make some changes? What would we say to get the others' attention, and how do we change things? What do you two do when one of you wants to make some changes, and how do you decide to make a change?"

☐ Manage Rules and Rule Sequences

When we focus on rules and rule sequences as a strategy to understand family processes, it makes it easier to understand why Satir (1972) compared family life to an iceberg where the majority of what is happening is beneath the surface. Families are aware of some sequences, and most families try to deliberately manage a few of them. The rules and rule sequences in family life become part of the package of beliefs, goals, aims, and worldview we label the family paradigm. It is important to remember that much of that paradigm and the totality of family life resides out of the awareness of the participants.

Even though most sequences and common family rules are submerged, families can become aware of some of them, and they can learn skills that help manage at least some of them. In fact, even families that are not well educated and not very resourceful find it relatively easy to modify vicious cycles when they become aware of them.

To summarize, there are several skills that can help families become aware of rule sequences. One skill is to occasionally try to "think sequences" or "think cycles" rather than just "think individuals" when problems occur in a family. Another strategy that sometimes helps is to explore the possibility that the "problem" is a reasonable response to a vicious cycle the family has not noticed. As Haley has observed, it is difficult for people in families to recognize cycles that are more complicated than three steps, but it is possible. Also, only identifying two or three steps in a cycle frequently is enough to be helpful. Often when families recognize two or three steps, these insights lead to the discovery of other steps that are not readily apparent.

Another skill that can help families recognize rule sequences is to ask people who are not in the middle of the situation if they see any vicious cycles operating. When we learn to think this way, members of the family who are not caught up in the vicious cycles can sometimes recognize what is happening and make suggestions that can help those who are involved recognize what is going on. The following situation illustrates how an undesirable rule sequence was repeated in a family many times before a family member that was not involved recognized it.

Step 1. The father's emotional distress would occasionally increase. Many incidents could be the ones to reactivate the cycle after a dormant period. For example, pressures at work, health frustrations, in-law troubles, a personal disappointment, and so on, could activate his stress.

Step 2. The father would behave in less patient and more critical or obnoxious ways. The first and second steps were a minicycle that would increase both conditions with the father getting more emotionally distressed, less patient, and more critical around the home. Eventually he would become angry or obnoxious enough that Step 3 would occur.

Step 3. The teenage daughter's room was usually messy and when the father was not upset, he would usually ignore it. However, when he was upset and noticed the daughter's room was messy he would get after the daughter to clean her room.

Step 4. The daughter would clean her room according to her father's standards rather than her own.

Step 5. The father's pressure on the daughter would increase her emotional distress. Often this was because she would feel angry and resentful.

Step 6. The daughter's behavior in some area of her life would be less desirable. This could take many forms. It could be she was more irritable or critical, did not do well at school, or misbehaved.

Step 7. The father's emotional distress would increase, and he would be less patient, and so on.

The cycle would repeat again and again until something occurred to disrupt it. The cycle also had several variations. For example, sometimes the mother would get involved instead of the father, and sometimes both parents would get upset before pressuring the daughter. During one of the family "scenes," an older brother happened to notice the connection between Steps 3 and 5. What he saw was 3 then 5 then 3 then 5 then 3 then 5 then 3 then 5, and so on. He described what he thought he saw and it was enough for the family to eventually recognize they had a rule-bound vicious cycle. Once the cycle was in the consciousness of the family, they were able to see the other steps and devise several ways to disrupt it.

One strategy they devised was to work harder to find a compromise on the standards of cleanliness for the daughter's room. They realized that the ongoing negative tension (remember the chapter on emotions) could be contributing to the cycle, and, if the father and daughter were more comfortable about the standards for the room, it might help disrupt the feedback loop.

A second strategy emerged from the belief that high levels of negative emotion were a key factor or at least a good barometer. A few strategies were then consciously devised to help each other find ways to reduce negative emotion when it was recognized. After that, the members of the family were a little more alert to their own moments of distress and the emotional distress in others, and they looked for ways to help each other calm down when upset.

This situation illustrates several important ideas. It illustrates that families can learn to manage at least some rule sequences that involve vicious cycles. It also illustrates several strategies that can be helpful in managing these sequences.

☐ Summary

This chapter discussed two types of rules that operate in family systems. One of these types is called family rules. Some of these rules are implicit and unknown to the family (even though they follow the rule). Other family rules are very explicit, negotiated and monitored by the group. Family rules come from many sources. Some are passed from one generation to another, and others are created by the group. Rules have many purposes. They regulate the way resources are managed, regulate emotional distance, clarify boundaries, control the implementation of decisions, clarify how to deal with exceptions and violation of rules, and so on.

The second type of rules is called rule sequences. These are patterned ways of behaving that involve sequences of behavior of several individuals. Rule sequences usually have a cyclic aspect to them, and most families are not aware of them. These sequences can be healthy and enabling, or they can be disabling and help keep a family "stuck" in earlier developmental stages.

Problems sometimes occur in the rule part of family systems, and when this occurs families need to consciously manage this part of their systems. Family scientists have discovered several strategies that can be helpful in managing this part of family life. When rules become developmentally inappropriate, too rigid, or disabling, learning to be adaptable is a helpful strategy. Usually the more implicit rules are, the better. Therefore, when families find it necessary to deal explicitly with their rules, it is desirable to deal with them as little as possible and then let them slide out of awareness.

☐ Study Questions

1. Define what a rule is.
2. How are rules and social norms different?
3. What is a rule sequence? Give an example of one.
4. Explain the concept of rule implicitness.
5. Name four different types of rules and how they could occur in family life.
6. Define social norm and give an example

7. What are some ways the text suggests to manage rule sequences in families?
8. What is the difference between an implicit rule and an explicit rule?

☐ Key Terms

Rules
Social norms
Rule sequences
Mores
Folkways
Distance regulation
Explicit
Implicit
Metarules

☐ Suggested Readings

Cigoli, V., & Scabini, E. *Family identity: Ties, symbols, and transitions.* Mahwah, NJ: Lawrence Erlbaum Associates.

Pleck, E. (2000). *Celebrating the family: Ethnicity, consumer culture, and family rituals.* Cambridge, MA: Harvard University Press.

Communicating in Families

☐ Chapter Preview

In this chapter, readers will learn:

- That we "have" to communicate with those around us, especially family members.
- That there are several important aspects of communication that we must attend to as we understand how families interact. These include the intent and content parts of a message.
- That there are several types or kinds of messages, including small talk, control talk, non sequitur, correcting and lecturing, superlatives, sarcasm and cutting humor, distancing, martyring, and meta-communication.
- About several types of positive communication styles, including straight talk, seeking clarification, reinforcing, seeking congruence, and appropriate self-disclosure.
- How gender differences play a large role in understanding family communication.
- About specific strategies one can use to ameliorate family communication.

☐ Introduction

Communication is at the heart of expressive family processes. Remember that family processes are strategies that families use to achieve goals, maintain ideological focus, and cope with life's changes and turbulence. Although some of those strategies are hidden from view, many goal-attaining strategies are more visible and expressive. How family members communicate, what they communicate about, and how they resolve differences are examples of these expressive family processes. In this chapter, we explore the power of family communication. In addition, we discuss several communication principles, along with suggestions for making family communication stronger.

"We converse our way through life" (Berger, Kellner & Hensfried, 1973). The most frequent activity you do with friends and family members is, most probably, talk. Communicating is a fundamental activity of life. We communicate about who we are, our dreams, our goals, and what we think is good or bad. We critique those around us, negotiate conflict, start fights, and try to find forgiveness. When we communicate, we reveal our weaknesses and strengths and explore our expectations, hopes, and disappointments (Duck, 1997).

PRINCIPLE 10.1   COMMUNICATION IS A FUNDAMENTAL ACTIVITY OF LIFE

We cannot avoid communicating. Communication is an essential and inescapable element of all relationships.

Obviously, communication is more than just talking. Communication is the process by which meaning is created and managed (Krauss & Fussell, 1996). As an early founder of the study of family communication once wrote, "We do not originate communication, we participate in it" (Watzlawick, Weakland, & Fisch, 1974). Watzlawick and his colleagues also described another important mantra of family communication: You cannot *not* communicate. In other words, it is impossible to avoid communicating with those in your world. Even if you decide you will never speak to someone again, that is still a type of communication. The point is that communication is a fundamental aspect of relationships; it is the way in which we discover each other, define relationships, and define who we are. We cannot avoid this important family process.

Communication begins when people meet and begin to establish a relationship. With each person in our world, we create a private and somewhat individualized message system (Tannen, 1986). As we become more involved and committed to a particular relationship, the rules and patterns of interaction take on a richer texture and fuller meaning.

We develop these special communication relationships from an early age. First, we watch and communicate with our parents and close family members. Then we branch out and watch the interaction of people on television and movies; we observe how our siblings solve problems and communicate with their friends; we continue to learn by watching our parents and other significant adults.

Each time a new friendship or relationship is formed, our ways of communicating and interacting change and adapt. The changes are not apparent and most of the time we do not talk about how we communicate to each other; the patterns just seem to unfold. Some have suggested that this unfolding is like peeling back the layers of an onion (and sometimes we even cry).

In this chapter, the goal is for you to consider the power of communication in primary relationships. We do not spend much time on how one communicates and builds ties with friends or the intricacies of communicating in the workplace. Instead we focus on the communication in families and other close relationships. Specifically, we explore the importance of communication in primary relationships, **types of communication**, communication styles that build stronger personal bonds, and the role of disclosure in important relationships. The problems inherent in relationship communication are covered only superficially. The next chapter is devoted to those issues. Additionally, a large section of this chapter deals with gender differences in communication: It has become apparent to researchers that men and women communicate differently in close relationships. It is important that we learn about these differences as we make decisions about how to build stronger bonds with family members. Finally, the latter part of this chapter focuses on several strategies for making partner and family communication more effective.

☐ The Importance of Communication

The goal in marriage is not to think alike, but to think together. (Robert C. Dodds)

The study of communication in families is like looking at a ray of light shining through a prism and projecting a rainbow pattern on the wall. The rainbow of information we see tells us about the hidden goals, deeply held beliefs, power differences, and expectations of daily life within families and close relationships. Communication is the process of making meaning: As we interact, the rainbow of feelings, dreams, and wants are exposed.

Most family scientists agree that effective communication is at the heart of understanding family strength. Conversely, when couples are experiencing relationship difficulty, it is often the communication style, content, and intent that one turns to for some understanding. Virginia Satir was an author and family therapist who wrote several books and articles about family communication. She showed us how communication is at the center of understanding family life: "Once a human being has arrived on this earth, communication is the largest single factor determining what kinds of relationships he makes with others and what happens to him in the world" (Satir, 1972, p. 30).

As mentioned earlier, when we enter into new relationships, a primary task in forming a new partnership is the development of an individualized, private message system (Tannen, 1986). As relationships are established, new rules and patterns of interaction take shape and emerge. In some ways, these emerging relational patterns are mysterious. That is, we do not sit and consciously plan them out; each conversational choice builds on the previous exchange.

The Parts of Communication

There are two fundamental elements of communication: **covert** and **overt messages** (Watzlawick et al., 1974). The word *overt* means obvious, explicit, observable, and visible. The content element of a message is the "report" part of the message. It is the explicit and obvious raw data of the message, often sent in words.

Intent Messages

The most powerful kinds of messages we send are the intent or covert messages. **Intent messages** are usually more concealed, not obvious, but implicit and hidden from view. The covert intent messages we send are much more subtle and harder to define than overt messages. However, these powerful intentional messages have the potential to override the actual words being used. The intent messages are carried in our tone of voice and things like the small sighs that slip out and the way our eyebrows curl down and tell the receiver we disapprove, for example.

After watching the first 2000 presidential debate between Al Gore and George Bush, many people commented about Al Gore's nonverbal facial gesturing, sighs of apparent impatience, and aggressive body posture. People seemed to remember the covert, nonverbal tone far better than they did the words that were spoken. From these intent messages, regardless of what words he used, Al Gore seemed to some to be impatient, aggressive, and rather uncaring. Before the second debate he had gotten feedback about his (probably unintended) intent messages and in the subsequent debate he changed his style of communicating. During the 2008 presidential debates, many commented on Barack Obama's smooth communication style and delivery and chided John McCain for his halting and uninviting speech delivery. If you simply read the words of either of these politicians, the messages are similar and often unremarkable. Delivery, however, can be a key to believability, trust, and how we vote.

Noller (1984) showed that the intent (nonverbal) element of communication can convey three important messages. First, intent messages can reveal our interpersonal attitudes toward the sender, toward the topic, or toward the situation. The intent messages provide small clues about assessment of the receiver. The receiver naturally extrapolates from those clues and has to guess what we think of them. The receiver does not have much to go on, but will make a guess about our judgment of them based on those limited observations. Most people are fairly skilled at picking up tones and facial clues that reveal our attitude toward them.

Second, intent messages tell the receiver how we feel about ourselves. Some of us have bad "poker faces." Whether we are having a miserable or great day seems to be written on our foreheads. Some people have the enviable skill of emotional constancy; even if they are having a rotten day, it is hard to tell. For most of us, though, our daily moods are frequently communicated in the message packages we send to those around us. Even if we don't intend on doing so, we tell people with our intent messages if we are depressed, confused, elated, excited, or bored. For most of us, those important intent messages about feelings seem to leak out and people collect the evidence and wonder if we are ill, what we are happy about, or why we are depressed. Especially in close relationships, partners and children read the mood messages that seem to be chained to the **content messages**.

The third aspect of intent messages focuses on our interactions with others. We monitor the gaze and posture of others, looking for clues of when to end the conversation, when to let them have a turn, when to laugh, and when to not respond. As Noller (1984) wrote, "One would expect that married couples who communicate well with one another would get to know each other's conversational patterns, and as well, get to know each other's nonverbal cues" (p. 6).

Some messages are sent and the receiver does not decode or interpret them in the same way we were hoping they would. At other times, neither the sender nor the receiver are able to send or receive what they intended. Being clear in one's messages and accurately **decoding** messages from others takes a fair amount of practice and skill for most of us. Few things in life are more puzzling and even aggravating to people than when the messages they send are lost, misunderstood, or misjudged.

We can judge the quality of a relationship by listening to the style of communication revealed in close relationships. To an astute observer, how we think and feel about the other person (and ourselves) is exposed by the way we communicate and talk with them. If we are condescending and hurtful, we have one type of intentions; if we are kind and gentle, we have another type of intentions.

☐ Types and Kinds

One way to begin to understand the various colors in the prism of communication is to explore other facets of the communication process. Thus far I have mentioned how the encoding and decoding process works, and I have mentioned the idea that communication contains an explicit report element and an implicit intent element. With those ideas in mind, let's turn to other features of the communication rainbow.

What do we talk about? Have you ever kept a diary of what you talk about with your friends? Activity 10.1 found in your workbook asks you to do some note taking about your conversations. What are the topics you spend the most time on? Who leads in choosing the topics? Who seems to decide when the topic should change?

Two researchers asked the same questions of married couples (Dickson-Markman & Markman, 1988). They asked couples with whom they had conversations and how much time they spent on a variety of topics. Not surprisingly, most couples spent far more time with their spouses than they did others (even friends or other family members). On average, couples had about 1.24 interactions per day that lasted long enough to be considered a conversational exchange. Those exchanges lasted an average of about 2 hours. The most frequent topics of discussion were work, home maintenance, children and other family members, conversations they had during the day with other people, and food. Notice what is missing from this list. These researchers found that couples rarely spend time talking about their own relationship. When they did talk about their relationship, it usually occurred after a sexual encounter or during an escalating conflict.

Another view of couples' interaction came from a study by Noller and Feeney (1998). These researchers found that couples reported an average of 22 conversations per week (about three per day) with each being about 20 to 30 minutes long. Of course, the length of time spent conversing with our partners is influenced by work schedules, number of children in the home, and the age and stage of family members. In another interesting study, (Roberts, 2000) found that couples who reported higher levels of marital satisfaction spent more time together at home and more time talking about personal topics. Of course, this question arises: Does good communication add to their feelings of couple satisfaction or do couples who like each other already stay home and talk more? No one has tackled that research yet.

☐ Kinds of Messages

Another way to explore the kinds of messages we send to our partners was illuminated by Miller, Wackman, Nunnally, and Miller (1988). These family scientists suggested that communication in close relationships could be organized into four types. I have reworded and updated their categories and call them small talk, competition and control talk, **meta-communication**, and cooperative or straight talk (Miller et al., 1988).

Small Talk

When we encounter a friend, stranger, or family member, we often just want to chat. Small talk topics usually focus on news items, the recent rainstorm, daily routines, something silly a child said, or what's for dinner. The purpose of this type of conversation is to build trust and establish bonds of connection. People who are not skilled at making small talk are sometimes seen as intrusive when they skip it and move immediately to requests, lectures, or inquiries. Conversely, if one only knows how to engage in small talk, then it is difficult to build lasting relationships with others.

Shop Talk

Another type of small talk is what Miller and associates labeled *shop talk*. Shop talk is really small talk that happens at or about the workplace. Often when we meet with friends or colleagues who work with us, we talk about office politics, work-related issues, and events related to employment. This type of small talk can become divisive or boring. Many people do not want to carry work into their home life or recreational settings.

Competitive and Control Talk

Frequently, we try to influence others. Control talk is about influence and change. When we praise, lecture, direct, request, or suggest things to family members we are using control talk. Parents often supervise their children, monitor their activities by asking where they have been, and teach them while the children are doing homework. All of these activities are control related.

As can be easily imagined, too much control talk can lead to trouble. Sometimes when we push too hard, expect too much, and demand multiple requirements of family members, they understandably fight back.

Fight talk is usually in response to someone pushing us to do or believe something when we do not want to. Both Gottman (1994, 1999) and Miller et al. (1988) found that when one partner provokes or pushes too hard to get something done or changed, about 80% of the time the other partner fights back. Most family scientists agree that using force to affect change in someone is ineffective. This idea is captured in the communication and change principle.

PRINCIPLE 10.2   COMMUNICATION AND CHANGE

The strategies we use to change someone or something a person is doing often make the situation worse and decrease the chance that the desired change will occur.

This principle tells us that the strategies we employ to get something done or change something or someone (even if the goal of the change is a worthy one) often make the situation worse and decrease the chance the desired change will occur. When we are aggressive, competitive, and punitive with others, they do not usually change; they just build up resentment toward us.

Any time we resort to compulsion, attempt to control someone, or try to dominate the situation with what we want to do, the generous spirit of cooperation leaves us. The following is a list of some kinds of destructive, competitive fight talk strategies that people often use that usually do not work and instead have the effect of making family life destructive.

Interrupting

Often when we are impatient and controlling, we interrupt the other person and try to redirect the conversation to go in the direction we want. Sometimes we become so unaware that we interrupt one another that it seems like the natural thing to do in conversation.

Kennedy and Camden (1983) showed that not all interruptions are a sign of dominating and controlling communication, only some kinds are. First, they found that women are far

FIGURE 10.1   Sometimes cutting someone off in conversations tells them that you really do not care much about what they are saying.

more likely to interrupt than are men. More important, they found that most of the interruptions that occurred in their study were *confirmation interruptions,* which occur when one seeks clarification, agrees with what is being said, or supports what is being discussed. Some interruptions, however, are not supportive. They are meant to change the subject, disagree, and disconfirm what is being discussed. Couples who have communication styles that build relationships make fewer combative, competitive, and dominating interruptions.

Non Sequitur

The non sequitur is another competitive fighting tool used effectively by partners who are trying to dominate others. The term *non sequitur* is a logical term indicating that one idea does not follow from the next. One partner might be talking about work or dinner; the other (maybe even in midsentence) interrupts the flow of the conversation and interjects a thought seemingly unconnected to the conversation. Again, such controlling and dominating communication strategies destroy relationship integrity.

Correcting and Lecturing

"If I've told you once, I've told you a million times," people often say. Most of us have been at the receiving end of controlling fight language that begins with sentences like that. Giving unsolicited advice, overrehearsing a topic, and attempting to change someone through sermonizing usually creates no positive advantage. Like most competitive communication, lecturing creates resistance and resentment. This is particularly true in parent–child relationships when accompanied by harsh discipline (Swinford, Demaris, Cernkovich, & Giordano, 2000). As Swinford et al. showed, using harsh forms of correction can have serious unintended effects. Children who grow up where there is frequent competitive, controlling, and dominating correction are much more likely to use violent behavior with their own intimate partners when they become adults. The unintended results of using harsh correction and lecturing can be increased resentment, hostility, and revenge by the recipient.

Superlatives

Another type of competitive fight talk is the use of superlatives. Superlatives are usually adverbs we throw into the conversation to exaggerate the point. These exaggerations and word-enhancing helpers are used to magnify our comment. Some examples are using *never, always,* "Ever since I've known you, you constantly . . . ," and "You are a total idiot." Here are some more examples of superlatives: *completely, continually, incessantly, utterly, absolutely, entirely, perfectly, thoroughly,* and *extremely.* In actuality, there are few instances in which the words *never, completely,* or *continually* are accurate; *always* is a long time and has not occurred yet. We use superlatives in our language to assert control, exaggerate a point, and dominate the conversation. The usual effect is that we push people to fight back. As with other competitive fight talk strategies, the use of superlatives is ineffective in changing someone's behavior or communicating a need or want. For the next few days, count how many times you use or hear someone use superlatives; you might be surprised at the number of times they slip into your conversations. As you count how many times people use them when communicating to you, you might also be surprised.

Sarcasm and Cutting Humor

Another common strategy for gaining control and dominating a relationship is using sarcasm and cutting humor to put others down. In current usage, the term *dissing* is popular. *Dis* is used as a short form of *disrespect* and means to make someone look foolish or unworthy. It also means to use wisecracks or make fun of what someone says or does. Current Western and American culture seem to thrive on the comedic repartee of dissing: This type of demeaning humor is frequently seen on situation comedies and talk shows. Again, when we use sarcasm and cutting humor in an attempt to better ourselves and make others look foolish, we are chasing away the spirit of harmony and unity in close relationships. It destroys trust and creates resentments that might be difficult to reconcile.

Distancing

When we give up on the other person, decide we have had enough, and disengage, we are distancing. Rather than battle with someone, we choose to retreat and build barriers.

Martyring

Closely tied to distancing is martyring. The martyr seeks control through a particular type of distancing strategy. He or she will say, "Okay, I see you don't care what I think at all; I'll just go into the kitchen where I belong and make dinner. I guess I'll leave the big decisions to you." The intent is clearly manipulative and controlling. It is designed to get the other partner to say, "Oh, honey, come on. That's not what I meant. No, please stay. Come on, what do you think?"

Interrupting, use of non sequiturs, correcting and lecturing, sarcasm and cutting humor, distancing, playing the martyr, and overuse or inaccurate use of superlatives are communication strategies that are likely to backfire. Any time we use overt or intent messages to manipulate and elicit responses from those around us, we are slipping into some form of competitive communication style.

PRINCIPLE 10.3   COMPETITIVE COMMUNICATION CAN BE DEADLY

There are several forms of competitive communication that, when employed, have the tendency to destroy relationships.

Meta-Communication or Search Talk

Miller et al. (1988) also listed search talk as an important type of relationship communication. When we talk about how we talk about things, we call this search talk or meta-communication. Meta-communication is important because it allows us to put the normal flow of decision making, problem solving, and conflict resolution on hold (see Chapter 9 for an example of meta-communication usefulness). Then we step aside and ask deeper questions like, "Why do we argue that way?" We might express appreciation for the kind tone in a partner's voice or find ways of adjusting how we interact. A good metaphor for meta-communication is the racetrack example used in Chapter 2. Most of the time the race car is zooming around the track. In terms of communication, we would be solving problems, scheduling our lives, making decisions, and attempting to understand the needs and wants of those around us. Occasionally, however, we must pull into the pit stop area and examine the process itself. We look under the hood, so to speak, change a tire, and refuel. We do not need to do that often, but it does need to happen.

If done effectively, meta-communication can be useful in building stronger relationships. However, if done too often or not frequently enough, it can be less than helpful. As new relationships are formed, one would expect the individuals to spend more time exploring how they do things in their relationships. As relationships mature, only infrequent "pit stops" are needed and couples spend the bulk of their time doing their relationship tasks instead of talking about how they do them. Spending too much time talking about how we talk irritates most people. In addition, if meta-communication is rare, opportunities are lost to build stronger, more effective communication bonds.

Cooperative or Straight Talk

Learning to take the "barbed wire and buckshot" out of our intimate communications with others is a lifelong effort for most people. Most of us are a bit competitive and controlling, and seek to dominate others too frequently. The following communication patterns come straight from the heart, are noncompetitive in their intent message, and tend to build relationship strength.

Seeking Meaning

One way to send nondefensive, noncombative, noncompetitive intent and content messages to those close to us is to seek meaning. When we seek meaning, we listen carefully, nonjudgmentally, and without thinking about what we want to say next. Listening with the intent of seeking meaning means we are studying and learning from the sender. We ask the other person to expand his or her thoughts, explore ideas, and express opinions. There is no hidden agenda; there is no impatience as we wait for a place to break into the other person's story so we can give our lecture, tell a better story, or make a joke of what is being said.

Instead, we look into the sender's eyes with affection, concern, and caring; we only want to hear what he or she has to tell us. For many people, this is surprisingly difficult. You might be surprised, however, that when you practice this skill, your appreciation for the other person is greatly enhanced. Additionally, we learn far more in these situations than when we are impatiently waiting for a spot to jump in and tell our stories. Satir (1972) suggested that the way we frame (or interpret) what others are saying tells a lot about us. For example, if we are jumping in, being competitive, or listening for only negative elements in someone's story or comments, it might mean that we have a lower sense of

FIGURE 10.2   Cooperative communication can build strength in relationships.

self-worth. Confident and mature listeners have little need to best someone's story, make fun, be sarcastic, or interrupt.

Seeking Clarification

When we seek clarification we go beyond seeking the meaning of the interaction. In this situation, we are listening closely and find some aspect of the message unclear. Good counselors are experts at knowing how to seek clarification. They gently encourage the sender to expand an idea or give examples of what they mean, or they will connect what is being said to some other part of the sender's message. When we do this, we encourage the sender and build trust. The sender cannot help but see that we really care and want to know what he or she feels or needs.

Reinforcing

As the sender is explaining an important message to us, it is important that we tell him or her (using both intent and content messages) that we appreciate the story or concern. We reinforce or reward the disclosure by saying simple things like "Uh-huh," "Sure," "I see," or "Really?" Remember that it is the intent part of the message that carries the relation-ship communication. When we encourage or reinforce people for telling us their story or expressing a need or want, we tell them that we want to be trusted, that what they want is important to us, and that we will take their story, request, or need seriously. Trust and connection are lost when we are uncaring or even lazy in developing these skills. Each new encounter during a day starts the relationship over (even if we have been married for 20 years). We define how we care for our partners each time we greet them, listen to their stories, respond to a request, or simply take note of the difficult day they are having. If we become lazy in these daily encounters, our close family and friends will begin to think we take that relationship for granted.

Seeking Congruence

According to Jacob (1987), congruency of messages leads to greater relationship satisfaction. Congruency occurs when we take the time to make sure that the intent and content aspects of messages are similar, or congruent. If one partner says, "I love you" with the content message, but the intent message is one of distance and coolness, then the messages are not congruent and the chances for building relationship strength decrease. On the other hand, if one's nonverbal (intent) language confirms that the partner does, indeed, love the other, the message package (both content and intent) builds the relationship. When congruence is missing, relationship confusion and anxiety are created.

When messages are congruent, family members are more likely to receive and send messages with greater clarity. Conversely, when there is less congruence (Satir, 1972; Sieburg, 1985; Wynne, 1984), family members might have problems with relationship ambiguity. The message confusion creates relationship ambiguity and can affect how we feel about ourselves. A child can experience doubt about what parents really think about him or her if the parents' messages are not authentic. When messages are congruent, authentic, and not confused, children (and spouses) are not left to wonder about how those important to them really feel about them.

Further, message congruence seems to have a significant effect on those within a relationship dyad (Sieburg, 1985; Wynne, 1984). These researchers suggest that when congruence is low it is more likely that family members would have poorer self-perceptions. It seems that message confusion creates relationship ambiguity and personal weakness. Additionally, when we are more confident of our own inner self, we are more likely to communicate with greater congruence. Apparently, this is one reason why clear, direct, involved, and open communication is associated with more functional marriages (Jacob, 1987).

Appropriate Self-Disclosure

One of the more powerful types of cooperative communication is the use of appropriate self-disclosure. This occurs when an individual reveals to one or more people some personal information they would not otherwise learn. We acquire information through daily interactions. As we become more confident in the reliability of those close to us, we reveal more and more about who we are, what our needs are, and what we need from others.

Waring and Chelune (1983) found that self-disclosure accounts for more than half of the variation in intimacy among couples. That is, although there are many factors that contribute to a feeling of intimacy with another, those feelings of closeness are tied to our ability to share special and private information about our inner lives. Therefore when researchers ask couples about how much they share with one another, the result is that the more a spouse engages in appropriate self-disclosure, the more likely both partners are to be satisfied with the relationship (Bograd & Spilka, 1996; Hansen & Schuldt, 1982; Rosenfeld & Bowen, 1991).

There is an important message in the self-disclosure research for men. Bell, Daly, and Gonzalez (1987) found that wives whose husbands self-disclose more (e.g., sensitivity, spirituality, physical affection, self-inclusion, and honesty) also reported much higher levels of marital satisfaction. They also found that what was disclosed to spouses was important. They wanted to know if secrecy was something that damaged marriages. They found that when men were able to disclose more about the relationship (with the partner), that was more important than whether or not they kept some secrets about their personal life.

They suggested that sometimes it is better to leave some things unsaid. A popular phase captures this idea: Which hill are you willing to die for? One must know the difference between being honest and open about relationship issues that really matter and keeping silent about those topics that will only makes things worse. Sometimes it is better to just let a topic drift away, unexplored and undiscussed.

For most of us, it takes concentration and practice to know when to comment and when to let go of a topic or issue. Baxter and Wilmont (1985) found that relationships could be strengthened when those in close relationships held back and did not "tell all." Sometimes partners' overdisclosures create a relationship threat and have the opposite of the intended effect. The intended message of the disclosure might have been to confide, build closeness, and connect. Instead, the message received is one of threat and confrontation.

On the other side of this coin, one should not keep secrets from partners as a way to deceive and manipulate. Vangelisti (1994) and Vangelisti and Caughlin (1997) found that the relationship between family secrets and family satisfaction depended on the reasons why the secrets were kept. If partners were keeping secrets to avoid evaluation or to keep from getting in trouble, these messages were perceived as divisive. However, when family members kept secrets to protect people, this strategy was seen as a sign of relationship strength.

As Sieburg (1985) found, learning the art of appropriate disclosure and secrecy are key elements of a good relationship. Timing is everything in building strong relationships. Over time, we learn when to disclose, when to hold back, and when to let the topic drop permanently. Learning when and how to employ these communication strategies takes higher levels of emotional maturity and years to perfect.

**PRINCIPLE 10.4   COOPERATIVE COMMUNICATION
BUILDS RELATIONSHIP STRENGTH**

There are several forms of cooperative communication that, when employed, have the power to enhance and enrich relationships.

☐ Gender in Communication

Much has been said about how men and women communicate differently in close relationships. Certainly, gender differences with respect to communication are an important topic for study. Men, generally, are socialized to communicate differently than women. They see the world of relationships with a slightly different hue. To learn how to strengthen relationship ties between men and women, one must attend to those differences. For example, Beck (1988) resubstantiated the idea that men do not talk about personal things as much as women do. He found that women think their marriages are stronger and working better when there is plenty of dialogue and exchange about the relationship. On the other hand, the men in this study generally felt the opposite. When communication turned to topics of relationships and marital evaluation, they felt the relationship was much more likely to be in trouble.

Similarly, Mackey and O'Brien (1995) found that a frequent source of tension between marital partners was the husbands' discomfort with talking about their inner thoughts and feelings. These husbands were not only uncomfortable talking about feelings, they also judged feeling-connected relationship messages as negative and harmful. Other researchers found that husbands actively try to control the amount of communication about feelings and personal topics. These researchers found that husbands are uncomfortable participating in what we labeled earlier as search talk. Correspondingly, their wives were unhappy with the lack of these relationship messages between them and their partners (Ball, Cowan, & Cowan, 1995).

In a popular book about this topic, Tannen (1990) emphasized that men approach life as a contest in which each party is striving to "preserve independence and avoid failure" (p. 25) Women, on the other hand, approach life as a community affair in which the goal is to connect, maintain intimacy, and avoid isolation. Men try to get out of relationships; women try to stay connected.

Similarly, several researchers have commented on the notion that men view relationships as a backdrop for attaining, maintaining, and evaluating status. When men interact, they are more likely to compare themselves to the other person, rating the position and social rank of the other, and protecting information about themselves that would diminish their status ranking with the other. Conversely, women, in general, are more likely to engage in relationships for connection and association.

In the same vein, when problems arise, women usually respond with more understanding; men tend to give advice and try to solve the problems (Tannen, 1990). This can result in relationship problems: In times of distress, what might be needed are supportive, encouraging, and nurturing responses. Men may be slower to realize those needs and, instead, be quicker to give a lecture, provide solutions, and sermonize. Some have suggested that this is because men see the world as more hierarchical; women see the world as cooperative and focus on connectivity (Olson & DeFrain, 1994).

As Tannen (1990) suggested, men spend more time thinking in terms of hierarchy; they are attuned to the process of evaluating. Men frequently evaluate to determine whether they are a notch up or a notch down vis-à-vis the other. Men like to keep score and tally how many bouts they lost and how many they won. A male colleague recently described a bad day by saying, "Some days you eat the bear; some days the bear eats you."

According to Tannen, a primary goal for women in relationships is to design their communication style so that it helps them avoid isolation. Therefore, women are the networkers of the world. They are fonder of association with others than they are of keeping score. They are also more likely to seek out friends and community members who will provide that expanded associative role.

Topical Differences

Bischoping (1993) found that men and women communicate about different topics in casual conversation. The primary small-talk topics that both men and women seem to discuss are money and work. However, men more frequently speak about leisure. This includes sports, personal fitness, movies, and so on. On the other hand, although women do talk some about leisure, they also talk about men more than men talk about women. In fact, in this study the women were four times more likely to talk about men than men were to talk about women.

Message Clarity

Another feature of gendered communication is that wives send clearer messages to husbands (Noller & Fitzpatrick, 1993; Thompson & Walker, 1989). These researchers also noted that husbands tend to give more neutral messages. A neutral message has an unclear or absent emotional or affective tone attached. Wives send more messages with some affective or emotional tone.

Additionally, wives set the emotional tone of arguments. They are more likely to escalate conflicts and use emotional appeals and threats. "Married couples who love each other tell each other a thousand things without talking" according to an Chinese proverb.

Interruptions

Interrupting was once considered a sign of dominance in relationships. Therefore, it was assumed that men would interrupt women more often because they are typically in a more dominant position relative to women. As our understanding of this important family process has become more sophisticated, it has become clear that not all interruptions are the same (see the earlier discussion). Sometimes we interrupt to show support, to seek clarification, to show concern, and even to voice agreement (Aries, 1996). Of course, interruptions can also be used to commandeer the relational space between communicating partners. Interruptions can also be used to demonstrate dominance and power. Again, the intent message in the interruption has to be gauged. The research in this area continues to grow but has several problems. First, we know little about couple interruptions in natural settings. Most of the research has been done with college students in laboratory settings measuring short periods of conversation (usually about 10–15 minutes). An important exception is Gottman's (1994) research. For the last 20 years he has been observing the same couples in a controlled setting as they resolve problems and conflict. Some of his findings are mentioned in the next section.

Most researchers agree (cf. Aries, 1996) that there is actually far less interrupting than family scientists once thought. Therefore, it is difficult to determine an accurate sense of what interruptions really mean to relationships when the research is based on short conversations between nonfamily members.

In addition, as Aries (1996) noted, the idea that men would dominate conversations and interrupt more than women has been discounted. In fact, this research indicates that men and women interrupt at about the same rates. However, when the couples are observed participating in personal casual conversation, women interrupt men more than men interrupt women. Again, most of that interruption is supportive and connective rather than competitive and aggressive.

Directness

One gender difference in communication style is how direct men and women are in conversation. Women usually approach conflict indirectly. This means they will try to solve the situation and possibly take some type of conflict-reducing measures that their partners do not recognize.

When men are faced with confrontation, conflict, and disagreements, they use direct approaches such as bargaining and negotiation. Note that the root word in *bargain* is *gain*. Men spend more time positioning themselves to secure gain. Women drop hints, suggest, mention, propose, and defer. Men ask, demand, seek closure, and stipulate (Noller & Fitzpatrick, 1990).

In like manner, men expect compliance, especially when talking to a woman. Women begin message exchanges expecting noncompliance (Falbo & Peplau, 1980). Another way that we see differences in directness is that women approach difficult situations in ways that involve and engage participants. Men approach similar situations expecting to promote, suggest, and even demand resolutions that feature autonomy and authority (Tannen, 1990). To that end, women are more accommodating, supportive, and socially responsive. Men, instead, provide suggestions and solutions to problems, as well as opinions and information (Aries, 1982).

An interesting window into the preceding differences can be found in the language structure women use to communicate. Women are more tentative in their language and use tag phrases such as "isn't it?" Men state things in ways that do not invite contradiction.

In sum, the approach men and women use in conversation and relationship connection is gendered. This means that men and women use different relationship strategies and, of course, implies that men and women might have different goals in relationships. Men typically see relationships as a feature of life necessary to attain other goals such as being a notch up at work, getting a better job, winning an argument, or closing a deal. Women are more likely to see the relationship as an end in itself. There is no secondary goal.

It is important to note that this section was written rather gingerly and carefully. The research on men and women's communication styles is still emerging and it is frequently changing in findings and emphasis. Certainly our notion about men and women's roles and strategies in close relationships is a fertile area for research.

☐ Making Relationships Stronger Through More Effective Communication Strategies

First, you have to want to change. All of the information in this chapter (and book) is relatively useless if you, the reader, do not want to change. Second, only reading this information will do little to assist you in developing stronger, more effective relationships with those you care about. Not only does one have to be highly motivated to change something as long-lasting as a relationship pattern, but also one has to put principles into action and make a serious effort.

Third, you can only change yourself. As we learned in Chapter 6, efforts to change others only end in frustration and disaster. It is difficult to change yourself if your partner is unwilling to participate and change as well.

☐ The Four Horsemen of the Apocalypse and Other Things That Plague Good Relationships

Gottman (1999) has been observing the same couples while they interact in a controlled laboratory setting for more than 20 years. During that time, as each couple returned for a weekend in the lab apartment, he has videotaped, recorded, and analyzed their interactions. The following ideas come from two of his books: *Why Marriages Succeed or Fail* (Gotman, 1994) and *The Seven Principles for Making Marriage Work* (Gottman, 1999).

In these books, he affirms that one of the primary keys to understanding why some couples remain together and others do not is the amount of conflict they exhibit in their daily interactions: "If there is one lesson I have learned from my years of research it is that a lasting marriage results from a couple's ability to resolve the conflicts that are inevitable"

Spotlight on Research 10.1

Predicting Marital Happiness and Stability in Newlywed Interactions

Gottman, Coan, Carrere, and Swanson (1998) conducted a study of 130 newlywed couples. The primary point of the study was to see if the researchers could tell over time if they way they interacted with each other initially predicted if they would stay married by the end of the study. The participants were initially screened and observed in a laboratory setting in which they resided for several days. The observers recorded what they said and did. In an important part of this study, the experimenter asked the couples (during the first interview shortly after marriage) to choose several topics to discuss that they rated as problematic. The couples discussed the chosen topics for 15 minutes and then viewed a recording of what had happened. Each individual rated the tapes as to the feelings they were having during the conversations.

An interesting finding in this and several other research studies conducted by Gottman is that anger is not very telling as a measure of marital problems. Instead, with these newlyweds, high levels of contempt, belligerence, and defensiveness were strong predictors of marital troubles later. These couples were asked to return to the lab each year for 6 years. Each time, it was confirmed that the power of contemptuous, belligerent, and defensive behavior has a major impact on the ability of the couple to meet their goals in a relationship.

Also of interest is the direct finding that active listening seems to be of little importance in building strong relationships. For many years, family life educators have tried to get couples to paraphrase what the other says as a way to get them to focus on the problem and show care. Gottman and his associates have repeatedly shown that this strategy has little effect on whether a couple is together years later.

This study also showed that a common Level II (see Chapter 5) pattern of interaction that seems to lead to divorce is when the wife uses some form of harsh startup. She says something like, "Why did you spend that money? We were saving it for our trip next summer. Are you a dope or what?" That is followed by the husband's refusal to be influenced by his wife. This pattern continues with pouting (low-intensity negativity) by the wife and no attempt by the husband to defuse the situation. The couple stews about issues for days at a time.

It was also clear that there were few if any relationships that did not have struggles. What seems to separate the group that was to be divorced from those who stay together was how much positive feeling happened during conflict. Conflict was unavoidable, but the intent message of ultimately caring for the other person is critical. Also, those who can deescalate a conflict were more likely to stay together. Someone would step forward and change the topic, tell a joke, or somehow break the ice. The couples who had the most trouble were those who could not let it go.

(Gottman, 1999, p. 28). He goes on to assert that many couples mistakenly believe that by simply reducing the struggles in marriage and tolerating low-level conflicts, they will be happy. He believes, instead, that having differences is normal and expected. The real test is whether couples can resolve their differences. He has found that there are at least three types of conflict resolution in marriage. The first is a *validating* style. In this type of marriage, the couples are quick to find ways of compromising and soothing each other. In addition, the validating couples help each other and find compromise a daily feature of their relationship.

The second kind of conflict-resolving relationships are what Gottman (1999) calls conflict-avoiding marriages. These couples run from conflict and rarely struggle together with the daily challenges of life. Because they rarely lock horns, they rarely explore the grievances that arise in daily family life. The final type of relationship is labeled the volatile marriage. For these couples, arguing and fighting are frequent, everyday events. They thrash about, resist the will of the other, and their communication often erupts into a fiery, passionate clash. Which type do you think is less likely to get a divorce? Surprisingly, Gottman found that all three styles are about equally stable and likely to end in divorce or not.

The 5 to 1 Ratio

More important, Gottman found that the ratio of competitive and control talk to cooperative or straight talk (to use the language of this chapter) was much more important in predicting marital breakup than was the overall style of the communication. In fact, he found that marriages that survived for many years contained partners who could maintain at least a five-to-one ratio of positives to negatives (Gottman, 1999, p. 29). Look back at the list of negative, competitive and control expressions presented earlier. At the top of this inventory are inappropriate interrupting, lecturing, scolding, using the non sequitur, being a martyr, and the use of sarcasm. Now look at the positive list of straight-talk communication forms. These include seeking meaning and clarification, communication congruence, and appropriate disclosure.

Harsh Startup

Gottman indicates that one of the most severe problems in communication styles is when we use competitive control communication to begin our exchanges with our partners. Let's label this idea the **harsh startup** principle.

PRINCIPLE 10.5   HARSH STARTUP

The tone and intent of the way we begin conversations is a sign of relationship strength. When we lead out with harsh, negative, and biting comments it is a sign our relationship is weaker. Conversely, if we lead out with a calm, generous, gentle, and civil intent, it is a sign we care more about our partner and that the relationship is stronger.

Look back at the list of controlling and competitive forms of communication. This principle tells us that not only are these strategies destructive, but their destructiveness is amplified when one of them is the first thing out of our mouths. Imagine a scene in which the wife walks in the door from work. The husband barely says hello, but then launches into a lecture: "I thought you said you were going to be home at 5:30. Did you remember that we are supposed to be at the Frogman's by 7:00? What were you thinking?" Gottman's (1999) research shows us that about 96% of the time when a conversation begins with a harsh startup from the control and competitive communication styles listed earlier, it will end with a negative tone. It does not seem to matter if you try to make it up, either. "Oh . . . okay, I am sorry, that was too blunt. Let me start over." Actually, you cannot start over. The damage for that encounter cannot be recalled.

Remember each contact with our partners is a new encounter (Ehrlich, 2000). We sometimes believe that our encounters with our close family members are continuous. Actually, they are not. Each time we meet and greet is a new scene in the relationship play. That does not mean it is a new play, but it is a new scene. Our partners read our intent tones, gather information about how we feel toward them, reflect on what information they want to disclose, and prepare messages to send to us. If we ignore this important rule and assume that context of the new encounter is not important, we are missing an important principle of life. As Ehrlich (2000) states, "Many of the defining moments of our lives can be traced to the impact of first encounters. . . . There is magic in the power in the first encounter . . . [his assertion is that] all human communication encounters are first encounters" (p. 5).

Our job in close relationships is to realize that each new day, each new encounter is manageable. We can and must manage those repeated first impressions. However, most of us get lazy and act as if the repeated first encounters do not matter much, so we simply blast

FIGURE 10.3 **T**his couple is slamming each other at the dinner table. Harsh startup (like slamming a tennis ball across the court at your partner) is usually met with the same kind of response: They slam it right back at you.

away with what is on our mind. If what is on our minds gets encoded into a nasty, controlling demand or lecture, it is almost certain that that segment of the relationship exchange will end on a negative tone and maybe even in a full-fledged fight. Most people, when challenged or pushed with a message that is confrontational, threatening, or demanding, do not repeatedly return the confrontation with generosity and openness. Instead, we eventually (or quickly) become resistant, combative, and even hostile.

Therefore, one place to start in building stronger relationship patterns with those you love is to plan more carefully how you express concerns, wants, wishes, requests, desires, and needs. Open the encounters with small talk that is at least neutral and, if possible, positive. Timing is crucial. Waiting for the right moment to express a need or want can make all the difference in the outcome.

The Four Horsemen

Gottman expands our list of competitive communication styles and includes four specific types of negative communication patterns he calls the "Four Horseman of the Apocalypse," a reference to the Biblical vision in which four horsemen usher in the final demise of the world. His assertion is that when we participate in these four deadly kinds of competitive interactions, our own world of marriage and family might come tumbling down on us.

FIGURE 10.4   The Four Horsemen of the Apocalypse is an image used by John Gottman and his coworkers to feature the four deadly patterns of relationship communication.

These four strategies of marital doom are criticism, contempt, defensiveness, and withdrawal. As you will note, they are similar to the types of control language listed earlier.

As you read about these four deadly communication styles, keep in mind they are presented with the idea that learning about them and how to avoid the use of them is an important way of building strong communication patterns in marriage.

Criticism

As a conversation begins to unfold after a harsh startup has occurred, what type of competitive or cooperative language happens next? Gottman (1999) claimed that, after a harsh startup, it is likely that more control and competitive language will follow. Specifically, he indicates that there are four types of competitive language that are damning to close relationships. The first is criticism. Criticism has many elements of destructive communication. This type of communication sends the messages of disapproval, condemnation, denigration, and denunciation. It is sometimes like a heated ping-pong match, hitting comments right back at the partner with as much force as possible.

We cannot go through life living with our partners without, at some time, being annoyed at something they do. It is a fact of life. The trick is deciding what type of message to send, how to encode it, and how to make sure it does not damage the relationship. Having a complaint is normal, natural, and predictable. Using criticism in response to an irritation does not help the situation; it makes things worse. It is one thing to say, "The way you talked to my mother last night concerns me. You seem to be annoyed with her lately."

It is another thing to take the annoyance or concern to another level of attack and make our words more global and general. "You are a socially clumsy oaf. Every time you get around my mother, you blow her off and make her feel like a moron." Once we become less specific and more general, we begin using more superlatives, personal attacks, lectures, and sarcasm. We are much less likely to use message clarity, seek meaning, and find congruence in our communication exchanges. Gottman (1999) indicated that harsh startups are often disguises for impending criticism. We slam someone quickly with a complaint (but it is not couched in the language of seeking meaning and congruence) and then move rapidly to the general, nonspecific criticism. The following is a true example of how this works. On a rainy Saturday night, a family decided that all of them (Mom, Dad, and 18-year-old Jacob) would go to a movie. Jacob had been up all the previous night watching movies with friends, waiting to go early in the morning to a ticket office to stand in line for tickets to a concert. After the ticket adventure, he and his friends played basketball for much of the day. Consequently, he was tired and fell asleep during the afternoon. He still wanted to go to the movie, however. Mom and Dad had some shopping to do before the movie. Jacob did not want to go shopping, but instead would meet Mom and Dad at the show at 7:30 p.m. The prepurchased ticket was left on the kitchen counter with a note to meet the parents at the movie.

Mom and Dad saved a seat for Jacob; the movie began, but no Jacob. After the movie, Mom and Dad returned home to find Jacob with a sour face in the kitchen. Dad said, "So, what happened? You didn't wake up in time for the movie?" (It was a bit of a harsh startup, a little sarcastic, and a bit critical.) Jacob took the bait and responded with a harsh startup of his own: "Well, if you guys would ever tell me what is going on, maybe I could figure out what to do." That took Dad by surprise. He thought the evening plans were quite clear. His startup with a critical intent inevitably led to a confrontation. Dad assumed Jacob simply did not get up in time and had wasted the $7.50 for the ticket. Jacob was annoyed because Dad had made a mistake and Jacob did not know what to do.

You see, Dad had purchased the tickets in the afternoon. Apparently, the ticket seller did not hear him correctly and had sold Dad three tickets for the afternoon matinee. Printed on the ticket was a 4:30 time for the movie. Jacob assumed that Mom and Dad had told him the wrong time, the movie was over when he awoke from his nap, and the theater would not let him in with an afternoon ticket. He was mad at Dad because of his mistake. Dad was mad at Jacob because he was being irresponsible.

All of the relationship trouble could have been avoided. If both Jacob and Dad had not blasted a harsh startup in the new encounter after the movie, several minutes of negative, relationship-destroying conversation could have been avoided. All Dad would have had to say was, "Gee, we missed you. What happened?"

Here are some other examples of complaints compared to criticisms:

Example of complaint: Looks like there is no milk this morning for cereal. I thought you were going shopping yesterday; did something come up?

Example of criticism: You never follow through with plans; you spend all day watching golf on TV then complain when there is no milk in the fridge.

Example of complaint: I just finished balancing the checkbook. I was kind of annoyed that you spent that extra $100 on buying more CDs. We could have made an extra payment on the credit card.

Example of criticism: We have got to sit down and talk about money. Every plan we make gets destroyed by this obsession you have with buying more and more CDs. Your financial irresponsibility is killing us. I can't believe you don't care enough about our relationship to pay attention to our finances.

Contempt

Often, the conversation boils over even more. Sometimes couples do not stop at criticism; they take it a notch higher and resort to words and intent messages that convey contempt (Gottman, 1999). Contempt can be defined as content and intent messages that convey disdain, scorn, and censure. When we see couples elevating a conflict to this level, there is a sneering and sniping tone to their voices. It often involves name-calling, eye-rolling, mockery, and sneering (Gottman, 1999). It often conveys more than just a competition, going one step further and sending a message of disgust. This type of demeaning conversation destroys trust, alienates us from our partners, and sends a message that we have no respect for the person. As Gottman indicates, a common response to contemptuous comments is belligerence and increased aggressive anger toward our partners.

Defensiveness

Both criticism and contempt result in sharp increases in defensive responses. Unfortunately, defensiveness does not work well. Resistance and self-protection often bring more attack rather than resolution. Attacking spouses are more likely to press on for resolution than they are to back down. Think for a minute: When was the last time someone criticized you and you respond with a defense ("I was not; I was only 20 minutes late"), and the attacking person said, "Oh, gee, that's right, I was wrong, sorry for bringing it up"? If you are like most people, that rarely happens. Defensiveness spawns more competitive exchanges and escalates conflicts. These three horsemen of the apocalypse work together, pushing us to attack, denounce, and defend.

Stonewalling

Rather than continue the confrontation, sometimes a partner will tune out: "Okay, that's it for me. Do whatever you want. I could not care less." Think back to our list of competitive and controlling communication patterns. Among them you will find distancing and martyring. Both of these are captured in Gottman's (1999) fourth deadly horseman. Stonewalling, distancing, and using the martyr strategy usually come later in relationships. Years of head-butting and competitive exchanges have conveyed the message that no change occurs in most of the relationship struggles that have occurred. So, one might conclude, what is the point of struggling? Gottman (1999) tells us that 85% of the time it is the husband who retreats and resorts to stonewalling. He decides that the aggravation is not worth the effort.

☐ Summary

In summary, let's explore what we can do to avoid the deadly effects of competitive and controlling communication in our close relationships. The following are a few suggestions. First, kindness seems to be more important than being an "effective" communicator. Couples who are more clumsy, more forgetful, and ineffective in communicating what they wanted in a relationship were able to meet family goals better (in spite of communication problems) when they were kinder and more generous. Couples who are good communicators (i.e., clear messages, precise directions, and accurate expectations) are probably not as successful with their family's goals if kindness is absent.

When family members think in terms of kindness rather than competition and control, we can begin to remove the criticism, contempt, defensiveness, and stonewalling from our response menus during the daily family contact. This chapter also emphasizes the idea that the more we try to change people, the more likely we will end up damaging close relationships. Remember, the only person you can try to change is yourself. This is difficult if a partner is a died-in-the-wool competitive communicator. One might try the approach of suggesting that you wish to try strengthening your relationship based on some material you have been reading. Then suggest that he or she read it also. Come together (meta-communication) and talk about how you talk about things. If that is unsuccessful, you might want to find a counselor who can guide you through ways of strengthening your communication strategies. Change is possible, but only if both partners are sincerely committed to change.

A key point of this chapter is that changing communication is an individual effort. Teaching yourself another way of communicating can dramatically change your life. It pays to take careful note about how many messages of kindness and generosity one is sending vis-à-vis how many negative, competitive, and controlling messages. It is also important for one to take note of what prompts you to retreat when attacked, when you are impatient with another, or when you want something changed in another person? This chapter also suggests that timing is a key element to understanding communication effectiveness. Gottman reminded us to make sure that each new encounter with a partner begins with sincere kindness, care, and loving connection. If we need to seek change, we should use carefully chosen words to express a complaint and avoid slipping into the minefield of superlatives, attacks, overgeneralizations, and sarcasm. Also, more effective couples avoid mimicking and other forms of clever repartee you see on television and in movies. Although possibly humorous to watch in a movie, the sarcastic, demeaning humor portrayed in the media will not build strong relationships.

Finally, it is important to remember that the style of communication you adopt with your partner will spill over into the type of messages sent to your children. In turn, they will pass those patterns of interaction along to their children and spouses.

☐ Study Questions

1. What is meant when we use the term *intent messages*?
2. What is a non sequitur?
3. Why do family scientists make the claim that "you cannot not communicate"?
4. What does *decoding* refer to?
5. What is meta-communication?
6. Name four ideas that reinforce the notion that it is critical to understand gender in the study of family communication.
7. Describe the harsh startup principle and explain how this idea can be used in families.

☐ Key Terms

Communication
Covert messages
Overt messages
Meta-communication
Decoding
Intent messages
Content messages
Types of communication (e.g., dissing, straight talk, control talk, etc.)
Harsh startup

☐ Suggested Readings

Booth, A., Crouter, A., & Clements, M. (2001). *Couples in conflict.* Mahwah, NJ: Lawrence Erlbaum Associates.

Gottman, J. M. (1994). *What predicts divorce?: The relationship between marital processes and marital outcomes.* Hillsdale, NJ: Lawrence Erlbaum Associates.

Gottman, J. M. (1999). *The seven principles for making marriage work.* New York: Crown.

Gottman, J. M. (2001). *The relationship cure.* New York: Crown.

Noller, P., & Fitzpatrick, M. A. (1993). *Communication in family relationships.* Englewood Cliffs, NJ: Prentice Hall.

Regulating Distance

☐ Chapter Preview

In this chapter, readers will learn:

- About the emotional climate in a family.
- How sometimes a family's emotional climate can create a situation in which family members become overly connected to the family system.
- That if family members are overconnected to their family, they might have a difficult time separating their emotions from their thinking selves.
- That there are at least two ways that a family's emotional climate can produce family members who feel overconnected. Both of these ways are examples of families who have a low tolerance for intimacy: chronic anxiety and emotional triangling.
- How chronic anxiety refers to long-term negative emotion in the family emotional system.
- That all families encounter important negative emotions such as despair, futility, and serious disappointment. Family emotional systems can be wisely managed by dealing with these negative emotions so they do not become chronic.
- How emotional triangles or triangling occurs when a family member has some anxiety about a family relationship and draws a third person into the problem as a strategy to solve the problem. Triangling is usually destructive in a family system.
- There are four ways one can use to cope with high levels of overconnectedness: using a genogram, understanding invisible loyalties, the benign assumption, and avoiding emotional cutoff.
- That the ideas about family emotional systems have several implications for families and those who try to help them.

☐ Introduction

Your family did not suddenly appear one day. Instead, who we are as families evolved from an ongoing, developmental, and historical process. For example, from my family of origin, I brought certain emotional and value-oriented ties. My wife also brought with her an orientation about how one should (or could) feel about another person or group of people within a family. One of the more important aspects of how our family system functions or fails to thrive is how each of us (my wife and I) manage the emotional relationships between us and between each of our five children. Families, who are better able to meet goals, maintain longer and more fulfilling relationships, and meet crisis are those families who have a capacity for tolerating intimacy and individuality (Farley, 1979; Gavazzi et al., 1993; Sabatelli & Anderson, 1991). An important aspect of understanding family processes is an awareness of how to balance these two ideas.

In this chapter, we focus primarily on the idea of learning to balance closeness in family life. Generally, family theorists and therapists refer to this topic as **differentiation** in families. Differentiation, or the ability to maintain appropriate emotional distance from other family members, is a key skill in successful family life. To differentiate means to appropriately separate, segment, and make different. When differentiation in families is problematic, families are either so emotionally close that there is little difference among the family members, or they are so emotionally separate that bonding, support, and connection are faint and removed.

☐ Building Individuality in Family Members

One of the key tasks of parenting is the process of encouraging and fostering personal individuality. During the course of this text, I have emphasized the idea that families can become a consensual community, working together, sharing a paradigm, and using their group strength to overcome problems. In this chapter, we take a slightly different angle on that theme and suggest that family strength is also achieved by building independence within the individuals who comprise the family. To some, that might sound paradoxical. How can you build group strength by building or creating strength in the person? Occasionally, we hear of families whose primary theme is to ask family members to surrender all they are individually and become subsumed into the collective of the family. These highly "enmeshed" families have constructed a family paradigm of beliefs, rules, rule sequences, and values that has as a core theme the idea that the family collective is more important than the strength and well-being of the individual.

A few years ago, there was a popular television program called *Star Trek: The New Generation*. In one episode, the crew of the starship encountered an alien culture that traveled through space completely consuming and absorbing any other culture, person, or thing that got in its way. This massive absorbing collective was called the Borg. The Borg captured all in its path. Once captured, victims became attached (literally) to the massive blob-like culture, tethered, undifferentiated, and unable to act for one's self. The voice of the Borg would announce, "Resistance is futile, you will be assimilated." In this way, the collective of space cyborgs assimilated and absorbed entire cultures and anyone who got in the way. This literary metaphor serves our discussion well. There are times when some families become like the Borg. This chapter is a distillation of about 50 years of research surrounding this topic. Past researchers identified one of the more destructive family processes known. This catastrophic process centers on what happens when families go past the boundary of loving and caring and journey into Borg-like behavior within which the group becomes a controlling, unstoppable collective that insists that the individual surrender any semblance of personal identity.

In general when we speak of tolerating or even building individuality, we often refer to the idea that a major task of families is to regulate distance. Regulating distance implies that families can be too close (Borg-like assimilation) and they can be too disconnected (every person for himself or herself). The feature of this process highlighted in this chapter centers on teaching families to learn how to effectively allow their children to develop an individualized self that can thrive independently.

A prime directive for parents is to find ways of staying connected, loving, caring, and interested, at the same time allowing children to become independent thinkers and allow them the freedom to make choices and have a sense of individuality. Family researchers and therapists have long taught that it is a sign of family strength when families create a climate of increasing independence in their children. The opposite situation is where families have little or no tolerance for individuality and instead demand conformity and compliance at any cost. Usually, to achieve this domination in children, overconnected parents create a climate of chronic anxiety, animosity, distrust, and conflict.

This type of family climate has the potential to create deep emotional problems for children who are raised with this type of parenting strategy. One early writer and originator of this concept was Bowen (1976). He authored several important research papers that describe how destructive unhealthy overconnection is in family life. At its most negative point, he suggested that occasionally family members become so connected to the family emotional system that this connection interferes with their ability to manage the other aspects of their lives.

According to several family researchers (Bowen, 1976; Gavazzi, 1993; Gavazzi & Sabatelli, 1990), our experience with family **connectedness** begins early in our lives. One of the jobs of a child is to resolve the inevitable strong connections between the child and his or her parents. We all are strongly connected to what happens in our families in early life, but the climate or tone of the family environment predicts whether or not we can build our own identity separate and apart from that of our parents and early family members. As we pass into early adulthood, one of the most important psychological tasks we approach is the search for independence, identity, or individuation. All of those terms mean essentially the same thing and refer to a person's need to separate from his or her family of origin and become a unique individual.

A term used by these family scholars to describe how connectedness and intimacy work in families is **differentiation**. The root of this term is *different*. In other words, to differentiate is to separate and become unique. This term is also used in biology and the idea is similar. For example, a primary difference between cancer cells and healthy cells is that healthy cells are differentiated. That means they know how to specialize and some cells become hair, others heart tissue, and still others know to become skin. Cancer cells, however, have forgotten what they are and are undifferentiated. Instead of becoming something specific and purposeful, they just grow and consume. A mass of undifferentiated cells is worthless to the body and even destructive. Researchers suggest that differentiation levels have been linked to the family's ability to prepare and successfully launch its offspring (Carter & McGoldrick, 1989; Farley, 1979; Gavazzi, 1994; Kerr & Bowen, 1988).

PRINCIPLE 11.1   DIFFERENTIATION IS A POWER TOOL IN FAMILY LIFE

Differentiation refers to appropriate separateness from one's family. The goal is to develop a differentiated self while remaining close (but not smothered) by one's family.

When the goal of a family is to create a mass of undifferentiated members who have forgotten or never knew a special purpose that resides outside of their families of origin (think of the Borg), children do not thrive. When we are young, no one really expects us to differentiate and become unique. As a child becomes a preteen, however, becoming differentiated is essential for the health of both the individual and the family so that each family member feels a sense of uniqueness, specialness, and individuality. Some individuals never really move beyond being emotionally connected to their parents. It is as if they have a very long emotional umbilical cord still attached to their mother, father, or both. In recent years, this has become more apparent with the invention and mass distribution of cell phones. Imagine parents using cell phone technology to monitor every movement of their child who is now an older teen—even at college. The mother (or father) is showing her love by calling several times per day, asking how a class went, inquiring about personal conversations, reminding the college student to eat a good lunch, and not eat unhealthy snacks, encouraging her to do her homework, and so on. The intrusion into the daily life by technology very well could be fueling a movement toward more unhealthy parent–child interactions.

On the other hand, families who know how to build differentiation allow individuals to express individuality and are still intimately connected (Gavazzi, 1993). As the child ages, the families are less intrusive and more supportive. Being differentiated does not mean that one disconnects from parents, nor does it imply rejecting the family's rituals, values, and beliefs. It does, however mean that the family allows children to become separated in a healthy and supported way as they grow into adulthood.

Poor Differentiation

Poorly differentiated families express a lower tolerance for the uniqueness of the individual family members. Think back to the chapter on ideologies. Families who are more

FIGURE 11.1 This drawing captures the idea that sometimes families are so fused and undifferentiated that it is hard to tell where one family member begins and is different from the others.

closed and have rigid boundaries with regard to the outside world are much more likely to be chronically anxious about making sure family members do not break any rules. However, inside the family walls, the boundaries are usually very blurred. That is, because undifferentiated families are so intrusive they might insist on opening everyone's mail, not letting children play behind closed doors, and forcing family members to participate in all family activities.

Intimacy

It is also the case that there is a low tolerance for intimacy in poorly differentiated families. The conflict that arises from intrusive attempts to maintain control and domination might completely squelch any kindness, generosity, or feelings of love. The overall result is a young person who is very unsure of his or her place in the world. The prevailing message is one of doubt, unresolved emotions, and a perpetual search for validation.

☐ Fusion

Family Fusion

The term **family fusion** (for our purposes here) refers to a situation within a family within which the patterns, rules, rule sequences, and family paradigm conspire together to negate family members' individuality. When someone in the family tries to break free of the "Borg," so to speak, their efforts at independence are seen as disloyal and the person's actions are seen as attempts to destroy the very integrity of the family. As a part of this process, highly fused families experience life as a Borgian group: Every experience resulting in anxiety, loss, joy, pain, or other emotional experience is felt and relived by the group. The daily stories of emotional highs and certainly all the lows are broadcast to the collective, experienced as a group, and processed by the whole. The person is not allowed to experience any feature of life in private, but must share all with the group.

PRINCIPLE 11.2   FUSION IN FAMILIES CREATES DEEP PROBLEMS

Often, fused family members feel trapped in the family ego-mass. This feeling of being trapped creates anxiety, dysfunction, and even mental illness.

Of course, we begin life emotionally connected and even fused to our parents (Reiss, 1988). This means infants and children are naturally and involuntarily caught up in the emotional processes of their parents and siblings. Early fusion has at least two possible outcomes. More effective families appropriately regulate the emotional climate in such a way that positive sentiment abounds: There are higher levels of trust, concern, confidence, and appreciation; children sense these emotions and respond to them positively. Within this supportive and more open climate, teenagers are more able to establish a clear and separate identity from their families of origin (Anderson & Fleming, 1986).

Internal Fusion

Not only can fusion be created at the larger social-group level, but fusion can spill over from the group process into the psyche of the individual. When family fusion exists, it is usually maintained by tension, anxiety, and even hostility. It takes high levels of energy (often negative energy such as control attempts, intimidation, cohersion, and even bullying) to keep family members connected and fused. This climate of tension and anxiety can have negative results for the inner well-being of the child. Sometimes when the anxiety and tension are chronic and high in family life, children have a difficult time learning how to separate their thinking world from their emotional world. Because much of their experience in family life is highly emotionally charged, they might not have been taught to pay attention to the thinking, rational aspect of their inner self. When home life is charged with resentment, animosity, and bitterness, children seem to lose the ability to separate their emotions from their intellect. Children who are raised in a climate of family fusion have more difficulty separating their thinking world from their feeling world.

To summarize this section, we are suggesting that the concept of fusion can be represented on a scale. On one end of the scale is differentiation. Children who are raised in a nonintrusive, nonfused family are encouraged to become independent and self-directed. At the other end of the family fusion scale is high fusion. In highly fused families, children are expected to become part of the collective, surrender personal identity, think and act like parents and other siblings or even grandparents, conform, and become absorbed into the family collective. Families who adopt a family paradigm that focuses on fusion usually use tactics like intimidation, high control attempts, physical force, higher levels of negativity, hostility, and animosity to achieve their goal of high conformity. It is important to note that often built into the constitution of this type of family paradigm is the idea that fusion and conforming is the ultimate family type. Family conformity and fusion are often presented as the highest ideal or even a sacred family form. As illustrated later, one of the outcomes of high family fusion is that children might lose the ability to think more rationally but, instead, will be consumed with an emotional, feeling world within which rational thought might be an infrequent visitor.

Results of Fusion

When a person grows up in a fused family within which anxiety and hostility are used to promote conformity and fusion, children have difficulty with effective problem solving (Papero, 1983) and have trouble with emotional regulation. They are more likely to have explosive tempers and bouts of depression, and less likely to form high levels of prosocial behaviors (like reaching out to help others). Likewise, research has found that in families where the climate was more positive and where there were fewer control attempts aimed at family conformity, children were much more likely to be able to separate their thinking selves from their emotional selves and they were generally less likely to experience problems with emotional reactivity. When people are more highly differentiated, they seem to be able to maintain more objectivity and to think carefully for longer periods of time in spite of the emotional arousal (Papero, 1983, p. 140).

Sauer (1982) listed several characteristics of families who are more intrusive, enmeshed, or fused. Check this list found in Activity 11.1 in your workbook and see if any of those questions fit how your family relates to one another.

Other researchers concur. For example, appropriate levels of differentiation in a family are more likely to produce teenagers who can build stronger relationships with other people (Sabatelli & Cecil-Pigo, 1985), have fewer problems with alcohol abuse (Bartle & Sabatelli, 1989), have higher levels of psychological maturity (Gavazzi et al., 1993) and were much less likely to have general problems at school, difficulty with peers, participation in illegal activities, and fewer problems with their families of origin (Gavazzi, 1993).

As mentioned earlier, when a person is raised in a climate of hostility—especially where the goal of the hostility is to promote group conformity—the child seems to lose his or her ability to think for himself or herself, solve problems effectively, and make good decisions (Nichols & Schwartz, 2007, p. 371). One of the original researchers to identify this problem said, "At the fusion end of the spectrum, the intellect is so flooded by emotionality that the total life course is determined by the emotional process and by what 'feels right' rather than by beliefs or opinions. The intellect exists as an appendage of the feeling system" (Bowen, 1976, p. 66).

Another family researcher, Kerr (1981), conducted several studies in which he found that calm people think more fairly, clearly, and objectively. However, when highly connected or fused individuals were placed in emotionally charged situations, they responded less calmly and, instead, more irrationally, and sought approval from others, placed blame on others, and tried to dominate others in the situation (Kerr, 1981, p. 237).

Therefore, one application of this principle is that when family climates have less conflict, family members develop a greater sense of differentiation or personal individuality and, consequently, they do much better at solving life's difficult problems. When a highly stressful event occurs, they are much more likely to be able to think clearly about their options and generate effective solutions. As Kerr and Bowen (1988) indicated, "An anxious family elevates a facet of a problem to the cause of the problem" (p. 61).

☐ Chronic Family Anxiety

There are at least two facets of inner family life that help us understand how family fusion operates. When there is family fusion there is a low tolerance for intimacy and individuality and there are usually higher levels of conflict, animosity, and anxiety. Researchers realized this many years ago and labeled this phenomena chronic family anxiety. This idea describes the seemingly perpetual bickering, nattering, intrusive control attempts that characterize fused families.

The second idea explored later is triangulation. In fused families, family members are more likely to try and recruit another family member to solve some problem they are having with a third family member. Often in fused families there are coalitions, teams, and partnerships who band together to effect some desired outcome. This topic is covered later and is labeled **emotional triangles**.

Defining Chronic Anxiety

Anxiety can be defined as a negative emotion that includes distress or uneasiness of mind caused by apprehension of danger or misfortune. Acute anxiety is different from chronic anxiety. Acute anxiety is usually a short-term response to a stressful situation, and most of the time it is a rational response to a real (rather than imagined) problem. For example, when a couple is told by a doctor their child has a serious disease, the natural emotional response is to have acute anxiety or feelings of "distress or uneasiness of mind caused by apprehension of danger or misfortune." Acute anxiety tends to leave after a person learns to cope with the stressful situation or the danger leaves. For example, the anxiety leaves a couple when they learn how to cope with the illness or if the diagnosis is not accurate.

All individuals and families encounter situations that create acute anxiety. It occurs whenever there are serious problems to be dealt with and whenever negative emotions such as despair, futility, inadequacy, inferiority, lack of fulfillment, discouragement, emotional hurt, or serious disappointments occur. One of the challenges all families face is to find ways to deal with these problems and their negative emotions so that they do not lead to chronic anxiety.

Chronic anxiety occurs when uneasiness, distress, or apprehension endures for long periods of time. Usually the sources of chronic anxiety are difficult to identify, as are the original causes, and it is an underlying condition that persists and colors many different situations.

There are some types of chronic anxiety that usually are not important in family systems. For example, people can have psychic fears or apprehensions that are related to their work, their education, or their friendships, and these forms or types of chronic anxiety often have little impact of family life. Also, people can have chronic anxiety about many other things that have little to do with family systems. They can have chronic anxiety about being in an elevator or being in dark places, and many of these chronic anxieties only occur outside the home and have little impact on family systems.

Bowen studied one type of chronic anxiety that is very important in family systems, long-term tension or resentment. This occurs when family members feel others in their family have been unjust to them in important ways. Emotional undercurrents can occur when family members love deeply, with close bonds, and then feel betrayed, abandoned, deceived, or ignored.

The solution is for families to find ways to deal with negative emotions such as resentment and disappointment so they do not lead to chronic ills in their system. The healing balm of such things as forgiveness, patience, and the willingness to let ourselves and others be frail and inadequate are strategies that can help families keep chronic anxiety low enough that it does not invisibly erode the basic structures of the family system.

Chronic family anxiety is a significant problem because it can lead to destructive emotional climates such as general feelings of animosity, malice, rancor, enmity, and hatred. Emotions such as these create seriously disabling processes in most families because they interfere with the most positive emotions that people seek (e.g., love, compassion, care, and nurturance).

Another reason this type of chronic anxiety is usually disabling is because it keeps family members "on edge," and even minor problems can be enough to create intense emotional reactions of anger, aggression, violence, and abuse. It is similar to having a pot of water simmering, where a slight increase in temperature is enough to make it boil.

When families do not have chronic anxiety in their emotional system they do not overrespond to minor problems, and they can marshal their resources to cope with the problems effectively. When they have ongoing tension, however, they have less ability to cope with even minor problems. The principle that Bowen developed can be called the chronic anxiety principle.

PRINCIPLE 11.3   CHRONIC ANXIETY PRINCIPLE

The higher the level of chronic anxiety in a family (or other relationship), the less likely they will be able to attain their goals or be adaptive.

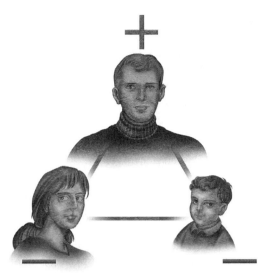

FIGURE 11.2   A triangle exists when one person does not like another person (or the actions of another)—the first person likes a third person—but the third person also likes the second person. The idea of triangles applies to likes and dislikes, difference of ideas, and even personality differences.

Emotional Triangles

The second outcome that frequently results in fused families is triangling. The creation of emotional triangles is a common occurrence in fused families. Triangling occurs when two parts of a family system have an ongoing conflict and they focus on something or someone else as a way of gaining control over the situation or stabilizing their problem. There are many targets for a triangling situation. Sometimes triangles are formed to control another family member. Other times, an attribute of a person is the target.

Emotional triangles have a number of rules that govern how they operate. Friedman (1985) said, "What Peter says about Paul tells you more about Peter than it does about Paul." In the concept of an emotional triangle, "What Peter says to you about his relationship with Paul has to do with his relationship with you" (p. 36).

Friedman (1985) developed several "laws" about emotional triangles that help us understand what they are and how they operate in families (pp. 36–39). His ideas have been edited and changed here to adapt them to family life.

1. Triangles are often used to create balance, but it rarely works: One family member might try to keep the relationship of two other family members in balance by intruding in the relationship of the two others. In this case, a family member will feel it is her (or his) responsibility to make sure that a child (for example) has a good relationship with his father or sibling. Or a child might feel a need to get two parents closer or stop high levels of conflict. In a family paradigm that uses fusion-creating strategies, one or more family members will try to force, dominate, control, or bully another to conform by trying to change the relationship between two family members.
2. The results are usually temporary. When Mary (the mother in our example) tries to change the relationship between Justin (the son) and Michael (the father), she might see some change, but rarely for more than a few days. It is almost always the case that

a relationship that is changed in this way (by the mother trying to make the son and father closer) will revert to the way it was before.

3. Triangulation makes things worse. When Mary tries to make Justin and Michael get along better, Mary's attempts almost always result in a worse relationship between Justin and Michael. The harder she tries to change their relationship (even though this is a good and wonderful goal), the more she gets an opposite result that she wanted.

4. The person who initiates a triangulation attempt feels worse. As Mary tries to get Justin and Michael to have a better relationship, not only is it less likely to get better, but Mary is more likely to feel worse about their relationship and take on the stress of them not being close to one another.

5. Stop using triangulation and things might get better. Mary has a greater chance at building stronger family relationships when she builds strong connections with Justin and Michael individually, rather than thinking she can force them to get along. She has to realize that the connection between Justin and Michael is not her responsibility but is best developed by the two of them. It usually turns out that intrusive attempts to make a relationship stronger by a third person make things worse (Friedman, 1985, pp. 36–39).

The roots of triangulation are ongoing, long-term anxiety (negative emotion) issues that are not resolved. The best alternative is to find ways to resolve the roots to the problem by finding ways to resolve the negative affect. The next best alternative is to find ways to manage the negative emotions so they do not disrupt healthy individual development, healthy family development, and attaining goals. (Friedman, 1985)

There are a number of practical implications of these ideas. One of the most obvious implications is that families can avoid emotional triangles or eliminate them if they can find ways to avoid long-term negative emotions such as resentment, tension, animosity, anger, fear, apprehension, and anxiety. Second, the use of triangulation in families is often a sign of attempts to create family fusion. Families who are anxious, worried, and distressed about lack of conformity to family paradigms often resort to these types of problematic strategies. Using triangulation as a way to solve family problems usually makes things worse.

A third implication is to try to be aware of how we might be part of family triangles. Often when someone solicits advice or help for a relationship problem, it is an attempt to triangle us into the problem situation. Being aware of the triangulation processes can provide useful ideas about how to help and how to avoid making the problem worse.

☐ Coping With Fusion

Family scientists suggest four ways of coping with emotional distress in families: It is useful to learn how to use and analyze a genogram and deal with insights it provides, to resolve invisible loyalties, to generate a **benign assumption** in family life, and to avoid a strategy many people try that is usually unsuccessful: **emotional cutoff**.

Using a Genogram

Genograms can provide insights about the amount of differentiation occurring in families. One reason they are helpful is that patterns of fusion and differentiation are often carried from one generation to another. Usually in each generation there are some children who tend to have a little more differentiation, and there are some children who tend to have a little less, but many children repeat the patterns of the earlier generations.

Using a genogram chart, first examine and evaluate the differentiation–fusion patterns that have existed over several generations in a family. This usually provides insights about how some people have been more fused than others, and it can provide clues about a particular individual's fusion. It also helps people think about their differentiation as part of a larger pattern.

Examining your own differentiation in the context of a genogram can make you become more aware of strategies you can use to become more differentiated. For example, it might help you realize you are an autonomous individual who needs to stand on your own two feet.

Being a transitional character can change the direction of a family. Learning about these important principles means that you have the groundwork for the first step of any change process: You have the knowledge. However, having the knowledge does not mean that the knowing will, by itself, change you. There are millions of people who know that smoking cigarettes will kill them, and yet the knowledge without a daily resolve to change means that they continue living their lives as they always have, using a product that probably will kill them. The same is true for those of us who eat too much. Change is difficult and only those who practice fighting the momentum of the past can really become a transitional character.

It also might help to realize that some feelings were appropriate when you were a child, but not when you are an adult. It also might help you realize how some of the family patterns that keep you "fused" to your family system were petty sibling rivalries you have now outgrown. It might help you be able to relate to your parents as individuals who also struggle with their limitations and circumstances.

Dealing With Invisible Loyalties

Boszormenyi-Nagy and his colleagues developed another strategy for resolving undesirable emotional connections in family systems. In their book *Invisible Loyalties,* Boszormenyi-Nagy and Spark (1973) described how families accumulate multigenerational patterns of obligations and rights. Some examples of positive things received are existence, love, nurturance, identity, heritage, values, bonds, and understanding.

Part of these patterns is obligations that are deeply felt emotional ties. These include such things as indebtedness, basic duties, and a sense of ethical responsibility. Boszormenyi-Nagy called these deeply felt connections invisible loyalties, and they involve such processes as giving and taking, helping and hindering, injustices and healing, teaching and receiving, and various combinations of hurting and acts of caring.

Boszormenyi-Nagy and Spark suggested that it is helpful to use the concept of a family ledger to think about these family processes. The ledger is a balance sheet of obligations and rights, debts and credits that accumulate over time. In more effective families, family members tend to balance the ledger with justice in the exchange of debts and obligations. Sometimes, however, the justice comes too slowly, or it is insufficient and there is too great an accumulation of injustices.

In other situations some individuals perceive the pattern has been unjust, and this is deeply troubling. When these inequities occur, it creates chronic anxiety, resentments, and animosities that are disruptive to family members individually and collectively. One of Boszormenyi-Nagy and Spark's examples of this process is a mother who is angry at being rejected by her mother. She tries to correct this injustice by offering total devotion to her own daughter. However, in the language of balance of payments, the mother assumes the daughter should reestablish family justice by being appreciative and giving to her mother the acceptance and understanding her own mother did not give her. In this type of situation, the mother often is excessively devoted to her daughter, creating resentment rather than appreciation. This can lead to the daughter having unexplained negative feelings toward the "loving" mother. Confusion and emotional disruption prevail between the mother and daughter. Improvement results when either the mother or daughter realizes how the mother is trying to "balance the payments" or make up for her own deprivation. This can help the mother and the daughter understand what is going on and free them from the invisible emotional processes.

Family fusion can be created because the emotionally based resentments are captivating and consuming. Often, according to Boszormenyi-Nagy and Spark, the main difficulty is the invisibility of these patterns of unfinished business. Therefore, when the patterns are discovered it is many times relatively easy to talk them through and resolve the emotional obligations.

The Benign Assumption

Another way that family theorists and therapists have suggested to combat the potential effects of negativity and chronic anxiety in families is to develop an emotional climate that has a benign tone (Beavers, 1982). Beavers and his associates suggested that one of the more important aspects of stronger families is that they build a climate that is void of malignant attitude. An example would probably best help to define how this works.

In families where there is a malignant or highly contentious tone, each daily event that annoys or even has the potential to annoy someone is responded to with far more negative response than the event should warrant. Suppose someone spills milk at the table. In a malignant climate the parent might say something like, "See, that is another example of how you always try to make my life miserable. You are a brat and deserve to be punished." Families in which there is a benign assumption would probably respond with something that is far less dramatic, histrionic, animated, and nasty. Instead, the parent does not assume that each time something happens (like the milk spilling, or the lost shoe) that it is a "federal case" (as my mom would say). Instead, they might even give a little laugh and say, "Oops, run and get a rag before it gets all over."

When there is no benign assumption, each day is filled with events that are interpreted as threatening and as attacks. It is as if the glass of life is always full of stress and accusation to overflowing and each creates a spill, so to speak. The application is, of course, to somehow break through the habitual overreactivity that too many families develop. They seem to be awash in a malignant assumptive world, filled with threat, anxiety, and unresolved anger. Although you might not be able to do much about your family of origin, you certainly can begin to work on your family of procreation. Literally nothing good comes from high levels of contention and a climate of the malignant assumption in family life. These two doses of strife only increase the distance between family members and decrease levels of intimacy.

Emotional Cutoff: An Undesirable Method

The fourth way one can cope with highly charged emotions in families is to face the problems in families head on and not use emotional cutoff as a method of trying to deal with fusion that is generally ineffective. Emotional cutoff refers to attempts to deny fusion rather than resolve it. The result is that people might stop interacting with their family, or they might move away from their family, but they are still emotionally fused. In these situations the fusion still has the same effects, even though the parental family might be thousands of miles away.

According to Bowen (1976), emotional cutoff is determined by the way people handle their unresolved emotional attachments to their parents. He claimed that all people have some degree of unresolved emotional attachment to their parents, and furthermore the more family fusion one experienced in childhood, the more likely one will experience the unresolved attachment and feelings of wanting to use emotional cutoff. Bowen indicated that the way an individual approaches the idea of cutoff greatly influences the way "people separate themselves from the past in order to start their lives in the present generation" (p. 83).

He further stated:

> The degree of unresolved emotional attachment to the parents is equivalent to the degree of fusion that must somehow be handled in the person's own life and in future generations. The unresolved attachment is handled by the intapsychic process of denial and isolation of self while living close to the parents; or by physically running away; or by a combination of emotional isolation and physical distance. (Bowen, 1976, p. 84)

He is also convinced that the more intense cutoff is, the more likely his own children are to do a more forceful cutoff with him in the next generation. There are many variations in the intensity of this basic process and in the way the cutoff is handled. The person who runs away from his family of origin is in serious need of emotional closeness, but at the same time, they are allergic to it.

Thus, emotional cutoff is always a less desirable solution than working through or resolving the emotional problems in a way that will promote healthy differentiation. In some situations, however, it might not be possible to differentiate; then emotional cutoff becomes one of the options to be considered. On several occasions students and professionals have challenged the tone of this paragraph. I have heard from several who say that if there is abuse of any kind (i.e., sexual, physical, or emotional) leaving and not looking back might be the best thing and usually a prime option to be explored.

☐ Summary

This chapter discussed two aspects of the family emotional differentiation—fusion and chronic anxiety—in which problems frequently occur, and suggested strategies for helping families deal effectively with them. Family fusion occurs when family members are excessively tied to the emotional system in their parental family. The result is that family members become victims of the emotionality in their lives, and when family fusion occurs it interferes with the ability people have to use their intellect.

Chronic anxiety comes about when feelings of resentment, apprehension, and rancor exist for long periods of time as part of the emotional climate (emotional field) in a family. Triangling and problems with health are two disabling processes in families that grow out of chronic anxiety.

☐ Study Questions

1. Define what is meant by the term *differentiation* in family life.
2. Give several examples of poor differentiation in families.
3. "What Peter says about Paul tells you more about Peter than it does Paul." Explain what this means within the context in which it was presented.
4. Define emotional triangle and give an example of how one might work in a family.
5. Is fusion different than differentiation? How, if it is?
6. Tell what is meant by the term *chronic anxiety* and give examples of how it works in family life.
7. Tell why emotional cutoff is a poor strategy for coping with family emotions.

☐ Key Terms

Differentiation
Connectedness
Family fusion
Emotional triangles
Emotional cutoff
Benign assumption

☐ Suggested Readings

Cox, M., & Brooks-Gunn, J. (1999). *Conflict and cohesion in families: Causes and consequences.* Mahwah, NJ: Lawrence Erlbaum Associates.
Holodynski, M., & Friedlmeier, W. (2006). *Development of emotions and emotional regulation.* New York: Springer.
Kerr, M. E., & Bowen, M. (1988). *Family evaluation.* New York: Norton.
Minuchin, S. (1996). *Mastering family therapy: Journeys of growth and transformation.* New York: Wiley.

CHAPTER

Building and Maintaining Family Rituals

☐ Chapter Preview

In this chapter, readers will learn:

- How family rituals and routines are similar in some ways and different in other ways.
- That when rituals are wisely managed they can help families attain important goals such as unity, closeness, intimacy, meaning, membership changes, and so on.
- That families can be wise or unwise in the ways they manage rituals and routines.
- That families can be creative in making new rituals and changing old ones.

☐ Introduction

We are all familiar with family **rituals**. Some of them occur on holidays such as Christmas, Thanksgiving, the 4th of July, Passover, Kwanzaa, or Three Kings Day. On these special days, families do a number of things in ways that are different from the ordinary. They trim trees, wrap and open presents, bake turkeys in a special way, color eggs, have religious ceremonies, go to parades, attend church, eat special foods, abstain from eating food, watch football games, and so on. Some rituals occur only once per lifetime (e.g., one's funeral).

Most family **routines** are more ordinary, and some of them are repeated on a daily basis. For example, we give each other kisses and hugs in special ways and wave goodbye as we leave for work and school. We tuck small children into bed, tell bedtime stories, eat certain meals at certain times and in certain ways, and have special places to sit and read.

Even though we are all familiar with family rituals and routines, when we try to study this part of the family realm we discover that the terms we use are fairly vague and elusive, and they also are complicated. For example, are rituals the same as routines, traditions, customs, and habits? Are they the same as family rules, or are they different? If they are different, what are the differences?

☐ What Are Rituals and Routines?

The term *ritual* is "an elusive concept, on the one hand transparent and conspicuous in its enactment, on the other, subtle and mysterious in its boundaries and effects on participants" (Wolin & Bennett, 1984, p. 401). Although scholars in many fields study rituals and routines, they have had difficulty agreeing about just what they are (Boyce, Jensen, James, & Peacock 1983; Friese, 2007). For example, anthropology, sociology, psychology, and family science all have a body of literature about them. Because the scholars in each of these disciplines have differing perspectives, they study different aspects of rituals and do not agree on how to define the terms (Gillis, 1996). For the purposes of this text, rituals are defined as a set of actions for behaviors that contain symbolic meaning, sacred meaning, or both. The act of performing ritual behavior provides utility to family group as they attempt to meet the demands of life and attain desired goals. In other words, families that have appropriate ritual systems are more efficient and effective in solving problems and attaining desired goals.

Commonalities of Rituals and Routines

There are several factors that are common to both rituals and routines:

1. Rituals and routines both always involve more than one member of a family.
2. They both have overt or visible behavior or action. Thus, just thinking about something is not ritual or routine.
3. There is repetition in the form and in the content of what is done. The form refers to how something is done and the content refers to what is done. Some rituals are repeated many times by the same family members, and some are just experienced once in the lifetime of a family member, but other individuals repeat them.
4. There is morphostasis and morphogenesis in both of them. This means they all have some continuity over time, but they also all evolve and change over time as individuals and families develop and as the external environment of families changes.

PRINCIPLE 12.1   RITUALS AND ROUTINES ARE ESSENTIAL BUT DIFFERENT

Families who are strong and efficient in goal attainment activities are also effective in creating and maintaining rituals. Rituals are different than routines.

Differences Between Rituals and Routines

Fiese (2007), Wise (1986), and Gillis (1996) prefer to divide rituals and routines into two separate groups. The following list of attributes helps us distinguish ritual from routine. To begin, we draw on the work of Fiese, who suggested that rituals and routines can be divided based on three dimensions: communication, commitment, and continuity.

1. Routines focus on communication styles that are functional and instrumental. That is, we know it is a routine if the communication about the activity communicates

something like, "this task needs to be completed before we leave for the movie." On the other hand, the communication that flows from a ritual tells the family members about identity and informs them about "who they are." Imagine a Jewish family performing the rituals associated with Passover. One of those activities is the spring megacleaning during which every morsel of chemetz is removed from the home. Chemetz is bread, grains, or leavened products that are not used during Passover. Following the cleaning, there is burning that takes place, during which any leavened products and segments, morsels, or pieces of bread are destroyed by burning. Following that, special unleavened bread is prepared, and other special items are made or obtained to be used during the Seder, the special meal taken by the family during the Passover feast. During the meal, traditional questions are asked by the youngest member of the family to the oldest family member, who answers with scripted responses that retell the story of the Jewish people leaving the land of Egypt. This special ritualized holiday communicates to the new generation a clear identity. It also helps remind the older generations who they are and what values they hold dear.

2. Rituals and routines are also different with regard to commitment. Routines require little commitment, are usually perfunctory, and take little thought. Taking a morning shower, for example, is not a ritual, per se. It is, however, a valued routine for many—but it requires no interpersonal commitment. Rituals capture the ideal of commitment. Remembering someone's birthday is a signal that you are committed to that relationship.

3. Ritual and routines are different with regard to continuity. Routines can change without fanfare. If someone decides to eat at 5:30 instead of 6:30, no one is really going to care much. But, if one changes the menu at Thanksgiving and decides to have spaghetti instead of turkey, there could be a revolt. Fiese (2007) says that the meanings created with rituals "extend across generations" (p. 11). She also says that rituals communicate across generations about who we (as a family group) will continue to be across generations.

In addition to these three fundamental differences between rituals and routines, there are several other differences that need to be discussed. First, they differ in the amount of emotion that is involved. There is a great deal of emotion during weddings, funerals, children leaving home to go to school, the birth of a new child, a Bar Mitzvah, and celebrations of important holidays such as Christmas and Thanksgiving. When these traditions involve important emotionality they become ritualized, and the best term for them is family rituals. There is relatively little emotion in the more ordinary events such as kissing each other hello when returning home each day, talking about the events of the day, vacuuming the carpet once a week, doing dishes, and helping children with their homework. There is routine in these traditions, but there is little ritualization, so they are called family routines.

A second way rituals and routines are different is in the amount of **symbolism**. Some traditions tend to have a large number of symbols. Weddings, for example, symbolize leaving the old households, being "given away," making important commitments and covenants, maturity, a **rite of passage** from being single to being married, and so on. Many other events such as a funeral, wake, Christmas, Bar Mitzvah, and christening have several different levels of symbolic meaning, and the symbolism in these events makes them rituals. When family events have less symbolism, they become more ordinary and are called family routines.

Some family scholars in recent years have used the term *metaphor* (Imber-Black & Roberts, 1992) to try to describe the symbolic aspect of family rituals. A metaphor in this

FIGURE 12.1 During the life course, we experience a rainbow of changes and events that are connected together by rituals and passages that define those transitions.

context refers to an abstract set of ideas or beliefs that is understood and shared but difficult to put into words. Rituals can provide a somewhat tangible representation of the more abstract idea in the metaphor, and thereby have a symbolism that provides meaning, purpose, and a sense of completeness and integration that is difficult to acquire in more rational ways of behaving or conversing.

The symbolism in the Thanksgiving holiday illustrates the metaphorical aspects of a typical American ritual. The unity of the family huddled together over a table of food is a metaphor for the unity of the family wherever they are in the world. They give thanks for the bounty before them as a symbol of the end of the harvest.

Some metaphors in family rituals are less desirable and less healthy. One family, for example, celebrated most holidays with alcohol as a prominent feature. Almost always harsh words were eventually spoken, tempers would flare, and the celebrations would turn into a living hell. Unintentionally, this reoccurring ritual was a miniversion of their entire life. The family was chaotic, and had unresolved conflicts that had gone on for several generations, but they were never brought into the open and dealt with. The family retreated into distance, anger, and hostility, and the dependency on the alcohol was an escape. All of the attempts to end the alcohol problem ended in disappointment. It was not until Bob, one of the sons, insisted on the abstinence from alcohol at holiday celebrations (even if it meant the absence of his drinking father) that the family was able to begin to have the healing effects of warm, peaceful holidays and a greater harmony and peace in general.

A third way rituals and routines are different is in how ordinary versus extraordinary their behaviors are. When traditions are part of the usual ways of behaving they are not special or "staged," and, the term *routine* is a good term to describe them. Rituals tend to have behavior that is relatively unique, unusual, or extraordinary (Fiese, 2007).

For example, when family members bow their head, are quiet, and say a prayer together in a reverent manner before eating a meal, these are "special" behaviors. Even if these special behaviors occur fairly frequently in the family, they still have a certain "uniqueness" or lack of "routineness" in them. When families get dressed up to celebrate the new year and they have a special meal, these are fairly unusual ways of behaving and they are therefore rituals. Routines involve more ordinary ways of doing things. For example, English families tend to use a knife and fork to eat vegetables, and American families just use a fork, and these patterns are part of the routines for family life. Getting up in the morning rather than the evening, eating three fairly sizable meals rather than 10 small meals, and turning the lights out before going to bed are routines.

Some rituals are so unusual and out of the ordinary that they are sacred or highly dramatic, and it is easy to tell them from routines. Other rituals are just barely unusual. For example, using the special china for certain meals, cleaning the house extra carefully when company is coming, and getting ready for a special date might be unusual enough that they become family rituals. Even events such as reading the daily newspaper or watching certain television programs can evolve from routine to ritual if they become unusual enough. For example, if family members like to get a certain combination of refreshments, lighting, seating, and emotional involvement while watching certain television programs, these become family rituals.

The fourth way rituals and routines are different is in the preparation for the event and the follow-up activities. "Ritual is not just the ceremony or actual performance, but the whole process of preparing for it, experiencing it, and reintegration back into everyday life" (Roberts, 1988, p. 8). Even rituals that are fairly frequent have a preparation phase and a back-to-normal phase, and these phases are important parts of the ritual. Routines do not have the same three phases because they are such a normal part of everyday life.

An example of these phases is the preparation for the ritual of Thanksgiving dinner. Many American families put a great deal of time into inviting relatives and preparing the food and their home. Many schedules are temporarily changed as miles and miles are traveled in preparation for the Thanksgiving feast and get together. If someone does not think these processes are important, witness the lack of students at college campuses during such holidays. When students cannot go to their own home, it is painful to stay alone, and hence many homes "adopt" these students who are unable to return home into their own family rituals.

In summary, rituals and routines both involve more than one individual, behavior rather than just thinking, repetition, morphogenesis, and morphostasis. Rituals are different from routines in that they tend to involve more emotion, symbolism, and stylized or staged behavior; and they have the three stages of preparing, experiencing, and shifting back into the ordinary.

Even though many rituals tend to be quite different from many routines, it is important to also realize that there are some situations where there is overlap and the differences are not clear.

Rituals and routines are different from family rules because **rules** are the "understandings" about how all kinds of things are done. Rules deal with such things as using dishes and utensils when we eat rather than putting the food on a table and eating with our hands. Rules define how we should do millions of daily things such as closing doors when it is cold and knocking on a door or ringing a doorbell rather than walking directly into someone's house. Rules are not rituals because they do not have several of the components of rituals. They have little, if any, symbolic meaning, and they are not emotional—even though emotion occurs when some rules are broken. Thus, rituals and routines are events, and rules are the beliefs that govern how these events are to be carried out in a family.

☐ Rituals and Family Paradigm

In Chapter 8, the concept of family paradigm was introduced. In that chapter, it was asserted that a family paradigm is "the shared, enduring, fundamental, and general assumptions or beliefs that family members subscribe to about the nature and meaning of life, what is important, and how to cope with the world they live in" (Reiss, 1981, ch. 4). Family rituals transcend the mundane, prosaic, ordinary features of life and become a seminal and elegant collection of shared, enduring, fundamental activities that make powerful statements about what our shared beliefs are, what is foundational, and what are the assumptive beliefs of a family group. Indeed, a window into the family paradigm is the kind, type, and style of the family rituals.

As clinical researchers, we have also found family rituals to serve as a window into a family's underlying shared identity, providing special access to the behavioral and emotional tenor characterizing each family (Wolin & Bennett, 1984, p. 401).

☐ How Are Rituals and Routines Created?

Bossard and Boll (1950) discovered that rituals originate in two ways in families. Some rituals are part of cultural traditions, and they are handed down from one generation to the next. Many of these "traditional" rituals involve holiday celebrations and religious activities such as having a Thanksgiving dinner, attending church, and sending Christmas cards.

The second way family rituals originate is for families to create or invent their own. These rituals arise out of immediate family interaction in a specific situation, such as going to bed, getting up, eating meals, doing household chores, relaxing over weekends, and vacationing in summertime. Whereas the traditional rites were usually rich pageants, the spontaneous ones were relatively simple. They were, however, more numerous, more frequently practiced, and related to a stricter utilitarian purpose. For this reason, they were often more quickly subject to change (Bossard & Boll, 1950; Fiese, 2007).

Developmental Processes

There are developmental processes in the way rituals are created and evolve over time in families (Fiese, 2007). When a new family begins with the union of two or more people, they pull from their past to develop unique family rituals. Also, during the formative stage of the family life cycle, there tends to be a searching for events that can be ritualized. For example, when a man and woman start dating, they usually create rituals around events that would otherwise be minor things. For example, they might pick out a song that is "their song" and whenever they hear it they enact their own special ritual of hugging, smiling, and commenting on it being something special to them. Or, they might have anniversary celebrations of things such as the day they met, their first date, the day they got engaged, the day they decided to live together, and so on. Other possibilities are they might develop rituals about certain places that had an unusual importance to them, such as the place where they decided to get married.

As families continue to acquire new rituals, some of the rituals they created in the formative stages of family development fade away and are not remembered. Also, the way rituals are emphasized changes at different stages of the family life cycle. When families have children between 2 and about 12 years old they find themselves creating and experiencing bathing rituals, bedtime rituals, eating rituals, and rituals as they visit certain friends and relatives. Also, during this childrearing stage of family development, many families find they emphasize some of the traditional holidays such as Easter and Christmas in elaborate ways that center around the children.

As families move into the stages where they have teenage children and are launching children, their rituals usually evolve. The young adults prefer lively rituals that involve friends, music, and action, and the parents usually find themselves preferring more sedentary and symbolic rituals.

Rituals and routines continue to evolve and change as families move into the postchild-rearing stages of the family cycle. Grandparenting brings rituals such as taking small children to parks and zoos, reminiscing, and telling stories about how things "used to be." Often the younger generations patiently, and sometimes not so patiently, listen over and over again to stories that become part of the family folklore. The routines and rituals of aging couples become even less energetic, but they remain an important part of the emotional and symbolic fabric of the family life of the elderly.

☐ Using Rituals and Routines to Meet Family Goals

The main principle about rituals and routines is summarized in Principle 12.2.

PRINCIPLE 12.2   RITUALS AND ROUTINES

Family rituals and routines are valuable resources, and when they are wisely used they can help families attain important goals such as unity, closeness, intimacy, meaning, membership changes, and so on.

Rituals tend to deal with the more cheerful and optimistic aspects of life providing positive emotional bonds. Rituals also provide a reservoir of such things as goodwill, feelings of "we can do it," "we're together," and trust. This helps families cope with the tragic and challenging aspects of life. They also can help provide a sense of "home" and a feeling that the world is, at least in some ways, a good and comfortable place. In addition, because rituals tend to help families deal with paradoxes and ambiguities and have guiding metaphors, they tend to help family members acquire meaning and purpose, explanation and coherence, and a sense of being in some control of life, or having life be somewhat predictable. They also provide memories that lead to the often-told stories and myths that create a mythology helpful to the sense of family. They help with life cycle transitions by providing rites of passage. They also include many soft, tender, and affectionate moments, thereby helping family members learn that emotionality is appropriate and desirable.

Family scientists have identified seven specific goals that rituals and routines can help with: (a) creating **healthy emotional ties**, (b) membership changes, (c) healing, (d) identity definition and redefinition, (e) belief expression and negotiation, (f) celebration, and (g) dealing with paradoxes and ambiguities.

Creating Healthy Emotional Ties

Several studies of family processes have found that rituals tend to help families create continuity, solidarity, integration, and bonds (Meredith, Abbott & Adams, 1986; Meredith,

1985; Meredith & Abbott, 1989; Schvaneveldt & Lee, 1983). There are many reasons rituals help families accomplish these goals. Meredith, Abbott, Lamanna & Sanders (1989) summarized some of these reasons in the following way:

> Family rituals, first and foremost, encourage contact between family members, usually in a relaxed, enjoyable setting. Family conflicts and problems are temporarily set aside. . . . Rituals may help to bridge the intergenerational gaps that separate family members by providing activity between parents and children and extended family members. A major theme of most family rituals is appreciation of one another and the enjoyment of life together; therefore commitment to the family may be renewed by the regular observance of family rituals. Family values and beliefs may be learned and perpetuated through rituals fostering a sense of unity and oneness. In sum, rituals may be family strengthening for many reasons. (p. 77)

Membership Changes

Families deal with membership changes in many ways. Some changes are major events such as births, deaths, marriages, and divorces; most cultures and families have rather elaborate rituals that help them deal with these major transitions (Gillis, 1996). For example, weddings help individuals, families, and friends make the adjustment of two families of origin coming together and a new family unit being created. Announcements, christenings, and other baby-naming rituals help new members be assimilated, and funerals and wakes help families cope with death. A Bar Mitzvah redefines membership in the family and in the Jewish community, and graduation ceremonies help families redefine the relationship of parents and children and their involvement with school systems.

There are some major changes in membership where families have few rituals that help them make the symbolic and emotional adjustments that are necessary. For example, there are few rituals associated with divorce and adoption. There are none when couples begin living together or stop living together, and there are none for beginning or ending homosexual relationships. Even though the number of stepfamilies has increased dramatically in recent years, there are few ways to ritualize the formation of a stepfamily. Weddings are used to create the marital part of stepfamilies, but the children have a peripheral role in the wedding, and sometimes they are even excluded. One consequence is that often the marital part of the new stepfamily is formed symbolically and emotionally, but the family system is not usually formed as gracefully and effectively.

An extreme example of this can be seen in a stepfamily that came for therapy due to stepparent–stepchild conflict that was rapidly leading to the exclusion of a child. This couple's wedding was celebrated with extended family and friends, but their five children from their prior marriage, ages 6 to 12, were barred from attending. The wedding ritual had publicly affirmed the new couple, but not the new stepfamily (Imber-Black, 1992, p. 69).

Healing

All individuals and families encounter situations in which healing is needed. Healing is needed after periods of conflict, when there is pain and grief, when there is reconciliation, when there is death, and when major changes occur such as retirement, disabilities, and midlife crises. Rituals provide a vehicle that can help healing.

Identity Definition and Redefinition

Rituals and routines can help individuals and families create, maintain, and change identities. Weddings, for example, do more than just redefine memberships. They transform identities by some members of the family becoming a spouse and others becoming in-laws. Rituals such as birthday celebrations, daily goodbyes and greetings, and goodnight kisses reaffirm who the individuals are, their importance to the family, and the emotional connections that maintain identity and create enduring intimacy.

Many of the religious, ethnic, and cultural rituals in which families participate have important implications for identity creation, change, and maintenance. In them specific foods, dress, and ceremonies might serve to symbolize the identity theme. Such celebrations define an individual's identity as part of a larger cultural group. In the multiethnic society of the United States, participation in such rituals as the Chinese New Year or Greek Orthodox Easter allow even highly assimilated persons to stay connected to their ethnic and religious identity. Cultural rituals, such as Veteran's Day, Mother's Day, and Father's Day, all involve the identity theme, as these mark and celebrate particular aspects of people's identities (Imber-Black, 1992, p. 73).

Rites of Passage

Some rituals provide the vehicle for rites of passage that facilitate growth and change. There are few rites of passage during adolescence in American culture, but some cultural groups such as Judaism and several Indian cultures have a number of rituals that help families and individuals mark the transitions from childhood to adulthood.

Rituals have the power to be therapeutic. For example, the ritual in funerals helps the participants move from one stage of life, through grief, and on to another stage of life. Doty (1986) explained that rituals have the power to transform, which is part of their wonderment and power. When transitions, catastrophes, and unexpected events occur in a family, rituals have a healing power that allows, encourages, and facilitates changes.

Meaning and Purpose

Fiese (2007) suggested that rituals help families deal with the deepest levels of shared meanings and values. Not only is it shared meaning of what things are now, but how things should be and can be. There are many abstract and ultimate concerns that are important to people that are difficult to understand, and clear answers are elusive. For example, questions about the origins of life, the purposes of even existing, the nature of reality, the role of birth and death, the role of the sacred, and the possibility of life after death are challenging concerns. They are challenging intellectually and emotionally because many of them are ultimate and profound, and it is difficult for individuals and families to come to terms with these concerns.

Rituals provide a vehicle that helps families find and maintain solutions to these complicated and ultimate concerns. The symbolism in rituals such as christening, baptism, celebrating the beginning of a new year, Thanksgiving, and Easter each help provide a sense of meaning and purpose that would be elusive and difficult to have without these or similar rituals.

Rituals also help with another aspect of meaning and purpose. Life has many forms of injustice and inequity. There also are many aspects of life in which there is little sense of control, and there are many contradictions and paradoxes. Rituals can help families deal with these complexities. As Roberts (1988) observed:

> Ritual can hold both sides of a contradiction at the same time. We all live with the ultimate paradoxes of life/death, connection/distance, ideal/real, and good/evil. Ritual can incorporate both sides of contradictions so that they can be managed simultaneously. For instance, a wedding ceremony has within it both loss and mourning and joy and celebration. People say, "You're not losing a daughter, you're gaining a son-in-law." Parents give their child away at the same time as they welcome a new member to their extended family. (p. 16)

Order and Predictability

Families can also use rituals and routines to help create a sense of order and predictability in life. They help create a sense of "home." For example, routines such as preparing and eating meals, leaving and returning home, dressing and undressing, preparing one's self to be dressed and groomed in an acceptable way, and having a favorite chair to relax in at the end of a day provide a sense of continuity, comfort, and peace that is an important part of life (Gillis, 1996).

It is likely that rituals and routines contribute in different ways to this goal. Rituals probably provide a sense of order and predictability about the more important issues, questions, and paradoxes of life, and routines seem to contribute in a different way. They help provide a sense of order in the daily rhythms and cycles, and contribute to a sense of comfort. The daily routines probably contribute to homes being a haven or place of refuge, a place where people can let their hair down, be "offstage" and escape from the competitiveness and aggression of the marketplace or school.

☐ Managing Rituals

Rituals and routines are not inherently healthy and facilitating. They can be unhealthy and destructive if families are not wise in the way they create them and carry them out. Research and clinical experience have identified five ideas that can help families be wise and effective: (a) it is enabling to have an adequate amount of ritualization—not too little or too much, (b) it is helpful to have **distinctive rituals** when there are problems that could be passed on to future generations, (c) families should have developmentally appropriate morphostasis and morphogenesis, and (d) they should avoid the inappropriate use of rituals and routines.

Have Moderate Ritualization

Research suggests a moderate amount of ritualization is helpful to families, and it is disruptive to have too much or too little emphasis on them (Bossard & Boll, 1950; Meredith et al., 1989). There is considerable variability in how many rituals families have and in the type of rituals they have, but being involved in rituals and being committed to them is helpful (Wolin & Bennett, 1984, p. 406).

Underritualization

Underritualization occurs when families have few or no rituals. Our fast-paced society that emphasizes economic, occupational, and materialistic parts of life creates a hustle-bustle attitude in which many families have little time with the whole family or even a majority of the family together at any time. Also, the emphasis in many families on passive entertainment such as watching television and listening to music with headphones on can lead to reduced attention to family rituals. The result of this is a loss of family and individual identity, loss of structure and stability, and little cohesiveness.

There are many important events in which rituals could help families cope when we do not have adequate ritualization. For example, there are few or no rituals to help families deal with events such as miscarriages, stillbirths, rape, and life-course transitions such as when one moves from childhood to adolescence or adolescence to adulthood. Rituals could help unite people, provide support, provide containment of emotions, and move participants on to acceptance and positive growth in these situations, but there tends to be an underritualization (Laird, 1988; Quinn, Newfield, & Protinsky, 1985).

Another example of how underritualization can be disabling is what happened when there was a stillborn birth in a family. The family had an unwritten rule that no one was to talk about the death. The body of the baby was taken from the mother soon after the birth. The mortuary flew the baby inside a casket, while the family drove in a car, from one state to a distant, desired state of burial. The casket was taken from the airport to the burial plot in the back of a station wagon, while the family rode in a separate car. The father declined to carry the casket from the car to the graveside before a very short memorial service. Few visits were made to the cemetery and talk about the little child was almost nonexistent.

What a change could have taken place if rituals had been used along the way, even one-time rituals. If only the family had been aware of the importance of touching and looking at the dead baby to help work through feelings of loss. If only they had realized the importance of talking about their grief and crushed expectations. There are many rituals that can help families work through the paradoxes, complexities, and ambiguities in these situations.

For example, if someone were in charge of transporting the casket and baby, it could help. If they had a more elaborate funeral or graveside ceremony that ritual would allow people to express consolation, support, and understanding, it would help. It would help if the funeral were followed by a luncheon, dinner, or time to visit where family and friends could gather to help express emotions and move forward. This would provide opportunities for the parents and children to express their deep-felt emotions, and allow

FIGURE 12.2   The death of a family member can shake the foundation of a family. It can also be a time of growth and healing.

for acceptance and moving on in the lives of this entrapped family. Rituals are one of the few ways we have to incorporate both sides of the contradictions involving living and dying, and rituals not only allow the participants to see both sides, but also to understand, experience, and cope with both sides.

Many difficult and tragic events are not well ritualized in our modern society. Incidents such as health changes that make it necessary to retire early, divorce, rape, and coping with physical abuse or incest are cases in which rituals could be used. Rituals in these areas could acknowledge the destructive aspects of these experiences and help create new structures for the future. They could help celebrate the survival of the participants, rather than leave them as victims, and this could help open communication about the events, use more of the family and community resources, and create cohesion rather than fragmentation in the families.

Overritualization

Overritualization can occur when families try to incorporate too much input from people or organizations outside the family. It can be too overwhelming if young couples try to incorporate all of the rituals from both parental families, and also try to include the rituals that are encouraged by various cultural, civic, religious, and fraternal groups. Couples need to selectively adopt and include rituals in their new family.

Overritualization also can occur when families never give up rituals that have lost their usefulness. For example, many families who have young children find it meaningful to have a large number of rituals around Christmas time. Later, however, as the children mature, some of the rituals are less relevant and important, and if some of the members of the family try to continue them, it can lead to being overwhelmed by the rituals.

People and families also differ in the amount of ritualization that is desirable. Some families find it helpful to have a relatively large number of rituals and others find it effective to invest less of their time and energy in rituals. There is some evidence that the parental and grandparental generations like more family rituals than teenagers and young adults (Meredith et al., 1989). It is possible that teenagers and young adults have so many other demands, challenges, activities, and developmental tasks they are trying to manage that this is a period of life when it is effective to be less involved in family rituals. Being less involved in family rituals might actually help young adults disengage from their parental family and create their own family. Then, as they create their own new family, they might find it enabling to get selectively reinvolved in some of the rituals in their larger family and create their own for their new family.

Distinctiveness of Rituals

A group of researchers have discovered an idea that can help families be wise in the way they manage their rituals. The idea has to do with the distinctiveness of family rituals. They found that when families have an undesirable characteristic such as alcoholism it is helpful to keep the rituals distinctive from or separated from the problem. Apparently, if family rituals can be separated from the family problems there tends to be less generational transmission of the problems. For example, if families are able to keep the alcohol problems separated from their holiday celebrations it decreases the likelihood the alcoholism will be passed on to future generations. If families are able to still have a pleasant dinner together, even though they have an alcohol problem in the family, it helps decrease the likelihood that the alcohol problem will be passed on.

This idea probably works with other kinds of family problems, too. For example, if families have problems such as physical abuse, fighting, closeness avoidance, aggressiveness, excessive competitiveness, or lack of intimacy, it is probably true that the more they can separate these problems from their family rituals the greater the likelihood the problems will not be passed on to future generations.

A practical implication of this is to try to agree to "not fight," "not drink," "be nice," or "be home" during family rituals—such as at Thanksgiving or birthdays.

Balance in Stability and Change

One of the paradoxes of rituals is that they are stable and change at the same time. They need to have some stability and be repeated over and over again to be rituals, but at the same time, individuals and families are continually developing and changing, and rituals need to adapt to these changes.

Healthy flexibility is seen when the way Christmas is celebrated is different when there are small children in a home than when there are just older people in a home. It also is illustrated when families with teenagers find themselves doing many of their rituals without the teenage children. Parents of small children and school-age children enjoy such rituals as family picnics and family reunions, but adolescents are in the middle of individuating, so forcing the teens to attend could have more undesirable effects than desirable ones.

Healthy flexibility occurs when the type of birthday parties given for children change as they grow older. Young children enjoy small family parties with games, cakes, and singing, but teens are different. They tend to want more friends over, or to go out somewhere for a movie or other activity. Rituals must be flexible enough to change over time so they are meaningful to the participants and carry the power that is potentially available in them. It is wise to "include" members of a family in rituals to promote the shared aspect of them, but this, too, should not be overdone.

Too much stability occurs when families get "stuck" in certain developmental stages and try to maintain rituals after they have outlived their usefulness. Some families maintain rituals in rigid, repressive, and degrading ways to preserve the status quo. These rigid patterns appear sometimes when families experience serious problems such as incestuous behavior, and they try to have rigid rituals to keep their secrets from getting out.

Another form of rigidity can occur when substance abuse such as alcoholism dominates rituals too much. When all of a family's activities end up with heavy drinking it can dominate what is done so much that new ways of doing things cannot emerge.

Family reunions also illustrate the need for balance in stability and variety. If the only activity in a family reunion ritual is to sit around and talk about ancestors not known to the young people, and the young people are forced to listen for hours, it soon becomes drudgery for them. Compare that to reunions in which food is part of the ritual, different activities are available such as short programs, games, prizes, treats, hiking, swimming, and so on. Which would attract future attendance at a family reunion?

Avoid Inappropriate Use of Rituals

There are many ways rituals can be abused. For example, parents can use rituals to try to control children long after the children should be in control of their own lives. Also, rituals can be used to perpetuate pseudomutuality, skeletons, cross-generational alliances, avoiding letting children go, avoiding independence, and so on. They are enormously powerful because they tap into a set of dimensions that are hard to identify, define, articulate, and understand because they deal with deep emotions that are dealt with implicitly and symbolically rather than with simple, overt, cognitive processes. Attempts to defy them can be defined as disloyalty.

Another way rituals can be abused is to adapt them to certain family members while ignoring others. For example, one wife emphasized her traditions and demanded that the husband's be eliminated. They visited her extended family, to the exclusion of the husband's, and her past family's rituals became the present family's rituals. Not only was the husband's wealth of experiences and memories lost, but also a number of new problems were created by the lack of balance.

☐ Guidelines When Creating or Changing Rituals

Family scientists have discovered that deliberately trying to create new rituals can help families accomplish their developmental tasks and cope with difficulties. One couple, for example, was struggling with past incidents of anger, mistrust, hurt, and lack of understanding. Extramarital affairs were present, as well as verbal declarations of wanting something different than what they had. A second wedding and honeymoon and a burning and burying of symbolic items from the dark past helped them create a new start. They ritualized the end of the past ways of doing things and creatively used new rituals to make things better and different, and the couple was able to change. It was a powerful way of getting "permission" to start over, while cutting off the old way.

Family scientists began in the 1970s to try to help families create new rituals as a strategy for dealing with problems and difficulties. This approach to helping families began when a group of Italian scholars started to prescribe rituals as a part of their family therapy (Palazzoli, 1977; Palazzoli et al., 1978). Gradually, as more and more family therapists and family life educators gained experience in helping families with rituals, a few guidelines were developed that are helpful in trying to create or modify rituals (van der Hart, 1983; Whiting, 1988).

The guidelines that have been developed in the field are mostly for how to design rituals as a part of family therapy or psychotherapy. However, I think if we generalize the guidelines a little bit they can be adapted so other family professionals can use them. We also believe families can use them without any professional assistance to find new ways to create and modify their family rituals.

There are at least three concerns when trying to deliberately create or modify rituals: (a) the goals, which are the purposes or objectives; (b) the form, which refers to how the rituals are carried out; and (c) the content, which refers to what is symbolized and what the behaviors are.

Goals

When someone wants to design or modify a family ritual, it seems helpful to have at least a vague idea about what it is he or she wants to accomplish. Imber-Black (1992) referred to this part of rituals as the "ritual theme." A large number of scholars refer to this part of rituals as the functions of the rituals (Doty, 1986). The term in ecosystems theory that describes this part of rituals is the term *goal.* Seven goals were described earlier in this chapter, but that list of goals is illustrative rather than exhaustive. There can be many other goals. Some additional examples are celebration, adventure, dealing with paradoxes and ambiguities, and preserving memories.

Most of the time when people want to design or change rituals they are dealing with more than one goal. Also, most of the time some of the goals are fairly vague and difficult to describe precisely, so it is helpful to not worry too much about getting a clear statement of the goals, how the goals will be quantified, or measured. Rituals are so "right brain" oriented that vague impressions, images, metaphors, and similes are sometimes enough.

Form

Counselors are not sure whether it is wise to focus on the form or the content first. They seem to both gradually evolve in a "chicken and egg" manner as ideas about what to do influence ideas about how to do it, and vice versa. Eventually, however, it is helpful to think through the form of the ritual. Whiting (1988) called this part of designing rituals the "design elements." It refers to issues such as how much the rituals will be open versus closed, how time and space will be used, and how much repetition will occur.

The open versus closed aspect of rituals refers to how much the ritual is rigid versus flexible. In rituals that are quite closed, there is little room for innovation or variation and there are understandings or rules that define fairly clearly what is to be done. There must, of course, be some closed or structured aspects. In rituals that are more open, there are fewer rules and more flexibility for innovation, creativity, and individual differences. Apparently, there can be wide variation in how closed versus open rituals are, and they should be tailored to different situations and to the family's personal preferences, values, and lifestyle.

I have learned that timing and placement of our family rituals is critical. Of course, this implies that one has to plan and organize these events and take care to choose timing and place with attention to the goals we have chosen (Whiting, 1988, p. 89).

Repetition

A third aspect of the form of rituals that must be dealt with is the amount of repetition. Many rituals are repeated frequently in families. For example, a prayer or period of silence before eating a meal and kissing each other hello and goodbye are two rituals that are performed daily in many families. Other rituals, however, are performed only once for the people involved. Giving a person a name and having a funeral for them are two examples. Also, a family might want to create a ritual that will occur once to help them deal with a unique situation.

An example of this type of ritual is a healing ritual that could be designed to help a family find a way to let go of a former relationship. These one-time rituals could be created for many situations, such as finding ways to accept a family member back into the family after the person has been excluded or finding ways to cope with a personal or financial failure.

Content

In many ways this is the most important aspect to consider when designing or modifying rituals because it gets to the heart of what rituals are about. The content deals with at least three different parts of rituals: (a) the behaviors that are performed, (b) the symbolism in what is done, and (c) the emotional aspects of the ritual.

The Behaviors

Whiting (1988) identified several ritual techniques or symbolic actions that help us understand the kinds of behavior or action that can be used in designing rituals. One of the categories he identified is letting go. By letting go we mean that during several kinds of rituals (death, marriage, graduation) there is a time when it is appropriate for the family members to express a willingness to release the individual(s) who are leaving. You will notice that in many rituals there is a time when final hugs are given, a flower is placed on the casket, or some other signal is given that it is time to let the person leave.

A second category of behaviors Whiting identified is giving and receiving. The exchanging of food, gifts, verbal expressions, and cards are the hallmarks of some rituals. For example, when a teenager is ready to begin driving, the parents could give the child a set of keys to the family automobile to symbolize the new status in an important step toward adulthood. When young adults are ready to leave home to attend college, families can use giving and receiving behaviors in rituals to help them accomplish this transition. The parents could give the student a computer that could say, "You're in charge of your life, and you can do it." I heard a story about one young adult who, on leaving home, gave his parents an apron to use during family barbecues. He had an extra string sewn on that was broken. He wanted to remind his dad that family life would go on even though he was moving away. In the United Kingdom, there is frequently a major birthday party for someone turning 21 years of age, sometimes called a key party. During this time the birthday person is symbolically given the "keys" to the house, indicating they have moved into the status of adult and no longer have to rely on someone else to let them in. Most birthday cards in the United Kingdom for this occasion will sport some type of key emblem.

A *third* category of behavior in Whiting's model is documenting. This is the process of writing something in an "official" way to document something such as an event, a change, or a transition. Sending thank-you cards is a simple example. Getting a marriage license and writing a will are other documenting processes that have enormous symbolism and can be used as rituals.

Love letters document commitment, care, concern, and interest. Many families have a ritual of sending notes of appreciation and love. Even something as subtle and minor as knowing that family members will place a long-distance telephone call to let others know they have arrived at a destination is a form of documentation, and when it is ritualized in a family it can have many positive effects.

Documenting rituals can be used to help family members remember pleasant experiences. For example, putting the pictures from a family vacation into a special album and making a place for it among other precious belongings documents and cements the positive aspects of the experience. Having a picture enlarged and hung in a special place in the home documents membership, importance, unity, and special events.

The Symbolism

The second part of the content is the symbolism, and it is one of the most important parts of rituals. As Turner (1967) argued, "the symbol is the smallest unit of ritual" (p. 19).

Symbols are tangible or observable things that represent something else. Many different things can be symbols. For example, they can be tangible objects, emblems, tokens, words, phrases, images, figures, or signs. The symbol derives its meaning from the object, idea, or other part of reality that it represents.

Families and individuals differ in the kinds of symbols that are important and can be important to them. Some families find symbols of the past, both of the current generation and of previous generations, to be important. Other families studiously avoid symbols of the past. Some families find religious symbols meaningful, and others find them empty and uncomfortable.

One way to try to understand the symbolism in a family is to try to identify the family paradigms that guide the family's thinking, images, and beliefs about what is important. Because family paradigms are highly abstract ideas, it is sometimes helpful to look at more specific parts of families to get clues about their paradigmatic beliefs. An examination of a family's main goals can provide helpful clues about these abstract ideals and beliefs. Also, clues can be acquired observing the tangible objects families put on their walls, the way they dress, the way they decorate their home, and the way they relate to their community.

A helpful clue about what is symbolized in a family is to identify the events or things that evoke strong emotion. It is my experience that when the parts of life that bring out strong emotions can be identified, an understanding of the family's symbols and things that are symbolized is close.

The Emotion

There are few ideas that all family scientists can agree on, but an idea where there is widespread agreement is that the emotional aspects of the family realm are extremely important. As a result, family theorists, family researchers, family therapists, and family life educators all pay great attention to the emotional processes as they try to understand and help families. This makes it doubly ironic that the literature in the field about rituals almost ignores the emotional aspects of rituals. All of the scholars who have studied rituals highlight the cognitive aspects: the symbolism, the meanings, the metaphors, and perceptions. They also pay a great deal of attention to the repetition, the staging, the functions, and the therapeutic and developmental value of rituals.

Unfortunately, however, the role of the emotional aspects of rituals is almost ignored in the literature about family rituals. Therapists and educators who use rituals to help families include the emotional aspects, but when they write books and papers to describe what they are doing and what rituals are, the emotional aspects are hardly ever mentioned. This is an unfortunate omission. I am convinced that it is the combination of the symbolism and emotionality that makes rituals such a rich and helpful part of the family realm.

Therefore, it is helpful to think about the emotional aspects of rituals whenever we try to help families develop or change rituals. Also, when families want to change or invent rituals they would be well advised to pay as much attention to the emotional aspects as any of the other aspects of rituals.

Emotional aspects deal with how people feel as they are involved with rituals. Are they attracted or repulsed? Do they experience feelings such as warmth, closeness, integrity, peace, or fulfillment? Or, are the feelings generally negative? For example, is a graduation experience an inconvenience or a fulfillment? Is a wedding and reception or open house viewed as a charade and superficially irrelevant experience? Are family celebrations of holidays an ordeal that is annoying or a fulfilling emotional experience?

Most family rituals involve some degree of emotional involvement, and some of them are extremely intense. One of the issues that is either overtly or covertly dealt with when designing and changing rituals is what type of emotion is expected and tolerated. How much intensity is desirable? At funerals, for example, the individuals in the immediate family often get carried away with their emotions and exhibit crying, wailing, and other forms of emotional distress. At weddings there are almost always tears.

The analog messages and the relationship messages that are sent with rituals help define what is appropriate emotionally, and occasionally it might be wise to turn these nonverbal communication processes into verbal communication. For example, when a family is designing a healing ritual to cope with a loss or serious problem, it might be helpful to observe that this is a time when it could be acceptable, even desirable, to experience some deeply felt emotions.

The neglect of the emotional aspect of rituals by family scholars means that thus far we have few ideas about how or when to deal with the emotional aspects of family rituals. I hope this deficiency will be corrected in the coming years.

☐ Summary

Family rituals and routines are valuable resources, and when they are wisely used they can help families attain important goals such as unity, closeness, intimacy, meaning, membership changes, and so on. Seven family goals with which rituals and routines can help are creating healthy emotional ties; making changes in family membership; healing, forming, and redefining the identities of individuals and families; providing rites of passage that help families and individuals make developmental transitions; helping families create a sense of meaning and purpose; and creating an adequate sense of order and predictability.

Rituals and routines can be enabling or disabling in families. Therefore, families should be wise in how they create and enact them. Four ideas that can help families be wise are to have moderate ritualization, to have distinctiveness when there are problems a family does not want to pass on to future generations, to have a balance of stability and change, and to avoid using rituals in inappropriate ways.

☐ Study Questions

1. What is a ritual?
2. Define the term *routine*.
3. Name three ways rituals and routines are different.
4. What is meant by overritualization?
5. How does staging make rituals important?
6. Why do rituals play an important role in building family strength?

☐ Key Terms

Ritual
Rules
Routines
Healthy emotional ties
Rite of passage
Overritualization
Underritualization

Distinctive rituals
Symbolism

☐ **Suggested Readings**

Fiese, B. (2007). *Family routines and rituals.* New Haven, CT: Yale University Press.

Smith, C. (2007). *Soul searching: The religious lives of American teenagers.* Oxford, UK: Oxford University Press.

Coping With Turbulence, Gains, and Losses

☐ Chapter Preview

In this chapter, readers will learn:

- That there are many "stressor events" that can create stress in family life.
- That some of the stressor events are more serious than others. Also, some of them come from the environment, and others come from inside the family.
- That there are developmental processes and predictable patterns in the way family stress is managed. Recent research has identified five different ways families respond to stress.
- How research about families has begun to identify coping strategies that families can use to deal effectively with stressful situations.
- That family stress theory has taken many forms. One of the most used is the ABC-X model of family crisis.
- That some simple coping strategies seem to be helpful and several can be less effective in certain stressful situations.
- How recent research has begun to identify coping strategies that deal with more fundamental changes in family processes.
- About some coping strategies that are helpful with certain types of stressor events (e.g., death or economic loss) but not helpful with other stressors.

☐ Introduction

Challenges such as death in a family, loss of a home, or a serious injury can create stress in individuals and also in family processes. In some situations the stress can be severe, disabling, and enormously difficult. In other situations, the stress is more temporary, fleeting, and easy to cope with. An important concept in this chapter is that stress and crisis are common occurrences. Most families find themselves coping with stressful situations. Additionally, it is not uncommon for a number of them to occur at the same time.

This chapter describes the various types of **stressor events** that families experience, and it describes the effects they have on family processes. It also summarizes what is known about enabling and disabling strategies that families tend to use. A central focus of this chapter is the **ABC-X model of crisis**. By understanding this theoretical idea, we can begin to not only understand crisis better, but understand how to better intervene as families experience crisis.

☐ Family Stress and Family Resilience Theory

There have been several theories and theoretical orientations presented in this text. The theory of **family stress and resiliency** has been considered by family researchers for more than 60 years and is a signature element of family process research. This research has an important element to it. Instead of focusing on a deficit approach to family well-being, this theoretical orientation focuses on the strengths and abilities of families. A deficit approach is much more common in family research: For example, researchers focus on how children suffer during divorce. When we focus on what is strong in families and how they use **resources**, we gain a different view into the way most families approach daily life.

Following the lead of Patterson (2002), we first define *resilience*, which has been defined in various ways by researchers, leading to some confusion. As Patterson reminded us, there are several problems in understanding this concept. First, the idea of resilience is sometimes used to denote an outcome. That is, we note that a family is doing well and we code them as resilient. Second, when thinking about resilience, is it in order to consider just the individual's well-being, or is it the family collective on which we should center our attention? Third, some researchers think of resilience in terms of protective factors. These are resources or attributes a family (or individual) possesses that keeps them from experiencing the force of a power stressor event. The concept of resilience began when researchers focused on children who were experiencing adversity (Garmezy, 1991; Masten, 1994; Patterson, 2002). McCubbin, Boss, Wilson, and Lester (1980) discovered the idea of resilience and used the concept in their emerging research about military families. They noted that families undergoing harsh stressor events (e.g., the loss of a husband in combat) could adapt to the situation when they had a larger bank of resources from which to draw. Following that tradition, Patterson (2002) stated that resilience is "the phenomena of doing well in the face of adversity" (p. 350). Families that do well in the face of adversity are ones who have a strong resource base and protective mechanisms in place. We cover the idea of resources later; protective mechanisms are such things as positive outlook on life, skilled problem-solving ability, and effective interpersonal communication skills.

☐ ABC-X Model of Family Stress

There have been several iterations of family stress theory models. Basically, all of them contain similar elements. Most of them stem from the work of a key family researcher, Rubin Hill. Hill (1958) was one of the first researchers to note similar processes when observing families experiencing stress. He developed the first family crisis model, the ABC-X model of crisis. In his work, he identified the four elements of the ABC-X model in the following way. First, he said that families experiencing a crisis perceived that there was a significant stressor event (the A part of the model). The stressor event (or events) could be in the form of a tornado, national money crisis, a war event, an automobile crash involving a family member, the birth of a child, and so on. The B element of the ABC-X model was referred to as the definition of the situation.

Remember that symbolic interaction theory (see Chapter 2) places a great deal of emphasis on how the person (or family collectively) defines the world and the daily events of life that surround them. When a person defines an event as real or as important, the effects of that event will be real to him or her (in spite of how others might view the same event). In like manner, the B aspect of this model focuses on the definition of the situation. The B of family crisis focuses on how the various family members (or the family collectively) view what is happening to them.

The C element of this model considers the resources available to them. When resources are high (money, skills, close relationship connections, spirituality, etc.) one would expect the family to be less impacted by even a more powerful stressor event. Of course, you can begin to see that the previous discussion of resilience is relevant here. Families are more resilient when they have high resources and are able to define the events of life in ways that make them more manageable.

PRINCIPLE 13.1   THE ABC-X MODEL OF CRISIS

The ABC-X model of crisis helps us organize how we think about stressor events, available resources, and how the stressor event is defined by the family or individual. These elements mix and shape the X part of the process, which is how much disruption results from the stressor event(s).

The remainder of this chapter is organized around the key concepts of the ABC-X model of crisis. First, we discuss the different types of stressor events. Then we examine the nature of resources that can make a difference. Woven within these discussions is the C part calculus. How family members, and the family collectively, define the events and resources they have impacts the level of disruption resulting from the stressor event(s).

☐ Types of Stressor Events

> In our view family stress is often greatest at transition points from one stage to another of the family developmental process, and symptoms are most likely to appear when there is an interruption or dislocation in the unfolding family life cycle. (Carter & McGoldrick, 1989, pp. 4–5)

A stressor event is something that happens to a family that cannot be managed effectively within the family's normal ways of doing things (McCubbin & Patterson, 1982). Some stressor events tend to cause more disruption in family processes than others. Holmes and Rahe (1967) developed a method of ranking the relative magnitude of various stressor events, and their ranking is shown here. The method they used was to ask 394 people to rate the seriousness of various changes people encounter. They gave marriage an arbitrary value, and asked them to compare other changes with this number.

The Holmes and Rahe list of events (some shown next) is instructive, albeit more than 40 years old, because it demonstrates there are a large number of stressor events families encounter. It also shows us that these events occur in many different times, transitions, and aspect of everyday life.

Stressor Events Originating Outside the Family

- War separation or reunion.
- Social discrimination.
- Economic depression.
- Natural disasters: floods, tornadoes, hurricanes, and so on.
- Home being robbed or ransacked.
- Banks going bankrupt and losing savings.
- Family member in an airplane crash.
- Political revolution.
- Member of family being sued or arrested.

Stressor Events Originating Inside the Family

- Alcoholism of a family member.
- Senility of a family member.
- A family member becoming mentally ill.
- Serious illnesses: cancer, heart attack, stroke, and so on.
- Rape of a member of the family.
- Family member in trouble with the law.
- Increased tasks and time commitments.
- Automobile accidents.
- Child running away.
- Family member contracting AIDS.
- Problems with schools.
- Desertion or return of a deserter.
- Unwanted pregnancy.
- Inability to bear children.
- Adolescent in family prematurely pregnant.
- Family member committing suicide.
- An affair or emotional triangle.
- Strained family relationships.
- Infidelity.
- Nonsupport.
- Physical abuse of a family member.
- Family member being sexually abused.
- Prolonged or serious depression.
- Child being born illegitimately.
- Relative coming to live with family.
- House burning.

When stressor events come one at a time, it is easier for families to cope with them. However, it is common for several stressor events to happen at the same time, and for new ones to occur while the family is still dealing with previous stressor events. When this happens, it increases the difficulty families have in coping effectively with the new inputs. McCubbin and Patterson (1982) used the term stress pile-up to refer to the stress that families experience from several changes occurring simultaneously, or several occurring in a short period of time before the initial stressor events are solved or resolved.

☐ Resources in Family Stress

Remember that the B part of the ABC-X model of crisis draws our attention to the resources families or family members can bring to bear during a crisis. A resource is a source of supply, support, or capability that can be drawn on in times of need. Resources are usually thought to be capabilities and supplies that are in reserve. We can, once a crisis occurs, garner new resources. However, the important starting point is understanding the level of resource reserve that exists prior to the identified trouble.

Further, resources can exist within the family or exogenous to the family group. Exogenous family resources are those that reside outside the family and are usually independent of the family's control. A simple example of an exogenous resource is your neighbor's pickup truck. You don't control it, per se. However, if you have a good relationship with her, you could use her pickup to haul the destroyed items following a fire in your garage. Your other neighbor, let's pretend, is a nurse and comes by to assist you and provide care after your teen has broken her ankle. You also have a local pastor that drops in with comfort and support as you struggle with the fire in the garage and your daughter's broken ankle.

Resources that reside within the family's control can be scant or vast in their quantity. A family with a good sum of money in the checkbook will have less trouble replacing the lawnmower destroyed in the garage fire. This family will also have less trouble if they have good insurance for the garage and for the broken ankle. Resources are not just financial, however. As has been mentioned in several places throughout this text, social capital is one of the most powerful resources a family can tap into. The social capital we have in reserve resides within the relationships we nurture and maintain. As we need the advice and assistance of our neighbor the nurse, that conversation will have a richer texture and potentially better outcome if we have invested in that relationship prior to the new stressor event. Although stress sometimes brings us together with our neighbors, those relationships can be much more powerful (as a resource) if the building blocks of trust, reciprocal friendship, and mutual sharing have occurred before the need arises.

FIGURE 13.1   The ABC-X model of crisis has been used in family research for about 50 years.

The depths of a crisis (the X factor) or the level of disruption felt during a crisis can be directly ameliorated by the bank of resources available. Again, these resources can include financial reserves and social capital, but they also include our capabilities such as our ability to make good decisions, think carefully and plan in times of stress, and problem solve during stressor events.

□ Family Stress as a Process: The X Factor

Systems theory has a number of concepts that help us understand how families are different when they are experiencing stress. To understand what happens when stressor events occur, it is helpful to review what happens in a system when families are not in stressful situations.

When life is "normal," a family system is in a process of transforming inputs into outputs with relative ease. The group can transform inputs such as money, energy, time, space, and behavior into love, attention, discipline, growth, development, satisfaction, bonds, heritage, closeness, learning, and security. To carry out these transformation processes, each family develops a large number of rules of transformation that govern the hourly, daily, and weekly routines and cycles of life. Some of the rules are explicit, but most of them are implicit "understandings" about how to do things. Each family is continually monitoring to see if the results are within the agreed upon standards or limits in attaining the family goals. As mentioned before, the choices a family makes during times of transition reflect deeply held elements of the core family paradigm (see Chapter 8 for a discussion of the family paradigm).

As individuals get older and pass through stages of development, we say that families experience morphogenesis. Importantly, however, during periods of morphogenesis there is a tendency for family members to try and stabilize the rate and intensity of change—this process we call morphostasis (see Chapter 4 for further discussion of these ideas). The result is a dynamic balancing of change and order, innovation and constancy, and creativity and predictability. There also is a continual balancing and rebalancing of the needs people have for togetherness and separateness, and the system is always responding to generational, emotional, affective, economic, social, and ecological factors outside and inside the family.

Even during those rare times when family life settles down and is relatively calm, family interactions evolve and change. Even in tranquil times there is a dynamic flow of energy, resources, activity, tension, agreements, diversity, consensus, love, anger, new information, and a refining of the patterns of interactions surrounding old and new traditions. Without stop, the age, knowledge, and connection of family members changes. As families evolve through time, they develop what systems theorists call *a requisite variety* of rules of transformation. This means they develop enough rules about how things should be done that they are able to transform the inputs into outputs that meet minimal standards in attaining goals.

Stress occurs when the families realize that that some of the events they experience push them to the edge of their resources and ability to cope. The old ways of solving problems do not seem to work in this new situation. For example, if a new infant is born and the family has the requisite variety of rules to cope with the new input, there is not as much resulting disruption from the stressor event. This, of course, does not mean that having a child born into a family is not a stressor event. Instead, what we watch for is when the new event tests the family to the point that the way they usually solve stressful problems does not work very well. The level of stress is exacerbated if there is yet another unanticipated stressor event piled on. Suppose the infant is born with a serious handicap; this event can threaten the ability to create some desirable outputs—such as to have healthy, normal children—and that creates stress.

All of these kinds of events cause some kind of change in a family life, but stressor events that the family does not know how to handle with its available rules, traditions, and patterns of interaction are particularly problematic to family members. They have to rethink how they approach such situations; they have to find new resources, learn new skills, and somehow adapt.

Imagine a family, for example, who has had no experience dealing with the juvenile courts. The family is sitting in front of the house when a police car drives up and an officer informs the family he is there to arrest their 17-year-old daughter. The event is foreign to them (in this case), and they might not have the requisite variety of experience, problem-solving skills, or resources to know how to deal with the situation. For most, this situation would be a life-changing stressor event. If it were to happen again with another child, chances are they would not be nearly as disrupted as in the first case. With experience and learning, we adapt, grow, and are better able to deal with similar future events.

☐ Patterns in Family Stress: How the X Factor Plays Out

When a stressor event occurs in a family, a number of processes can evolve. If the family is able to cope quickly, the normal family processes will not be as disrupted, and the family will be able to resume their normal routines and traditions. However, if the stressor event is serious enough that the family is not able to adjust quickly, other patterns will emerge.

There are two kinds of patterns that can emerge when a stressor event is so severe that the old ways of solving things do not work: an acute phase in which energy is directed toward minimizing the impact of the stress, and a reorganization phase in which the new reality is faced and accepted (McCubbin & Dahl, 1985, p. 154).

The acute stage of family stress is usually a short period of time. During this time families try to examine the breadth and width of the problem, they try to get routines back to "normal," and they might attempt breaking the situation into manageable parts, getting their emotions under control, and trying to get information about the problem. During the reorganization stage they are creating new rules, changing the ways they relate, gradually coming to terms with their emotions, getting help from others if they need it, trying to be adaptable, and learning how to accept the new realities.

When family scientists first began to study family stress in the 1930s and 1940s, they assumed that all families went through the "rollercoaster" pattern of adjustment that was first described by Koos (1946). After the stress occurs a family moves into a period of disorganization during the acute stage. During this period of time, some of the normal transformation processes are disrupted as the family's attention is diverted to dealing with the stress. If the family is able to make adjustments that cope effectively with the stressor event, they move into a period of recovery.

During the reorganization phase, families rearrange their rules and transformation processes so they gradually recover. In some situations they are eventually better off than they were before the stressor event. For example, it might be stressful to move, but if the economic condition of the family improves after the move, the "normal" level of organization for the family might be higher. In other situations, a family might never recover fully from a stressor event, and the new "normal" level might be lower than before the crisis. This often occurs with problems such as a child in a family running away, conflict that

FIGURE 13.2 Crisis can be like a rollercoaster. The downside of the rollercoaster is sometimes used to depict the idea that as the stressor events occur, the family becomes more disorganized.

cannot be resolved, loss of trust in a relationship, alcoholism and other forms of substance abuse, and economic losses.

There is some recent research that suggests that Koos's (1946) rollercoaster pattern is an accurate description of the developmental pattern for some but not all families. Burr et al. (1994) interviewed families who had experienced six different types of stress, and they found the rollercoaster pattern was the response pattern only about half of the time. They found the five different developmental patterns. About 18% of their families experienced a pattern they called increased effectiveness, in which family life became better as a result of the stressful situation, and the families did not experience a period of disorganization. In 10% of the families the response pattern was no change; family life did not improve or get worse. About 5% of the families experienced decreased effectiveness, and 11% had a mixed pattern where they initially were better off and then experienced the rollercoaster pattern. The Harker and Taylor research helps us realize there are several different developmental patterns in the way families respond to stress.

There is a paradox in these insights. We usually do not think about stressful situations being desirable. We assume they bring pain, discomfort, anxiety, frustration, and anguish. Therefore, we usually assume it is better if we can avoid problems. Although it is true that life would be simpler and less painful, it also is apparently true that when we back off and take a long-term view of life, we realize that stressful situations also can have beneficial aspects. Ironically, when we look at the total life span and its experiences, we realize that some stress and problems help us grow, develop, learn, and become stronger.

One reason it is often "desirable" to encounter difficulties and stress is that sometimes when we experience pain, frustration, disappointment, tragedies, and other adversities we are able to experience the deepest and most satisfying joy, happiness, and sense of accomplishment and fulfillment, such as the joy that comes from being needed and from nursing loved ones who are ill. For example, the challenge of caring for a handicapped child can bring bonds of closeness, learning about the richness of sacrificing, abilities to be patient and loving, and insights about the subtle beauties of the human spirit that can be deeply rewarding.

☐ Coping with the X Factor: Strategies Families Use

One of the goals of the scientists who have studied family stress has been to identify the **coping strategies** families find helpful in dealing with stressful situations. This research began in the 1930s (Angell, 1936), and there are now a large number of studies that have discovered many helpful strategies (Boss, 1987; McCubbin, Boss, Wilson & Lester, 1980; McCubbin, Balling, Possin, Frierdich & Bryne, 2002).

Coping strategies are processes, behaviors, or patterns of behaviors that families go through to adapt to stress (McCubbin & Dahl, 1985). According to Pearlin and Schooler (1982), having a large repertoire of coping strategies is more important than using one or two strategies well. They stated:

> It is apparent from the foregoing analyses that the kinds of responses and resources people are able to bring to bear in coping with life-strains make a difference to their emotional well-being . . . (there is no magic wand). The magical wand does not appear in our results, and this suggests that having a particular weapon in one's arsenal is less important than having a variety of weapons. (Pearlin & Schooler, 1982, p. 127)

☐ Strategies That Are Generally Enabling or Disabling

Research has been conducted on a large number of stressor events, and there are several strategies that seem to be helpful in dealing with all of them and in all of the developmental stages of family stress.

Cognitive Strategies

Cognitive strategies are things families can do intellectually or mentally to help them cope with stress. Having an optimistic or positive attitude when faced with problems is an effective coping strategy (Innstrand, 2008). Practical methods of keeping a positive attitude include focusing on the positive aspects of life, visualizing a good outcome, and finding ways to help feel in control of the situation.

Part of the reason this strategy is helpful is because the attitude families have about stressful situations tends to become a self-fulfilling prophecy. Recall the perception as reality principle from Chapter 2. In this principle, an idea is expressed that says simply this: If people define situations as real, they are real in their consequences.

Therefore, when the members of a family develop a positive attitude and believe they can cope effectively, they tend to cope effectively. When they believe a situation is too difficult to cope with, it tends to actually make it more difficult than it would be if they had different beliefs.

When people have confidence in their ability to cope with a situation they tend to have different "striving behaviors" than when they believe they are defeated. They invest more energy and try harder. They tend to focus on solutions rather than the overwhelming aspects of the problem situation, and this makes them more effective in finding and implementing solutions. These attitudes often are contagious, and others often work harder and more effectively when a positive attitude prevails.

This principle does not mean that families should be unrealistic in their attitudes, and it does not mean that merely having a positive attitude will do everything that needs to be done to cope with stressor events. A positive attitude can simultaneously exist with realism, a good knowledge of the realities of situations, and efforts toward solving problems. What this idea means is that the definition of the situation tends to have a predictable influence on how seriously stressor events influence families and on how families tend to cope.

Another of the cognitive strategies is getting accurate information. Kaplan, Smith, Grobstien, and Fischman (1973) found in their research about how families cope with serious illnesses, such as leukemia, that it helps families if they get accurate information as soon as possible. It seems as though this would be an obvious thing to do, but research about how families actually operate in stressful situations indicates a large number of families do not do this well.

Of the families studied, 87% failed to resolve successfully even the initial task of coping; that is, the tasks associated with confirmation of the diagnosis. Parents' reactions vary but fall into certain recognizable classes. Their most common reaction is to deny the reality of the diagnosis in as many ways as possible. Such parents avoid those who refer to the illness as leukemia. They themselves use euphemisms (e.g., virus, anemia, blood disease) in speaking of the child's illness. They might even be fearful that the child will hear the news from someone outside the family (Kaplan et al., 1973).

In addition, the Kaplan research team found that it is helpful if all of the family members who are mature enough to understand are informed about the nature of the problem and the seriousness of it. All of the family having accurate and prompt information allows the family to properly mourn if necessary, to face up to future consequences, to make plans, and to take realistic action (Kaplan et al., 1973).

Without knowledge about details of the stressor event and how it might affect the family, none of these things can be done. Without information at the first, it is difficult to engage in short-term or long-term coping strategies such as finding ways to acquire social and emotional support and construct a realistic but positive definition of the situation. In addition, people who do not receive information promptly tend to become anxious and angered when a stressful situation is occurring. Often they concentrate on the worst possible alternatives, invent unrealistic expectations and explanations, and jump to false conclusions. Thus, the lack of information tends to make situations worse than they should be.

Another aspect of cognitive strategies is that when stressor events are precipitated by events outside the family, families seem to be able to deal with them more easily and effectively. This finding has several implications for the acute stage of coping. One implication is to try to externalize blame if possible. Another is to realize that, when it is not possible to attribute the blame outside the family, the stressor event is an important issue for the family that needs to be dealt with carefully. If someone in the family is blamed for the stressor event, the blaming itself tends to be another stressor event that can create a number of emotional, interpersonal, and perceptual reactions.

Communication Strategies

There are a number of communication-oriented strategies that families seem to find helpful. Just having someone to "listen" and "try to understand" can be enormously helpful. Trying to be honest and open in communication also tends to be helpful in most families. Two other communication strategies that tend to be helpful are to be empathetic and sensitive to nonverbal messages (McCubbin & Figley, 1983).

Emotional Strategies

Research about family stress documents that stressor events tend to create strong emotional reactions. For example, when disasters strike, people become frantic in their attempts to locate members of their family. When couples discover they are not able to bear children it usually takes years to adjust to the deeply felt emotional reactions (Snowden & Snowden, 1984).

Another aspect of managing emotions is that with some stressor events, such as chronic illnesses, families find themselves dealing with the painful emotions over and over again. They get their feelings resolved at one stage of the illness, but as the illness moves to a new stage or new experiences occur, the emotional reactions resurface, and they need to deal again and again with feelings such as helplessness, loss, and "why does this happen?"

According to McCubbin et al. (1988), the management of emotions involves two fairly different processes: (a) being aware of the emotions and fatigue, and (b) finding constructive ways to release or come to terms with the emotions.

The differentiation/fusion principle that was described in Chapter 11 helps us realize that when emotions become intense they tend to "take over." When emotions get intense, they can incapacitate a family, and interfere with the process of coping with the stressful event. Families who are effective at coping with stress gradually learn that when emotions become intense, the attempts to "be sensible" and "reasonable" and "get things done" need to be set aside temporarily while the emotional reactions are dealt with.

To ignore the emotions, pretend they do not exist, or tell people they "shouldn't feel that way" does not eliminate them. It just forces the emotions into the part of the family iceberg that is below the surface, where family members are not aware of what is going on. Usually what happens in these situations is the emotions find a way to surface in other ways. Some examples of other ways emotions can surface are people getting angry at minor incidents, losing their temper often, developing physical illnesses such as having an upset stomach or always being tired or depressed, turning to excesses with alcohol or sex, and so on. Therefore, emotions that are involved in a stressful experience need to be dealt with so they do not make coping more difficult. This can be facilitated by using the family as a collective support group, hugging, talking with others, being close, crying, reassuring, listening, getting feelings out, and being around loved ones.

Changing Relationships

The first generalization that was developed in the research about family stress is the idea that being flexible, pliable, or willing to change is helpful. Usually family scientists use the term *adaptability* to describe this. One of the first studies was by Angell (1936), and this idea was the main conclusion his book contributed to the field. Since then, this idea has been found again and again to be an important coping strategy (Boss, 1987; McCubbin et al., 1988).

Adaptability is in essence the ability to be flexible and try something new. Families with this ability tend to be more accepting of change and therefore roll with the punches, so to speak. Families who are relatively adaptable are also more willing to try other coping strategies at all levels of change. In addition, this willingness to try more coping strategies will end up helping the family be more proficient at the use of a wider variety of coping strategies, which increases their requisite variety.

The various parts of family life tend to be intertwined. Therefore, changes in one part of the family tend to influence other parts. Kaplan et al. (1973) recognized this interdependence and suggested that it is helpful if the individuals in families can cope and mourn together when serious stressor events occur. A family can offer its individual members the potential for mutual support and access to its collective coping experience. According to Hill (1958), when helping an individual cope or handle stress, the individual should be treated as a family member not as an independent individual. Thus, the idea that the family realm has more impact than most people realize emerges again. Here again, the emotional, generational, and other ties to the family are so great that they are dealt with the most effectively when there is a network of family members who are involved.

Thus, families who can emotionally lean on each other have an advantage when dealing with life's problems. As McCubbin (1988) observed, maintaining family togetherness, even by taking the time to do little things with the children and plan family outings, is an effective coping strategy for dealing with family stress.

Spiritual Strategies

Many families find it helpful to turn to spiritual sources for strength, meaning, and assistance when they are experiencing family stress. These strategies include such things as praying, trying to have more faith, seeking help from one's God, and becoming more involved in religious activities.

Strategies That Focus on the Environment

Families can do many things with their environment to help them cope with stress. Support can come from family members, friends, work, clubs, police, churches, and so on. In addition to varying in source, social support also can vary in its type. It can be emotional, financial, physical, mental, and so forth.

Many studies indicate that social support makes individuals and families less vulnerable when they experience such stressor events as losing a job or participating in a difficult line of work (Cobb, 1982; Gore, 1978; Maynard et al., 1980), raising a chronically ill child (Holroyd & Guthrie, 1986), recovering from a natural disaster (Scaramella, Sohr-Preston, Callahan, & Mirabile, 2008), or adjusting to war-induced separations (Campbell & Demi, 2000).

Cobb (1982) stated that social support was an exchange of information between the family and environment that provided families with (a) emotional support, leading the recipients to believe they are cared for and loved, (b) self-esteem, leading them to believe they are valued; and (c) network support, which gives them a sense of belonging.

Bronfenbrenner's (1979) review of the research in this area added an important new insight to the role of supportiveness inside families and in the amount of support families receive from the community and friends. When individuals and families are not coping with stressful events, it is growth producing to have considerable independence and autonomy and to have relatively little overt help, assistance, or support. However, when things are not going well, it then is helpful to have more supportiveness inside the family and between the family and the community. Another way of stating Bronfenbrenner's idea is that high supportiveness tends to be enabling when dealing with serious stressor events, but it can actually be disabling when things are going well.

PRINCIPLE 13.2   THE STRATEGIES USED MATTER

The choice of strategies that families use in times of crisis matters greatly. Families who learn or can be taught to use more effective strategies in response to crisis will necessarily do better at recovering.

Individual Development

There is limited research that suggests it can be helpful to focus on some aspects of individual development. Some of these strategies are such things as trying to promote self-sufficiency (without overdoing it), working out to keep physically fit, and being sure to keep up one's obligations to other organizations such as one's employment.

Disabling Strategies

Research has identified a number of ways of responding to stressor events that seem to usually have disabling or destructive effects. One of these is to react with violence. A number of research studies have found people tend to be more violent when experiencing stressful situations such as undesirable behavior by a child, unemployment, unhappiness in their marriage or in their employment, or illnesses (McCubbin et al., 1988). The violence, however, tends to make the situations worse. It destroys positive emotional feelings toward the violent individuals and creates a number of negative emotions such as mistrust, anger, confusion, shame, and hate.

Other strategies that usually are disabling are denial, avoidance, rejection, increased use of alcohol, hostility, producing garbled and dishonest communication about the problem, preventing communication, prohibiting and interrupting individual and collective grieving within the family, and weakening family relationships precisely when they most need to be strengthened (Kaplan et al., 1973, p. 67; McCubbin et al., 1988). These strategies usually aggravate the original problem and create other problems such as less connection to family members and decreases in problem solving effectiveness.

Boss (2007) introduced another concept into the field that deals with coping strategies. The concept is boundary ambiguity. This occurs when families are uncertain in their

FIGURE 13.3 Sometimes stressor events come at very inconvenient times. This mother cannot really take time off to recover because many of her mothering duties and even work duties outside the home have to continue.

FIGURE 13.4 Some crises are very devastating and create a multitude of cascading stressor events.

perception of who is in or out of the family or who is performing what roles and tasks within the family. Her initial research was with military families and families who experience Alzheimer's disease. Military families find this problem especially severe when the father is listed as missing in action (MIA). The problem also occurs with families experiencing divorce, joint custody, desertion, and some chronic illnesses.

When families, or professionals working with families, understand this concept, they can use it to help families cope because they can try to get the ambiguity within tolerable limits. Some strategies for helping families deal with their boundary ambiguity are to talk about who is in and out of the family, whether family members will be in or out for an identifiable period of time, and what the boundaries inside the family should be. Other strategies are to avoid keeping a physically absent family member psychologically present when it is disruptive for the family.

In some situations, families are not able to manage the new events with these strategies. When this occurs, the family gradually slips into a deeper and more serious crisis situation.

When this happens, the very fabric of the family is in trouble, and the paradigmatic assumptions are called into question. The family's basic philosophy and orientations to life are examined, and these basic beliefs can evolve, change, be discarded, or be reconstructed.

Examples of this would be changes in the way a family relates to its environment, changes in beliefs about who the family can "count on" when the chips are down, changes in beliefs about God and the role of the spiritual part of life, changes in beliefs about whether people are inherently good or bad, and differentiation from kin.

If a family that did not believe in drug use found themselves in a situation where a teenage boy was adopting a lifestyle that they did not understand, this could be a serious stressor event. The first strategies this family would tend to use involve trying to create simpler levels of change. For example, the parents could talk to the son about his life and why he is making these choices. If these simple methods do not work, the family might try enforcing rules about coming home earlier, grounding him, and taking away resources such as his access to money, and so on.

If the simple rule changes do not work, the family would eventually resort to more fundamental changes. They might try to change their basic parenting methods, try to get professional assistance to make other changes, change where the child lives, or change the basic structure of the family.

If these methods do not work, the family will tend eventually to question some of their basic beliefs. For example, they might adopt a more fatalistic view of life and conclude that things will happen as they will and they have less control over their world than they thought they had. They might rearrange their priorities in life and become more or less involved in trying to change their community values and structure. They might reevaluate their beliefs about the choices their children make try to understand them more fully.

☐ Coping Strategies That Are Relevant for Specific Situations

Some stressor events are relatively different from other stressor events, and some of the strategies that are helpful in one context are not helpful in others. We have only begun to discover what is unique about different types of stressors, but a few ideas have been developed. This section of the chapter reviews some of the strategies that are helpful in coping with specific types of stressful processes.

Coping With Death

Death is a very important part of family life. As Freedman (1988) observed, "Death is the single most important event in family life. From an individual point of view it marks the end; from a family point of view it is often a beginning that initiates processes in the family that can continue for generations" (p. 168).

With most stressor events, it is helpful if families to try to eliminate the stress process as quickly as possible. For example, if someone has lost his or her job, the speed with which a new job is found correlates with the stress levels. If families acquire a new member, lose a member, have an accident, have an illness, and so on, the family tends to have less disruption, and the crisis is coped with best if it is resolved quickly.

Death, however, is an exception to this general rule. When a member of a family dies, it creates a wide range of emotional reactions, and the emotions are so deep and fundamental that it takes a long period of time to work through them. As Walsh and McGoldrick (1988) observed, "the process of mourning is likely to take at least 1 to 2 years, with each new season, holiday, and anniversary revoking the loss" (p. 311).

One way family scientists think about this principle is to talk about the "angle of recovery" in the bottom of the rollercoaster diagram. A number of research studies have found that, with most stressor events, the smaller the angle of recovery the better for the family (Hill, 1958; Waller and Hill, 1951, p. 468). With death, however, a larger angle is more effective because it allows the family time to experience the mourning and bereavement that is necessary.

Another activity that is helpful in coping with death is assembling family members to provide a time when they can work through unresolved concerns and begin the process of reorganizing family processes.

Interpersonal and Occupational Stressors

Different resources are helpful in situations where the main concerns are emotional rather than when occupational and economic stress occurs. Pearlin and Schooler (1982, p. 134) found that with relatively impersonal stressor events, such as those stemming from economic or occupational experiences, the most effective forms of coping involved the manipulation of goals and values in a way that increases the emotional distance of the individual from the problem. On the other hand, problems arising from the relatively close interpersonal relations in the family realm are best handled by coping mechanisms in which the individual remains committed to, and engaged with, the relevant others. In other words, when dealing with stress in the family, it is better to keep close relationships and not to avoid the individuals, the relationships, or the stress.

Because people can move in and out of the business world relatively easily, it is relatively easy and helpful in public realms to make changes that will distance stressful situations. However, because the family realm is unique in that there is a certain permanence to family relationships, it is more difficult and even unhealthy to avoid or distance oneself from most problems inside the family realm.

☐ Summary

There are numerous events that create stress in families, and some stressor events are more serious than others. Also, some of them come from the environment, and others come from inside the family. The process of family stress has phases and there seem to be five different patterns in the way families respond to stress: a rollercoaster pattern where some families experience disorganization followed by reorganization, a descending pattern where some families become disorganized and stay there, an ascending pattern where some families get better off in a stressful situation and stay there, a no-change pattern, and a mixed pattern where some families are better off and then have the rollercoaster experience. Research about families has begun to identify coping strategies that families can use to deal effectively with stressful situations and seven different types of coping strategies were discussed.

☐ Study Questions

1. Name four types of stressor events.
2. Name three stressful events that can originate outside the family.
3. What are the primary elements of the stress process?
4. Give an example of a serious stressor event and then tell how a family could generate a coping strategy to match.
5. Why would the suicide of a family member be so devastating? Use the information in this chapter to explain your answer.

☐ Key Terms

Stressor events
Coping strategies

Resources
ABC-X model of crisis
Family stress and resiliency

☐ Suggested Readings

Boss, P. (1998). *Ambiguous loss.* Cambridge, MA: Harvard University Press.

Burr, et al. (1994). *Reexamining family stress: New theory and research.* Thousand Oaks, CA: Sage.

Cherlin, A. J. (1992). *Marriage, divorce, and remarriage.* Cambridge, MA: Harvard University Press.

Duncan, G., & Brooks-Gunn, J. (1997). *Consequences of growing up poor.* New York: Russell Sage Foundation.

L'Abate, L. (1990). *Building family competence.* Newbury Park, CA: Sage.

Walsh, F. (1998). *Strengthening family resilience.* New York: Guilford.

REFERENCES

Ahmed, S. S., & Bould, S. (2004). One able daughter is worth 10 illiterate sons. *Journal of Marriage and Family, 66,* 1332–1341.

Allport, G. (1937). *Personality: A psychological interpretation.* New York: Holt.

Anderson, S. A., & Fleming, W. M. (1986). Late adolescents' identity formation: Individuation from the family of origin. *Adolescence, 21,* 785–796.

Angell, R. C. (1936). *The family encounters the depression.* New York: Scribner.

Aries, E. (1982). Verbal and nonverbal behavior in single-sex and mixed-sex groups: Are traditional sex roles changing? *Psychological Reports, 51,* 127.

Aries, E. (1996). *Men and women in interaction: Reconsidering the differences.* New York: Oxford University Press.

Babbie, E. (2006). *The practice of social research.* New York: Wadsworth.

Bader, E., Microys, G., Sinclair, C., Willet, E., & Conway, B. (1980). Do marriage preparation programs really work? A Canadian experiment. *Journal of Marriage and Family Therapy, 6,* 171–179.

Ball, F. L., Cowan, J. P., & Cowan, C. P. (1995). Who's got the power? Gender differences in partners' perceptions of influence during marital problem-solving discussions. *Family Process, 34,* 303–321.

Baron, B. (1991). The making and breaking of marital bonds in modern Egypt. In N. Keddie & B. Baron (Eds.), *Women in Middle Eastern history* (pp. 26–43). New Haven CT: Yale University Press.

Bartle, S. E., & Sabatelli, R. M. (1989). Family system dynamics, identity development, and adolescent alcohol use: Implications for family treatment. *Family Relations, 38,* 258–265.

Bavelas, W. R., & Segal, L. (1982). Family system theory: Background and implications. *Journal of Communication, 32,* 99–107.

Baxter, J., Hewiit, B., & Haynes, M. (2008). Life course transitions and housework: Marriage, parenthood, and time on housework. *Journal of Marriage and Family, 70,* 2, 259–272.

Baxter, L. A., & Wilmont, W. (1985). Taboo topics in close relationships. *Journal of Social and Personal Relationships, 2,* 253–269.

Beavers, W. R. (1982). Healthy, midrange and severely dysfunctional families. In F. Walsh (Ed.), *Normal family processes* (pp. 45–66.). New York: Guilford.

Beavers, W. R. (1985). *Successful marriage.* New York: Norton.

Beck, A. (1988). Anxiety and depression: An information processing perspective. *Anxiety Research, 1,* 23–36.

Becker, G. (1991). *A treatise on the family.* Cambridge, MA: Harvard University Press.

Bell, R. A., Daly, J. A., & Gonzalez, M. C. (1987). Affinity-maintenance in marriage and its relationship to women's marital satisfaction. *Journal of Marriage and the Family, 49,* 445–454.

Bennett, L. A., Wolin, S. J., Reiss, D., & Teitelbaum, M. A. (1987). Couples at risk for transmission of alcoholism: Protective influences. *Family Process, 26,* 111–129.

Berger, P., Kellner, & Hansfried. (1973). Marriage and the construction of reality. In N. Glazer-Malbin & H. Y. Waehrer (Eds.), *Woman in a man-made world: A socioeconomic handbook* (pp. 22–58). New York: Rand McNally.

Berscheid, E. (2006). *Dynamics of romantic love: Attachment, caregiving, and sex.* New York: Guilford.

Bischoping, K. (1993). Gender differences in conversation topics. *Sex Roles, 28,* 1, 1–18.

Blood, R. O., & Wolfe, D. M. (1960). *Husbands and wives.* New York: Free Press.

Blumberg, R. L., & Coleman, M. T. (1989). A theoretical look at the gender balance of power in the American couple. *Journal of Family Issues, 10,* 225–251.

Bochard, G., Lussier, Y., & Sabourin, S. (1999). Personality and marital adjustment: Utility of the five-factor model of personality. *Journal of Marriage and Family, 61,* 3, 651–660.

Bograd, R., & Spilka, B. (1996). Self-disclosure and marital satisfaction in mid-life and late-life remarriages. *International Journal of Aging & Human Development, 42,* 161–172.

Booth, A., Carver, K., & Granger, D. A. (2000). Biosocial perspectives on the family. *Journal of Marriage and the Family, 62,* 1018–1034.

Booth, A., Johnson, D., & Granger, D. (2005). Testosterone, marital quality, and role overload. *Journal of Marriage and the Family, 67,* 483–503.

Boss, P. (1987). Family stress. In M. B. Sussman & S. K. Steinmetz (Eds.), *Handbook of marriage and the family* (pp. 22–42). New York: Plenum.

Boss, P. (1998). *Ambiguous loss.* Cambridge, MA: Harvard University Press.

Boss, P. (2007). Ambiguous loss theory: Challenges for scholars and practitioners. *Family Relations, 56,* 105–112.

Bossard, J. S., & Boll, E. S. (1950). *Ritual in family living.* Philadelphia: University of Pennsylvania Press.

Boszormenyi-Nagy, I. & Spark, G.M. (1973). *Invisible Loyalties.* Levittown, PA: Brunner/Mazel.

Boszormenyi-Nagy, I., & Spark, G. M. (1973). *Invisible loyalties: Reciprocity in intergenerational therapy.* New York: Gardner.

Botwin, M. D., Buss, D. M., & Shackelford, T. K. (1997). Personality and mate preferences: Five factors in mate selection and marital satisfaction. *Journal of Personality, 65,* 107–136.

Bowen, M. (1976). Theory in the practice of psychotherapy. In P. Guerin (Ed.), *Family therapy* (pp. 42–61). New York: Gardner.

Boyce, W. R., Jensen, E. W., James, S. A., & Peacock, J. L. (1983). The family routines inventory: Theoretical origins. *Social Science Medicine, 17,* 193–200.

Broderick, C. B. (1993). *Understanding family process: Basics of family systems theory.* Newbury Park, CA: Sage.

Brody, N., & Ehrlichman, H. (1998). *Personality psychology: The science of individuality.* Upper Saddle River, NJ: Prentice Hall.

Bronfenbrenner, U. (1979). *The ecology of human development.* Cambridge, MA: Harvard University Press.

Buehler, C., Krishnakumar, A., Stone, G., Pemberton, S., Gerard, J., & Barber, B. (1998). Interparental conflict styles and youth problem behaviors: A two-sample replication study. *Journal of Marriage and Family, 60,* 119–132.

Bumpass, L., & Lu, H. (2000). Trends in cohabitation and implications for children's family contexts in the United States. *Population Studies, 54,* 29–42.

Burke, P. (2006). *Contemporary social psychological theories.* Stanford CA: Stanford University Press.

Burr et al. (1994). *Reexamining family stress: New theory and research.* Thousand Oaks, CA: Sage.

Burr, W. R., Leigh, G. K., Day, R. D., & Constantine, J. (1979). Symbolic interaction and the family. In W. R. Burr, R. Hill, F. I. Nye, & I. L. Reiss (Eds.), *Contemporary theories about the family* (Vol. 2, pp. 42–111). New York: Free Press.

Burr, W. T. (1973). *Theory construction and the sociology of the family.* New York: Wiley.

Buss, D., Shackelford, Kirkpatrick, L., & Larsen, R. (2001). A half century of mate preference: The cultural evolution of values. *Journal of Marriage and Family, 63,* 491–503.

Caine, L. (1974). *The personal crisis of a widow living in America.* New York: Morrow.

Campbell, C., & Demi, A. (2000). Adult children of father missing in action: An examination of emotional distress, grief, and family hardiness. *Family Relations, 49,* 267–277.

Carlson, M., McLanahan, S., & England, P. (2006). Union formation of fragile families. *Demography, 41,* 237–262.

Carter, B., & McGoldrick, M. (Eds.). (1989). *The changing family life cycle: A framework for family therapy* (2nd ed.). New York: Allyn & Bacon.

Cherlin, A. J. (1999). *Public and private families: An introduction* (2nd ed.). New York: McGraw-Hill.

Cobb, S. (1982). Social support and health through the life course. In H. I. McCubbin, A. E. Cauble, & J. M. Patterson (Eds.), *Family stress, coping and social support* (pp. 351–372). Thousand Oaks, CA: Sage.

Coleman, J. S. (1988). Social capital in the creation of human capital. *American Journal of Sociology, 94*(Suppl.), S95–S120.

Coleman, J. S. (1990). *Foundations of social theory.* Cambridge, MA: Belknap Press of Harvard University Press.

Coleman, J., & Hoffer, T. (1987). *Public and private high schools.* New York: Basic Books.

Condry, J., & Condry, S. (1976). Sex differences: A study of the eye of the beholder. *Child Development, 47,* 812–819.

Constantine, L. L. (1986). *Family paradigms.* New York: Guilford.

Cook, K. S., Coye, C., & Gerbasi, A. (2006). Power-dependence and exchange networks. In P. Burke (Ed.), *Contemporary social psychological theories* (pp. 95–121). Stanford, CA: Stanford University Press.

Cook, K., & Emerson, R. M. (1978). Power, equity, and commitment in exchange networks. *American Sociological Review, 43,* 721–739.

Cook, K. S., Emerson, R. M., Gillmore, M. R., & Yamagishi, T. (1983). The distributions of power in exchange networks: Theory and experimental results. *American Journal of Sociology, 89,* 275–305.

Cook, K. S., & Rice, E. R. W. (2001). Exchange and power: Issues of structure and agency. In J. H. Turner (Ed.), *Handbook of sociological theory* (pp. 221–260). New York: Kluwer.

Coontz, S. (1992). *The way we never were: American families and the nostalgia trap.* New York: Basic Books.

Cottrell, L. S., Jr. (1942). The adjustment of the individual to his age and sex roles. *American Sociological Review, 7,* 617–620.

Crider, A. (2005, September 3). Stories from Hurricane Katrina. Retrieved Feb. 24, 2009, from http://dir.salon.com/story/news/feature/2005/09/03/katrina_stories/index.html?pn=1

Cronen, V., Pearce, W., & Harris, L. (1979). The logic of the coordinated management of meaning: A rule-based approach to the first course in inter-personal communication. *Communication Education, 23,* 22–38.

Dalaker, J. (2001). *Current population report.* Washington, DC: U.S. Census Bureau.

Day, R. D., Gavazzi, S., & Acock, A. (2001). Compelling family processes. In A. Thornton (Ed.), *The well-being of children and families: Research and data needs.* Ann Arbor: University of Michigan Press.

Dickson-Markman, F., & Markman, H. J. (1988). The effects of others on marriage: Do they help or hurt? In P. Noller & M. A. Fitzpatrick (Eds.), *Perspectives on marital interaction* (pp. 33–63). Philadelphia: Multilingual Matters.

D'Onofrio, B. M., Turkheimer, E. N., Emery, R. E., Harden, K. P., Slutske, W., Heath, A., Madden, P. A. F., & Martin, N. G. (2007). A genetically informed study of the intergenerational transmission of marital instability. Journal of Marriage and Family, *69,* 793–803.

Doty, W. G. (1986). *Mythography: The study of myths and rituals.* Tuscaloosa: University of Alabama Press.

Downs, B. (2003). *Fertility of American women: June 2002* (Current Population Reports, No. P20-548). Washington, DC: U.S. Census Bureau.

Driver, J., & Gottman, J. (2004). Daily marital interactions and positive affect during marital conflict among newlywed couples. *Family Process, 43,* 301–314.

Druckman, J. M. (1979). *Effectiveness of five types of pre-marital preparations programs.* Grand Rapids, MI: Education for Marriage.

Duck, S. (1997). *Handbook of personal relationships: Theory, research, and interventions.* Chichester, UK: Wiley.

Duvall, E. (1955). *Family development.* New York: Lippincott.

Duvander, A., & Andersson, G. (2006). Gender equality and fertility in Sweden: A study on the impact of father's uptake of parental leave on continued childbearing. *Marriage and Family Review, 39,* 121–142.

Ehrlich, F. (2000). Dialogue, couple therapy, and the unconscious. *Contemporary Psychoanalysis, 36,* 483–503.

Elder, G. (1985). *Life course dynamics.* Ithaca, NY: Cornell.

Etizoni, A. (1993). *The spirit of community.* New York: Crown Publishers.

Eysenck, H. J. (1952). *The scientific study of personality.* New York: Praeger.

Fagot, B., & Leinbach, M. (1987). Socialization of sex roles within the family. In D. Carter (Ed.), *Current conceptions of sex roles and sex typing: Theory and research* (pp. 111–144). New York: Praeger.

Falbo, T., & Peplau, L. A. (1980). Power strategies in intimate relationships. *Journal of Personality and Social Psychology, 38,* 618–628.

Farley, J. (1979). Family separation-individuation tolerance: A developmental conceptualization of the nuclear family. *Journal of Marital and Family Therapy, 5,* 61–67.

Fiese, B. (2007). *Family routines and rituals.* New Haven, CT: Yale University Press.

Fisher, T.D. & McNulty, J.K. (2008). Neuroticism and marital satisfaction: The mediating role played by the sexual relationship. *Journal of Family Psychology, 22,* 1, 112–122.

Ford, F. R. (1983). Rules: The invisible family. *Family Process, 22,* 135–145.

Freedman, J. (1988). Families in death. In C. Falicov (Ed.), *Family transitions: Continuity and change over the life cycle* (pp. 166–190). New York: Guilford.

Friedman, E. H. (1985). *Generation to generation.* New York: Guilford.

Galston, W. (1998). A liberal-democratic case for the two-parent family. In A. Etzioni (Ed.), *The spirit of community.* (pp. 96–131).

Galvin, K., & Brommel, B. (1991). *Family communication: Cohesion and change* (3rd ed.). Glenview, IL: Scott & Foresman.

Garmezy, N. (1991). Resilience and vulnerability to adverse developmental outcomes associated with poverty. *American Behavioral Scientist, 34,* 416–430.

Gavazzi, S. M. (1993). The relation between family differentiation levels in families with adolescents and the severity of presenting problems. *Family Relations, 42,* 463–468.

Gavazzi, S. M. (1994). Advances in assessing the relationship between family differentiation and problematic functioning in adolescents. *Family Therapy, 21,* 249–259.

Gavazzi, S. M., Anderson, S. A., & Sabatelli, R. M. (1993). Family differentiation, peer differentiation and adolescent adjustment in a clinical sample. *Journal of Adolescent Research, 8,* 205–225.

Gavazzi, S. M., & Sabatelli, R. M. (1990). Family system dynamics, the individuation process and psychosocial and adolescent adjustment in a clinical sample. *Journal of Adolescent Research, 5,* 500–519.

Geist, R., & Gilbert, G. (1996). Correlates of expressed and felt emotion during marital conflict: Satisfaction, personality, process, and outcome. *Personality & Individual Differences, 21,* 49–60.

Gillis, J. (1996). *A world of their own making: Myth, ritual, and the quest for family values.* New York: Basic Books.

Goldberg, S. (1990). Attachment in infants at risk: Theory, research, and practice. *Infants and Young Children, 2,* 11–20.

Gontang, R. & Erickson, M.T. (1996). The relationship between Million's personality types and family systems functioning. *American Journal of Family Therapy, 24, 3,* 215–226.

Goode, W. J. (1960). A theory of role strain. *American Sociological Review, 35,* 483–496.

Gore, S. (1978). The effect of social support in moderating the health consequences of unemployment. *Journal of Health and Social Behavior, 19,* 157–165.

Gottman, J. M. (1994). *What predicts divorce? The relationship between marital processes and marital outcomes.* Hillsdale, NJ: Lawrence Erlbaum Associates.

Gottman, J. M. (1999). *The seven principles for making marriage work.* New York: Crown.

Gottman, J., Coan, J., Carrere, S., & Swanson, C. (1998). Predicting marital happiness and stability from newlywed interactions. *Journal of Marriage and the Family, 60,* 5–22.

Greenberg, G. S. (1977). The family interactional perspective: A study and examination of the work of Don D. Jackson. *Family Process, 16,* 385–412.

Guerney, B., & Guerney, L. (1981). Family life education as intervention. *Family Relations, 30,* 591–598.

Gupta, S. (2007). Autonomy, dependence, or display? The relationship between married women's earnings and housework. *Journal of Marriage and Family, 69,* 399–417.

Haley, J. (1963). *Strategies of psychotherapy.* New York: Grune & Stratton.

Haley, J. (1976). *Problem solving therapy.* San Francisco: Jossey-Bass.

Haley, J. (1987). *Reflections on therapy and other essays.* Washington, DC: The Family Therapy Institute.

Hall, A. D., & Fagen, R. E. (1956). Definition of system. *General Systems Yearbook, 1,* 18–28.

Hansen, J. E., & Schuldt, W. J. (1984). Physical distance, sex, and intimacy in self disclosure. *Psychological Reports, 51,* 3–6.

Hellmuth, J.C. & McNulty, J.K. (2008). Neuroticism, marital violence, and the moderating role of stress and behavioral skills. *Journal of Personality and Social Psychology, 95, 1,* 166–180.

Hess, R. D., & Handel, G. (1959). *Family worlds.* Chicago: University of Chicago Press.

Hewlett, B. S., Lamb, M. E., Shannon, D., Leyendecker, B., & Scholmerich, A. (1998). Culture and early infancy among Central African foragers and farmers. *Developmental Psychology, 34,* 653–661.

Hill, R. (1958). Generic features of family under stress. *Social Casework, 49,* 139–150.

Hill, R. L., & Hansen, D. A. (1960). The identification of conceptual frameworks utilized in family study. *Marriage and Family Living, 22,* 299–311.

Hobbes, T. (1947). *Leviathan.* New York: Macmillan. (Original work published 1651)

Holmes, T. H., & Rahe, R. R. (1967). The social readjustment rating scale. *Journal of Psychosomatic Research, 11,* 213–218.

Holroyd, J., & Guthrie, D. (1986). Family stress with chronic childhood illness. *Journal of Clinical Psychology, 42,* 552–568.

Imber-Black, E., & Roberts, J. (1992). *Rituals for our time.* New York: Harper Perennial.

Innstrand, S. (2008). Positive and negative work–family interaction and burnout. *Work & Stress, 22,* 1, 1–15.

Jackson, D. D. (1957). The question of family homeostasis. *Psychiatric Quarterly Supplement, 31,* 79–90.

Jackson, D. D. (1963). Suggestion for the technical handling of paranoid patients. *Psychiatry, 26,* 306–307.

Jackson, D. D. (1965). Family rules: Marital quid pro quo. *Archives of General Psychiatry, 12,* 589–594.

Jackson, D. & Yaom, I. (1965). Family rules: Marital quid pro quo. *Archives of General Psychology, 12,* 3, 589–594.

Jacob, T. (1987). Family interaction and psychopathology: Historical overview. In T. Jacob (Ed.), *Family interaction and psychopathology: Theories, methods, and findings* (pp. 242–283). New York: Plenum.

Kantor, D., & Lehr, W. (1975). *Inside the family.* San Francisco: Jossey-Bass.

Kaplan, D. M., Smith, A., Grobstien, R., & Fischman, S. E. (1973). Family mediation of stress. *Social Work, 18,* 60–69.

Keirsey, D. (1998). *Please understand me.* New York: Prometheus Nemesis Press.

Kennedy, C., & Camden, C. (1993). Interruptions and nonverbal gender differences. *Journal of Nonverbal Behavior, 8,* 44–52.

Kerr, M. (1981). Family systems theory and therapy. In A. S. Gurman & D. P. Kriskern (Eds.), *Handbook of family therapy* (pp. 212–244). New York: Brunner/Mazel.

Kerr, M. E., & Bowen, M. (1988). *Family evaluation.* New York: Norton.

Klein, D. M., & White, J. M. (1996). *Family theories: An introduction.* Thousand Oaks, CA: Sage.

Klonsky, J., & Bengston, V. L. (1996). Pulling together, drifting apart: A longitudinal case study of a four-generation family. *Journal of Aging Studies, 10,* 255–279.

Koos, E. (1946). *Families in trouble.* New York: King's Crown Press.

Krauss, R., & Fussell, S. (1996). Social psychological models of interpersonal communication. In E. Higgins & A. Kruglanski (Eds.), *Social psychology: Handbook of basic principles* (pp. 44–82). New York: Guilford.

Kuhn, T. (1969). *The structure of scientific revolutions* (3rd ed.). Chicago: University of Chicago Press.

Laing, R. D. (1972). *The politics of the family.* New York: Vintage Books.

Laird, J. (1988). Women and ritual in family therapy (pp. 69–102). In E. Imber-Black & J. Roberts (Eds.), *Rituals in families and family therapy.* New York: Norton.

Landale, N. (2002). Contemporary cohabitation: Food for thought. In A. Booth & A. Crouter (Eds.), *Just living together* (pp. 111–131). Mahwah, NJ: Lawrence Erlbaum Associates.

Larson, J., Parks, A., Harper, J., & Heath, V. (2001). A psychometric evaluation of the family rules from the past questionnaire. *Contemporary Family Therapy, 23,* 83–104.

Lidz, T. (1963). *The family and human adaptation.* New York: International Universities Press.

Mackey, R. A., & O'Brien, B. (1995). *A lasting marriage: Men and women growing together.* Westport, CT: Praeger.

Marsiglio, W., Amato, P., Day, R. D., & Lamb, M. E. (2000). Scholarship on fatherhood in the 1990's and beyond. *Journal of Marriage and the Family, 62,* 1173–1191.

Masten, A. (1994). Resilience in individual development: Successful adaptation despite risk and adversity. In M. Wang & E. Gordon (Eds.), *Educational resilience in inner-city America: Challenges and prospects* (pp. 3–25). Hillsdale, NJ: Lawrence Erlbaum Associates.

Maynard, P.E. & Hultquist, A. (1988). The circumplex model with adjudicated youth's families. *Journal of Psychotherapy and the Family, 4,* 1, 249–266.

Mazur, A., & Michalek, J. (1998). Marriage, divorce, and male testosterone. *Social Forces, 77,* 315–330.

McCrae, R. R., & Costa, P. T. (1991). Adding Leibe und Arbeit: The full five-factor model and well-being. *Personality and Social Psychology Bulletin, 17,* 227–232.

McCubbin, M., Balling, K., Possin, P., Frierdich, S., & Bryne, B. (2002). Family resiliency in childhood cancer. *Family Relations, 51,* 103–111.

McCubbin, H., Boss, P., Wilson, L., & Lester, G. (1980). Developing family vulnerability to stress: Coping patterns and strategies wives employ. In J. Trost (Ed.), *The family and change* (pp. 89–103). Sweden: International Library.

McCubbin, H. I., & Dahl, B. (1985). *Marriage and family.* New York: Wiley.

McCubbin, H. I., Dahl, B., Lester, G., Benson, D., & Robertson, M. (1976). Coping repertoires of adapting to prolonged war-induced separations. *Journal of Marriage and Family, 38,* 461–471.

McCubbin, H. I., & Figley, C. (1983). *Stress and the family: Vol. 1. Coping with normative transitions.* New York: Brunner & Mazel.

McCubbin, H. I., Thompson, A. I., Pirner, P. A., & McCubbin, M. A. (1988). *Family types and strengths: A life cycle and ecological perspective.* Edina, MN: Burgess International Group.

Meredith, W. H. (1985). The importance of family traditions. *Wellness Perspective, 2,* 17–19.

Meredith, W., Abbott, D., & Adams, S. (1986). Family violence: Its relation to marital and parental satisfaction and family strengths. *Journal of Family Violence, 4,* 75–88.

Meredith, W., Abbot, D., Lamanna, M.A., & Sanders, G. (1989). Rituals and family strengths: A three-generational study. *Family Perspectives, 23,* 75–84.

Merton, R. K. (1968). *Social theory and social structure.* Glencoe, IL: Free Press.

Miller, S., Nunnally, D., & Wackman, S. (1988). *Alive and aware: Improving communication in relationships.* Minneapolis, MN: Interpersonal Communication Programs.

Minuchin, S. (1981). *Family kaleidoscope.* Cambridge, MA: Harvard University Press.

Minuchin, S. (1996). *Mastering family therapy: Journeys of growth and transformation.* New York: Wiley.

Molm, L. D. (2003). Theoretical comparisons of forms of exchange. *Sociological Theory, 21,* 1–17.

Monroe, P. A., Bokemeier, J. L., Kotchen, J. M., & Mckean, H. (1985). Spousal response consistency in decision-making research. *Journal of Marriage and the Family, 47,* 733–738.

Nasir, J. (1990). *The Islamic law of personal status.* London: Graham & Trotman.

The National Marriage Project. (2006). *The state of our unions: The social health of marriage in America.* Retrieved Feb. 24, 2009, from http://marriage.rutgers.edu/Publications/SOOU/TEXTSOOU2006.htm

Nichols, M. P., & Shwartz, R. C. (2007). *Family therapy: Concepts and methods* (8th ed.). Needham Heights, MA: Allyn & Bacon.

Noller, P. (1984). Clergy marriages: A study of a uniting church sample. *Australian Journal of Sex, Marriage and Family, 5,* 187–197.

Noller, P., & Fitzpatrick, M. (1990). Marital communication in the eighties. *Journal of Marriage and the Family, 52,* 832–843.

Norman, W.T. (1963). Toward an adequate taxonomy of personality attributes: Replicated factor structure in peer nomination personality ratings. *Journal of Abnormal and Social Psychology, 66, 3,* 574–583.

Oakley, D. (1985). Premarital childbearing decision making. *Family Relations, 34, 2,* 225–266.

Okun, B., & Rapport, L. J. (1980). *Working with families.* Belmont, CA: Wadsworth.

Olson, D. H., & DeFrain, J. (1994). *Marriage and the family: Diversity and strengths.* Mountain View, CA: Mayfield.

Olson, D. H., & McCubbin, H. I. (1982). The circumplex model of marital and family systems VI: Applications to family stress and crisis intervention. In H. I. McCubbin, A. C. Cauble, & J. M. Patterson (Eds.), *Family stress, coping and social support* (pp. 132–150). Springfield, IL: Thomas.

Palazzoli, M. (1988). *Family games: General models of psychotic processes in the family.* New York: Norton.

Palazzoli, M. S., Boscolo, L., Cecchin, G., & Prata, G. (1978). *Paradox and counterparadox.* New York: Jason Aronson.

Papero, D. V. (1983). Family systems theory and therapy. In B. B. Wolman & G. Stricker (Eds.), *Handbook of family and marital therapy* (pp. 144–190). New York: Plenum.

Parke, R., Kim, M., Flyr, M., McDowell, D., Simpkins, S., Killian, C., et al. (2001). Managing marital conflict: Links with children's peer relationships. In J. Grych & F. Fincham (Eds.), *Interpersonal conflict and child development: Theory, research, and applications* (pp. 207–257). New York: Cambridge University Press.

Patterson, J. (2002). Integrating family resilience and family stress theory. *Journal of Marriage and Family, 64,* 349–360.

Palazzoli, M.S. (1977). Family rituals: A powerful tool in family therapy. *Family Process, 16, 4,* 445–453.

Pearlin, L., & Schooler, C. (1982). The structure of coping. *Journal of Health and Social Behavior, 19,* 2–21.

Pears, K., Capalidi, D., & Owen, L.D. (2007). Substance use risk across three generations: The roles of parent discipline practices and inhibitory control. *Psychology of Addictive Behavior, 21, 3,* 373–386.

Phillips, J., & Sweeney, M. (2005). Premarital cohabitation and marital disruption among White, Black, and Mexican American women. *Journal of Marriage and Family, 67,* 296–314.

Pinello, D. R. (2006). *America's struggle for same-sex marriage.* New York: Cambridge University Press.

Pines, A. M. (1998). A prospective study of personality and gender differences in romantic attraction. *Personality & Individual Differences, 25,* 147–157.

Polmin, R. (1994). *Genetics and experience: The interplay between nature and nurture.* Thousand Oaks, CA: Sage.

Quinn, W. H., Newfield, N. A., & Protinsky, H. O. (1985). Rites of passage in families with adolescents. *Journal of Family Processes, 24,* 101–111.

Reiss, D. (1981). *The family's construction of reality.* Cambridge, MA: Harvard University Press.

Reiss, D. (1995a). Genetic influence on family systems: Implications for development. *Journal of Marriage and the Family, 57,* 543–560.

Reiss, D. (1995b). Genetic questions for environmental studies: Differential parenting and psychopathology in adolescence. *Archives of General Psychiatry, 52,* 925–936.

Reiss, I. L., & Lee, G. R. (1988). *Family systems in America* (4th ed.). New York: Holt, Rinehart, & Winston.

Roberts, J. (1988). Setting the frame: Definition functions, and typology of rituals. In E. Imber-Black, J. Roberts, & R. A. Whiting (Eds.), *Rituals in families and family therapy* (pp. 3–46). New York: Norton.

Roberts, L.J. (2000). Fire and ice in marital communication: Hostile and distancing behaviors as predictors of marital distress. *Journal of Marriage and Family, 62, 3,* 693–707.

Rogers, F. (1983). Mr. Rogers talks with parents. Berkley, CA: Berkley Books.

Rosenfeld, L., & Bowen, G. (1991). Marital disclosure and marital satisfaction: Direct-effect versus interaction-effect models. *Western Journal of Speech Communication, 55,* 112–133.

Rowe, D. C. (1994). *The limits of family influence: Genes, experience, and behavior.* New York: Guilford.

Sabatelli, R. M., & Anderson, S. A. (1991). Family systems dynamics, peer relationships and adolescents' psychological adjustments. *Family Relations, 40,* 363–369.

Sabatelli, R. M., & Cecil-Pigo, E. F. (1985). Relational interdependence and commitment in marriage. *Journal of Marriage and the Family, 47,* 931–938.

Sabatelli, R. M., & Shehan, C. L. (1993). Exchange and resource theories. In P. Boss, W. Doherty, R. LaRossa, W. Schumm, & S. Steinmetz (Eds.), *Sourcebook of family theories and methods: A contextual approach* (pp. 385–411). New York: Plenum.

Satir, V. (1972). *Conjoint family therapy: A guide to theory and technique.* Palo Alto, CA: Science and Behavior Books.

Sauer, R.J. (1982). Family enmeshment. *Family Therapy: The Bulletin of Synergy, 9,* 298–304.

Sauber, R., L'Abate, L., Weeks, G., & Buchanan, W. (1993). *Dictionary of family psychology and therapy.* Newbury Park, CA: Sage.

Scanzoni, J. (1988). Joint decision making in the sexually based primary relationship. In D. Brinberg & J. Jaccard (Eds.), *Dyadic decision making* (pp. 143–165). New York: Springer-Verlag.

Scaramella, L. V., Sohr-Preston, S. L., Callahan, K. L., & Mirabile, S. P. (2008). A test of the family stress model on toddler-aged children's adjustment among Hurricane Katrina impacted and nonimpacted low-income families. *Journal of Clinical Child & Adolescent Psychology, 37,* 530–542.

Schvaneveldt, J. D., & Lee, T. R. (1983). The emergence and practice of ritual in the American family. *Family Perspectives, 17,* 137–143.

Seccomb, K. (2008). *Families and their social worlds.* Boston: Allyn & Bacon.

Seltzer, J. (2004). Cohabitation and family change. In M. Coleman & L. Ganong (Eds.), *Handbook of contemporary families* (pp. 57–78). Thousand Oaks, CA: Sage Publications.

Shaffer, D. R. (1989). *Developmental psychology.* Pacific Grove, CA: Brooks/Cole.

Sherif, B. (1999). The prayer of a married man is equal to seventy prayers of a single man. *Journal of Family Issues, 20,* 617–633.

Sieburg, E. (1985). *Family communication: An integrated systems approach.* New York: Gardner Press.

Simmons, T., & O'Connell, M. (2003). *Married-couple and unmarried partner households: 2000* (Census Special Report No. CENSR-5). Washington, DC: U.S. Census Bureau.

Smith, C. (2005). *Soul searching: The religious and spiritual lives of American teenagers.* New York: Oxford University Press.

Snowden, R., & Snowden, E. (1984). *The gift of a child.* London: George Allen & Unwin.

Sprey, J. (1979). Conflict theory and the study of marriage and the family. In W. R. Burr, R. Hill, F. I. Nye, & I. L. Reiss (Eds.), *Contemporary theories about the family* (Vol. 2, pp. 130–159). New York: Free Press.

Sprey, J. (2000). Theorizing in family studies: Discovering process. *Journal of Marriage and the Family, 62,* 18–31.

Steinglass, P., Bennett, L. A., Wolin, S. J., & Reiss, D. (1987). *The alcoholic family.* New York: Basic Books.

Stephen, E., & Chandra, A. (2006). Declining estimates of infertility in the United States: 1982–2002. *Fertility and Sterility, 86,* 516–523.

Sternburg, R. (1986). A triangular theory of love. *Psychological Review, 93,* 119–135.

Swinford, S. P., Demaris, A., Cernkovich, S. A., & Giordano, P. C. (2000). Harsh physical discipline in childhood and violence in later romantic involvements: The mediating role of problem behaviors. *Journal of Marriage and the Family, 62,* 508–519.

Tannen, D. (1986). *That's not what I meant! How conversational style makes or breaks your relations with others.* New York: Morrow.

Tannen, D. (1990). *You just don't understand: Women and men in conversation.* New York: Morrow.

Thompson, L., & Walker, A. J. (1989). Gender in families: Women and men in marriage, work, and parenthood. *Journal of Marriage and the Family, 51,* 845–871.

Tucker, J. (1991). Ties that bound: Women and family in eighteenth- and nineteenth-century Nablus. In N. Keddie & B. Baron (Eds.), *Women in Middle Eastern history* (pp. 242–261). New Haven, CT: Yale University Press.

Turner, V. (1967). *The forest of symbols: Aspects of Ndembu ritual.* Ithaca, NY: Cornell University Press.

U.S. Census Bureau. (1998). *Current population report* (Table 69). Washington, DC: Author.

U.S. Census Bureau. (2003). *Current population report* (Table 66). Washington, DC: Author.

U.S. Department of Education. (2008). 1.5 million homeschooled students in the United States in 2007. (National Center for Educational Statistics, Issue Brief NCES 2009-030). Washington, D.C.: U.S. Government Printing Office.

van der Hart, O. (1983). *Rituals in psychotherapy: Transitions and continuity.* New York: Irvington.

Vangelisti, A. (1994). Family secrets: Forms, functions and correlates. *Journal of Social & Personal Relationships, 11,* 113–135.

Vangelisti, A., & Caughlin, J. (1997). Revealing family secrets: The influence of topic, function, and relationships. *Journal of Social & Personal Relationships, 14,* 222–243.

Waerdahl, R. (2005). Maybe I'll need a pair of Levi's before junior high? Child to youth trajectories and anticipatory socialization. *Childhood: A Global Journal of Child Research, 12,* 201–222.

Waite, L. (1995). Does marriage matter? *Demography, 32,* 483–507.

Waller, W., & Hill, R. (1951). *The family: A dynamic interpretation.* New York: Dryden.

Walsh, F. & McGoldrick, M. (1988). Loss and the family life cycle. In C. Falicov (Ed.) *Family Transitions.* NY: Guilford.

Waring, E., & Chelune, G. J. (1983). Marital intimacy and self-disclosure. *Journal of Clinical Psychology, 39,* 183.

Watzlawick, P., Weakland, J. H., & Fisch, R. (1974). *Change: Principles of problem formation and problem resolution.* New York: Norton.

White, J. (2005). *Advancing family theories.* Thousand Oaks, CA: Sage.

Whiting, R. A. (1988). Guidelines to designing therapeutic rituals. In E. Imber-Black, J. R. Roberts, & R. A. Whiting (Eds.), *Rituals in families and family therapy* (pp. 96–139). New York: Norton.

Wise, G. W. (1986). Family routines, rituals, and traditions: Grist for the family mill and buffers against stress. In S. Van Zant (Ed.), *Family strengths 7: Vital connections* (pp. 45–66). Lincoln, NE: Center for Family Strengths.

Wolfson, E. (2004). *Why marriage matters: America, equality, and gay people's right to marry.* New York: Simon & Schuster.

Wolin, S., & Bennett, L. A. (1984). Family rituals. *Family Process, 23,* 401–420.

Wynne, L. C. (1984). The epigenesis of relational systems: A model for understanding family development. *Family Process, 23,* 297–318.

Xu, X., Hudspeth, C., & Bartkowski, J. (2006). The role of cohabitation in remarriage. *Journal of Marriage and Family, 68,* 261–274.

GLOSSARY

ABC-X model of crisis: A theoretical model used to explain and understand how families are affected by stressful events and situations: A refers to the stressor event, B refers to the family members' definition of the situation, C refers to the resources available to the family, and X refers to level of stress experienced by the family.

Agreeableness: A personality trait referring to how warmhearted, trusting, and kind an individual is. Agreeable individuals also tend to be high on empathy and compassion.

Agreement reality: The tendency of individuals to conform to or adopt views or opinions that most closely resemble their own without consideration of additional viewpoints.

Ambivalence: The state of experiencing two opposing affective states simultaneously. For example, the birth of child is usually a very happy and exciting experience. However, there might also exist fear and anxiety regarding the transition to parenthood.

Anticipatory socialization: The process of learning the norms, values, and so on, of a role or roles before one is expected to take on that particular role.

Behavioral genetics: The study of the genetic influence on individual behavior as opposed to environmental influences.

Benign assumption: Emotional climate that has a benign tone, it is assumed that there is no hostile intent in what people do, but that things just happen and should simply be dealt with.

Biased: Favoring one person (or group of people) over another. In research this refers to the over- or underrepresentation of a segment of the population in a sample. If the bias is created by a characteristic of the sampling procedure, then the sample is said to contain systematic distortion. Often this distortion is unintentional and unknown to the researcher.

Boundaries: The borders within a family between subsystems that help to define family membership and an individual's roles within a family system.

Cohabitation: An intimate relationship in which partners live together without being formally married either legally or religiously; sexual involvement is usually part of such relationships.

Commitment: The state of being bound emotionally to another person or group of people; one's degree of devotion to such a relationship. Commitment is a construct of Sternburg's triangle theory of love.

Communication: Symbolic and transactional process through which we create and share meaning.

Connectedness: The degree to which families value spending time together and associating with one another; families can have healthy connectedness and unhealthy connectedness (either disconnected or overconnected).

Conscientiousness: A personality trait referring to the level of one's personal organization and tendency to plan ahead.

Constructs: An idea or formulation deemed relevant to a particular theory or research question.

Content messages: The overt, explicit aspect of a message; most often sent in words.

Continuum of abstraction: The concept that certain processes or interactions occur in visible, obvious ways, whereas other processes and interactions are more subtle or implied, based on unspoken rules and ideologies.

Coping strategies: Processes, behaviors, or patterns of behaviors that families go through to adapt to stress; types of strategies can include emotional, cognitive, social, and spiritual forms of coping.

Covenant marriage: In some states (e.g., Louisiana), it is legal to obtain a marriage within which the couple agrees to premarital counseling and accepts a much more limited list of grounds for divorce. This type of marriage has been promoted by the religious right in American politics in an effort to stem the tide of high divorce rates and as a pro-marriage stand that holds marriage as a theologically sacred institution.

Covert messages: *See* intent messages.

Cross-generational (or intergenerational) alliance: Instances in which family members from separate generations (e.g., mother and child) form a relational alliance to the exclusion of other family members of that generation. Such an alliance often occurs because of the failure or absence of normal generational bonds (e.g., father is unable to keep a job or is an abusive alcoholic).

Decoding: The process by which a message is received and the meaning and intent are interpreted. Because communication is a symbolic process, received messages must always be decoded to understand what is intended by the message.

Defense of Marriage Act (DOMA): Federal law passed on September 21, 1996, stating that no state need treat a relationship between people of the same sex as a marriage, even if the relationship has been approved in another state. For example, currently Massachusetts allows same-sex marriage. If a same-sex couple married in Massachusetts moved to Montana, Montana would not be obligated to recognize that marriage. This law has far-reaching effects on topics like insurance coverage, hospital rights, and other issues within which litigation is possible. The law also mandates that the federal government may not treat same-sex marriage as viable—even if one of the states does.

Demographics: The statistical data of a population, especially those showing age, income, education, and so on.

Differentiation: The ability to maintain appropriate emotional distance from other family members; to appropriately separate, segment, and make different.

Distinctive rituals: Rituals that define a family or that are unique or specific to them.

Economic dependency theory: The theory that women are economically dependent on men not out of choice, but as a result of cultural discrimination.

Emotional cutoff: An attempt to deny fusion rather than resolve it, an ineffective method that results in disconnecting from the family but still produces all the feelings of the effects of fusion.

Emotional triangles: When two parts of a family system have an ongoing conflict and they focus on something or someone else as a way of gaining control over the situation or stabilizing their problem. Examples include bringing a child into the parents' fight or focusing on dishes or finances rather than parental relationship.

Empiricism: The philosophical tradition suggesting that to really know our world we have to rely on objective experience.

Entity: Something that exists as a particular and discrete unit (persons, groups, etc.).

Equifinality: The idea that multiple origins can yield the same outcome. This construct also suggests that one single origin (or cause) can yield many different outcomes.

Equilibrium: In families, the state of maintaining a balanced organization, structure, and system of interactions.

Exaggeration under stress principle: When under stress, families have a tendency to increase their efforts in promoting the ideologies and strategies they are already comfortable with rather than trying to find of new way of dealing with the problem.

Experiential reality: An individual's perception of the world based on his or her own personal life experiences.

Explicit rule: The beliefs that are recognized, acknowledged, and known by a family; these can often be talked about overtly because they have been formalized.

Extroversion: A personality trait characterized by outgoing behavior and a desire to be surrounded by and involved with large numbers of people.

Family-involved mate selection (FIMS): Systems of courtship in which mate selection is directed primarily by members of an individual's family; may include smaller, more private interactions between parents and the potential mate or more elaborate public arrangements involving extended family members and kin.

Family of orientation: One's family of orientation centers on the family group within which one was raised. Your family of orientation would include your parents and you as a child or grandchild.

Family of origin: *See* family of orientation.

Family of procreation: One's family of procreation involves forming a close relationship (usually through marriage) and then adding children to that relationship.

Family processes: The strategies families use to attain goals. These strategies include, for example, the enactment of routines, creation and maintenance of rituals, adoption of key ideological orientations, use of communication, decision making and problem-solving styles, parenting approaches, and ways couples and family members resolve power issues and conflict.

Field research: A form of research that focuses on natural events, interviews, and case study analyses.

Fixed biological connections: Biologically based familial connections, such as father, mother, or child, that are definite and cannot be undone.

Folkways: Social norms dealing with behaviors that are preferred but are generally optional.

Fusion: A situation in a family within which the patterns, rules, rule sequences, and family paradigm conspire together to negate family members' individuality.

Gender: Socialized characteristics regarding what is and is not appropriate behavior for boys or men and girls or women.

Generation: One's place or position within a kinship structure (i.e., parent, child, grandparent, etc.).

Genogram: A tool used for understanding family processes that employs charts and symbols to map out several generations of family relationships. Genograms can also be used to identify significant events that might have an influence on families and individuals.

Head Start: A government program started in the 1960s under the leadership of President Lyndon Johnson as part of the Great Society initiative. Head Start targeted the early education of disadvantaged children.

Healthy emotional ties and rituals: Present in families with healthy differentiation, rituals are used for the appropriate purpose and are not so rigid as to prevent change and flexibility.

IIuman Genome Project: A multibillion-dollar effort begun in 1990 to attempt to identify all of the 20,000 to 25,000 genes in human DNA.

Ideologies: Similar to paradigms, ideologies encompass the beliefs, values, attitudes, and assumptions of an individual or group that represent one's understanding of the world and how things are organized.

Implicit rule: Beliefs that remain hidden from view and are generally not discussed. Families are often unaware of their implicit rules because that is simply "the way things are."

In-depth interviews: A type of field research in which the researchers select a relatively small number of individuals who share a common experience and then conduct lengthy interviews with each individual, taking detailed notes, to obtain as much information from those individuals as possible.

Intent messages: Subtle, implicit, usually nonverbal messages that may accompany overt content messages and that are usually conveyed through one's tone of voice, posture, and so on; intent messages might often override or send a different message than the words that are actually being said.

Intergenerational transmission: The transfer of information from older generations to the new generation by means of relational processes.

Intimacy: An aspect of personal relationships that refers to the disclosure of personal information such as goals, dreams, aspirations, fears, and so on. Intimacy is a construct of Sternburg's triangle theory of love.

Introversion: A personality trait that, in contrast with extroversion, is characterized by quieter, more reserved behavior and an affinity for smaller groups and more intimate connections with others.

Invisible loyalties: Unspoken ethical obligations between generations to provide affection, care, nurturance, and appreciation.

Land grant school: In the 1800s, most states created state universities (sometimes called agriculture schools) that offered degrees in farming, animal husbandry, mechanics, and frequently home economics for women.

Love-based mate selection (LBMS): Refers to systems of courtship in which mate selection is based on feelings of love and attraction between the two parties involved in the relationship; family involvement is generally minimized and limited. (This term is unique to this book.)

Love Lab: Gottman's research was centered in an apartment-like situation within which couples spent several days a year for many years while being observed by researchers.

Meta-communication: A searching form of communication in which individuals talk to each other about how they communicate and what is or is not effective.

Metarule: Rules regarding how new rules are created and how old rules are eliminated or changed.

Mores: Social norms dealing with behaviors that are considered especially important or serious.

Morphogenesis: The tendency of a system (a family system in our case) to need to adapt and change to new circumstances and ever-changing development of family members.

Morphostasis: The tendency of a system (in our case a family system) to maintain order and sameness.

Neuroticism: A personality trait referring to how emotional, anxious, or "high-strung" an individual is as opposed to being even-tempered or self-assured.

No-fault divorce: During the 1970s, there was a cultural surge to dramatically alter the list of reasons why a person could sue for divorce. For example, prior to the no-fault divorce era, many states required the person seeking the divorce to prove abandonment, infidelity, insanity, or that he or she had committed a felony. Each state had a list of faults under which one could apply for divorce. In no-fault divorce, the couple merely has to say "We don't love one another and we want a divorce." The concept of no-fault divorce was pioneered by the Bolsheviks during the Russian Revolution of 1917 and brought to the United States in 1969 by then governor of California, Ronald Reagan.

Openness: A personality trait referring to how open an individual is to new experiences and ideas.

Overgeneralizing: To take the opinions of a person (or of a small, nonrepresentative group of people) and assume that what those people think or how they behave is representative of a larger group.

Overritualization: When families try to incorporate too many rituals from their families of origin and from organizations outside the family.

Overt messages: *See* content messages.

Paradigms: The enduring, fundamental, shared, and general assumptions families develop about the nature and meaning of life, what is important, and how to cope with the world they live in; types of family paradigms include open, closed, random, and synchronous.

Participant observation: A type of field research in which researchers immerse themselves in situations, family groups, tribes, or communities, and record, in detail, their observations.

Passion: Intense emotions based on sexual drive and attraction. Passion is a construct of Sternburg's triangle theory of love.

Personal experiential reality: *See* experiential reality.

Personality: Individual characteristics or temperament traits that are generally stable throughout time and across various situations.

Polygyny: The Greek for many is *poly* and *gyny* means women. Polygyny is a specific form of polygamy and features situations where a man has more than one wife.

Power: The ability to influence others to behave in a manner they normally would not.

Prosaic: The root word is *prose* (as opposed to poetic). The prosaic of daily living is about the ordinary prose of life, or the daily living that involves routines, rituals, and rules of life.

Qualitative research strategy: Research methods are often exploratory, usually involving observation or careful probing interviews and in-depth coding of what is observed. This type of research usually focuses on the deep underlying story of the lived experience rather than a numerical summation of people's attitudes or beliefs about their lived experience.

Quantitative research strategy: Research methods in which individual responses are reduced to a series of numbers and then analyzed using statistical methods. This research strategy often focuses on responding to identified hypotheses formulated by researchers.

Quotidian: The quotidian of life focuses on the ordinary aspects of life. In our case, the quotidian of family life refers to the ordinary elements of daily living.

Reciprocal obligation: A situation in which the person with the most power asks the partner in the position of greatest interest for compensation of some sort.

Reductionism: An orientation toward research in which complex systems are studied primarily through the analysis of their most basic parts.

Reliability: The degree to which a measure used in a study can repeatedly obtain similar results.

Reporting inaccuracy: The tendency of people to give an inaccurate representation of reality because of poor memory or the simple human tendency to interpret what we see and hear through the lens of our own personal experiences.

Research goals: The overarching research questions researchers ask.

Research strategies: The plans and methods used to solve a specific research goal.

Research tactics: Procedures or modes of approaching and solving a research problem.

Resources: Any means whereby a situation or obstacle may be dealt with. This includes physical resources such as money, physical goods, and so on, as well as psychological and social resources such as personal talents, character traits, community programs, supportive relationships, and social connections. Resources are an important construct of several theories used in studying families, including social exchange theory, conflict theory, and family stress theory.

Rites of passage: Rituals that mark a significant change in a person's social status.

Rituals: Involve more than one family member, overt behavior, repetition in the form and content of what is done, they have continuity and change, more symbolism, more emotion, and more extraordinary behaviors.

Role strain: The felt difficulty experienced when trying to conform to the demands of a new role or roles.

Roles: The specific function(s) and purpose(s) that an individual has within a family structure.

Routines: Involve more than one family member, overt behavior, repetition in the form and content of what is done, they have continuity and change, less symbolism, less emotion, and more ordinary behaviors.

Rule sequences: Implicit interactions that gradually develop into patterns of interaction and that create a framework for future interactions.

Rules: Principles or regulations guiding conduct or behavior; includes social norms, laws, mores, and so on, and might or might not be enforceable; understandings about how all kinds of things are done, some are implicit and some are explicit.

Same-sex marriage: Marriage between two members of the same sex. Same-sex marriage is available in some states but not in most at the current time.

Sample bias: Occurs when a certain group of people from a population is over- or underrepresented in a sample. Data collected from a biased sample will not be representative of the total population.

Sex: Biological, chromosomal configuration resulting in physically observable sex characteristics.

Social capital: A social resource that is inherent in social connections and quality relationships; the connections one has and maintains with others.

Social norms: Arbitrarily agreed-on rules that govern and inform how individuals are to behave in certain social environments.

Stressor: Any event, expected or unexpected, that happens to a family that cannot be managed effectively with the family's normal ways of doing things.

Subsystems: Subunits within the family comprised of one or more family members (e.g., parental subsystem, sibling subsystem, etc.).

Symbolism: The practice of representing things with symbols or of investing meaning into events or objects.

Temporary Assistance to Needy Families (TANF): The current government program to provide assistance to needy families. It is different from past welfare programs in that benefits are time-bound and limited in scope.

Thesis, antithesis, synthesis: Primary aspects of conflict theory: *thesis* is an original idea expressing a specific point of view; *antithesis* is another point of view in direct opposition to the thesis; *synthesis* refers to a newly formed position created through the struggle of trying to reconcile the two opposing viewpoints embodied in the thesis and antithesis.

Trajectory: The path or course one follows through life, which is different for each person.

Transitions: Periods of rapid change in which new roles are adopted, old roles are abandoned, or both.

Underritualization: Occurs when families have few or no rituals.

Validity: The degree to which a measure used in a study is assessing what it was intended to measure.

Variable: Some aspect of the measured experience that varies or changes. Variables are subject to change and hopefully responsive to measurement during which researchers attempt to assess a construct.

AUTHOR INDEX

SUBJECT INDEX